Game Theory with Economic Applications

H. SCOTT BIERMAN
Carleton College

LUIS FERNANDEZ
Oberlin College

ADDISON-WESLEY PUBLISHING COMPANY, INC.

Reading, Massachusetts • Menlo Park, California • New York
Don Mills, Ontario • Wokingham, England • Amsterdam • Bonn • Sydney
Singapore • Tokyo • Madrid • San Juan • Milan • Paris

This book is dedicated to
Barbara, Melody, Emily, Danielle, Lauren, and Rachel
for their patience and love

Library of Congress Cataloging-in-Publication Data

Bierman, Scott.
   Game theory with economic applications / H. Scott Bierman, Luis
Fernandez.
      p.   cm.
   Includes bibliographical references and index.
   ISBN 0-201-56298-7
   1. Game theory. 2. Decision-making.   I. Fernandez, Luis
Florentin. II. Title.
   HB144.B54   1993   92-15414
   330'.01'5193—dc20   CIP

1 2 3 4 5 6 7 8 9 10–HA–95949392

Preface

The growing use of game theory by economists has led to near agreement among the best graduate programs that a professional economic education is incomplete without a firm understanding of this new tool. Yet, most undergraduate economics majors currently graduate with little knowledge of game theory beyond the Prisoner's Dilemma. We believe one reason game theory is not a more integral part of the undergraduate economics curriculum is the lack of a textbook designed with undergraduates in mind. Our book was written to satisfy this need.

This textbook presents the theory of non-cooperative games in extensive form. We have limited ourselves to noncooperative games for two reasons. First, noncooperative games have yielded more economic insights than has cooperative theory. Second, noncooperative and cooperative game theory employ different methods and ideas, and so are difficult to combine in an introductory book. Game trees and backwards induction have been used from the very beginning. The primary solution concepts developed are Nash equilibrium, subgame-perfect equilibrium, and Bayesian equilibrium. Because this is an introductory textbook, we have avoided discussions of refinements of Nash equilibrium and non-Nash solution concepts such as rationalizability. We provide some references to these topics in the end-of-chapter readings.

In writing this book we have tried to avoid trivializing either the economics or the game theory. When the economics is made too trivial, an application often looks contrived and applicable to only a narrow set of circumstances. When the game theory is made too trivial, on the other hand, it is easy to lose sight of its role in the analysis. In each of the applications in this book both the game-theoretic and the economic foundations have been laid out in detail. Although we have provided fewer examples than some other recently published game theory texts, we have tried to give a more thorough presentation.

In order to accommodate a wide variety of institutional settings and student interests we have chosen applications from many fields—from labor economics, economics of the public sector, natural resource economics, regulation, international economics, macroeconomics, finance, and, of course, industrial organization. A student who studies this entire book will learn not only quite a bit of game theory, but quite of bit of economics as well.

Prerequisites

Most of the economics in the book will be understandable to students who have only had a Principles of Economics class. There are, however, a few places in the text where a course in Intermediate Microeconomics will be very useful. The book has been used at both Oberlin College and Carleton College without an Intermediate Microeconomics prerequisite, but lack of that background certainly slowed down the pace of the class. Those faculty teaching a course on game theory and economics for the first time will probably want to have an Intermediate Microeconomics prerequisite.

When we began writing this text, we hoped that calculus would not be necessary. Alas, we were unable to write a book in which the economics was not horribly unrealistic without some minimal use of calculus. There were simply too many examples in which the decision variables were continuous. Students are expected to know how to take derivatives of simple functions (i.e., polynomials and exponentials) of one and two variables and to be able to use the chain rule.

Probabilistic and statistical concepts (conditional probability, expected value, variance, Bayes' theorem) are used extensively. We have tried to include enough background material about probability so that students who have not had a previous course in probability and statistics will not be at much of a disadvantage.

An Overview

The book is divided into five parts. In Part One we introduce a number of tools used throughout the book: decision trees, information sets, expected utility, conditional probability, and Bayes' theorem. The expected utility hypothesis is developed in some detail. Much of the material in Part One can be skipped if the students have covered it in an introductory statistics or intermediate microeconomics course.

The analysis of games really begins in Part Two. Parts Two through Five each begin with one or two chapters of theory and methods and conclude with two to five chapters of economic applications. The application chapters are (with one exception) independent of each other. This modular structure allows the instructor to pick and choose among them. The applications have been designed both to reinforce the concepts and methods introduced in the theory chapters and to teach important economic ideas.

Games with perfect information are the subject of Part Two. Nash equilibrium, subgame perfection, and the method of backwards induction are introduced. The first application is a simple model of alternating-offer bargaining over a trading surplus. The second and third applications examine the problem of moral hazard in the labor and insurance markets. We show how moral hazard can lead to suboptimal market outcomes such as involuntary unemployment and incomplete insurance. The fourth application is a location model in which firms use patents to impede market entry by competitors. Patents, in this model, serve not to limit entry, but to influence the location of the entrant. The fifth application looks at the problem of obtaining low inflation and full employment when the central bank cannot credibly commit itself to maintaining low money growth.

Simultaneous-move games in which the players are otherwise fully informed are the subject of Part Three. Payoff matrices are introduced along with the concepts of dominant strategies and mixed strategies. The first application uses iterated dominance to analyze the validity of the Coase theorem in the presence of bargaining costs. The second application looks at the historically important duopoly models of Cournot and Bertrand. The third application provides an explanation for the large amount of intraindustry trade across countries. It also shows why a country might enact an export subsidy and then negotiate with its trading partners to eliminate it. The fourth application is from the public-choice literature. It demonstrates how the chair of a committee could be made worse off by being given the power to break ties. The problem of the overuse of a common resource is the topic of the fifth application.

Some of the most interesting work done by economists in the last decade has involved games in which players have private information. Such games are the subject of Part Four. The central solution concept is Bayesian equilibrium. The first application is Milgrom-Robert's model of predatory pricing in which a monopolist tries to signal to a potential entrant that it should not enter the market. Signaling is also the topic of the second application. The signal is the imposition of a strike, and its purpose is to convince the firm that the worker will not accept a low wage offer. The third application examines the problem of adverse selection in the credit market. We show how a competitive market equilibrium can exist in which there is an excess demand for loanable funds. The fourth application examines the ways in which management efforts to fight off a hostile takeover, such the payment of "greenmail," may be in the best interest of shareholders. The fifth application brings us back to the economics of the public-sector literature. The problem is to induce people to reveal the intensity of their preferences for a public good. The solution proposed is the Clarke tax.

The last section of the book, Part Five, provides an introduction to repeated games. Issues of reputation and credibility are at the fore, and subgame perfection is given its full power. There are two applications. The first examines the difficulties faced by a cartel in enforcing output restrictions. The second application looks at Professor Ronald Coase's conjecture that a monopolist producing a durable good will charge a price far below the classical monopoly price.

Acknowledgments

This book has benefited from the advice, help, and encouragement of a large number of people. The initial impetus for the book came from a summer workshop on game theory in the social sciences sponsored by the Alfred P. Sloan foundation. The workshop was a part of the New Liberal Arts program—an effort to give quantitative methods a more central place in undergraduate liberal arts education—and was directed by Professor Alan Taylor of Union College and Professor Steven Brams of New York University. By the end of the workshop it was clear to the economists in attendance that game theory needed to be included among the analytical tools taught undergraduate economic students. Steven Brams, Samuel Goldberg at the Sloan Foundation, and our colleagues at Carleton and Oberlin College encouraged us to develop and teach an undergraduate game theory course. From the lecture notes of those first courses came this book.

The preparation of a complete textbook moved into high gear when a grant from the Danforth Foundation allowed one of the authors to spend a year visiting the Cowles Foundation at Yale University. We wish to give special thanks to William Brainard, William Nordhaus, and Peter Crampton for their hospitality and many suggestions and ideas. They are absolved, however, from responsibility for any errors or omissions.

First drafts of this book were foisted on students at Oberlin and Carleton College during 1990–1991. We are grateful to them for their willingness to act as guinea pigs and endure countless typos, last-minute substitutions, and a general air of creative chaos. Many of their suggestions have been incorporated in this book.

We have benefited from the support and advice of our colleagues at Oberlin and Carleton College—David Cleeton, Barbara Craig, Michael Henesath, Mark Kanazawah, Hirsch Kasper, George Lamson, Peter Montiel, Martha Paas, Robert Piron, Steve Sheppard, Stephen Strand, Robert Will, Douglas Williams, and Jim Zinser—and the secretarial assistance of Che Gonzalez, Tracy Tucker, and Betty

Kendall. We also wish to thank Nadim Haider, Nathan Corson, and Pasha Mahmood for their help with the proofreading.

The book was greatly improved as the result of reviewer comments solicited by Addison-Wesley. We wish to thank our reviewers: Kyle Bagwell, Northwestern University; Jeff Baldini, Colgate University; Jonathan Hamilton, Duke University; Ignatius Horstmann, The University of Western Ontario; Dan Kovenock, Purdue University; David Levine, California Institute of Technology; Jeffrey Weiss, The City University of New York; and Kealoha Widdows, Wabash College.

A small army of people at Addison-Wesley have been very supportive of this effort. Special thanks goes to Executive Editor Barbara Rifkind, who first approached us about writing our book for Addison-Wesley and encouraged us to us sharpen our initial ideas. The professionalism of everyone at Addison-Wesley with whom we have worked has been evident from the beginning. Our editor Marjorie Williams and assistant editor Kari Heen helped us through the revisions and into production. Although we don't know all who have worked on this book, we wish to give special thanks to production editor Helen Wythe for making this process so smooth (at least to us). We also wish to thank Judy Ashkanez and David Ershun of Total Concept Associates for their book design, copyediting, typesetting, and artwork.

Our final thanks is to our wives and children, Barbara, Melody, Emily, Danielle, Lauren, and Rachel. They endured postponed and canceled vacations, countless refrains of "I can't play with you right now," and "I won't be able to go to the zoo with you and the kids this Sunday after all," with patience and understanding.

Contents

What is Game Theory?

Late on a Saturday evening at an all-campus party, Ted and Beth are talking. More accurately, Ted is droning on endlessly about his senior thesis on nonlinear Hamiltonian oscillators and Beth is waiting for a chance to get away from him. When the band takes a break, Beth sees her chance. As she ducks out the doorway, Ted yells from across the room that he'll see her at tomorrow night's basketball game. In the silence that suddenly falls over the room, she manages to mutter loudly enough for Ted and everyone else to hear, "Not if I can help it," and heads out the door.

On the way back to her dorm, Beth begins to realize she is in a quandary. Running into Ted tomorrow night is the last thing she wants to do. As much as she loves basketball, if Ted is going to be at the game, she would much rather go to the library and study for next week's calculus exam. Yet because of her nasty parting words, she knows that Ted knows she wants to avoid him. He may be a jerk, but he is no dummy. If Ted expects her to go to the library instead of the game, he will probably go to the library also. But if Ted goes to the library, then she should go to the game. Of course, if Ted expects her to expect him to go the library, then he will go to the game also. She is back where she began. What is she going to do?

Beth is not the only one who has been doing some thinking. Ted realizes from Beth's final words that he has not made a good first impression. But he is certain he can change her opinion of him if only he can see her again before her feelings have had time to harden. Ted realizes Beth may not go to the game in order to avoid him. In that case, he can probably catch her at the library. But if Beth expects him to go to the library, then she will go to the game. He seems to be going around in circles. What is he going to do?

If Ted can predict where Beth will go, he will find her. And if Beth can predict where Ted will go, she will avoid him. This means each wants to be as unpredictable to the other as possible. This is easily accomplished: They each flip a coin, which gives them a 50% chance of meeting. If Ted makes his choice in this way, Beth cannot reduce the probability of meeting Ted below 50%; and if Beth makes her decision in this way, Ted cannot increase the probability above 50%.

Now let's consider a second situation with which you may be familiar. Amy, Betty, Charles, David, and Emily are enrolled in Professor Smith's senior seminar in industrial organization. This is the last class they will take together. Over the next five weeks, they have to give a classroom presentation, which will count for half the seminar grade. All five students have similar abilities and care about only two things: their course grade and how much time they spend preparing for their presentation. The higher the grade and the less time spent preparing, the happier they will be. Yet, each student is willing to spend a lot of time if this will result in a higher grade. Professor, Smith has announced that the best presenter will receive an A, the second best an A−, the third best a B+, the fourth best a B, and the worst a B−. In the event of a tie, the tied students get the average of the grades for which they are tied. In the interest of fairness, the student has their topic assigned to them only a week before the presentation. As a result, when each student begins preparing for the presentation, each knows how well those who have gone before have done. How much time will each student spend preparing? The answer is as simple as it is surprising: They will all spend a full week preparing.

The answer is surprising because, clearly, if they all spend a full week preparing, they will all do equally well and get a B+ (the average of an A, A−, B+, B, and B−). But the same thing will happen if they all spend no time preparing. Because Amy is the first presenter, it would seem that it is up to her to establish a benchmark. If Amy spends no time preparing, it would seem the rest of the class should follow suit. Oddly enough, however, all of them are at the mercy of Emily, who goes *last*.

Emily's position is critical because she is the only student who will make her decision with full knowledge of how well the others did. If none of the other four students spends the full week preparing, then Emily can guarantee herself an A by spending a little more time preparing and thereby doing better than the rest. On the other hand, if her classmates all do their best, then Emily will have to follow suit or receive a poor grade. Although David, who goes right before Emily, doesn't know what she will do, he can foresee what is rational for her to do. With this knowledge he can see that his best strategy is to spend the full week preparing and force a tie for first place. And so it goes. As with a stack of dominoes, all the students can see they must spend the full week preparing in order not to be outdone by those who follow.

The common feature of these two examples—in fact, the common feature of all the situations we will examine in this book—is that the decisions of one person affect the welfare of others and vice versa. Such situations are called *games* and the decisions of the participants are called *strategic decisions*. Game theory aims to predict the strategic decisions made by the participants in any game. Over the last twenty years game theory has become an increasingly important tool for economic analysis. It has offered a rigorous way to look at economic issues that heretofore have been treated informally. But game theory has done more than simply confirm results obtained with traditional methods. It has also produced many remarkable new economic insights.

Economists studying industrial organization have been in the forefront of the move toward game-theoretic analysis. Using these methods they have been able to find the circumstances under which a monopoly can retain substantial market power in the face of potential entry, and the circumstances under which the threat of entry will force a monopoly to act as if it were a perfect competitor. Game theory has also become the central tool in the relatively new subfield of *public choice*. One important concern of public choice theorists is the behavior of individual voters in different voting systems. Game-theoretic analysis of many common voting systems has produced many apparently paradoxical results. For example, it may be disadvantageous to chair a committee if the chair is given a tie-breaking vote. Game theory has also been used to design mechanisms that will induce voters to reveal honestly the intensity of their preferences for goods and services. This, in turn has uncovered some limits in the ability of governments to improve on market outcomes even when there is "market failure."

With each passing day, game theory is proving useful in every field of economics, not just industrial organization and public choice. Game-theoretic models of bargaining can account for bluffing, delay, and "walking away from the table." This has changed the way in which labor economists think about strikes, lockouts, and arbitration. Game-theoretic models of the insurance market can account for the absence of privately provided unemployment insurance and the current problems with privately provided medical insurance. Game-theoretic models of international trade can explain why countries impose tariffs on exports and then sit down and negotiate with other countries to reduce them; how everyone in a country can benefit from subsidizing exports to other countries; and why the largest trading countries tend to trade similar goods with each other. Economists working on the economics of natural resources have used game theory to explain why common resources are depleted too rapidly. Banking and financial analysts have found game theory useful in explaining why the savings and loan industry collapsed and why banks sometimes will refuse to extend credit to borrowers who are willing to pay a higher interest rate than the bank is currently charging. Game theory can also explain why corporate managers who pay bribes to deter potential takeover attempts may be acting in the best interest of their shareholders.

Macroeconomists have also made very productive use of game theory. They have used it to show why the promise by a central bank to reduce the rate of inflation may not be credible. In addition, they have revealed how "involuntary unemployment" can be consistent with competitive market equilibrium. This result offers hope for reconciling traditional Keynesian macroeconomics with standard microeconomic analysis without resorting to ad hoc arguments about "sticky prices" and "sluggish expectations."

Game theory has been critically important in understanding the role of information in the market mechanism. It has long been suspected that "perfect information" is necessary in order for perfectly competitive markets to have the efficiency properties attributed to them. But only recently have economists confirmed this using game theory. Indeed, only recently have economists even begun to understand what is meant by information One subtlety about information that you may not be able to use it without revealing it. The ability of actions to reveal information has important effects on how people behave.

The union of game theory and economics has been difficult. The two disciplines were first brought together in 1944 by John von Neumann and Oskar Morgenstern in their path-breaking work, *The Theory of Games and Economic Behavior*. The notion that strategic behavior could be modeled rigorously appealed to many economists and much time and effort was spent trying extend the theoretical tools invented by von Neumann and Morgenstern. Unfortunately, little progress was made. As late as 1970 game theory was only a tangential part of the training of most economists.

Then things quickly began to change. Some neglected articles were dusted off and found to be very helpful in analyzing strategic situations; some very creative economists showed the profession how to harness new mathematical developments in game theory; and most important, the profession learned that by tying game theory together with information theory, surprising and unorthodox results could be generated and many unexplained empirical anomalies could be now be accounted for. Today, graduate schools in economics are requiring their students to learn substantial amounts of game theory, and more and more published economic research assumes a familiarity with game-theoretic ideas.

You are about to embark on an intellectual journey that will greatly expand your understanding of economics and will change the way you view your behavior and the behavior of those around you. Have a great trip!

PART ONE

Decision Theory

• CHAPTER 1 •

Making Optimal Decisions

1.1 • Decision theory

The players in a game must decide how to act given that the welfare of each depends on the actions of all. Before we get embroiled in determining how to behave in a game, we will first examine how to make intelligent decisions when the mutual interdependency of a game is absent. This is the subject of classical **decision theory**. Many of the tools and ideas of decision theory will form the basis for our analysis of games.

To make our discussion more concrete, we will consider the hypothetical case of Sonya Jimenez, an entrepreneur who wants to build a factory to manufacture child safety seats. Ms. Jimenez believes that during the next year she can sell 100,000 seats for $40 each and incur a constant marginal manufacturing cost of $20 per seat. This means her projected net operating revenue will equal ($40 − $20) • 100,000 = $2,000,000 per year. Since this revenue will not be earned until the end of the year, we must first convert this future income into its **present value**. Since the market interest rate is 11.11%, the present value of $1 one year from now equals $1 ÷ (1 + 11.11%) = $0.90. The present value of Jimenez's net revenue equals $2,000,000 ÷ (1 + 11.11%) = $1,800,000. The venture will be profitable as long as this present value is greater than the initial outlay required to build and furbish the factory.

Jimenez commissions two architectural firms to design a factory with a manufacturing capacity of 100,000 seats per year. We will refer to the first design as "Factory A" and the second design as "Factory B." Jimenez must decide whether to build a factory at all and, if so, which factory design to use She wants to make the decision that will earn her the highest profit.

Factory A will cost $1.4 million to build and Factory B will cost $1.5 million to build. For the moment, we will assume the factory will last one year before it has to be completely overhauled. We will also assume that Jimenez wants to make the decision that results in the highest discounted profits. Discounted profits are the difference between the *discounted* net operating revenue (either $0 or $1.8 million depending on whether she builds the factory or not) and the *immediate* construction costs (either $1.4 million or $1.5 million depending on the design she chooses). Since the construction outlays must be made immediately, they are not discounted.

Jimenez's very simple decision problem can be depicted by the diagram in Figure 1.1, which is called a **decision tree diagram**. The vertex of the sideways "W" denotes a choice. This vertex is called a **decision node**. The decision maker, in this case Sonya Jimenez, has three options—that is, three branches she can travel along. At the end of each branch is shown a final **terminal node** and next to it the discounted profit Jimenez will earn if she selects the corresponding branch. A terminal node represents the outcome of a sequence of decisions. Without question, the rational choice for Ms. Jimenez is to build Factory A.

Let us now add some complexity to this deliberately simple setup and assume the factory will last two years. Suppose Jimenez believes the demand for child car seats will increase between the first and second year, allowing her to sell up to 200,000 seats at $40 each. Marginal manufacturing costs will remain at $20 for output levels below capacity. At the beginning of the second year, the factory's manufacturing capacity can be doubled, but at a cost. If Factory A is built, then the construction cost of the expansion will be $1.9 million. If Factory B is built, then the construction cost of the expansion will be $1.6 million.

So Jimenez now has two decisions to make: First she must decide whether to build a factory and, if so, what design to use. Second, assuming she decides to build a factory, she must decide whether or not to expand the factory's capacity in the second year. Together, this results in five possible sequences of decisions: (1) Don't build the factory, (2) build Factory A and expand it in the second year, (3) build Factory A but don't expand it in the second year, (4) build Factory B and expand it in the second

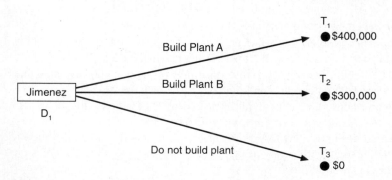

FIGURE 1.1 • Sonya Jimenez's decision tree.

year, (5) build Factory B but don't expand it in the second year. The new decision tree is shown in Figure 1.2. This tree has three decision nodes (labeled D_1, D_2, and D_3) and five terminal nodes (labeled T_1, T_2, T_3, T_4, T_5). The first decision node, D_1, corresponds to the construction decision in the first year, and the next two decision nodes, D_2 and D_3, correspond to the construction decision in the second year, where the expansion decision depends on the design decision made in the first year.

All decision nodes have branches emanating from them, and alongside each branch is the present value of the profit earned from the decision taken. The figures listed to the right of each of the five terminal nodes are the present values of the profits earned in both years given the particular sequence of construction decisions that lead to each node. For example, should Sonya Jimenez choose design A and then decide to expand the factory in period 2, she will earn a discounted profit in the first year of $400,000 and will earn a discounted profit in the second year of $1,530,000. The second number equals the present value of the revenues earned at the *end* of the second year ($4,000,000 ÷ 1.1111^2 = $3,240,000) minus the present value of the construction costs incurred at the *beginning* of the second year ($1,900,000 ÷ 1.1111 = $1,710,000). The other numbers are obtained in a similar fashion. The total discounted profit of $1,930,000 is shown next to terminal node T_2.

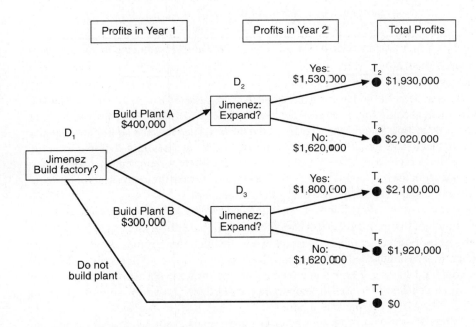

FIGURE 1.2 • Ms. Jimenez's two-period decision tree.

A comparison of the profit outcome at the five terminal nodes shows that the best outcome is T_4. This implies that the best decision is to build the factory using design B and then expand the factory's capacity in the second year.

1.2 • Decision trees: A formal description

Decision trees are such powerful decision-making tools that we will pause for a moment and examine them more formally.

As you have already seen, decision trees are diagrams made up of **nodes** and **branches.** We will denote nodes by upper-case roman letters (A, B, etc.) and will denote branches by lower-case Greek letters (α, β, etc.). Every branch α connects two nodes, one of which is the **parent** $P(\alpha)$ and the other of which is the **child** $C(\alpha)$. The interpretation is this: At the node $P(\alpha)$ the decision maker must make a decision, which consists of choosing among the branches emanating from that node. The branch α may be one of many branches that can be taken from that node. When the branch α is chosen, the decision maker then reaches the node $C(\alpha)$. At $C(\alpha)$ she either faces a new decision or makes no further decisions. We will say that the node $P(\alpha)$ is a **parent** of $C(\alpha)$ and, not surprisingly, that the node $C(\alpha)$ is a **child** of $P(\alpha)$. A fundamental requirement of a decision tree is:

RULE 1.1   Every node has at most one parent and is connected to the parent by one branch.

To see why Rule 1.1 must be imposed, consider Mary, who must make the hypothetical commuting decision depicted in Figure 1.3. Mary can go to work either by car or by bus. Should she decide to take the bus, she faces the additional decision of whether to take the express bus (which costs $2.00 but takes only 30 minutes) or the local bus (which costs $1.00 but takes 45 minutes). Node A represents her decision to use the car or the bus, node B represents her decision to take the express bus or the local bus, and node C represents her final work destination.

In this diagram, node C is the destination node of three decision branches: β, τ, and μ. Although Figure 1.3 is correct in one sense—all three travel modes get Mary to her job—it is incorrect in that it hides the ways in which these routes *differ* from each other. Mary is interested in more than simply arriving at work. She is also interested in how tired she is and how much money she has left when she arrives. By attaching all three decision branches to the common child node C, two of the dimensions in which Mary is "traveling" are ignored.

Figure 1.4 shows how the original decision tree can be redrawn to conform to Rule 1.1 by simply giving each of the branches β, τ, and μ its own destination node. Node

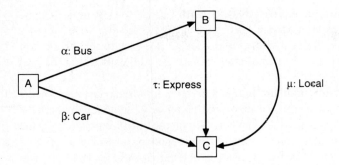

FIGURE 1.3 • A decision tree for Mary that violates Rule 1.1.

C represents "getting to work by car," node C' represents "getting to work using the express bus," and node C" represents "getting to work using the local bus."

When Rule 1.1 is satisfied, it makes sense to speak of one node "coming after" another node. Informally, node B *comes after* node A if it is possible for the decision maker to get to node B by making a sequence of decisions originating at node A. Formally, node B *comes after* node A if and only if there exists some sequence of nodes, N_1, N_2, ..., N_K, such that $A = N_1$, $B = N_K$, and each node is a child of the previous node in the sequence and a parent of the next node in the sequence. When one node comes after another node, there must be a series of decisions leading from node to node that will take the decision maker from the earlier node to the later node.

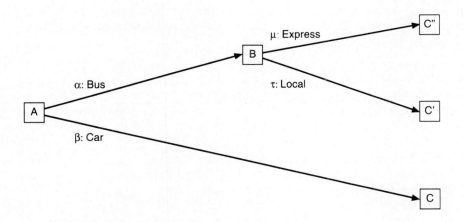

FIGURE 1.4 • A modified decision tree for Mary that satisfies Rule 1.1.

This sequence of nodes will be referred to as the **path** from A to B. Rule 1.1 can be shown to imply that there is at most one path between any two nodes. Node A comes before node B if and only if node B comes after node A. It is easy to see that both of these orderings are **transitive**: If C comes after (before) B and B comes after (before) A, then C comes after (before) A.

Consider another decision problem. Simon's favorite author has just published a new work in hard cover to great critical acclaim and has already negotiated a paperback edition of the book for release one year from now. Simon can buy the book today at the high hard-cover price or wait a year and buy it at the cheaper paperback price. Figure 1.5 shows a decision tree for Simon's decision problem that satisfies Rule 1.1. But notice that in this diagram decision node A is both the origin and the destination of branch ß. As a result, A comes both before and after itself!

Decision trees with circular loops introduce ambiguity about the order in which decisions are made. They also cause distinct outcomes to be treated as if they are the same. In Simon's case, for example, the diagram treats access to the book today and access a year from now as identical, whereas they are actually very different. In order to eliminate this ambiguity, we will avoid decision trees that have circular loops by requiring that all trees obey Rule 1.2.

RULE 1.2   No node comes after itself.

Figure 1.6 shows how Simon's decision tree can be redrawn so as to satisfy both Rule 1.1 and Rule 1.2. The solution now is to add more decision nodes. At his first decision node, Simon must choose either to buy the hard-cover edition or to delay his purchase until next year. If he chooses to delay, then next year he will find himself at a *new* decision node, where the choice will be either to buy the paperback edition or not to buy the book at all. This implies there are three possible sequences of actions:

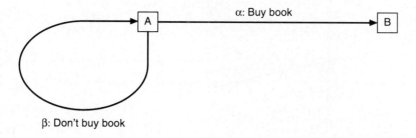

FIGURE 1.5 • A decision tree for Simon that has a circular loop.

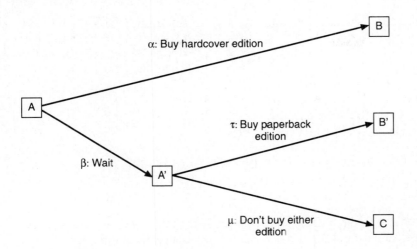

FIGURE 1.6 • A decision tree for Simon that satisfies both Rule 1.1 and Rule 1.2.

(1) Simon buys the hard-cover edition immediately, (2) Simon buys the paperback edition a year from now, (3) Simon never buys the book.

If node B comes after node A, then A is called an **ancestor** of B and B is called a **successor** of A. The ancestors of a node consist of the node's parent, the parent's parent, and so on; and the successors of a node consist of the node's children, its children's children, and so forth. A terminal node has no successors, and an **initial node** has no ancestors. We will reserve the term **decision node** for a node that is not terminal.

Figure 1.7 shows a decision tree that satisfies Rules 1.1 and 1.2 but has no initial node. Unfortunately, "headless" decision trees are capable of generating logical ambiguities and so must be avoided. An example of such a logically ambiguous tree can be found in exercises 1.4 at the end of this chapter. For this reason, we require that our decision trees satisfy Rule 1.3:

RULE 1.3 Every node has an ancestor that is an initial node.

Rules 1.1, 1.2, and 1.3 imply that every node comes after exactly one initial node. But what if there is more than one initial node? Fortunately, whenever this happens the nodes can be divided into disjoint sets according to which initial node they follow. We claim (and you are asked in an exercise to prove) that each of these disjoint subsets of

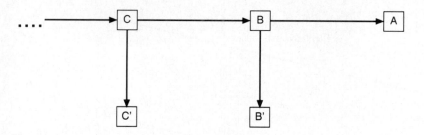

FIGURE 1.7 • A decision tree with no initial node.

nodes (together with the branches that connect them) can be viewed as a separate decision tree that satisfies Rules 1.1, 1.2, and 1.3. Yet, each of these sub-trees has only one initial node by construction. This means that any decision problem that is represented by a decision tree with many initial nodes can be broken down into independent decision problems, each of which is represented by a decision tree with exactly one initial node. So there is no loss of generality, but a gain of simplicity, in our final requirement:

RULE 1.4   Every decision tree has exactly one initial node.

1.3 • Finding the optimal decision

Once Sonya Jimenez forms her decision tree, she must decide what to do. A quick comparison of the five terminal nodes shown in Figure 1.2 reveals that she should build Factory B and then expand capacity in the second year. There is nothing technically difficult in figuring out why this decision makes sense. In more realistic problems, however, there may be scores of terminal nodes, and calculating the pay-offs at each one can become exceedingly tedious. In such cases the task of finding the optimal decision can be simplified by using the technique of **backwards induction**. The idea is to begin with each of the final decision nodes on the decision tree and determine the optimal decision to make at each of these points. For example, it is easy to see that if Jimenez builds Factory A, then she shouldn't expand capacity in the second year; whereas if she builds Factory B, then she should expand its capacity in the second year. We have marked these two optimal decisions in Figure 1.8 by circling their respective branches.

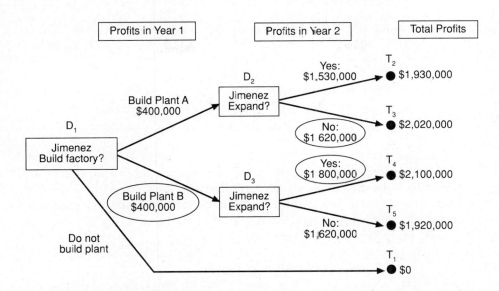

FIGURE 1.8 • Jimenez's decision tree showing the best choice to make at *every* decision node.

We have now simplified Jimenez's problem from choosing among five possible sequences of actions to choosing among only two. This simplification is the point of backwards induction. By working backward starting from the *end* of the decision tree, you can lop off branches right and left. You reduce a big decision problem to a sequence of small decision problems. The best Jimenez can do if she builds Factory A is to earn a discounted profit of $2,020,000, and the best she can do if she builds Factory B is to earn a discounted profit of $2,100,000. Plant B wins.

If Jimenez were to make her decision by starting at the *beginning* of the decision tree and choosing the factory design on the basis of the profits in the first year—while ignoring the question of expansion in the second year—then she would choose Factory A. Factory B will be chosen only if Jimenez *looks ahead* and recognizes that by building the more costly Factory B, she can profitably expand the factory in the second year. Once she builds Factory A, she is saddled with such large expansion costs that she must forego expansion in the second year. Looking ahead saves her $80,000 in the long run.

The point we want to make is that when a decision maker is making a series of decisions in sequence, it is necessary to look at the consequences of the later decisions *before* deciding on the earlier decisions. We do not mean to imply that we are saying anything particularly clever here. As children we were told to "look before you leap," and this is really the same principle.

1.4 • Summary

Decision theory is a set of methods by which a single, isolated decision maker can reach intelligent decisions when faced with a complex sequence of choices. One of the important tools that decision theorists have developed is the decision tree. The larger the number of decisions you must make, or that are made by someone or something else, the larger the number of branches on the tree. In order to be unambiguous, decision trees must satisfy four rules: (1) Every node must have a parent, (2) no node can come before itself, (3) every node must have an ancestor that is an initial node, and (4) this initial node must be the only initial node of the tree.

Backwards induction provides a simple algorithm for finding the optimal sequence of decisions in a multistage decision tree. This algorithm embodies an overriding principle of decision theory: Look before you leap.

Clearly, however, the type of decision problem we have considered so far is too simple to capture even the most commonplace decisions. For example, our assumption that the decision maker knows *for certain* the outcome of every action she makes is almost never satisfied in the real world. Either the outcome depends partly on events outside the decision maker's control, or the decision maker simply does not know exactly what the final outcomes will be. Indeed, we have all experienced situations in which we undertook a costly action in order to gain information about the likely outcome of another decision. We cannot hope to make predictions about the behavior of people enmeshed in complex strategic interactions until we can handle decision making under conditions of uncertainty and with incomplete knowledge. These are the topics of Chapters 2 and 3.

1.5 • Exercises

Exercise 1.1   The Electa Company has to ship 10,000 television sets from its factory in Manila to an American importer in New York City. As can be seen in Figure 1.9, the firm can either ship the sets by boat directly to Los Angeles or ship them via the Panama Canal to either New Orleans or New York City. From Los Angeles it can ship the sets to New York by truck or to New Orleans by truck or train. From New Orleans it can ship the sets to New York by either truck or train or boat. Draw the firm's decision tree.

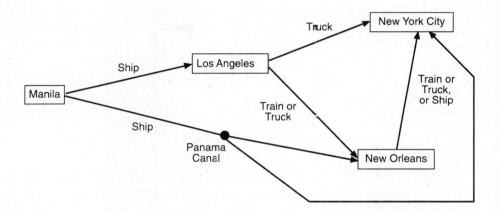

FIGURE 1.9 • The routing possibilites between Manila and New York City for Electa's television sets.

Exercise 1.2 This is a continuation of Exercise 1.1. Listed here are the freight charges (in dollars per television set) for each mode of transportation and each route:

Transportation Costs (Dollars per television Set)

By boat:
Manila–Los Angeles	$30
Manila–New Orleans	$50
Manila–New York	$75
New Orleans-New York	$25

By truck:
Los Angeles–New York	$50
Los Angeles–New Orleans	$30
New Orleans–New York	$35

By train:
Los Angeles–New Orleans	$20
New Orleans–New York	$20

In addition, every time television sets are transferred between carriers, Electa incurs a cost in paid labor time, in damage, and in theft. This transfer cost (in dollars per set) is as follows:

Transfer costs (dollars per television set)

Boat–train	$6
Boat–truck	$2
Train–truck	$4
Boat–boat	$4
Train–train	$1
Truck–truck	$1

The Electa Company wants to minimize total shipping cost per set (transportation plus transfer). From the transportation and transfer costs, determine the total cost (in dollars per set) of using each possible routing between Manila and New York City. Find the firm's best shipping route and modes of transport.

Exercise 1.3   Continuation of Exercise 1.1. Use the tables in problem 1.2 and the method of backwards induction to find the best decision at *every* decision node on its decision tree.

Exercise 1.4   Consider the decision tree in Figure 1.10. This tree has no beginning node. Instead, it extends backwards into the infinitely remote past. The nodes are labeled "node 1," "node 2," and so on. At node n there are two choices: move {down} and get a payoff p_n or move {across}. At every node other than the last one, choosing {across} leads to another decision node. At the last decision node, {across} leads to a payoff of 0. The {down} payoffs satisfy the following recursive relation:

$$p_n = \begin{cases} 1/2 & \text{if n is even} \\ 1 & \text{if n = 1} \\ p_{n-2} + 1/2 & \text{if n is odd and n > 1} \end{cases}$$

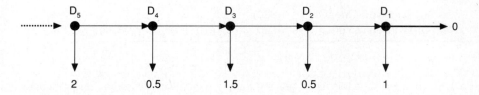

FIGURE 1.10 • A decision tree with no initial node.

(a) Use backwards induction to find the optimal strategy for this decision tree.

(b) Explain why the optimal strategy you found in (a) provides the decision maker with an ambiguous sequence of actions.

Exercise 1.5   Every time a motion is brought before the Oberlin City Council, the council can either "approve the motion as read," "amend" it, or "defeat" it. In order for a motion to be officially adopted by the Oberlin City Council, the council must approve the motion as read in two successive meetings. If the motion is approved for the first time, or is amended, then it must be brought up at the next council meeting. Once approved, a motion cannot be amended later. A motion can be amended only once. If the motion is defeated, it cannot be brought up again during the current council's term. Draw the decision tree for this legislative process.

Exercise 1.6   Let T be a decision tree that satisfies Rules 1.1, 1.2, and 1.3, but has two initial nodes, N_1 and N_2. Prove:

(a) The set S_1 that contains the decision nodes that come after N_1 is disjoint from the set S_2 that contains the decision nodes that come after N_2.

(b) No branch connects a decision node in S_1 with a node in S_2.

Use these two results to prove that S_1 and S_2 (together with the branches that connect them) are essentially two separate decision trees that satisfy Rules 1.1, 1.2, 1.3, *and* 1.4.

• CHAPTER 2 •

Choosing Among Lotteries

2.1 • Introduction

In Chapter 1 we assumed Ms. Jimenez knew with certainty the full consequences of every action she took. It is much more likely, however, that she is ignorant of many variables outside her control that also affect the outcome of her actions. For example, she is unlikely to know in advance exactly how much it will cost to build the factory, or exactly how much it will cost to expand the capacity of the factory in the future, or exactly what the future price of child car seats will be. Instead, she must make educated guesses about all of these important parameters and explicitly take into account the possibility that some of her decisions may, with hindsight, turn out to be bad ones. In this section we will explain how we can incorporate uncertainty and risk into our decision-making apparatus.

Let us go back to our first example in Chapter 1 where we assumed the car seat factory lasted exactly one year and the choices were only three: (1) Don't build the factory, (2) Build Factory A, or (3) Build Factory B. We have reproduced our original decision tree in Figure 2.1. Now we will add a new twist. Factory A uses new construction materials whose future prices are very uncertain, whereas Factory B uses very common materials whose prices have fluctuated little for many years. There is a 60% chance that Factory A will cost $1 million to build and a 40% chance the factory will cost $2 million. Factory B, in contrast, has a 50% chance of costing $1.4 million and a 50% chance of costing $1.6 million. Sonya Jimenez will not know exactly what the cost of each type of factory will be until *after* she has to decide on the design. There is a 60% probability that Factory A will be cheaper to build than

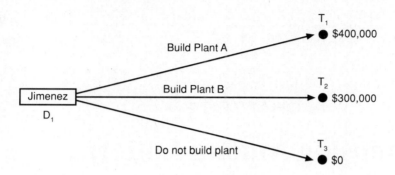

FIGURE 2.1 · Sonya Jimenez's decision problem when she is certain of the consequences of her actions.

Factory B, but there is a 40% chance that Factory B will be cheaper to build than Factory A. As a result, there is no obvious way for her to tell which factory is the more cost-effective.

One approach she could take would be to choose the factory that has the lowest expected construction cost. By **expected costs** we mean the arithmetic average of the costs of constructing a large number of factories at different points in time using a given design. For example, if 1,000 firms were to build factories at different times over the next few years using Factory A, then we would expect 600 of them to incur construction costs of $1 million and expect 400 of them to incur construction costs of $2 million. The arithmetic average of the construction costs of these hypothetical 1,000 firms equals $0.60 \cdot \$1,000,000 + 0.40 \cdot \$2,000,000 = \$1,400,000$. This is the expected construction cost of Factory A.

Notice that probabilities can be used for the "expected" proportion of firms that would incur each of the two possible construction costs. Similarly, the expression for the expected cost of building Factory B equals $0.50 \cdot \$1,600,000 + 0.50 \cdot \$1,600,000 = \$1,500,000$.

In some ways the term *expected cost* is a misnomer. Ms. Jimenez certainly does not "expect" Factory A to cost $1.4 million. She expects it to cost either $1 million or $2 million. Nevertheless, for better or worse, this terminology has become standard and we will go along with the convention. We will often denote the expected value of an outcome, say C (for cost), by E(C). Because the expected cost of Factory A is less than the expected cost of Factory B, it is reasonable for Ms. Jimenez to choose Factory A . But it is also reasonable for Ms. Jimenez to choose the "safer" Factory B over the "risky" Factory A . In order to predict Ms. Jimenez's choice, we need to incorporate into our decision theory framework the possibility that the outcome of a decision can depend on more than her actions.

2.2 • Modeling uncertainty

The set of all outside factors that affect the outcome of a decision maker's actions will be called the **state-of-the-world**. The outcome of a decision depends on the actions taken by the decision maker and the state-of-the-world. In Jimenez's case, the relevant states-of-the-world are two: Either the price of construction materials is high, or the price of construction materials is low. The two states-of-the-world and three possible decision choices result in five possible outcomes. The new decision tree is depicted in Figure 2.2.

At the root of the tree is an initial node corresponding to Ms. Jimenez's choice of factory. Subsequently, something or someone else "chooses" the state-of-the-world. We will call this something or someone else **Nature**. What makes Nature so different from a decision maker is that Nature has no goals and chooses completely at random. Although Nature may be very influential in determining the outcome of any decision maker's choice, it functions as a "dumb" automaton.

To keep Jimenez's decisions distinct from Nature's "decisions," we have labeled decision nodes where she must make a decision with the word *Jimenez* and labeled the nodes where Nature makes a "choice" with the word *Nature*. Since Nature makes its choice blindly using known probabilities, we have added these probabilities to the labels for the branches that originate from Nature's decision nodes. Finally, at the end of the tree we have added the construction costs for all five outcomes, as well as the expected cost of each factory.

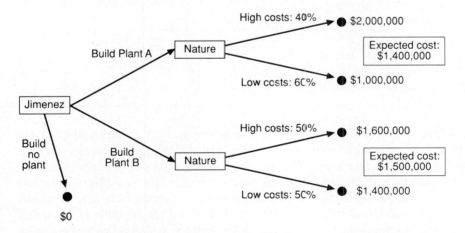

FIGURE 2.2 • Sonya Jimenez's decision problem when she is uncertain about the cost of building the two types of plants.

In this model, Sonya Jimenez is deciding which factory to build under conditions of **imperfect information**. This means that when she makes her decisions she does not know enough about the state-of-the-world to be certain of the outcome of her actions. In her case, when she has to decide which factory to construct, she does not know what the construction costs will be. One way to model this lack of information is to draw the decision tree so that Nature chooses the state-of-the-world *after* Jimenez makes her decision.

Figure 2.2 seems to suggest that choices are made in a chronologically sequential fashion—Jimenez chooses a factory, then Nature chooses the cost of construction. It is far more likely that the sequence of actions takes place in reverse chronological order: Nature first determines the cost of construction materials, but this information is not revealed to Jimenez until after she has made her choice. Up until now we have implicitly assumed that the ordering of nodes on a decision tree corresponded with the chronological order in which the decisions are made. Once we have another decision maker in the picture, however, this may no longer be true. Now the ordering of nodes must correspond to the order in which decisions *become known to the decision maker*. Regardless of when the construction costs are determined in real time, because this information is not revealed to Jimenez until after she has made her decision, the appropriate place to put Nature's decision is *after* Jimenez moves, not before.

Reminder The ordering of nodes in a decision tree does not necessarily correspond to the chronological ordering in which choices are made. Instead, this ordering corresponds to the order in which decisions are revealed to the decision maker.

2.3 • Ordinal utility

To date we have made two simplifying assumptions. First, we have assumed that decision makers rank their choices according to some single observable characteristic of the outcomes of those choices. For example, in Jimenez's case, this characteristic is the present value of her profits from building different factories. Second, when the outcomes are also determined by the random actions of Nature, we have assumed that decision makers rank their choices according to the expected value of this single outcome characteristic. Unfortunately, there is ample evidence that both of these simplifying assumptions are often false.

Fortunately, it is simple to relax both of the foregoing assumptions. The first assumption can be replaced by the weaker assumption that people can rank the outcomes of their choices from worst to best. This ranking is called an **ordinal utility ranking** of the outcomes and the assumption is the **ordinal utility hypothesis**. The utility function U can be thought of as converting the relevant attributes of the outcome A into a single ordinal measure, U(A). We can relax the second assumption by assuming that, whenever the decision maker is operating under conditions of uncertainty or imperfect information, choices are ranked according to the **expected utility** of their outcomes. That is, we assume the outcomes can be assigned a numerical ranking such that the best choice always corresponds to the one that generates the highest utility *on average*.

More formally, the ordinal utility hypothesis states that it is possible to assign to every outcome T_i a number, U_i, such that the outcome T_i is preferred or indifferent to the outcome T_j if and only if $U_i \geq U_j$. The function $U(T_i) = U_i$ is called an **ordinal utility representation** of the decision maker's preferences over the set of outcomes $\{T_1, \ldots, T_n\}$. We will often refer to U simply as the decision maker's **utility function**. In short, the decision maker has a ranking over the outcomes of her decision-making process, and this ranking is completely captured by assigning a single number to every outcome. The higher the number assigned to an outcome, the higher that outcome ranks against the others.

The ordinal utility hypothesis implies that the decision maker's preferences over outcomes satisfy three properties. First, these preferences must be **complete**, meaning that for *any two* outcomes A and B, either A is preferred to B, or B is preferred to A, or both. If A is preferred to B while at the same time B is preferred to A, then the individual is said to be **indifferent** between A and B. Second, these preferences must be **reflexive**, meaning that the individual is indifferent between any outcome and that same outcome. Finally, these preferences must be **transitive**, meaning that if the outcome A is preferred to the outcome B and if B is preferred to the outcome C, then A is preferred to C.

When the set of outcomes is finite (which will normally be the case) and the decision maker's preferences over the outcomes are complete, reflexive, and transitive, then the ordinal utility hypothesis is satisfied. The proof is simple. Completeness and transitivity imply that the outcomes can be completely ordered from the least preferred to the most preferred.[1] It is easy to see that the resulting ordinal ranking is an ordinal utility representation. When the set of outcomes is infinite—as would be the case, for example, if the possible outcomes were represented by all real

---

[1] There are many algorithms for doing this. If you have not seen such procedures before, you might find it fun to develop one yourself.

TABLE 2.1   Two ordinal utility functions

Outcome	Utility 1	Utility 2
T_1: $1,000,000	85	4,225
T_2: $1,400,000	78	3,084
T_3: $1,600,000	55	25
T_4: $2,000,000	50	−500

numbers between 0 and 10—then further restrictions on the preferences are required in order to ensure that there exists an ordinal utility representation.

If a decision maker's preferences have one ordinal utility representation, then they will have many. For example, suppose the set of outcomes are: (1) costs of $1 million, (2) costs of $1.4 million, (3) costs of $1.6 million, (4) and costs of $2 million. And suppose Ms. Jimenez prefers (1) to (2), prefers (2) to (3), and prefers (3) to (4). Then her preferences can be represented by either of the two utility functions shown in Table 2.1.

In fact, it turns out that given any ordinal utility function that satisfies the ordinal utility hypothesis, $U(x)$, and any strictly increasing function, $f(u)$, then the function $V(x) = f(U(x))$ of that ordinal utility function will also maintain exactly the same ranking. Therefore, the individual's preferences captured by the original ordinal utility function will also be captured by the later. It is precisely this feature of the ordinal utility function that makes it ordinal (as opposed to cardinal).

A wide variety of implications follow from this fact. Among them is that we cannot expect to observe anyone's ordinal utility function, but we might reasonably expect to observe the ordinal ranking implied by this function (at least if it is revealed to us through the choices made). By collecting information about preferences, we can construct *an* ordinal utility function, but we can never hope to construct *the* ordinal utility function.

Furthermore, properties such as diminishing marginal utility cannot be empirically verified if the only observations are of choices over certain outcomes. Fortunately, choices over *uncertain* outcomes reveal information about the relative intensity with which one outcome is preferred over another. Before we can show this, however, we must first develop a language for describing uncertain outcomes.

2.4 · Lotteries

You are probably very familiar with **simple lotteries** in which people buy tickets with a number printed on them, at an appointed time one number is chosen publicly at random, and the owner of the ticket having the selected number printed on it wins a prize (money, a car, a Caribbean cruise, etc.). There are many variations on this description of a lottery. In some lotteries, ticket buyers can choose their lottery number; in some lotteries, the prize money increases with the number of tickets sold; and in some lotteries, the winner is automatically entered in a second special lottery with an even bigger prize. Lotteries have been used to determine the order in which men were drafted into the army, to ration tickets to the first Beatles concerts in the United States, and to select which applicants would receive state-subsidized mortgages.

Decision theorists have found that any uncertain outcome can be modeled as a lottery. As a result, in order to find out how a decision maker will rank different uncertain outcomes, it is enough to know how she will rank different lotteries. In this section we will present the terminology and notation for modeling uncertain outcomes as lotteries, and in the next section we will examine certain behavioral hypotheses about preferences concerning these lotteries.

Given a set of possible outcomes $X = \{T_1, T_2, ..., T_N\}$, a simple lottery over X is simply a random selection from the elements of X with fixed probabilities $\{p_1, p_2, ..., p_N\}$. These probabilities are nonnegative numbers that sum to one, and p_i is the probability that the outcome T_i is chosen. A simple lottery will be represented as follows: $(T_1: p_1, T_2: p_2, ..., T_N: p_N)$. For example, suppose you are in a lottery in which you pay \$2 to get access to a die. You roll the die and get reimbursed \$1 for each point that is rolled. If you pay to play and roll a 5, then you will be \$3 wealthier, but if you roll a 1, you will be \$1 poorer. In this case $X = \{-\$1, \$0, \$1, \$2, \$3, \$4\}$. If the die is "fair," then all outcomes are equally likely, with a probability of 1/6. This means the lottery can be represented as $(-\$1: 1/6, \$0: 1/6, \$1: 1/6, \$2: 1/6, \$3: 1/6, \$4: 1/6)$.

We can also construct **compound lotteries** in which some of the outcomes are themselves lotteries. An example of a compound lottery is the process of applying to U.S. colleges. In the first round of the lottery, high school students (and their parents) apply to colleges for admission; the colleges then inform the students whether they have been accepted, rejected, or put on the school's waiting list. A student who has been accepted at one college but wait-listed at another more preferred college must decide whether to accept the first college's offer by the cutoff date or wait and hope to be accepted later at the second college. If she chooses to wait, she has essentially entered herself in a second lottery. The entire process, from initial application to eventual enrollment, is a compound lottery.

In general, the first round of a compound lottery determines which of the lotteries $\{L_1, L_2, ..., L_K\}$ will be played next. If the lottery chosen in the first round is a simple lottery, then in the second round this lottery is played, an outcome is selected, and the lottery ends. If the lottery chosen in the first round is itself a compound lottery, then in the second round the compound lottery is played, which results in the selection of a *third* lottery. This third lottery is played in the third round, and so forth. Compound lotteries will be denoted as $(L_1: p_1, L_2: p_2, ..., L_K: p_K)$, where the numbers $\{p_1, p_2, ..., p_K\}$ are positive numbers that sum to one. The number p is the probability of selecting the lottery L_i in the first round.

Consider once again the decision Jimenez is making about her factory's design. Let T_1, T_2, T_3, and T_4 denote factory construction costs of $1 million, $1.4 million, 1.6 million, and $2 million, respectively. If A is chosen, then there is a 60% chance that construction costs will be T_1 and a 40% chance that construction costs will be T_4. Once Jimenez makes a decision to choose Factory A , she faces the simple lottery (T_1: 0.6, T_4: 0.4). We will refer to this lottery as L_A. Similarly, if she chooses Factory B she faces the simple lottery (T_2: 0.5, T_3: 0.5), which we will refer to as L_B. An example of a compound lottery is $L^* = (T_1: 0.60, L_B: 0.40)$. L^* represents a situation in which Jimenez only knows the cost of Factory A before she has to make her choice, and will choose Factory A if the cost of Factory A is low and will choose Factory B if the cost of Factory B is high. There is a 60% chance she will choose Factory A and the outcome will be T_1, and there is a 40% chance she will choose Factory B and the outcome will be that of the lottery L_B.

2.5 · Expected utility

In order to have any hope of extending our decision theory framework to a world with uncertain outcomes, decision makers must have a method for ranking lotteries. In this book we will assume that the preferences of decision makers over lotteries satisfy the **expected utility hypothesis**. Simply put, this hypothesis states that decision makers rank lotteries according to their "expected utilities." Lotteries with higher expected utility are preferred over lotteries with lower expected utility.

More precisely, the expected utility hypothesis is as follows:

Expected Utility Hypothesis   There exists a function U(.) over the final outcomes $\{T_1, \ldots, T_N\}$ such that:

1. A simple lottery $L_1 = (T_1: p_{11}, T_2: p_{12}, \ldots, T_N: p_{1N})$ is preferred to a simple lottery $L_2 = (T_1: p_{21}, T_2: p_{22}, \ldots, T_N: p_{2N})$ if and only if $EU(L_1) \geq EU(L_2)$, where $EU(L_i) = \sum_{k=1}^{n} p_{ik} U(T_k)$ for i = 1,2;

2. a compound lottery $L_1^* = (L_{11}: q_{11}, \ldots, L_{1N}: q_{1N})$ is preferred over a compound lottery $L_2^* = (L_{21}: q_{21}, \ldots, L_{2N}: q_{2N})$ if and only if $EU(L_1^*) \geq EU(L_2^*)$, where $EU(L_i^*) = \sum_{j=1}^{n} q_{ij} EU(L_{ij})$ for i = 1,2.[2]

---

[2] This definition is to be understood recursively. If any of the lotteries that make up the compound lottery are all simple then the expected utility is defined by part 1 of the definition. If any of these lotteries are themselves compound lotteries, then shuld be applied the formula recursively to each of them.

The function $U(T_i)$ is called a **von Neumann–Morgenstern utility representation** (VNMU) for the decision maker's lottery preferences, and the number EU(L) is the **expected utility** of the lottery L based on the von Neumann–Morgenstern utility function U.

In order to illustrate the concept of expected utility, consider your purchase of a $2 state lottery ticket. If it is your lucky day, you win back $10 million; otherwise, you are out the $2. The chances of your winning are 1 in 15 million. If losing the $2 only results in a loss in utility of 0.01, whereas winning $10 million results in a gain in utility of 12 million, then the expected gain in utility from buying the lottery ticket is equal to $(-0.01) \cdot (14,999,999/15,000,000) + (12,000,000) \cdot (1/15,000,000) = 0.79$. Because, on average, your utility will be higher by 0.79 if you buy the ticket than if you don't, we assume you will buy the ticket. That is, we assume you choose the option with the highest expected utility.

Like the ordinal utility hypothesis, the expected utility hypothesis implies that preferences over lotteries satisfy certain conditions. The restrictions on preferences implied by the expected utility hypothesis are much stronger and more controversial than those implied by the ordinal utility hypothesis. As a result, the empirical validity of this hypothesis is an area of current research interest among economists.

Because choosing among lotteries confronts a decision maker with subtle trade-offs between the various outcomes, such choices reveal more information about her preferences than would a simple ordinal ranking of them. In particular, when a VNMU utility function exists, it reveals in a limited sense by *how much* she prefers one alternative over others. Such information is called a **cardinal measure** of her preferences. Temperature, acidity, and pressure are other examples of cardinal measures. Two cardinal measures are equivalent if they differ only in their choice of units and origin; for example, the Celsius and Fahrenheit scales are equivalent measures of temperature.

Because the VNMU function cannot be observed directly, the expected utility hypothesis cannot be tested directly. What can be observed are the choices people make when they have to choose among pairs of lotteries. Fortunately, in 1949 the mathematician John von Neumann and the economist Oscar Morgenstern showed that the expected utility hypothesis is satisfied if and only if the decision maker's preferences over lotteries satisfy five directly testable conditions. Not surprisingly, these five conditions are known as the **von Neumann–Morgenstern axioms,** and the mathematical theorem that establishes their equivalence with the expected utility hypothesis is called the **expected utility theorem**. In the rest of this section we will examine these axioms in detail and prove the expected utility theorem. Although this material is somewhat technical and dry, it is important because the expected utility hypothesis forms the behavioral foundations on which much else in this book rests.

The expected utility hypothesis implies that the decision maker's preferences over lotteries can be represented by an ordinal utility function. We already know from our earlier discussion of ordinal utility functions that this implies that these preferences are complete, reflexive, and transitive. These three properties, therefore, must be satisfied in order that the expected utility hypothesis holds.

Axiom 2.1 (consistency)   There is a complete, reflexive, and transitive preference ordering over the elements of the set L of lotteries constructed from the finite set of outcomes X.

The consistency axiom implies it is possible to order the elements of X from the worst to the best. The reason is that every outcome in X, say T, can be identified with the "trivial" lottery $L_T = (T: 1)$ in which the outcome T occurs with certainty. As a result, any preference ordering over lotteries implies the obvious preference ordering over elements of X: the outcome T is preferred to the outcome T' if and only if the lottery L_T is preferred to the lottery $L_{T'}$. It is easy to see that if the preference ordering over lotteries is complete, reflexive, and transitive, then so is the implied preference ordering over the outcomes in X. Because X is finite, there exists a best and worst outcome in X. We will denote the worst outcome in X as T_W and the best outcome in X as T_B. For example, according to Table 2.1, Jimenez ranks T_1 as the best outcome and T_4 as the worst.

Consider a special lottery $L(u) = (T_B: u, T_W: 1 - u)$ in which only the best or worst outcomes are selected with probabilities u and 1 - u, respectively. As we increase u from 0 to 1, T_B becomes increasingly more likely to occur and T_W becomes increasingly less likely to occur. As a result, it seems reasonable that as u increases, the lottery L(u) becomes more desirable. This is the meaning of the second von Neumann-Morgenstern axiom.

Axiom 2.2 (monotonicity)   L(u) is preferred to L(v) if and only if $u \geq v$.

If T is any other outcome in the set X, then, by assumption, the trivial lottery $(T_B: 1, T_W: 0) = L(1)$ is preferred to T, and T is, in turn, preferred to the trivial lottery $(T_B: 0, T_W: 1) = L(0)$. Monotonicity implies that as u increases, L(u) becomes more and more preferred. The third von Neumann-Morgenstern requirement is that as u increases, eventually there comes a point where the decision maker is exactly indifferent between the lottery L(u) and the given outcome T. Otherwise, there would exist a discontinuity in the preference ordering.

Axiom 2.3 (continuity)   For every outcome T in X, there exists a unique number U(T), called the **normalized von Neumann-Morgenstern utility function**, such that the decision maker is indifferent between the (certain) outcome T and the lottery L(U(T)).

To see what the continuity axiom implies, let T_1, T_2, T_3, and T_4 denote, respectively, factory construction costs of $1 million, $1.4 million, $1.6 million, and $2 million faced by Sonya Jimenez. The outcomes T_1 and T_4 are, respectively, the best and the worst. As a result, we assign to T_1 the normalized von Neumann-Morgenstern utility of 1 and to T_4 the normalized von Neumann-Morgenstern utility of zero. *Suppose* Jimenez is indifferent between the outcome T_2 with certainty and the lottery (T_1: 70%, T_4: 30%)—a 70% chance of having a construction cost of $1 million and a 30% chance of having a construction cost of $2 million—then T2 has a normalized von Neumann-Morgenstern utility of 0.70. Likewise, if Jimenez is indifferent between T_3 and the lottery (T_1: 20%, T_4: 80%), then the normalized von Neumann-Morgenstern utility of T_3 equals 0.20 (Table 2.2).

The final two von Neumann–Morgenstern axioms concern "inconsequential" changes in a lottery. By this we mean changes that do not alter the lottery's relative attractiveness. These last two axioms have been the subjects of more controversy than the first three. The first type of "inconsequential" change is the substitution for one outcome in a lottery of another outcome that the decision maker finds equally attractive.

Axiom 2.4 (substitution)   Suppose the decision maker is indifferent between the certain outcome T and the lottery L, and two lotteries L_1 and L_2 differ only in that wherever T appears in one, L appears in the other. Then the decision maker is also indifferent between L_1 and L_2.

The second type of "inconsequential" change involves the replacement of a compound lottery by a simple one. This fifth axiom implies two things: (1) that the decision maker is interested only in the probability that each outcome will occur and not in the specifics of the mechanism by which the final outcomes are selected, and (2) that the decision maker believes the random selections that occur at each stage of a compound lottery are stochastically independent.

TABLE 2.2   Normalized von Neumann–Morgenstern utility function for Sonya Jimenez

Outcome	Utility
T_1	1
T_2	0.7
T_3	0.2
T_4	0

Axiom 2.5 (simplification)   Suppose L is the compound lottery, $(L_1: q_1, L_2: q_2, ..., L_M: q_M)$, where each of the lotteries L_i is simple and $L_i = (T_1: p_{i1}, T_2: p_{i2}, ..., T_K: p_{iK})$, $i = 1, ..., M$. Then the decision maker is indifferent between L and the simple lottery $(T_1: r_1, T_2: r_2, ..., T_K: r_K)$, where $r_j = \sum_{i=1}^{M} p_{ij} \cdot q_i$.

The whole point of specifying the von Neumann-Morgenstern utility function and the von Neumann-Morgenstern axioms is to prove

Theorem 2.1 (Expected Utility)   The expected utility hypothesis holds if and only if the five von Neumann-Morgenstern axioms are satisfied.

Proof   The proof that the expected utility hypothesis implies the five von Neumann-Morgenstern axioms is left as an end-of-chapter exercise. We will show below that the von Neumann-Morgenstern axioms imply that the normalized von Neumann-Morgenstern utility function is a von Neumann-Morgenstern utility representation of the decision maker's preferences over lotteries. But this means the expected utility hypothesis holds.

Suppose the five von Neumann-Morgenstern axioms are satisfied and the set of final outcomes is $X = \{T_1, ..., T_K\}$. The consistency axiom implies that these outcomes can be ordered from the worst, T_W, to the best, T_B. Let L(u) denote the simple lottery $(T_B: u, T_W: 1 - u)$ and let S be an arbitrary simple lottery $(T_1: p_1, ..., T_K: p_K)$. The continuity axiom implies that for every outcome T_i there exists a number $U(T_i)$ such that T_i is equivalent to the lottery $L(U(T_i)) = (T_B: U(T_i), T_W: 1 - U(T_i))$. The heart of the proof is the demonstration that every simple lottery S is equivalent to the lottery L(EU(S)), where $EU(S) = \sum_{i=1}^{k} p_i U(T_i)$. Once this is shown, the monotonicity and consistency axioms imply that any simple lottery L_1 is preferred to another simple lottery L_2 if and only if $EU(L_1) \geq EU(L_2)$. This is the first part of the expected utility hypothesis. The second part of the hypothesis now follows from the first part and the simplification axiom. We leave this as an end-of-chapter exercise for the reader.

Because T_1 is equivalent to the lottery $L(U(T_1))$, the substitution axiom implies that S is equivalent to the lottery $(L(U(T_1)): p_1, T_2: p_2, ..., T_K: p_K)$. Repeated use of the substitution axiom implies that S is equivalent to the lottery

$$(L(U(T_1)): p_1, L(U(T_2)): p_2, ..., L(U(T_K)): p_K). \tag{2.1}$$

The only outcomes of this compound lottery are T_B and T_W. It follows from the simplification axiom that this lottery is equivalent to the lottery

$$(T_B: \sum_{i=1}^{k} p_i U(T_i), T_W: \sum_{i=1}^{k} p_i (1 - U(T_i))). \tag{2.2}$$

But

$$\sum_{i=1}^{k} p_i(1 - U(T_i)) = \sum_{i=1}^{k} p_i - \sum_{i=1}^{k} p_i U(T_i)) \tag{2.3}$$

$$= 1 - EU(S)$$

because the outcomes T_i are exclusive and mutually exhaustive events. It follows from the transitivity of indifference that S is equivalent to the lottery $(T_B: EU(S), T_w: 1 - EU(S)) = L(EU(S))$, as we claimed. This proves the theorem. ■

The expected utility hypothesis simply says that there is *some* von Neumann-Morgenstern utility representation for the decision maker's lottery preferences. It says nothing about how many such representations there are or what relation, if any, each one has to the normalized von Neumann-Morgenstern utility (VNMU) function. It is easy to see that if U is a VNMU, then so is the function V obtained from U by multiplying U by some positive constant b and then adding another constant a.

The surprising fact is that these alterations of scale and origin are the *only* transformations of the utility function that will completely preserve the decision maker's preferences. That is, if the VNMU function U cannot be transformed into the VNMU function V by a simple change of scale or origin, then it is possible to find two lotteries L_1 and L_2 such that $EU(L_1) > EU(L_2)$ but $EV(L_1) < EV(L_2)$. This second stronger property of a VNMU means the function is a cardinal measure of the decision maker's preferences in the same way that temperature is a cardinal measure of the heat being radiated by a body.

Take the hypothetical VNMU for Jimenez given in Table 2.2, U. Any other VNMU for her preferences, say V, will differ from the function tabulated in Table 2.2 only by the addition or subtraction of a constant and multiplication or division by a positive constant. In particular,

$$= \frac{V(T_2) - V(T_1)}{\$1,400,000 - \$1,000,000} \div \frac{V(T_3) - V(T_2)}{\$1,600,000 - \$1,400,000} \tag{2.4}$$

$$= \frac{U(T_2) - U(T_1)}{\$1,400,000 - \$1,000,000} \div \frac{U(T_3) - U(T_2)}{\$1,600,000 - \$1,400,000}$$

$$= 0.30.$$

This ratio measures the *marginal* disutility of having the costs of the factory increase from \$1,000,000 to \$1,400,000 relative to the *marginal* disutility of having the costs increase from \$1,400,000 to \$1,600,000. This ratio will be the same for every VNMU representation of Jimenez's preferences. Since the ratio in this case is less than one, we can say the marginal disutility declines as costs increase.

Contrast what we can say about marginal utility when we know the decision maker's VNMU with what we can say when we only know the ordinal ranking of the outcomes. Marginal utility is meaningless for an ordinal utility function. When someone's preferences are described by a VNMU, however, we can talk intelligently about whether marginal utility is increasing or decreasing.[3] We will now relate the shape of the VNMU to the degree to which the decision maker will shun risky situations.

2.6 · Risk neutrality and risk aversion

Suppose a person's utility depends only on his purchasing power—that is, on his real income.[4] The **marginal utility** of income is defined as the *additional* utility received from an *additional* dollar of income. This number will normally be different at different levels of income. For example, if your income is very low and you are often hungry, then an additional dollar with which to buy food may result in a large increase in your utility. On the other hand, if your income is high enough that you are never deficient in food, shelter, or seasonally appropriate clothing, then an additional dollar of income may well be frittered away on minor amusements that improve your welfare only slightly. Risk neutrality turns out to be directly related to the way the marginal utility of income changes as income increases.[5]

Let us be more concrete. Imagine a very simple lottery, L_1, in which a coin is flipped. If the coin comes up heads, you win $100, but if it comes up tails, you lose $100. A second "lottery," L_2, consists of doing nothing. Suppose that some potential gambler, call him Kenny Peterson, is perfectly indifferent between the two lotteries. Assuming that his preference over lotteries satisfies the expected utility hypothesis, this indifference implies $EU(L_1) = EU(L_2)$. Because expected values carry with them a precise mathematical meaning we can express the previous equation as

$$0.5 \cdot U(Y_0 + \$100) + 0.5 \cdot U(Y_0 - \$100) = U(Y_0), \qquad (2.5)$$

---

[3] We still cannot talk intelligently about how much it absolutely increases or decreases, nor can we make utility comparisons between people.

[4] Traditionally, utility depends on a set of consumable goods and services. To describe utility as a function of real income amounts to assuming that the individual's ability to buy bundles of goods and services is a good proxy for the vector of individual goods and services themselves.

[5] Once again, a warning is in order. It does make sense to talk about the marginal utility of real income for a *single individual* rising or falling. It does *not* make sense to make interpersonal comparisons of utility. For example, we cannot logically argue that because person A is poor and therefore has a high marginal utility of income and B is rich and has a low marginal utility of income, therefore a redistribution of income from B to A will make the world a better place. That argument relies on ethics.

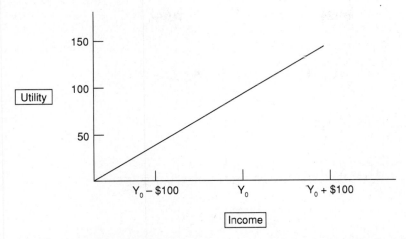

FIGURE 2.3 · Kenny Peterson's von Neumann–Morgenstern utility function

where Y_0 is Mr. Peterson's current income. The left-hand side of equation (2.5) simply says that there is a 50% chance that Mr. Peterson's income will rise by \$100 and a 50% chance that it will fall by \$100 if he takes part in L_1. Arbitrarily set $U(Y_0)$ = 100 and $U(Y_0 - \$100) = 50$.[6] Using this calibration we find that $U(Y_0 + \$100) = 150$. As Mr. Peterson's income rises from $Y_0 - \$100$ to Y_0, his utility rises by 50. That is, his marginal utility equals 50/100, or 0.5. Similarly, as his income rises from Y_0 to $Y_0 + \$100$, his utility increases by 50, implying a marginal utility of 50/100 or 0.5. Therefore, Mr. Peterson, through his preferences among lotteries, has shown that he has a constant marginal utility of income. Figure 2.3 shows that as income rises between $Y_0 - \$100$ and $Y_0 + \$100$, his utility increases along a straight line.

Suppose there is a second gambler, Ms. Safe, who prefers to do nothing rather than to play Lottery L_1. Once again, as long as Ms. Safe's preference over lotteries satisfies the expected utility hypothesis, we know that $EU(L_1) < EU(L_2)$, which says that the expected utility from Lottery 1 is less than the expected utility from Lottery 2. Therefore,

$$0.5 \cdot U(Y_0 + \$100) + 0.5 \cdot U(Y_0 - \$100) < U(Y_0). \tag{2.6}$$

Once again, arbitrarily setting $U(Y_0) = 100$ and $U(Y_0 - \$100) = 50$ reveals that $U(Y_0 + \$100)$ is less than 150. As Ms. Safe's income rises from $Y_0 - \$100$ to Y_0, her

---

[6] Remember that a VNMU is only defined up to a linear transformation, so you can arbitrarily set the origin and the scale.

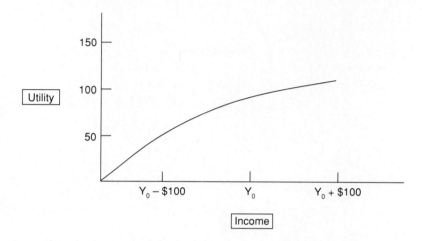

FIGURE 2.4 · Ms. Safe's von Neumann–Morgenstern utility function.

utility rises by 50, implying a marginal utility of 50/100, or 0.5. As her income rises from Y_o to $Y_o + \$100$, however, her utility must rise by less than 50, implying that her marginal utility of income is less than 0.5. We can determine from Ms. Safe's choice between the two lotteries that as her income rises, her marginal utility of income must fall. A possible utility function with this property is shown in Figure 2.4.

The lottery L_1 offers a 50% chance of winning \$100 and a 50% chance of losing \$100. On average, across many bets, you would exactly break even playing this lottery. More formally, the expected additional income from this lottery is zero. Such lotteries are called **fair lotteries**. When the expected additional income from a lottery is negative, the lottery is called **unfair**; and when the expected additional income is positive, the lottery is called **superfair**.

If a person is indifferent between playing a fair lottery and doing nothing (what we have been calling L_2), then that person has a constant marginal utility of income in that income range. Conversely, a person with a constant marginal utility of income will be indifferent between a fair lottery and doing nothing. This person will also jump at the chance to play any superfair lottery and will steer clear of any unfair lottery. Anyone who behaves in this way is said to be **risk-neutral**.

If, however, this person is not willing to play any fair lottery, but only superfair ones, then, as we have seen, she must have a diminishing marginal utility of income. In this case, she would be said to be **risk-averse**.[7] A third possibility is that the person is willing to accept unfair lotteries. Such an individual must have an increasing marginal utility of income and is called **risk-loving**. A risk lover gets some type of thrill from increasing her exposure to risk.[8]

We can be a little more general about the implications of being risk-neutral, risk-averse, or risk-loving. So far we have considered only comparisons of two lotteries where one of the lotteries was really just the status quo. Unfortunately, life is filled with situations where the status quo is not an option. Even when you do nothing, the world moves on around you, time passes, and your wealth and income change through no fault of your own.

Consider now the following two lotteries. In Lottery 1 a fair coin is flipped; if it lands heads up you win $10, and if it lands tails up you lose $10. In Lottery 2 the same fair coin is flipped; if it comes up heads you win $1,000, and if comes up tails you lose $1,000. In both lotteries the expected change in wealth is $0. But as you can see there is a big difference between them. Lottery 1 involves relatively modest gains or losses, whereas Lottery 2 results in much more dramatic changes in wealth.

Consider a risk-neutral, expected utility–maximizing gambler, such as Mr. Peterson again. We know that Mr. Peterson will be indifferent between either lottery and doing nothing. It follows that he is also indifferent between the two lotteries themselves.

What about a risk-averse gambler? Recall that risk aversion is characterized by a diminishing marginal utility of income. In this example there are four possible levels of income. In order of magnitude they are:

$$Y_1 = Y_0 - \$1,000,$$
$$Y_2 = Y_0 - \$10,$$
$$Y_3 = Y_0 + 10,$$
$$Y_4 = Y_0 + \$1,000. \qquad (2.7)$$

Because the marginal utility of income is assumed to fall as income increases, we know that

$$\frac{U(Y_4) - U(Y_3)}{Y_4 - Y_3} < \frac{U(Y_2) - U(Y_1)}{Y_2 - Y_1}. \qquad (2.8)$$

---

[7] A common misconception is the belief that risk-averse people do not take any risks. This is not correct. Risk-averse people simply must be compensated before they will willingly assume additional risk. The more risk-averse a person is, the more they must be compensated.

[8] Complicating things even more is the fact that most people are risk-loving when the stakes are small and risk-averse when the stakes are high. Think of the person who simultaneously buys life insurance and lottery tickets. What do you think this must imply about the shape of the person's utility function?

Since $Y_4 - Y_3 = Y_2 - Y_1 = \$990$, this inequality implies

$$U(Y_4) - U(Y_3) < U(Y_2) - U(Y_1). \tag{2.9}$$

Rearranging equation (2.9) and multiplying both sides by 0.5 results in

$$0.5 \cdot U(Y_4) + 0.5 \cdot U(Y_1) < 0.5 \cdot U(Y_2) + 0.5 \cdot U(Y_3). \tag{2.10}$$

The left-hand side of equation (2.10) is the expected utility of Lottery 2, and the right-hand side is the expected utility of Lottery 1. Because Lottery 2 has a larger dispersion in its outcomes than Lottery 1 (even though the expected dollar gains are the same for both lotteries), Lottery 2 is said to be *riskier* than Lottery 1. The expected utility hypothesis, combined with risk aversion, implies that the less risky Lottery 1 is preferred. The intuition behind this result makes a great deal of sense. Lottery 2 will result in either a large gain or a large loss. Because of the diminishing marginal utility of income, the gain in utility from the large gain in income is small compared to the large loss in utility from the large loss in income. A risk-averse person wants to minimize the swings in her income. As a result, she worries about more than the expected income from playing a lottery. She is interested also in how much her lottery income will deviate from this expected income.

2.7 • Summary

Frequently the decision maker is faced with the prospect of making choices without full knowledge of their outcomes. Alternatively, we can say the choice is made without knowing the state-of-the-world. We can incorporate this lack of knowledge into the decision tree by assuming that after the decision maker makes her choice, the state-of-the-world is chosen by a second decision maker, whom we call Nature. As a consequence, the decision maker is faced with having to choose among different random selections of the final outcomes. These random selections we call lotteries.

If the expected utility hypothesis is satisfied, then the decision maker can rank these lotteries according to their expected utility. The expected utility of a lottery is simply the weighted sum of the utility of each lottery outcome, where the weights are the lottery probabilities. The utility function is called a von Neumann–Morgenstern utility (VNMU) function because of the early research by these two game theory pioneers. John von Neumann and Oscar Morgenstern showed that the expected utility hypothesis is satisfied if and only if the decision maker's preferences over lotteries satisfy five conditions, called the von Neumann–Morgenstern axioms.

When the expected utility hypothesis is satisfied, the VNMU is a cardinal measure. That is, like temperature, the VNMU is completely determined once you choose the scale and point of origin. When the final outcomes consist of changes in the decision maker's wealth, the VNMU is often referred to as the utility of wealth. The decision maker's preference over wealth-altering lotteries reveals whether the decision maker's marginal utility function is constant, increasing, or decreasing in wealth.

If the marginal utility decreases as wealth increases, then the person is risk-averse and will not accept gambles whose expected payoff is zero; if the marginal utility is constant, then the person is risk-neutral and is exactly indifferent between accepting and rejecting gambles whose expected payoff is zero; and if the marginal utility is increasing as wealth increases, then the person is risk-loving and will accept any gamble whose expected payoff is zero.

In order to calculate the expected utility from a given decision, an expected utility maximizer must know the probabilities associated with each of Nature's actions. In this chapter we have completely ignored the question of how the decision maker determines these probabilities or alters them in the light of new information. This is the subject of the third and last chapter of this preparatory section.

2.8 • Further reading

The expected utility hypothesis comes from John von Neumann and Oscar Morgenstern, *Theory of Games and Economic Behavior* (Princeton, NJ: Princeton University Press, 1944), Chapter 3. The proof given here is based on those by C. J. McKenna, *The Economics of Uncertainty* (New York: Oxford University Press, 1986), and R. D. Luce and H. Raiffa, *Games and Decision* (New York: Wiley, 1957).

Experimental evidence against the expected utility hypothesis was first reported by M. Allais, "Le Comportement de l'Homme Rationnel Devant le Risque: Critique des Postulates et des Axiomes de l'École Américaine," *Econometrica* 21 (1953), pp. 503–546. The current state of knowledge is surveyed in M. Allais and O. Hagen, eds., *Expected Utility Hypothesis and the Allais Paradox* (Boston: Reidel, 1979). This empirical evidence has led to a number of alternatives to expected utility, including the **regret theory** of G. Loomes and R. Sugden, "Regret Theory: An Alternative of Rational Choice under Uncertainty," *Economic Journal* 92 (1982), pp. 805–824, and the **prospect theory** of D. Kahneman and A. Tversky, "Prospect Theory: An Analysis of Decisions Under Risk," *Econometrica* 47 (1979), pp. 263–291.

Measures of risk aversion have been developed by Kenneth Arrow, *Some Aspects of the Theory of Risk Bearing* (Helsinki: Yrjo Jahnssonin Saatio, 1965) and John Pratt, "Risk Aversion in the Small and in the Large," *Econometrica* 32 (1964), pp. 122–136.

2.9 · Exercises

Exercise 2.1   Show that if the expected utility hypothesis is satisfied, then the decision maker's preferences over lotteries must satisfy the five von Neumann–Morgenstern axioms.

Exercise 2.2   Suppose the von Neumann-Morgenstern axioms hold, the set of possible outcomes $\{T_1, ..., T_K\}$ is ordered from best (T_1) to worst (T_K), and every simple lottery L is equivalent to the lottery $(T_1: EU(L), T_K: 1 - EU(L))$, where $EU(L) = \sum_{i=1}^{k} p_i U(T_i)$. Let L^* be a compound lottery $(L_1: q_1,..., L_m: q_m)$ in which each lottery L_i is simple. Show that L^* is equivalent to the lottery $(T_1: EU(L^*), T_K: 1 - EU(L^*))$, where $EU(L^*) = \sum_{i=1}^{k} q_i EU(L_i)$.

Exercise 2.3.   What must the VNMU utility function look like for a person who both buys a \$1 state lottery ticket each week and simultaneously insures his house against loss by fire or flood. (*Hint*: Can a person be risk-averse over some wealth levels and risk-loving over others?)

Exercise 2.4   An executive at a publishing house has just received two *stock options* as a bonus. Each of these options gives the executive the right (but not the obligation) to purchase one share of the publishing company's stock for \$50. The executive can exercise both options today, or exercise one option today and one tomorrow, or exercise both options tomorrow, or choose to exercise neither option. Whatever she does, however, after tomorrow the two options expire and become worthless. If the executive exercises either option, she must then immediately sell the stock bought from the company at the market price in effect at the time. The stock price today is \$54. The stock price tomorrow will be either \$49 or \$59 with equal probability.

Draw a decision tree for this executive, taking care to label the action taken along each branch, to label who moves at each decision node (the executive or Nature), and to label the change in wealth at each terminal node. Assume there are no brokerage commissions or taxes.

Exercise 2.5. Suppose the executive in Exercise 2.4 is risk-neutral. Use backwards induction to determine her optimal course of action.

Exercise 2.6. A randomly chosen college student is presented with the following three lotteries:

(1) A 50% chance of winning $5 and a 50% chance of winning nothing,

(2) A 25% chance of winning $10 and a 75% chance of winning nothing,

(3) A 75% chance of winning $3.33 and a 25% chance of winning nothing.

The student prefers 1 to 2 and prefers 2 to 3. Assume the student is an expected utility maximizer and let U be her von Neumann–Morgenstern utility function. Setting U($0) = 0 and U($10) = 1, use her reported lottery preferences to find upper and/or lower bounds for U($5) and U($3.33). What can you say about the risk aversion of this student from these bounds? (*Hint*: Try plotting her utility function. Where is it concave? Where is it convex?)

• CHAPTER 3 •

Using Information

3.1 • Introduction

As you saw in Chapter 2, when you make a decision it is extremely important to take advantage of everything you know. Frequently, what you "know" you do not know with certainty. I do not know whether a tossed coin will and with the head side facing up or the tail side facing up. But I know the head side wi l face up 50% of the time and the tail side will face up 50% of the time.[1] Much of our knowledge is probabilistic. That is, it is knowledge about the probability something either is or will be true.

In the case of a tossed coin, most people will have the same assessment of the probability that the coin will land face up. But for some of the examples in Table 3.1, different people could very well have very different probability assessments. For example, Keynesian economists are likely to have different assessments of the probability that the economy will experience high inflation during the coming year than will monetarist economists. These differences occur for many reasons. Different people have access to different information. Or, as is the case with Keynesians and monetarists, they have different beliefs about how the world works. When we talk about "knowledge," we are not referring to absolute truths about the world but, rather, to the *beliefs* people have about the world; and some of these beliefs are probabilistic. For our purposes, **information** refers to any observation or knowledge that would lead someone to reevaluate her probability assessments. In order for information to be valuable to a decision maker, two things must be true: (1) the information must alter that decision maker's optimal action at some decision node,

---

[1]In this case the coin is called "fair".

43

TABLE 3.1 Examples of probabilistic knowledge

1. The probability you will encounter a traffic jam on the way to work during the rush hour is 0.70.
2. The probability that a competing bidder at an art auction is willing to pay more than $10,000 for the painting up for sale is 0.5.
3. The probability the XYZ Corporation will default on their $500,000 loan is 0.01.
4. The probability that a randomly chosen mainframe computer salesman earned more than $100,000 last year is 0.10.
5. The probability that the inflation rate will exceed 10% during the coming year is 0.05.

and (2) the information must be revealed to the decision maker before that critical decision node is reached. As a result, it is extremely important *when* information is revealed to a decision maker relative to when certain decisions must be made.

For example, suppose you are a sales supervisor for a firm and your initial assessment of a new salesperson is that there is a 70% chance she is a hard worker. Over time you get to observe her sales record. Unfortunately, her sales record depends on more than her effort. It also depends on a group of events we will simply lump together under the name "luck." If you observe a good sales record, you don't know if it was the result of hard work or simply good luck. Likewise, a poor sales record could be due to a lack of hard work or due to bad luck. Intuitively, however, the higher her sales during the year, the higher is the probability that she is a hard worker. It is less clear, however, by exactly how much you should alter your initial assessment of the effort she gives to her job on the basis of her subsequent sales record.

In this chapter we will present a method of altering probability assessments in the light of new information. This method uses the concepts of *information sets* and *conditional probability.* We will use appropriately modified decision trees to show how a decision maker can use recently acquired information to make more intelligent decisions.

3.2 • Information sets

The outcome of a decision problem usually depends not only on the actions a player takes but also on events beyond her control. In order to incorporate the effect of outside events into the decision tree, in Chapter 2 we introduced the fiction that these events are due to the actions of another decision maker we labeled "Nature." Nature randomly selects a state-of-the-world. The decision maker's welfare depends both on her actions and on the state-of-the-world.

The decision maker often will not know the state-of-the-world or the outcome of her actions with certainty at the time when she has to make her decisions. In Chapter 2 we represented this ignorance by having Nature randomly select the state-of-the-world *after* the decision maker chose her action. Partial ignorance was modeled by having Nature make some choices before the decision maker moved and by having Nature make other choices after she moved. For example, we can model the situation in which Jimenez knows the cost of Factory A before she makes her choice, but not the cost of Factory B, by having Nature move both before and after Jimenez. The first time Nature moves it selects the cost of Factory A, and the second time Nature moves it chooses the cost of Factory B.

One problem with modeling the acquisition of information by having Nature take some action is that the method breaks down when we go on to model multiperson decision problems in which the decision makers are privy to different information. A second problem is that even a small change in the specification of the decision maker's knowledge will often necessitate a complete redrawing of the decision tree. For these reasons, in this book we will model the acquisition of knowledge using a new tool: information sets.

We will illustrate the notion of an information set using the reformulation of Ms. Jimenez's decision problem shown in Figure 3.1.[2] The first decision node belongs to Nature. At this node Nature determines the cost of building both types of factories. Because there are two possible costs for each type of factory, there are four possible choices: (1) The cost of both types of factories is low, (2) the cost of both types of factories is high, (3) the cost of Factory A is high and the cost of Factory B is low, and (4) the cost of Factory A is low and the cost of Factory B is high.

Each of Nature's four "choices" leads to a decision node for Jimenez. Each of the five decision nodes has been numbered, and we will refer to them by their numbers. From each of Jimenez's decision nodes emanates two branches, each of which represents one of the two types of factories. Suppose Jimenez can observe whether the cost of Factory A is high or low but knows nothing about whether the cost of Factory B is high or low. Then Jimenez can distinguish between nodes where the cost of A is high (nodes 4 and 5) and those where the cost of A is low (nodes 2 and 3). Because she does not know whether the cost of B is high or low, she cannot distinguish between nodes 4 and 5, nor can she distinguish between nodes 2 and 3.

We can describe this situation by saying nodes 4 and 5 are in one **information set**, I_1, and nodes 2 and 3 are in another information set I_2. That is, I_1 = {node 4, node 5}

---

[2]Because we want to concentrate on the choice of factory, we have eliminated the choice of not building the factory at all. After choosing the type of factory to build, Jimenez can compare the expected costs with the expected revenues and decide whether or not to go ahead with the project.

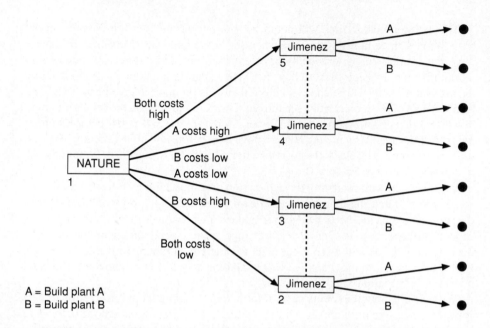

FIGURE 3.1 · Mrs. Jimenez's modified decision tree with five decision nodes, eight terminal nodes, and two information sets.

and $I_2 = \{node\ 2,\ node\ 3\}$. Simply put, an information set is a set of decision nodes between which Jimenez cannot distinguish.[3] When a decision maker reaches a decision node in some nontrivial information set, she does not know which node she has reached. For example, once Jimenez learns that the construction costs for Factory A will be high (but learns nothing about Factory B), she knows she is at either node 4 or node 5, and is *not* at node 2 or node 3. Similarly, if she were to learn that the costs of building Factory A are low (again, learning nothing about Factory B), then she knows she is either at node 2 or at node 3, and is definitely *not* at node 4 or node 5.

When two decision nodes are in an information set, we will display this by connecting the two nodes with a dotted line. This new feature can be found in Figure 3.1. One dotted line connects decision nodes 2 and 3, and the other connects decision nodes 4 and 5.

---

[3]There might be nodes not included in the information set that are also indistinguishable from those in the information set.

The collection of information sets constitutes the **information partition** for the decision maker. In Figure 3.1, the information partition for Jimenez comprises the information sets I_1 (consisting of nodes 2 and 3) and I_2 consisting of nodes 4 and 5).

Having defined what an information set is and how it will be depicted, we will now consider some *invalid* information sets. The following information sets are invalid because in each case it is possible for the decision maker to deduce logically which node she has reached using her knowledge of the decision tree and her previous decisions. The first example of such an ill-formed information set is shown in Figure 3.2.

In Figure 3.2 nodes A and C are designated as members of an information set. By definition this means that the decision maker should not be able to distinguish between node A and node C. But node C can be reached only from node A—and then only if the lower branch is chosen. The decision maker will know when she reaches node C by dint of her knowledge of Figure 3.2 and her action at node A. Therefore, nodes A and C cannot be in the same information set. Similarly, it would be incorrect for Figure 3.2 to show nodes A and B within the same information set, and it would be incorrect for nodes A, B, and C to be included in a common information set. The point is that an information set cannot contain nodes that the decision maker could distinguish by reason of their *following* one another on the decision tree.[4] We will therefore require:

Information set rule 3.1   If decision node B is an ancestor to decision node A, then A and B cannot be contained in the same information set.

Consider now the somewhat different situation shown in Figure 3.3. Suppose decision node C allows a decision maker to choose only between actions 1 and 2 and decision node B allows a decision maker to choose only between actions 1 and 3. If the decision maker reaches node C, then she knows her options are actions 1 or 2.

Because she knows 3 is *not* an option, she knows she *cannot* be at B. Therefore, C and B are logically distinguishable and cannot be in the same information set. This motivates:

Information set rule 3.2   Exactly the same set of actions can be taken at each of the decision nodes in an information set.

---

[4]It could be argued, however, that this diagram depicts a situation of "lost memory" or *imperfect recall*. When the decision maker reaches C, there is no longer any recollection of the choice made at A. As a result, it may be perfectly plausible for nodes A and C to "look the same." We will always assume decision makers have *perfect recall*

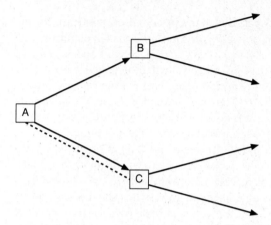

FIGURE 3.2 • An information set that contains two nodes that follow each other on the decision tree.

The representation of information with information sets allows us to simplify our decision trees. It is now possible to have Nature move first and completely determine the state-of-the-world. The decision maker's acquisition of information about the state-of-the-world can now be represented by her information partition. A further

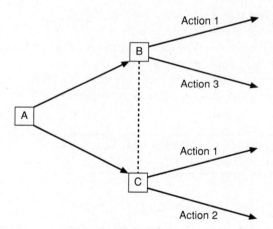

FIGURE 3.3 • An information set that contains two decision nodes that allow the decision maker to take different sets of actions.

benefit is that an alteration in our specification of the decision maker's knowledge does not require that we reorder the nodes and branches on the decision tree. Instead, we need only to alter the information partition.

3.3 • Marginal and conditional probabilities

When Ms. Jimenez finds herself at a decision node that is contained in a nontrivial information set, before she can intelligently determine what to do, she must first make a probabilistic assessment of where she is on her decision tree. In order to make such an assessment, Ms. Jimenez needs to have some model of how construction costs are determined and how they change over time.

In Chapter 2 we made no assumptions about how the costs of building the two types of designs were related. We simply assumed that the cost varied in some random way. In any given year, Factory A had a 60% chance of having a construction cost of $1 million and a 40% chance of costing $2 million, and Factory B had a 50/50 chance of having a construction cost of either $1.4 million or $1.6 million. Realistically, however, we would expect the construction costs of building the two factories in any given year to be related. In particular, if the cost of building Factory A is high, then the cost of building Factory B will *probably* be high as well—though not necessarily—and vice versa. As a consequence, information about the cost of building one type of factory provides useful (probabilistic) information about the cost of building the other type of factory. In statistical jargon, the costs of building the two factories are not **stochastically independent**. Two random variables x and y are independent if for every possible pair of values a and b, $P\{x = a \text{ and } y = b\} = P\{x = a\} \cdot P\{y = b\}$.

The relationship between the costs of building either factory can be fully captured by the **joint probability distribution** shown in Table 3.2. Each row of the table corresponds to a cost for Factory B, and each column of the table corresponds to a cost for Factory A. Each table entry shows the probability that a particular mix of costs will occur simultaneously. For example, the probability that the construction costs for both factories will be high equals 0.35. In addition, the probability that the construction costs of both factories will be low equals 0.45. This means there is an 80% (35% + 45%) chance that the construction cost will be high or low for both factory designs simultaneously, and there is only a 20% chance that one design will have a high cost when the other has a low cost.

The sum of each row or column in Table 3.2 is called a **marginal probability**. These are the probabilities that one design will have a particular construction cost in the face of complete ignorance about the cost of constructing a factory using the other

TABLE 3.2 Joint probability of costs for factory designs A and B

		Factory A	
		Low Cost	High Cost
Factory B	Low Cost	0.45	0.05
	High Cost	0.15	0.35

design. For example, the marginal probability that Factory B has a high cost is 0.15 + 0.35 = 0.50, and the marginal probability that Factory B has a low cost is 0.45 + 0.05 = 0.50. Notice that the two marginal probabilities sum to 1.00. The marginal probabilities are shown in Table 3.3.

Back in Chapter 1 we asserted that Factory B is designed to use standard materials. Because of this, it seems reasonable to suppose that Jimenez can learn the cost of building Factory B by observing the cost of constructing other B-type factories. Suppose, prior to making her decision, Jimenez observes that other companies that are currently building factories using a B-type factory design are all incurring high construction costs. Then she can be very confident—we will assume she is perfectly confident—that Factory B will cost $1.6 million to build.

More important, this information allows her to reassess the probability that she will incur high construction costs with the A design. She can perform such a reassessment by calculating the **conditional probability** that the cost of building Factory A will be high given that the cost of building Factory B is high. This is denoted symbolically as: P{Cost of A is high | Cost of B is high}. The conditional probability is defined by the following expression:

P{Cost of A is high | Cost of B is high}   (3.1)

    = P{Cost of A is high AND Cost of B is high} ÷ P{Cost of B is high}
    = 0.35 ÷ 0.50
    = 0.70

where P{Cost of B is high} is the marginal probability that the cost of building Factory B is high. Since, by assumption, the cost of building Factory A is either high or low, it must be the case that P{Cost of A is low | Cost of B is high} + P{Cost of A is high | Cost of B is high} equals one. This is easily verified using Table 3.3 and the definition of conditional probability:

P{Cost of A is low | Cost of B is high}   (3.2)
   = P{Cost of A is low AND Cost of B is high} ÷ P{Cost of B is high}
   = 0.15 ÷ 0.50
   = 0.30
   = 1 − 0.70
   = 1 − P{Cost of A is high | Cost of B is high}.

Of course, it could have been the case that the other companies were currently incurring low construction costs building B-type factories. In this case, Jimenez would want to calculate the conditional probability that the cost of building Factory A is high given that the cost of building Factory B is low, denoted P{Cost of A is high | Cost of B is low}. This conditional probability is defined as

P{Cost of A is high | Cost of B is low}   (3.3)
   = P{Cost of A is high AND Cost of B is low} ÷ P{Cost of B is low}
   = 0.05 ÷ 0.50
   = 0.10

where P{Cost of B is low} is the marginal probability that the cost of B is low. As before, we can immediately deduce that the conditional probability that Factory A has a low cost given that Factory B also has a low cost, denoted P{Cost of A is low | Cost of B is low}, equals 1 − 0.10 = 0.90.

Table 3.4 summarizes our calculations. Before you go further, be sure you understand how each of these numbers was obtained and what it means.

TABLE 3.3 Joint and marginal probabilities for factory designs A and B

		Factory A		Factory B Marginal Probability
		Low Cost	High Cost	
Factory B	Low Cost	0.45	0.05	0.50
	High Cost	0.15	0.35	0.50
Factory A	Marginal Probability	0.60	0.40	1.00

TABLE 3.4 Conditional probability of the construction costs for factory A given prior knowledge of the cost of constructing factory B

		Factory B		
		Low Cost	High Cost	Unknown Cost
Factory A	Low Cost	0.90	0.30	0.60
	High Cost	0.10	0.70	0.40
	Column Sum	1.00	1.00	1.00

3.4 • Decision trees

If Jimenez knows what it will cost to build Factory B before she has to choose which design to use, then her decision problem can be modeled using the tree displayed in Figure 3.4. In this new decision tree, Nature moves twice. First, Nature decides the cost of building Factory B. The probabilities used are the *unconditional* probabilities from Table 3.3. Jimenez makes her decision after observing Nature's move. As a result, Jimenez has two decision nodes. After Jimenez makes her choice, Nature moves again and chooses the construction costs of Factory A.[5] The probabilities associated with Nature's second choice are the *conditional* probabilities in Table 3.4, *not* the marginal probabilities given in Table 3.3.

At Jimenez's two decision nodes, she knows exactly how much it will cost to build Factory B, but she does not know exactly how much it will cost to build Factory A. Let us assume Jimenez is risk-neutral and ranks the two factory designs according to their expected construction costs. These **conditional expectations** are calculated as follows. The expected cost of building Factory A conditional on Factory B having high construction costs, denoted as E(Costs of Factory A | Costs of Factory B are high), is defined as

E(Costs of Factory A | Costs of Factory B are high)   (3.4)
    = \$1,000,000 · P{Costs of A are low | Costs of B are high}
    + \$2,000,000 · P{Costs of A are high | Costs of B are high}
    = \$1,000,000 · 0.30 + \$2,000,000 · 0.70
    = \$1,700,000.

---

[5] Another interpretation is that Nature reveals the costs for building factory A to Jimenez at this point.

Similarly, the expected cost of building Factory A conditional on Factory B having low construction costs, denoted as E(Costs of Factory A | Costs of Factory B are low), equals

E(Costs of Factory A | Costs of Factory B are low)   (3.5)
= $1,000,000 · P{Costs of A are low | Costs of B are low}
   + $2,000,000 · P{Costs of A are high | Costs of B are low}
= $1,000,000 · 0.90 + $2,000,000 · 0.10
= $1,100,000.

We can now use backwards induction to determine what Jimenez should do. If Jimenez learns that the costs of building Factory B are high, then she should select B. If she learns the construction costs of building Factory B are low, then she should select A. Of course, if Jimenez fails to learn of the costs of building Factory B and has to make her decision without this information, then she should choose Factory A.

Is it worthwhile for Jimenez to inform herself about the costs of building Factory B? Since there is a cost to doing so—for example, she may have to pay someone to conduct a survey of other firms—Jimenez must compare this cost with the benefits. The knowledge that Factory B's costs are low does not alter Jimenez's choice. As a result, such information confers no benefit to her. On the other hand, prior knowledge that the cost of building Factory B is high does alter her choice and thereby reduces

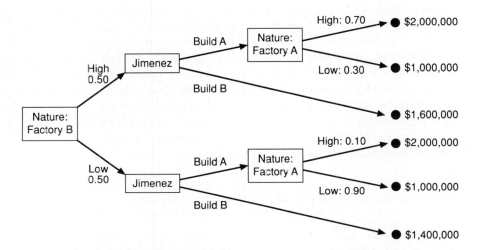

FIGURE 3.4 · A decision tree for Jimenez when she knows the cost of building Factory B at the time she makes her decision, but not the cost of Factory A.

TABLE 3.5   Expected cost of building factories A and B conditional on information about factory B

Information	Factory A	Factory B
None	$1,400,000	$1,500,000
Cost of B is low	$1,100,000	$1,400,000
Cost of B is high	$1,700,000	$1,600,000

her expected construction costs by $100,000 ($1,700,000 − $1,600,000). Since there is a 50% chance that Factory B's costs will be high, the expected value of the information equals $50,000 (= $0 • 0.50 + $100,000 • 0.50). If it costs less than $50,000 to obtain this information, then she should obtain it; otherwise, she shouldn't. This serves to illustrate a more general proposition: *It is not always rational to be fully informed.*

3.5 • Bayes' theorem

Decisions often reveal some of the information on which they were based. When that happens, other decision makers will want to update their own probability assessments to take this new information into account.[6]

For example, suppose another firm has just decided to build a car seat factory after hiring an engineering firm to determine the construction costs of the same two factory designs Jimenez is considering. Although the other firm's construction costs will be somewhat different than those of Jimenez, these costs are perfectly correlated with hers: The costs of either design are low (high) for the other firm if and only if they are also low (high) for Jimenez. If she knew the rival's costs, she would know her own. For obvious competitive reasons, the rival firm is not going to share its proprietary cost information with Jimenez. But the rival firm cannot prevent her from learning which factory design it chose. Suppose Jimenez knows that the other firm will choose design A if and only if it believes the cost of building Factory A is low and the cost of building Factory B is high. Any other cost combination will lead it to adopt a B-type factory.[7]

---

[6]This material can be skipped if the reader does not plan to cover the material in Parts 4 and 5. It is not used in Parts 2 and 3. It can also be delayed until the class reaches the material in Part 4 on games with imperfect information.

[7]The other firm will behave this way if, for example, the cost of building an A-type factory is either $1.000,000 or $2.000,000 and the cost of building a B-type factory is either $1,200,000 or $1,600,000 .

TABLE 3.6   The rival firm's decision, conditional on its private cost information

| | | Factory B | |
		Low Cost	High Cost
Factory A	Low Cost	Design B	Design A
	High Cost	Design B	Design B

If Jimenez learns that the other firm chose to build an A-type factory, then she knows the costs of both factories with certainty. As a result, she can see that Factory A will cost less than Factory B. In contrast, the knowledge that the other firm chose a B-type factory is consistent with both low and high costs for either design. As a result, such information seems to be useless. We will now show that this conclusion is incorrect. When the rival firm chooses Factory B, Jimenez cannot determine *with certainty* what each factory will cost to build. But she can revise the joint probability distribution over the three possible cost combinations. The tool for performing this revision is a theorem concerning conditional probabilities called **Bayes' theorem**.

Theorem 3.1 (Bayes')   Suppose the event F has a nonzero probability of occurring. Then for each event i,

$$P(E_i \mid F) = P(F \mid E_i) \cdot P(E_i) \div P(F) \text{ and} \qquad (3.6)$$

and

$$P(F) = \sum_{i=1}^{N} P(F \mid E_i) \cdot P(E_i). \qquad (3.7)$$

Bayes' theorem allows a decision maker to reassess the probability of the events E_i after learning that the event B has occurred using only the conditional probability that F will occur given that E_i has occurred and the unconditional probabilities of the events E_i.

We will use Bayes' theorem to revise Jimenez's beliefs after she learns the other firm's construction decision. Let E_{HH} denote the event "the cost of both types of factories is high," let E_{LH} denote the event "the cost of Factory A is low and the cost of Factory B is high," and so forth. Let F be the event "The rival firm chose to build a B-type factory." Jimenez wants to determine $P(E_{ij} \mid F)$. From Bayes' theorem we have

$$P(F) = P(F \mid E_{HH}) \cdot P(E_{HH}) + P(F \mid E_{HL}) \cdot P(E_{HL}) \tag{3.8}$$

$$+ P(F \mid E_{LH}) \cdot P(E_{LH}) + P(F \mid E_{LL}) \cdot P(E_{LL})$$

$$= 1 \cdot 0.35 + 1 \cdot 0.05 + 0 \cdot 0.15 + 1 \cdot 0.45$$

$$= 0.85$$

and

$$P(E_{ij} \mid F) = P(F \mid E_{ij}) \cdot P(E_{ij}) \div 0.85. \tag{3.9}$$

The joint probabilities $P(E_{ij})$ are those in Table 3.3. The conditional probabilities $P(F \mid E_{ij})$ can be inferred from Table 3.6: $P(F \mid E_{HH}) = P(F \mid E_{LL}) = P(F \mid E_{HL}) = 1$ and $P(F \mid E_{LH}) = 0$. The resulting revised probabilities $P(E_{ij} \mid F)$ are shown in Table 3.7.

Suppose the other firm chooses to build a B-type factory. If Jimenez incorrectly assumed there was no useful information in that fact, and made her choice on the basis of the unconditional expected cost of both factories, she would choose Factory A. In fact, however, the knowledge that the other firm chose a B-type factory is useful. As Table 3.8 shows, with this information the expected cost of Factory A is $1,470,000—*not* $1,400,000—and the expected cost of Factory B is $1,482,000—*not* $1,600,000. Not making use of Bayes' theorem will lead her to choose the more costly factory and, on average, will cost her $12,000.

Proof of Bayes' Theorem   From the definition of conditional probability we have

$$P(E_i \mid F) = P(E_i \text{ and } F) \div P(F) \tag{3.10}$$

TABLE 3.7   Revised joint probability of factory costs given the rival firm chose design B

		Factory A		Factory B Marginal Probability
		Low Cost	High Cost	
Factory B	Low Cost	0.53	0.06	0.59
	High Cost	0	0.41	0.41
Factory A	Marginal Probability	0.53	0.47	1.00

TABLE 3.8 Expected cost of building factories A and B conditional on the design choice of the rival firm

Information	Factory A	Factory B
Rival chose Factory A	$1,000,000	$1,600,000
Rival chose Factory B	$1,470,000	$1,482,000

and

$$P(F \mid E_i) = P(E_i \text{ and } F) \div P(E_i). \tag{3.11}$$

Multiplying both sides of equation (3.11) by $P(E_i)$ results in the identity

$$P(F \mid E_i) \cdot P(E_i) = P(E_i \text{ and } F). \tag{3.12}$$

Substituting the left-hand side of equation (3.12) for $P(E_i \text{ and } F)$ in equation (3.10) yields equation (3.6). Multiplying both sides of equation (3.6) by $P(F)$ yields

$$P(E_i \mid F) \, P(F) = P(F \mid E_i) \, P(E_i). \tag{3.13}$$

Summing both sides of equation (13) over the index i gives

$$\left[\sum_{i=1}^{N} P(E_i \mid F) \right] P(F) = \sum_{i=1}^{N} P(F \mid E_i) \, P(E_i). \tag{3.14}$$

Since the events $\{E_1, \ldots, E_N\}$ are assumed to be mutually exhaustive and exclusive, the term within brackets on the left-hand side of equation (3.14) equals 1. The result is equation (3.7), which proves the theorem.

Bayes' theorem often yields results that are counterintuitive. An example arises in the current debate over universal screening for infection by the virus that causes acquired immune deficiency syndrome (AIDS), known as the human immunodeficiency virus (HIV). HIV screening consists of a laboratory test for the presence of antibodies to the HIV virus using a sample of blood. This test is not foolproof. Like all medical tests, there is a chance for both false negative and false positive results.

The test is said to generate a *false negative* result if the laboratory claims to detect no antibodies to the HIV virus when the person is in fact infected. This will occur if the person has only recently been infected because it takes some time for the body to manufacture antibodies to the virus. The current false negative error rate is so low that we will assume it to be zero. The test is said to generate a *false positive* result if it detects the presence of antibodies to the HIV virus when the person is, in fact, not infected. The probability of a false positive result depends on the test used. For example, the ELIZA test has been reported as having a false positive error rate of about 7%. But if it is combined sequentially with the Western blot test, the error rate can be reduced to 0.005%.

It is currently estimated that about 1% of the adult population of the United States is infected with the HIV virus. But this overall infection rate disguises sizable differences among subgroups. For example, screening of military recruits and blood donors has shown an infection rate among women of 0.06% and 0.01%, respectively. Assume the infection rate among all women is 0.01% and we institute universal HIV testing using a test whose false positive error rate is 0.005%. What is the probability that a woman randomly chosen from the general population will be infected with HIV if the test result is positive? Before we go further, write down your guess. Let us now use Bayes' theorem to find the answer.

Let E be the event "infected with the AIDS virus" and let F be the event "the test is positive." We want to compute $P(E \mid F)$, the probability of infection given a positive test result. We know the probability of testing positive when the person is infected, $P(F \mid E)$, equals (nearly) 100% and the probability of testing positive when the person is not infected, $P(F \mid \text{not } E)$, equals 0.005%. We also know that the probability the person is infected, $P(E)$, is 0.01%. It now follows from Bayes' theorem that

$$P(E \mid F) = P(F \mid E) \cdot P(E) \div P(F)$$
$$= 100\% \cdot 0.01\% \div P(F)$$
$$= 0.01\% \div P(F)$$

and

$$P(F) = P(F \mid E) \cdot P(E) + P(F \mid \text{not } E) \cdot P(\text{not } E)$$
$$= 100\% \cdot 0.01\% + 0.005\% \cdot 99.99\%$$
$$= 0.015\%.$$

Substituting $P(F)$ into the expression for $P(E \mid F)$ gives

$$P(E \mid F) = 0.01\% \div 0.015\%$$
$$= 33\%.$$

This means that 67% of women who test positive for the HIV virus will, in fact, not be infected! If you don't believe this answer, check the arithmetic.

Figure 3.5 may help you visualize why the probability of infection is so small among those who test positive. The figure shows two circles. The smaller circle

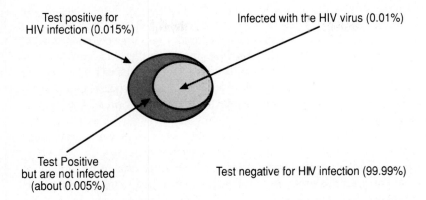

Test positive for
HIV infection (0.015%)

Infected with the HIV virus (0.01%)

Test Positive
but are not infected
(about 0.005%)

Test negative for HIV infection (99.99%)

FIGURE 3.5 · The size of the group of HIV-infected women relative to all women who will test positive for the virus.

represents the 0.01% of women estimated to be infected with HIV virus. The larger circle represents the 0.015% of the population who will obtain a positive test result: all of the infected population plus 0.005% of the noninfected population. The small circle is contained within the larger one because of the negligible proportion of false negative results. The probability of infection among those who test positive, P(E | F), is the area within the small circle divided by the area within the large circle. As you can see from Figure 3.5, this ratio is about 1 : 3.

3.6 · Summary

This has been a fairly technical chapter and probably tough sledding if you have not already taken a course in probability and statistics. What we have seen is that information concerning the choice Nature makes about one variable can, in certain circumstances, reveal information about Nature's choices concerning other variables. The revelation of that information to a decision maker, coupled with the clever use of conditional probability, allows the decision maker to generate a better perspective of where she is on the decision tree. Even when this information does not allow the decision maker to pin down where she is with absolute certainty, it will often allow her to reassess the probability of being at any node on the decision tree. Armed with this new information—and, as always, remembering to "look before you leap"—more intelligent decisions can be made.

In our analysis of Ms. Jimenez's decision problem, the construction costs of the two factory designs have been assumed to be exogenous. But recall that these two designs were submitted by two competing architectural firms. Viewed more broadly, the cost characteristics of the two designs were *chosen* by the two firms as their submission in a *contest*. In choosing what designs to submit, the two firms had to consider both Ms. Jimenez's and each other's decision-making process. In the terminology of this book, the designs submitted were the outcome of a *game*. The analysis of such games is the subject of the remainder of this book.

One reason game theory has proven so useful to economists is that it has enabled them to model the revelation of information in a coherent way. A very brief introduction to information sets and conditional probability, although a painful reminder of the difficulty of abstract analysis, sets the stage for some of the more interesting and challenging economic applications in this book. But before we can get to those applications, we must develop a framework for representing games and extending our single-person decision-making apparatus to these more complicated multiperson decision problems. To that we now turn.

3.7 • Further reading

A more advanced presentation of Bayesian updating can be found in Chapter 13 of C. Holloway's textbook, *Decision Making under Uncertainty* (Englewood Cliffs, N.J.: Prentice-Hall, 1979).

A good discussion of the likely consequences of universal testing for HIV infection is K. Meyer and S. Pauker, "Screening for HIV: Can We Afford the False Positive Rate?" *New England Journal of Medicine* 317 (1987), pp. 238-241.

3.8 • Exercises

Exercise 3.1   In Figures 3.6 and 3.7 we have presented two possible information partitions for Jimenez. What economic interpretation can you find for each of them?

Exercise 3.2   No employee at a department store stays more than three years. In an effort to find out why, the personnel manager of the store examined the personnel files of past employees and found the following (empirical) joint probability distribution between the number of letters in an employee's last name and the duration of the employee's employment at the store.

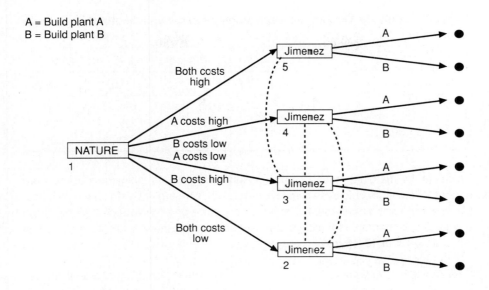

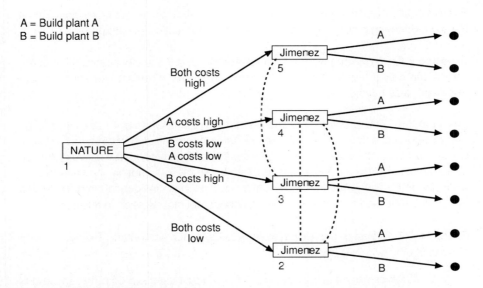

FIGURES 3.6 and 3.7 • Two other decision trees for Jimenez.

Joint probability distribution between length of name and length of employment

	Number of Letters in Last Name			
Years of Employment	2-6	6-10	11-15	16-20
1	5%	20%	15%	10%
2	4%	16%	12%	8%
3	1%	4%	3%	2%

Calculate the marginal probability distributions for years of employment at the store and for letters in an employee's last name. Use these marginal distributions to calculate the expected employment duration at the store and the expected length of an employee's last name. In the case of the latter, assume every employee's name has either 4, 8, 13, or 18 letters.

Exercise 3.3   Continuation of Exercise 3.2. Calculate the conditional probability distribution of an employee's length of employment given the length of her name. Use this conditional probability distribution to calculate the expected duration of an employee at the store conditional on the length of her name.

Exercise 3.4   Continuation of Exercise 3.2. Show that the length of employment at the store and length of an employee's name are stochastically independent.

Exercise 3.5   Prove that two random variables X and Y are stochastically independent if and only if the conditional distribution of X given Y equals the unconditional (marginal) distribution of X.

Exercise 3.6   This problem is based on Exercise 2.4 in Chapter 2. Use information sets to construct a decision tree for the executive in which Nature moves *first*—that is, out of chronological sequence. Alter only the information sets in your tree diagram so as to depict the executive's decision problem under the assumption she knows today what the firm's stock price will be tomorrow (i.e., has "insider information"). Use backwards induction to determine the executive's optimal decision in this case.

Exercise 3.7   Continuation of Exercise 3.6. Use your answers to Exercise 3.6 to determine

   (a) Whether the executive's actions today could be used to predict the firm's stock price tomorrow.
   (b) Whether his actions today and tomorrow could be used to show he had insider information at the time he acted.

Exercise 3.8 At a small midwestern college, a student who registers for a course is either "admitted" into the course or "closed out" of the course. In addition, students are allowed to register for no more than one course in a department each semester. The chairman of the Economics Department is worried that economics majors are being closed out of the department's courses because of competition from nonmajors. Unfortunately, the college registrar cannot provide the joint distribution of major/nonmajor status and closed out/admitted status among those who registered for the department's courses last semester. All the registrar can say is that, last semester, 20% of all students who registered for economics courses were closed out; 61% of all the students who were admitted into economics courses were economics majors; and 55% of all the students who registered for economic courses were economics majors. Use Bayes' theorem to calculate the proportion of economics majors who were closed out when they applied for an economics course.

PART TWO

Games with Perfect Information

• CHAPTER 4 •

The Elements of A Game

4.1 • An introduction to games

From the time we were children all of us have played games: hide-and-seek, Monopoly, chess, tennis. When economists talk about games, however, they have a much larger class of activities in mind. Besides the examples just mentioned, all of the social and economic interactions listed in Table 4.1 would be considered games by economists.

What the games listed in Table 4.1 have in common with the garden-variety games you have been playing since you were a child is that they are all situations in which a decision maker must take into account the actions of other decision makers. A chess player who does not take into account the past and expected future moves of her

TABLE 4.1   Examples of market games

1. Two television stations in a small city are setting their advertising rates for the coming year.
2. United Airlines and the Airline Pilots Association are negotiating a new labor contract.
3. A board of directors is deciding on a stock option plan for the top managers of the corporation.
4. A physician is making an out-of-court settlement offer to a patient who is suing her for malpractice.
5. The members of the House Ways and Means Committee are deciding whether to send a bill to the full House of Representatives.

opponent would be very foolish. Similarly, a television affiliate in Minneapolis would be foolish not to consider the advertising rates that other Minneapolis television stations are likely to charge when it sets its own rates. This interdependency between decision makers is the essence of a game.

Game theory is concerned with how individuals make decisions when they are aware that their actions affect each other and when each individual takes this into account. It is the interaction between individual decision makers, all of whom are behaving purposefully, and whose decisions have implications for other people, that makes **strategic decisions** different from other decisions. Decision theory is concerned with problems like the following: Mary must choose one of two numbers, 1 or 2. Simultaneously a machine will, with known probability, also choose one of these two numbers. If the numbers match, Mary wins some money; if not, she wins nothing. To determine what choice of number will maximize her wealth, Mary needs only to perform a few calculations. Now suppose the situation facing Mary changes. She must still choose a number, 1 or 2. But now another individual, Sue, must also choose 1 or 2. If the numbers match, then Mary wins some money, and if they do not match then Sue wins some money. What Mary should do depends on what she thinks Sue will do; and what Sue does will depend on what she thinks Mary will do. Less obviously, this means that what Mary does depends on what Sue thinks Mary will do. But what Sue does depends on what she thinks Mary thinks Sue thinks Mary will do, and so on. This is a problem for game theory.[1]

Almost all decision problems can be thought of as games. For example, consider the textbook case of a consumer deciding how much milk to buy at the grocery store. Because the consumer knows her purchase decision will have a negligible effect on the store's and the milk producer's profits, she probably ignores the interaction and takes the price of milk as a given, like the weather. As you know, this is called *price-taking behavior*. But when aggregated together with other consumers, her behavior is an important component of the milk-pricing game played between area grocery stores and milk producers. Although it makes sense to think of the individual consumer as a price taker, it may not be realistic to think of either the grocery stores or the milk producers as price takers. Small towns may have only two or three grocery stores from which residents can choose. Even in larger cities, the cost to potential customers of traveling around the city gives most grocery stores some local monopoly power. If we are interested only in understanding the consumer's behavior and preferences, the game-theoretic aspects can be ignored. But if we are interested in understanding the behavior of the grocery stores and the milk producers, we need to take the interaction into account.

---

[1] In fact, this is a problem you will be asked to solve in Chapter 11.

Games sometimes appear where you might not expect them. Consider the pricing decision by the publisher of a new mystery thriller written by a very popular author. Since each individual reader's purchase has no effect on the publisher, it would at first appear that demanders can be treated as simple nonstrategic "price takers" and that the publisher can be modeled as a classical monopolist. But if the reader believes the publisher will lower the price of the book in the future, then the reader faces a choice as to whether to purchase immediately or wait for the price to drop. Because book buyers know that the publisher can change the price of the book at any time, the quantity of books the publisher will sell today at the current price will depend on the price the public expects to be charged in the future. As a result, the publisher finds herself playing a game *against herself*.[2] This strategic interaction is crucial to understanding not only the publisher's pricing behavior, but also the consumers' demand behavior.

4.2 • A more formal description of a game

To this point we have been vague about what constitutes a game. To develop a true theory of games, we need to provide more structure. A game, more formally, consists of the following: (1) a set of **players**, (2) an **order of play**, (3) a description of the **information** available to any player at any point during the game, (4) a set of **actions** available to each player whenever called upon to make a decision, (5) the **outcome** that results from every possible sequence of actions by the players, and (6) a von Neumann-Morgenstern utility ranking (VNMU) for every player over the set of outcomes. The VNMU ranking of an outcome to a player is that player's **payoff** from that outcome. Any description of a strategic situation must have all six elements to be considered *well defined*.

4.2.1   Cooperative and noncooperative games

This book is devoted entirely to **noncooperative games**. Noncooperative games are characterized by the fact that the players cannot enter, ahead of time, into binding, enforceable agreements with each other. This distinguishes such games from **cooperative games**, in which the players can do so. For example, suppose you are deciding whether to get immunized against the flu. Your decision to do so will have implications for your roommates. Similarly, their decision to get immunized will have implications for you—if they choose to get immunized you are less likely to get the flu. The haggling

---

[2]Actually, the game pits the monopolist *today* against herself in the *future*.

(or lack thereof) between you and your roommates over whether you should be immunized is frequently cast as a cooperative game.

Formally, any cooperative game *can* be modeled as a bargaining session in which the players enter into enforceable commitments with each other, followed by a noncooperative game. Because the bargaining session can also be modeled as a noncooperative game, any cooperative game can be modeled as a noncooperative game, at least in principle. Doing so, however, has proved to be extremely difficult. As a result, analysts of cooperative games have developed tools that are very different from those used by noncooperative game theorists. For this reason and also because in our opinion noncooperative games have proved more useful *so far* in economic analysis, we have chosen to restrict ourselves to noncooperative games.

4.2.2 Players in a game

The **players** in a game are simply decision-making entities. Individuals, families, firms, and governments can all be considered players. **Nature**, a nonpurposeful entity, is a special type of player in a game. Nature chooses among its actions according to fixed probabilities. All players except Nature will be called **strategic players** and are assumed to be rational decision makers.

4.2.3 Rationality and common knowledge

Many psychologists and philosophers devote their entire professional careers to studying rationality. We will not attempt a summary of the debate. In decision theory, decision makers are assumed to make their choices according to internally consistent criteria. Such behavior is called **rational behavior**. Game theorists also assume that all players are rational. In addition, however, they have found it necessary to make two further assumptions. The first assumption is that the rationality of every player is **common knowledge**. A "fact" in a game is said to be "common knowledge" if every player knows it, every player knows that every other player knows it, every player knows that every other player knows that every other player knows it, and so on. Although this infinite regress may sound strange, it is important. Because decisions are going to depend not only on facts, but also on how other decision makers respond to those facts, the common knowledge assumption is crucial.

The second assumption game theorists usually make is that the complete description of the game—players, actions, strategies, order of play, information, and payoffs—is also common knowledge. This second assumption is *very* strong—much stronger than simply assuming that every player is rational. We will relax this assumption in Part Four when we examine games where players have different information about the environment in which they are playing.

4.2.4   The order of play

Players will be called on to make decisions at various points in a game. These points are called **decision nodes.** The sequence in which decisions are made is referred to as the **order of play**. If all players make their decisions in a sequence, one after another, then the game is called a **sequential-move game**. Chess is an example of a sequential-move game.

Alternatively, the players in a game may have to make their decisions at the same time. Such a game is called a **simultaneous-move game**. A sealed-bid auction is an example of a simultaneous-move game. You will have to wait until Part Three of this book before you will see a simultaneous-move game. Naturally, there are also games in which some of the decisions occur simultaneously and other decisions occur sequentially.

We can display the order of play using a diagram very similar to the decision tree introduced in Chapter 1. This diagram is called a **game tree**. A game tree can be thought of as a joint decision tree for the players in the game. Like a decision tree, a game tree is a picture composed of nodes and branches that satisfies the four rules given in Chapter 1. Each node in the game tree represents a decision point for one of the players; each branch represents a possible action for a player at that point in the game. The decision node is said to *belong* to the player that moves at that point in the game. All the concepts that were introduced in Chapter 1 for decision trees can be extended to game trees: path, parent, child, ancestor, successor, initial node, decision node, and terminal node. As with decision trees, we require of every game tree that each node has at most one parent, that there are no "loops," and that the tree has exactly one initial node. We will refer to this unique initial node as the **root** of the tree.

4.2.5   Information

In Chapter 3 you were introduced to information sets. You recall that an information set consists of decision nodes between which the decision maker cannot distinguish. In decision theory, nontrivial information sets represent situations in which the decision maker has not observed a previous action taken by Nature. In game theory, nontrivial information sets represent situations in which a player has not observed previous moves by either Nature *or other players in the game*. In order to be consistent with this interpretation, all the decision nodes in any information set must belong to the same player and must provide that player with the same set of actions.

Almost all games in economics are games of **perfect recall.** A game has perfect recall if no player forgets any information she once knew, and all players know the actions they previously took. This places two restrictions on the player's information sets. First, if two decision nodes are in the same information set, then neither node is a successor of the other. Unfortunately, this is not sufficient to capture fully the idea that players do not forget their previous moves. We must also rule out game tree diagrams such as the one in Figure 4.1. In this diagram, decision nodes D_1, D_2, D_3 and D_4 all belong to Player 1, and the information sets are $\{D_1\}$, $\{D_2\}$, and $\{D_3, D_4\}$. This means that Player 1 can distinguish nodes D_1 and D_2, but she cannot distinguish nodes D_3 and D_4. But D_3 is reached by taking action R at node D_1 and D_4 is reached by taking action L at node D_2. So the diagram implies that when Player 1 gets to D_3 or D_4, she has "forgotten" her previous action.

If every player at every decision node knows the actions taken previously by every other player (including Nature), then the game is one of **perfect information**. It is easy to see that a game is one of perfect information if and only if every information set contains only one decision node. In Part Two we will restrict our attention to games with perfect information, and we will consider games with imperfect information in Parts Three, Four, and Five.

4.2.6 Actions and strategies

The set of choices available at each decision node in a game is referred to as the player's **actions**. If a player has the option of "doing nothing," then this "nonaction" must be included as one of the player's actions. A **pure strategy** for a player is a rule that tells the player what action to take *at each* of her information sets in the game. Put another way, a pure strategy is a detailed plan that tells the player what action to take under *every* contingency. Because decision nodes and information sets coincide in a game of perfect information, a pure strategy for such a game is a rule that tells the player what action to take at every decision node.

For example, consider two people, Mary and Sam, who have met each other recently at a party. They are walking toward each other on the same sidewalk. Mary

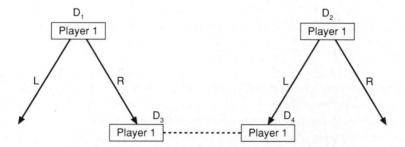

FIGURE 4.1 • A game tree diagram that implies a player has forgotten the action she took at a previous decision node.

is looking up and Sam is looking down, so Mary sees Sam first. When she sees him she can take two actions: (1) Smile at Sam and say hello, or (2) Do not smile at Sam but say hello anyway. Regardless of which action Mary takes, Sam, at this stage, has two possible actions: (1) Reply, or (2) Do not reply. If Sam replies, then Mary can either: (1) Ask him to join her for a movie, or (2) not ask him to join her for a movie. If Sam does not reply, then she can either: (1) Keep walking down the street, or (2) Kick him in the shin. One possible strategy for Mary is: Smile at Sam and say hello; if Sam replies, then ask him to join her for a movie; but if Sam does not reply, then kick him in the shin. Many other strategies are possible, some of which may be better than the one just described. It would have been incorrect for us to say that Mary's strategy is: Smile at Sam and say hello, and if Sam replies, then ask him to join her for a movie. This is not a strategy because it is incomplete: We do not know what Mary will do if Sam does not reply.

In contrast to pure strategies, we will also allow players to choose randomly between the actions available to them at every information set. Strategies that allow this type of randomizing behavior are called **mixed strategies.** More formally, a mixed strategy for a player consists of a probability distribution over the set of pure strategies.

Unfortunately, though easy to define, mixed strategies are often cumbersome to work with. Fortunately, in games with perfect recall, every mixed strategy is equivalent to a more intuitive type of strategy called a **behavioral strategy**. A behavioral strategy for a player specifies a probability distribution over the set of actions available *at each information set* that belongs to that player. Because all the games in this book are games with perfect recall, there is no loss of generality in restricting players to behavioral strategies.

A pure strategy can be viewed as a behavioral strategy in which all the probability assignments are either zero (the action is never taken) or one (the action is taken for sure). From now on, whenever we use the phrase *mixed strategy*, we will mean a behavioral strategy. A collection of pure or mixed strategies, one for every strategic player, is called a **strategy profile**.

4.2.7. Payoffs

Players are assumed to have a von Neumann–Morgenstern utility (VNMU) ranking over the set of possible outcomes of the game. This VNMU ranking constitutes the players' **payoffs** in the game. These payoffs are assumed to be common knowledge.

If Nature is not a player in a game and the strategic players all execute pure strategies, then they will choose a sequence of actions that leads to a determinate final outcome. This outcome results in a payoff for each player. As a result, every pure strategy profile can be associated with a collection of payoffs, one for each player. This association is called a **payoff schedule**.

If Nature is a player, or the strategic profile includes a mixed strategy, then the outcome from executing this strategy profile is not determinate but random. Put another way, the execution of the strategy profile results not in one outcome but in a *lottery* over the set of possible outcomes. Fortunately, we can readily extend the definition of a payoff schedule to handle this case. Since each player has a VNMU ranking over the outcomes, every player has an expected utility ranking over lotteries constructed from these outcomes. This collection of *expected* utilities, one for each player, is the "payoff" we will associate with the strategy profile. In this way the notion of a payoff schedule can be extended to all games and all strategy profiles.

Notice two things about this very general notion of "payoff." First, payoffs must incorporate *all* the relevant consequences of reaching a particular terminal node or outcome. As a result, the payoffs can differ substantially from the changes in income or wealth that the players experience at the conclusion of the game. Second, the payoff associated with an outcome can incorporate the means (that is, the sequence of actions) by which the players have reached that outcome. For example, if ethical values make some strategy reprehensible to a player, this can and must be reflected in the payoffs for that player. In addition, if players are not totally selfish but are affected by the welfare of other players, then this too must be reflected in the payoffs. This said, ethical and fairness considerations are ignored in most economic applications of game theory. In principle, however, they could be incorporated into the analysis.

4.3 • A detailed example of a game: The software game

Consider the following strategic situation: The Macrosoft Corporation, a computer software firm, is considering the marketing strategy to use for a new computer game they are currently developing. After much research, the company has pared its choices to two: (1) a "Madison Avenue" (MA) campaign or (2) a "word-of-mouth" (WOM) campaign.

Macrosoft knows that total sales of the computer game will be the same regardless of the campaign chosen, but the *timing* of these sales will be different. As long as Macrosoft is the sole provider of the game, employing a MA campaign results in very high sales in the first year as a result of an advertising blitz, smaller sales in the second year, and no further sales after the second year because of the saturation of the market. Using a WOM campaign results in relatively small sales in the first year, large sales in the second year due to initial users of the game telling their friends (by "word of mouth") how good the game is, and then no further sales because of complete saturation of the market. The present value of net profits in each year under

TABLE 4.2 Macrosoft's profits

Year	MA Campaign	WOM Campaign
1	$ 900,000	$ 200,000
2	$ 100,000	$ 800,00
Gross profit	$1,000,000	$1,000,000
Ad cost	$ 570,000	$ 200,000
Net profit	$ 430,000	$ 800,000

either ad campaign are shown in Table 4.2.Obviously if Macrosoft decides not to market the game, then the additional profit earned will be zero.

Relying entirely on Table 4.2 makes it appear that Macrosoft's optimal decision is to use the cheaper WOM campaign and rely on the reputation of the game to boost sales in the second year. But this conclusion ignores the potential entry of competitors. Unfortunately for Macrosoft, a second company, Microcorp, possesses the technical capability to produce a legal clone of Macrosoft's program within a year of the game's introduction at a time-discounted cost of $300,000. If Microcorp decides to introduce a clone, then the two firms will split the market in the second year.

Because of the interdependency between the two companies, Macrosoft and Microcorp are playing a game. In order to analyze this game coherently, we will need a complete description of it. That is, we need to specify carefully the players, the order of play, the actions and strategies for all of the players, the information the players possess and when they possess it, the outcomes from every strategy profile, and the payoffs.

4.3.1 The players in the software game

The players of our software game are Macrosoft and Microcorp. Although the buying public is affected by the actions taken by these two firms, no single buyer's purchase decision has any appreciable affect on either firm. As a result, we will treat the buyers as nonstrategic price takers and incorporate their choices indirectly into each firm's sales.

4.3.2 The order of play in the software game

In our software game the order of play is *sequential*: (1) Macrosoft decides what ad campaign to adopt, and (2) Microcorp decides whether or not to clone the game and enter the market. Because we have *assumed* that the two firms will split the market once they both have a product on the market, we have begged other strategic issues such as pricing and output decisions by the two firms. These are probably best treated as decisions made simultaneously. We will develop the tools needed to deal with these issues in Part Three.

Figure 4.2 displays the game tree for the software game. Decision nodes for each player are represented by rectangles labeled with their owner, terminal nodes are represented by circles, actions are denoted by labeled arrows, and payoffs are listed after the terminal nodes. By having Macrosoft's single decision node come before any of Microcorp's decision nodes, we show that Macrosoft must make its advertising decision without any knowledge of whether Microcorp will introduce a clone or not. In contrast, Microcorp can make its decision with full knowledge of Macrosoft's choice of ad campaign. A shorthand way of describing the order of play in this game is to say that Macrosoft is the **first mover**.

4.3.3   Actions available in the software game

Macrosoft has exactly three actions from which to choose: (1) Use a MA campaign, (2) use a WOM campaign, or (3) do nothing. We will refer to these three actions as MA, WOM, and IDLE, respectively. Microcorp has exactly two actions: (1) Clone the game

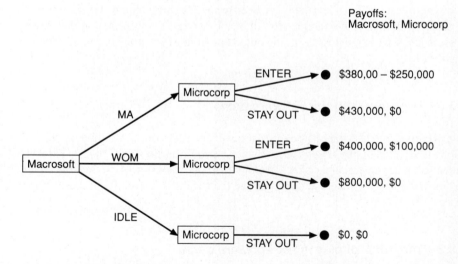

FIGURE 4.2 · The game tree for the software game between Macrosoft and Microcorp. Decision nodes, terminal nodes, actions, and payoffs are all depicted.

and enter the market, or (2) don't clone the game and stay out of the market. These two actions will be denoted ENTER and STAY OUT. Microcorp's first action is possible only if Macrosoft markets the game. That is, if Macrosoft chooses IDLE, then Microcorp must choose STAY OUT.

4.3.4 Strategies available in the software game

We will limit the strategies under consideration to pure strategies. Recall that a strategy is a detailed set of plans. Because Macrosoft has only one decision to make, a strategy for Macrosoft simply consists of choosing one of its available actions. Hence, three strategies are available: (1) Choose the MA campaign, (2) choose the WOM campaign, or (3) do nothing. Because strategies are *sets* of actions, the first strategy can be written {MA}, the second strategy {WOM}, and the third strategy {IDLE}.

A strategy for Microcorp is more complicated because a detailed plan for Microcorp must include contingency actions for any action that Macrosoft chooses. As a result, a strategy for Microcorp consists of decisions to enter or stay out of the market *conditional* on all possible choices Macrosoft might make regarding an ad campaign. One possible strategy for Microcorp would be to choose the action ENTER if Macrosoft chooses MA, choose STAY OUT if Macrosoft chooses WOM, and choose STAY OUT if Macrosoft chooses IDLE. We will write this strategy as follows: {ENTER | MA, STAY OUT | WOM, STAY OUT | IDLE}. The first word within the brackets (ENTER|MA) states what Microcorp will do *if* Macrosoft chooses MA; the second word (STAY OUT | WOM) states what Microcorp will do *if* Macrosoft chooses WOM; and the third word (STAY OUT | IDLE) gives Microcorp's action *if* Macrosoft chooses IDLE. This is just one possible strategy; Microcorp has three more distinct strategies. We have left it as an exercise to determine what these other strategies are.

It is common to confuse strategies and actions. In part, this is because, in the simple games frequently encountered in textbooks, strategies are in a one-to-one correspondence with actions. This is the case, for example, with Macrosoft in the software game. But it is crucial to understand that strategies are *not* the same as actions. A strategy maps out a plan of attack under *all* eventualities. Many different strategies can give rise to the same sequence of actions. For example, both of the following pairs of strategies result in actions whereby Microcorp enters the market and clones Macrosoft's game:

1. Macrosoft's strategy: {WOM}
   Microcorp's strategy: {ENTER | MA, ENTER | WOM, STAY OUT | IDLE}
2. Macrosoft's strategy: {MA}
   Microcorp's strategy: {ENTER | MA, STAY OUT | WOM, STAY OUT | IDLE}

TABLE 4.3   The payoffs for the software game

Microcorp's Action	Macrosoft's Action		
	MA	WOM	IDLE
ENTER	$380,000	$400,000	NA
	–$250,000	$100,000	NA
STAY OUT	$430,000	$800,000	$0
	$0	$0	$0

Top is Macrosoft's payoff, bottom is Microcorp's.

4.3.5   Information in the software game

In sequential-move games with perfect information, at the time a player makes a decision, all information about the actions other players have taken is known to that player. Therefore, although Macrosoft does not know what Microcorp will do when Macrosoft has to make a decision, Microcorp does know what action Macrosoft has taken.

4.3.6   Outcomes and payoffs in the software game

We will suppose both firms care only about the expected profits they earn under different strategy profiles. Thus, profits are the VNMU payoffs for both players. Macrosoft's and Microcorp's payoffs in the software game are shown in Table 4.3.

This table has six cells. Each cell lists the payoffs for Macrosoft on top and those for Microcorp on the bottom. Table 4.3 tells us, for example, that if Macrosoft chooses MA and Microcorp chooses ENTER, then Macrosoft will earn a profit of $380,000 and Microcorp will suffer a loss of -$250,000. The cell that corresponds to Macrosoft choosing IDLE and Microcorp choosing ENTER has no payoffs listed because Microcorp cannot enter the industry unless Macrosoft has developed the software game. To be perfectly accurate we should have described the payoff schedule giving each player's payoff for every pure strategy profile (of which there are 12). That, however, seems to let technique dominate reason.

4.4 · Summary

In this chapter the essential elements of a game were carefully laid out. What distinguishes game theory from decision theory is its attention to situations in which the outcome depends on the decisions of more than one strategic decision maker. A complete description of a game must include the following: a list of the players; a description of the order of play; a statement about the information each player possesses; a list of the actions each player can take, the strategies available to each player, and the payoffs attained by each player at each possible game outcome.

A simple device for describing games is a game tree. Much of what we learned about decision trees in Part One holds for game trees. Implicit in the analysis of a game is the assumption that the game tree is common knowledge, as is the rationality of all the players. By common knowledge we mean anything that is known to all the players, which all the players know is known to all the players, which all the players know all the players know is known to all the players, and so on.

4.5 • Further reading

In recent years the assumption of common knowledge has come under fire, particularly by Ken Binmore. His views on this topic as well as on game theory in general have been collected in *Essays in the Foundations of Game Theory* (Cambridge: Basil-Blackwell, 1990).

4.6 • Exercises

Exercise 4.1   Write down all four strategies for Microcorp in the software game detailed in section 4.3.

Exercise 4.2   During the Vietnam War, the U.S. government wanted to motivate teenagers to register for the military draft. The problem faced by the government was that it would be impossible to punish everyone involved in any large-scale draft evasion. If the odds of being punished were too low, many people would be willing to risk being prosecuted to avoid the draft. To make the problem more stark, suppose Congress allowed the Selective Service to prosecute *only one* person who failed to register. Suppose also that the Selective Service announced it would go after draft evaders *in alphabetical order*. That is, the Service would begin at the beginning of the alphabet with, say, Abraham Aaabbot. If he failed to register, he would be prosecuted and sentenced to a five-year jail term. If he registered, however, they would move up the list to, say, Aaabot Aaron, and prosecute him if he turned out not to have registered. And so on.

(a)   Draw the game tree for this game under the assumption that there are only three potential registrants—Aaron, Burns, and Cheng—and the game is one of perfect information.

(b) Suppose the Supreme Court ruled it unconstitutional to single out people for punishment because of the alphabetical order of their names, but ruled that the Selective Service could prosecute draft evaders in some other random order, such as the order of their social security numbers. Would such a change alter the game being played? If so, how? If not, why not?

Exercise 4.3   Professor Brown announces he is going to auction off a dollar. Bids proceed in increments of 50 cents, bidders cannot bid twice in a row, and once a bidder passes she does not get to bid again. The highest bidder gets the dollar, but *both* the highest and the second highest bidders pay their bids to him. Draw the game tree under the assumption that Mary and Tom are the only two bidders, it is common knowledge that they each have only $2.00 in their wallets, and Mary gets to make the first bid.

• CHAPTER 5 •

Nash Equilibrium I

5.1 • Nash equilibrium and backwards induction

Once we have described the strategic situation, we need to predict the strategies that will be chosen by the players in a game. A **solution concept** is a methodology for predicting player behavior. One of the intriguing and frustrating aspects of game theory is that there does not yet exist a universally accepted solution concept that can be applied to every game. There has emerged, however, wide agreement about some of the properties an acceptable solution concept should have

First, any solution of a noncooperative game must be a **Nash equilibrium** for that game. The name derives from its originator, John Nash, who was a pioneer of game theory. A Nash equilibrium for a game is a collection of strategies, one for each player, such that every player's strategy is optimal *given that the other players use their equilibrium strategy*. The last phrase has been italicized to emphasize the limited sense in which each player's strategy is optimal. Change the strategy of any single player and the proposed strategies of the other players will often become suboptimal.

In order for a player to make an intelligent decision as to which strategy to adopt, she must form a belief about the strategies the other players will adopt. If she is maximizing her well-being, then her strategy must be optimal given her beliefs about the other players. Only when the strategies form a Nash equilibrium can the players have a *common* belief about the strategy each of them will adopt. This belief will turn out to be correct. So requiring a solution to be a Nash equilibrium is tantamount to requiring that the players act as if they shared a common belief about what strategy each of them will adopt.

Unfortunately, in many instances games have more than one Nash equilibrium. If we are trying to predict as accurately as possible how the players will behave, we will need some mechanism for selecting which of the Nash equilibria are most reasonable.

The first method we propose for finding "reasonable" Nash equilibria is an extension of the methodology we employed in Chapter 1 to solve single-player decision problems: **backwards induction**. Since you have seen this approach before, you will probably read the next page or so far too rapidly. Here is some advice: *Never read about a solution method quickly and without thought*. You can save yourself a great deal of confusion, time, and agony by thinking carefully about each of the six steps that follow. When applied to games with perfect information, the method of backwards induction works as follows:

1. Start at the terminal nodes of the game tree and trace each one back to its parent. Each of these parent nodes is a decision node for some player.
2. Find the optimal decision for that player at that decision node by comparing the utility ranking the player assigns to the terminal nodes that are reached from this decision node.[1] Record this choice at each node; it will constitute part of the player's optimal strategy.
3. "Prune" from the game tree all the branches that originate from the decision nodes selected in step 1. This pruning turns each of these decision nodes into a terminal node. Attach to each of these new terminal nodes the payoffs received when the optimal action is taken at this node.
4. You now have a new game tree that is smaller than the original one. If this new tree has no decision nodes, you are done.
5. If the new tree still has decision nodes, then loop back and apply step 1 to this new tree. In this way, you can work your way step by step up the game tree.[2]
6. For each player, collect together the optimal decisions at every decision node that belong to that player. This collection of decisions constitutes that player's optimal strategy in the game.

We will now apply this method to the software game described in Chapter 4. The game tree is reproduced in Figure 5.1. The last three decision nodes belong to

---

[1] If there is more than one optimal decision, then we need to reevaluate the payoff assignments and find a way to break the purported tie. If the modeler believes the tie is a correct formulation of the game, then we next need to determine whether or not there are "social conventions" that would make one choice much more likely than the other. If so, we use these social conventions to break the tie. Finally, if there are no conventions to fall back on, then we must acknowledge that the player's behavior will contain an element of unpredictability.

[2] Notice the remarkable terminology. We start at the end of the game tree and work our way "up" toward the root of the tree.

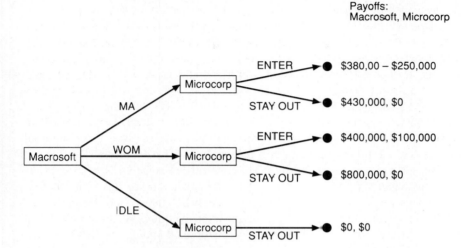

Payoffs:
Macrosoft, Microcorp

FIGURE 5.1 • The game tree of the software game

Microcorp. If Macrosoft chooses the action MA, then Microcorp earns a $0 profit if it chooses STAY OUT and suffers a loss of $250,000 if it chooses ENTER; the optimal decision in this case is STAY OUT. If Macrosoft chooses WOM, then Microcorp earns a profit of $100,000 if it responds by choosing ENTER and, of course, $0 if it chooses STAY OUT. The optimal decision for Microcorp in this case is ENTER. The last possibility is that Macrosoft chooses IDLE in which case Microcorp must choose STAY OUT. Because these are Microcorp's only decision nodes, we have found its optimal strategy: {STAY OUT | MA, ENTER | WOM, STAY OUT | IDLE}.

By pruning all of Microcorp's decision nodes and replacing them with terminal nodes, we are left with only one decision node, which belongs to Macrosoft. According to our strategy of solving the game by backwards induction, we will loop back and evaluate Macrosoft's possible actions *under the assumption that Microcorp chooses its optimal strategy.* If Macrosoft chooses the {MA} strategy,[3] then Microcorp will stay out and Macrosoft will earn a profit of $430,000. If Macrosoft chooses the {WOM} strategy, then Microcorp will enter and Macrosoft will earn a profit of $400,000. Finally, if Macrosoft chooses {IDLE}, then it earns a profit of $0. Clearly, Macrosoft's optimal decision is to adopt the more costly Madison Avenue campaign,

---

[3]Recall that actions and strategies are identical for Macrosoft.

so the optimal strategy for Macrosoft is {MA}. *Looking ahead* and taking Microcorp's entry decision into account prevents Macrosoft from making a $30,000 mistake.

The strategy profile that results when both players choose their optimal strategies is {{MA},{STAY OUT | MA, ENTER | WOM, STAY OUT | IDLE}}. This is a Nash equilibrium. If Microcorp believes Macrosoft will choose {MA}, then it can do no worse than to choose {STAY OUT|MA, ENTER|WOM, STAY OUT | IDLE}. Similarly, if Macrosoft believes Microcorp will choose {STAY OUT|MA, ENTER | WOM, STAY OUT | IDLE}, then Macrosoft will be best off choosing {MA}. Therefore, when each player plays his or her Nash equilibrium strategy, their beliefs about each other are confirmed. It is an important proposition in game theory that all strategies derived from using backwards induction are Nash equilibria.

In our software game, the costly Madison Avenue campaign is best *precisely because* it induces Microcorp not to enter the market. To see this more clearly, consider what would happen if it cost Microcorp only $10,000 to clone the game. It is now profitable for Microcorp to enter the market regardless of the ad campaign chosen by Macrocorp. As a result, Microcorp's optimal strategy is {ENTER|MA, ENTER | WOM, STAY OUT | IDLE}. Since Microcorp will clone the software as long as Macrosoft develops it, then Macrosoft might as well choose the cheaper advertising campaign. So Macrosoft's optimal strategy is {WOM}. Similarly, suppose the cost of cloning the program were $500,000. Then Microcorp would always suffer a loss if it entered and its optimal strategy would become {STAY OUT | MA, STAY OUT | WOM, STAY OUT | IDLE}. In this case, Macrosoft can ignore the threat of entry and should choose its advertising campaign solely on the basis of cost. Once again, the optimal strategy is {WOM}.

5.1.1 Threats and credible threats

Implicit in our analysis of the software game was the assumption that Microcorp and Macrosoft never talk with each other. But suppose they *do* talk with each other about their strategies. It turns out that our previous conclusions do *not* depend on a lack of communication between Macrosoft and Microcorp. The conclusions only depend on their inability to make *enforceable* commitments with each other. Suppose, for example, that Microcorp were to tell Macrosoft that it will clone the software regardless of the advertising choice made by Macrosoft. In other words, Microcorp tries to get Macrosoft to believe that it will adopt the strategy {ENTER | MA, ENTER | WOM, STAY OUT | IDLE}. When one player attempts to get other players to believe it will employ a specific strategy, it is called a **threat**.

Clearly, the threat is intended to induce Macrosoft to adopt a word-of-mouth campaign. If Macrosoft were to believe Microcorp's threat, it would earn $400,000 by employing WOM and only $380,000 by choosing MA. If Macrosoft actually chooses MA, then nothing stops Microcorp from carrying out the threat to enter—except the knowledge that by doing so it is harming itself.[4] Macrosoft would be wise to ignore the threat made by Microcorp.

This shows that the method of backwards induction incorporates the following principle:

A threat by a player is not **credible** unless it is in the player's own interest to carry out the threat when given the option. Threats that are not credible are ignored.

It is important to note the words "when given the option." If Microcorp *cannot* back down from its threat, we will say that the threat is **binding**.[5] The proper way to model the software game if Microcorp can make binding threats is to have Microcorp move *first* and issue its threat, and then to have Macrosoft move second and choose its ad campaign knowing Microcorp's threat. The game tree that corresponds to this new game is shown in Figure 5.2. To make the diagram simpler, we have dropped IDLE from Macrosoft's possible actions.

In the exercises at the end of the chapter you will be asked to confirm that Macrosoft's optimal strategy in this new game is: Select MA only if Microcorp threatens to STAY OUT should Macrosoft select MA and to ENTER should Macrosoft select WOM; select WOM in response to any other threat. Microcorp's optimal strategy is to promise to ENTER no matter what Macrosoft does. The outcome when both firms adopt their optimal strategies is that Macrosoft chooses the cheaper word-of-mouth campaign and Microcorp clones the software. Microcorp ends up $100,000 better off by becoming the first mover, whereas Macrosoft becomes $30,000 worse off.

There is an important relationship between credible threats and Nash equilibrium. As we just saw, if Macrosoft really believes that Microcorp will employ the strategy {ENTER | MA, ENTER | WOM, STAY OUT | IDLE}, then Macrosoft should choose {WOM}. But it is also true that if Microcorp believes Macrosoft will choose {WOM}, then it can do no worse than to choose the strategy {ENTER | MA, ENTER | WOM, STAY OUT | IDLE}. Therefore, the strategy profile {{WOM},{ENTER | MA, ENTER | WOM, STAY OUT | IDLE}} is a Nash equilibrium. It is, however, a Nash equilibrium that relies on an *incredible* threat, namely that of Microcorp entering if Macrosoft employs the Madison Avenue campaign. We will hereafter ignore such Nash equilibria.

---

[4]It is tempting to say that Microcorp might want to make the threat real so that future threats to Macrosoft will be taken seriously. But then the terminal nodes in Figure 5.2 are not the real terminal nodes. The game goes on. We will examine such repeated games in Part Five.

[5]If you have seen the movie *Fail Safe,* you know what such a binding threat means.

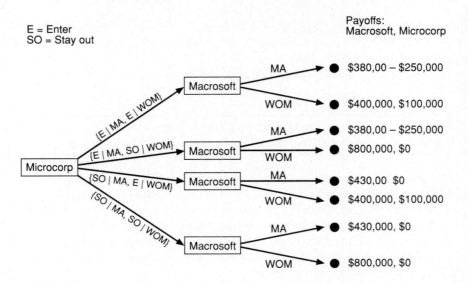

FIGURE 5.2 • If Microcorp can commit to an entry strategy before Macrosoft makes its decision, then that commitment should be reflected in the game tree, as it is here.

5.2 • Subgames and subgame-perfect equilibrium

The idea that a Nash equilibrium that incorporates incredible threats will be a poor predictor of how people will behave is almost universally accepted by game theorists. It is an idea usually attributed to Reinhard Selton, who formalized his idea by inventing the concept of a subgame and the solution concept called subgame perfection.

A **subgame** is essentially a smaller game within a larger game with two special properties. First, once the players begin playing a subgame, they continue playing the subgame for the rest of the game. Second, the players all know when they are playing the subgame. Because it is a game, a subgame has one initial node, which is a **subroot** of the larger game. The first property of a subgame is met if the subgame consists of the subroot and all its successors. The second requirement is met if every information set that contains a decision node of the subgame *does not* contain decision nodes that are not part of the subgame.

More formally, we require of any subroot x that every information set that contains x or a successor of x only contains other successors of x. Whenever a subroot of a game is reached, thereafter every player that moves can deduce that this has happened from the fact that the information set consists only of successors of the subroot. The subgame G_S of the game G_T is a game constructed as follows:

1. G_S has the same players as G_T, although some of these players may not make any moves in G_S.
2. The initial node of G_S is a subroot of G_T, and the game tree of G_S consists of this subroot, all its successor nodes, and the branches between them.
3. The information sets of G_S consist of those information sets of G_T that contain a decision node of G_S.
4. The payoffs of each player at the terminal nodes of G_S are identical to the payoffs in G_T at the same terminal nodes.

These four conditions amount to saying that the set of players, the order of play, the set of possible actions, and the information sets in the original game are preserved in the subgame. This definition implies that every game is a (trivial) subgame of itself.

One subgame of the software game is shown in Figure 5.3. This subgame begins with the node labeled D_2 and includes the two subsequent terminal nodes T_1 and T_2, the two branches between these three nodes, and the payoffs ($380,000, -$250,000) and ($430,000, $0). In games with perfect information, such as the software game, every decision node is a subroot. Since every game is a subgame of itself, the software game has four subgames.

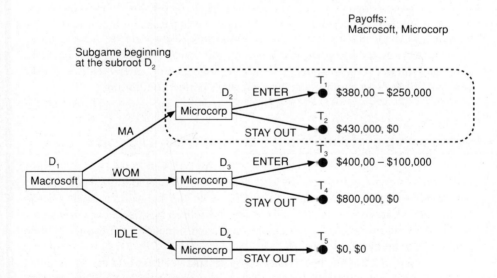

FIGURE 5.3 • The software game and one subgame.

Whenever the players begin playing any subgame of a game, this fact is common knowledge. As a result, rational behavior for the players in the overall game should also appear rational when viewed from the perspective of this subgame.

Return for a moment to the software game. We have already seen that the strategy profile {{WOM},{ENTER | MA, ENTER | WOM, STAY OUT | IDLE}} is a Nash equilibrium. But it is a Nash equilibrium that involves the incredible threat by Microcorp to ENTER no matter what type of ad Macrosoft chooses. Consider now the subgame in Figure 5.3 that begins at D_2. This subgame has only one Nash equilibrium in which Microcorp chooses STAY OUT. But, the strategy profile shown above requires Microcorp to choose ENTER at D_2. It is this nonoptimality in the subgame that makes the threat incredible. Microcorp's incredible threat is eliminated if we demand of Nash equilibrium strategies that they remain a Nash equilibrium when applied to any subgame. A Nash equilibrium with this property is said to be subgame-perfect.

Definition   A strategy profile is a **subgame-perfect equilibrium** of a game G if this strategy profile is also a Nash equilibria for *every* subgame of G.

In games with perfect information, the subgame-perfect equilibria consist precisely of those selected using backwards induction. The reason is straightforward. If we look at any subgame that begins at the last decision node for the last player who moves, the only Nash equilibrium of that subgame is the action that results in the highest payoff for the last decision maker. But this is precisely the action chosen using backwards induction. As we move up the game tree, backwards induction eliminates all the incredible threats, so that the collection of actions selected constitutes not only a Nash equilibrium, but a subgame-perfect equilibrium.

5.3 • Games with perfect information and uncertain outcomes

In the software game, every action by Microcorp and Macrosoft results in a determinate outcome. As we have already mentioned in Part One, the real world is usually not so predictable. The outcome of any game will depend both on the strategies of the players and on the state-of-the-world; usually the latter, and sometimes the former, will be impossible to predict ahead of time.

As you saw in Part One, uncertainty about the state-of-the-world can be modeled by introducing a new player, Nature. Nature is assumed to "choose" among the states-of-the-world according to probabilities that are known to all the players at the beginning of the game. We will continue to call a game with uncertainty a game with "perfect information" as long as *all* the information sets are single decision nodes. This means one of two things: Nature moves after every strategic player has moved; or Nature moves before some of the strategic players move, but Nature's move is observed by all of them.

As long as the game remains one of perfect information, it is possible to use the method of backwards induction to find subgame-perfect equilibria as follows (remember to pay careful attention to any solution concept):

1. Start at the terminal nodes of the game and trace each one back to its parent. If the parent node is the decision node of a player other than Nature, go on to step 2. If the parent node belongs to Nature, then move up the tree to its parent until the decision node of a player other than Nature is reached.

2. You are now at the decision node of some player other than Nature. Each action the player can take at this node results in a lottery (possibly trivial) over the final outcomes. Find the optimal decision for that player at that decision node by calculating the expected utility of each lottery that results from an action that can be taken at that node. Record the optimal choice at each node; this choice will form part of the player's optimal strategy.

3. Prune from the game tree all the branches that originate from the decision nodes reached in step 1. This turns each of these decision nodes into terminal nodes to which you assign the expected utility payoff to each player that results from the lottery selected when the optimal decision is taken at this node.

4. You now have a new game tree that is smaller than the original one. If this new tree has no decision nodes, you are done.

5. If the new tree still has decision nodes, loop back and apply step 1 to this new tree. In this way, you work your way step by step up the game tree.

6. For each player, collect together the optimal decisions for all the decision nodes that belong to that player. This collection of decisions constitutes that player's optimal strategy in the game.

5.4 • Games with perfect information and continuous strategies

To date, we have considered only strategies that involve discrete choices. In the software game, for example, Macrosoft had only three actions to choose among and Microcorp only two. Many decisions, however, involve choices among a continuum of options. For example, it would be more realistic to recast the software game as one in which Macrosoft chooses *how much to spend* on advertising. Other examples of continuous choices include the productive capacity of an electrical power plant, the salary to offer a prospective employee, or the insurance premium to charge a prospective client. The six-step solution procedure outlined here assumes that the game tree has a finite number of decision nodes. If the choice set of one of the players is infinite, however, then the game tree may spawn an infinite number of decision nodes as well. One way to handle the problem is to approximate the continuous set of choices with a discrete set. Fortunately, there is a way to solve such games without resorting to discrete approximations.

As an illustration we will examine a **duopoly**—that is, a market where the good or service is supplied by exactly two firms. A duopoly is a type of industry that is a subset of a larger class of industry structures referred to as **oligopolies**. Markets that are not characterized by either perfect competition or perfect monopoly are often referred to as oligopolies. Economists working in the subdiscipline of economics called industrial organization spend a good deal of their time trying to understand better how firms in oligopolistic markets behave. Because firms in oligopolies are nearly always involved in strategic decisions, economists in the field of industrial organization have been at the forefront of the developments in game theory. The model that we will present here owes its development to the pathbreaking work by Heinrich von Stackleberg in 1934. Von Stackleberg did not have access to modern game theory, so we have taken the liberty of cleaning up the game theory embedded in his duopoly model. The general ideas in this section, though, are his.

Our duopolists are the Sparkling Water Company and Clearwater, Inc. They sell exactly the same product, bottled water, in the same market. Both firms are private suppliers of bottled water to a community that has no municipal water company. Both firms must decide how much water to put up for sale. They constitute the players in the game. Subsequently, the price of water is set "by the market" so as to equate the quantity supplied with the quantity demanded by consumers.[6] Because the two firms produce a homogeneous product, the price of bottled water will be the same for both.

The technology for producing bottled water requires firms to set production levels and then contract with input suppliers to hire the necessary resources to produce the production target. Once these contracts are set, changes in output are prohibitively expensive. Sparkling Water has superior management and can contract with input suppliers before Clearwater can. Therefore, Sparkling Water can effectively set its production target before Clearwater does. This fact is known to both firms, the fact that this fact is known to both firms is also known by both firms, and so on. Furthermore, there are enough corporate leaks that once an output target has been set, both firms know about it, both firms know that both firms know about it, and so on. Therefore, the order of play is that Sparkling Water chooses its output first and this is observed by Clearwater, which then sets its output levels. The order of play and the output choices are common knowledge.

---

[6]Unfortunately, the price-setting mechanism will not be formally modeled. With the right theoretical tools, we could cast the process of price determination as a subgame of our game.

We will suppose that prior to hiring inputs each firm has an unlimited production capacity. If we let Q_1 and Q_2 represent the output for Sparkling Water and Clearwater, respectively, then the possible actions either firm can take are represented by any real number greater than or equal to zero.

The only thing left for us to do to describe the game fully is to define the payoffs. Assume both firms maximize profits. Our assumption of how the price of water is determined implies two important things: (1) the impossibility of excess demand (except when both firms choose to produce nothing) or excess supply (except when both firms produce an output greater than what is demanded at a price of $0), and (2) that neither firm has any direct discretion over the price at which its product sells in the marketplace. The market price depends on the *total* quantity of product put up for sale. As a result, the price—and remember that both firms get exactly the same price for their products—depends on the outputs chosen by *both* firms.

More concretely, suppose the inverse market demand function for bottled water can be written as

$$P = \begin{cases} 10 - Q_T & \text{for } Q_T < 10 \\ 0 & \text{otherwise,} \end{cases} \tag{5.1}$$

where Q_T is the *sum* of the outputs from the two water companies, and P is the price (in dollars per bottle) received by both firms. Given that $Q_T = Q_1 + Q_2$,

$$P = 10 - (Q_1 + Q_2). \tag{5.2}$$

Each firm can produce any output at a constant marginal cost of $3 per bottle. That is, there are no fixed costs to the production of bottled water. This gives us a total cost function for each firm, denoted by TC and TC_2, of

$$TC_i(Q_i) = 3 \cdot Q_i, \text{ for } i = 1,2. \tag{5.3}$$

Profit for each firm is just the difference between total revenue and total cost, so

$$\pi_i(Q_1, Q_2) = (10 - (Q_1 + Q_2)) \cdot Q_i - 3 \cdot Q_i, \text{ for } i = 1,2. \tag{5.4}$$

5.4.1 Isoprofit Curves

The profits of each firm depend on the outputs of both. As a result, there are many combinations of outputs for Sparkling Water and Clearwater that will generate the same level of profit to either firm. A relationship that describes the combinations of outputs that produce the same level of profit for one firm is called an **isoprofit** curve for that firm. For example, one possible profit level for Clearwater is $2. If Clearwater produces an output of 1 and Sparkling Water produces an output of 4, then equation (5.4) tells us that Clearwater's profits will equal $2. But Clearwater will also earn a profit of $2 if Clearwater produces an output of 4 and Sparkling Water produces an output of 2.5.

More generally, the answer to the question "Which combinations of outputs generate a profit of $2 for Clearwater?" is given by equation (5.5):

$$2 = (10 - (Q_1 + Q_2)) \cdot Q_2 - 3 \cdot Q_2. \tag{5.5}$$

Notice that the only free variables in equation (5.5) are the outputs of the two firms, Q_1 and Q_2. Solving equation (5.5) for Q_1 as a function of Q_2 yields

$$Q_1 = (- Q_2^2 + 7 \cdot Q_2 - 2) \div Q_2. \tag{5.6}$$

The graph of this function is shown in Figure 5.4, along with the graphs of three other isoprofit curves. There is a different isoprofit curve for each level of profit. With one exception, all the isoprofit curves have the same parabolic shape. The exception is the isoprofit curve corresponding to a profit of $0, which is a straight, downward-sloping line. This line is defined by the equation

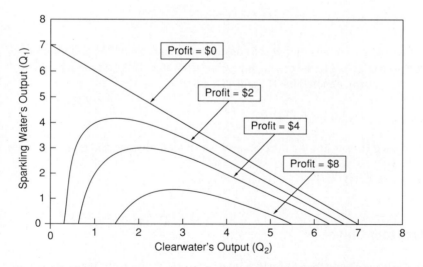

FIGURE 5.4 · Four isoprofit curves, depicting combinations of outputs that generate the same profit for Clearwater, are drawn.

$$0 = (10 - (Q_1 + Q_2)) \cdot Q_2 - 3 \cdot Q_2, \qquad (5.7)$$

or, equivalently,

$$Q_1 = 7 - Q_2. \qquad (5.8)$$

Notice that the zero-profit isoprofit curve lies above the $2-profit isoprofit curve, which lies above the $4-profit isoprofit curve, which lies above the $8-profit isoprofit curve. This raises an important technical point—namely, that isoprofit curves closer to the horizontal axis correspond to higher levels of profit for Clearwater. Indeed, the isoprofit curve for Clearwater associated with the highest level of profit is found when Sparkling Water produces an output of 0 and Clearwater produces an output of 3.5. You will be asked to verify this in the end-of-chapter exercises.

Sparkling Water also possesses a series of isoprofit functions. Because of the assumed symmetry between the two firms, the algebra of deriving an equation for these functions should be clear, but the graphical depiction requires a little caution. Because Clearwater's output is measured along the horizontal axis whereas Sparkling Water's output is measured along the vertical axis, Sparkling Water's isoprofit curves should simply be an inverted version of Clearwater's isoprofit curves. Two of these curves are shown in Figure 5.5. Higher profit levels for Sparkling Water will be those closer to the vertical axis.

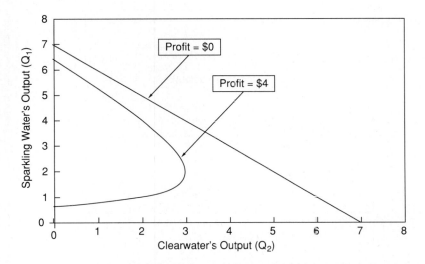

FIGURE 5.5 · Two isoprofit curves for Sparkling Water are drawn. Isoprofit curves associated with higher profits will lie closer to the vertical axis.

Because Clearwater's zero-profit isoprofit line is coincidental with Sparkling Water's zero-profit isoprofit line, any output pairs that lie above this line generate a loss for *both* firms. Because both firms can guarantee themselves a profit of zero by producing no output, the equilibrium pairs of output of the two firms must lie below this line. Hence we eliminate any strategies from consideration that result in output combinations to the northeast of this line.

5.4.2. Reaction curves

Yet another extremely useful technical construct is the **reaction function**, whose graph is called the **reaction curve**. A reaction function assigns to every fixed output level for one firm the profit-maximizing output level for the other. Because Clearwater must make its output decision after Sparkling Water has made its output decision, it makes sense to derive the reaction function for Clearwater.

To see how to derive graphically Clearwater's reaction curve, consider Figure 5.6. Suppose Sparkling Water were to produce an output of 3 units. Having made this output decision, Clearwater knows that it cannot be changed. As a result, the only possible pairs of outputs for the two firms are those that lie on the horizontal line through $Q_1 = 3$ (Q_1 being the output for Sparkling Water). Being constrained by this

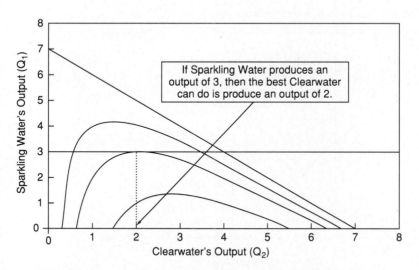

FIGURE 5.6 • Assuming Sparkling Water chooses an output of 3, then the isoprofit curve tangent to the horizontal line at a height of 3 will maximize Clearwater's profit.

line, the profit-maximizing output level for Clearwater s where this horizontal line is *tangent* to one of Clearwater's isoprofit curves. All other points on this line lie on isoprofit curves associated with *lower* profit. This tangency point is shown in Figure 5.6 and corresponds to an output of 2 bottles of water and a profit of $4 for Clearwater.

Clearwater's reaction curve consists of the collection of all output combinations that maximize Clearwater's profits given a specific output choice by Sparkling Water. Graphically, the curve consists of the "top" of each of Clearwater's isoprofit curves.

To derive the reaction function for Clearwater analytically, we need to maximize Clearwater's profit function, holding Sparkling Water's output constant. This requires taking the partial derivative of equation (5.4) with respect to Q_2 and finding the value of Q_2, denoted Q_2^*, which makes the expression zero:

$$\partial \pi_2 / \partial Q_2 = (10 - (Q_1 + Q_2^*)) - Q_2^* - 3 = 0. \tag{5.9}$$

The solution is

$$Q_2^* = \begin{cases} (7 - Q_1)/2 & \text{if } Q_1 \leq 7 \\ 0 & \text{if } Q_1 > 7, \end{cases} \tag{5.10}$$

whose graph is displayed in Figure 5.7.

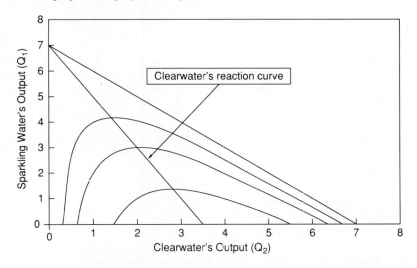

FIGURE 5.7 • The profit-maximizing output decision for Clearwater given any output choice by Sparkling Water is captured by a reaction curve.

5.4.3 Rational output choice

Equation (5.10) is a rule detailing what action Clearwater should take conditional on the output choice by Sparkling Water. As such it is a *strategy*—that is, a detailed set of plans. Not only is it a strategy, it is the *profit-maximizing* strategy. Because we have assumed there is complete information and common knowledge, Sparkling Water rationally believes that Clearwater will behave as described by equation (5.10). Sparkling Water's problem is to choose the point on Clearwater's reaction curve that maximizes Sparkling Water's profits. This corresponds to the point on Clearwater's reaction curve that is also tangent to one of Sparkling Water's isoprofit curves (Figure 5.8).

We can calculate this optimal output analytically as follows. First, substitute Clearwater's reaction function into Sparkling Water's profit function, thereby making the firm's profits depend only on its output, Q_1.

$$\pi_1 = (10 - (Q_1 + (7 - Q_1)/2)) \cdot Q_1 - 3 \cdot Q_1 \qquad (5.11a)$$

Second, calculate the derivative of this "concentrated" profit function with respect to Q_1 and find the value of Q_1 for which it is zero.

$$d\pi_1/dQ_1 = 3.5 - Q_1 = 0. \qquad (5.11b)$$

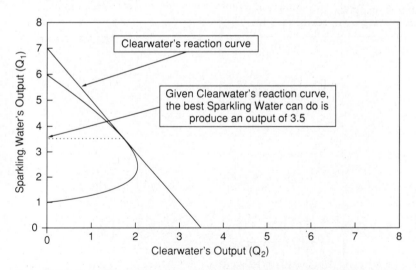

FIGURE 5.8 • Sparkling Water, knowing that Clearwater will rationally choose an output on its reaction curve once it learns the output Sparkling Water has chosen, will choose an output where its isoprofit curve is tangent to Clearwater's reaction curve.

The solution is obviously 3.5 bottles. At this profit-maximizing output level, Sparkling Water will earn a profit of $6.125. Clearwater reacts to this decision by producing 1.75 bottles, on which it earns a profit of $3.06. Sparkling Water earns twice the profit of Clearwater. So the **first-mover advantage** in this game results in additional profit of $3.065.

When von Stackleberg was writing about this model, he referred to the firm that chooses its output first as the industry **leader** and the firm that chooses its output second as the **follower**.[7] Because the leader in a von Stackleberg game has a first-mover advantage over the follower, what bars the follower from moving first and becoming the leader? In our example, the barrier was assumed to be contracting difficulties.

Another way one firm could gain a leadership position would be if the firm was particularly innovative in introducing new products. In this case, the leader would be a monopolist in the short run who faces the threat of entry from another firm. In order to maintain its Stackleberg leadership, however, this innovating firm must find it prohibitively costly for it to alter its output. Otherwise, the entrant would expect a reaction by the monopolist to its entry and therefore will no longer act as a Stackleberg follower. One way the leader could make it very costly for it to alter its own output would be to enter into very long term contracts with suppliers and/or consumers. Such contractual obligations reduce the leader's flexibility and make it more credible that it will not alter its output in response to entry. Of course, long-term contracts are risky in that they make the firm more vulnerable to changes in taste or technology. As a result, Stackleberg competition is more likely where the technology is very mature and demand is very stable, and much less likely where the technology is changing quickly or where demand is highly variable.

5.5 • Summary

In this chapter we have discussed the most important solution concept for noncooperative games: Nash equilibrium. The strategies chosen by the players in a game constitute a Nash equilibrium if no player can do better by unilaterally adopting some other strategy. Because there will often be more than one collection of Nash equilibrium strategies, we then proposed a procedure for selecting among them: backwards induction. The idea is to look ahead to the end of the game and determine what the player who moves last will do. Having done that, we can now determine what the player

---

[7] Von Stackleberg actually thought of the two firms as being run by managers with different temperaments, one of whom was a leader and the other a follower. We have followed modern convention in recasting von Stackleberg's model as a game of perfect information in which both players are rational.

who moves next to last will do, and so on. Backwards induction allows the analyst to prune branches from the game tree until the root of the game tree is reached.

Backwards induction will eliminate any Nash equilibria that involve incredible threats. Another way of saying the same thing is that backwards induction selects the subgame-perfect equilibria. These are the Nash equilibria that are also Nash equilibria in every subgame.

We noted that many games that give the players a continuum of actions at their discretion are not easily analyzed using game trees. As an example we considered a game-theoretic interpretation of the Stackleberg model of duopoly. To solve this game we introduced the concept of an isoprofit curve and showed how isoprofit curves allow us to determine the Stackleberg follower's optimal response to the leader's output. This response can be represented diagrammatically by a reaction curve. The leader's optimal output is simply the point on the opponent's reaction curve that maximizes the leader's profits. At this optimal point, one of the leader's isoprofit curves is tangent to the reaction curve.

5.6 · Further reading

For a good nontechnical modern introduction to game theory, the reader should see Avinash Dixit and Barry Nalebuff, *Thinking Strategically* (New York: Norton, 1991). The classic work on game theory, chock full of wonderful examples, is Thomas Schelling, *The Strategy of Conflict* (New York: Oxford University Press, 1960).

The original source for the concept of Nash equilibrium is John Nash's seminal paper "Non-Cooperative Games," *Annals of Mathematics* 51 (1951), pp. 286-295. His work has spawned much literature, most of it quite technical. For those with strong German skills, the original development of subgame perfection by Reinhard Selton is in "Spieltheoretische Behandlung eines Oligopolodells mit Nachfragetragheit," *Zeitschrift für die gesamte Staatswissenschaft* 121 (1965), pp. 301–324, 667–689.

Von Stackleberg first put forth his duopoly models in *Marktform und Gleichgewicht* (Vienna: Julius Springer, 1934), which has been reprinted in *The Theory of the Market Economy*, translated by A. T. Peacock (London: William Hodge, 1952).

5.7 · Exercises

Exercise 5.1   The Nash equilibrium of the software game depends, in part, on how much it costs Microcorp to clone Macrosoft's game. Denote this cost by C. For what values of C will Macrosoft's Nash equilibrium strategy be {MA} and for what values of C will its equilibrium strategy be {WOM}? What is Microcorp's Nash equilibrium strategy in each case?

Exercise 5.2   Use backwards induction to determine the optimal strategy for Aaron, Burns, and Chen in the draft evasion game described in Exercise 4.2. Assume all three teenagers would prefer to register than to be convicted of draft evasion and to spend five years in prison.

Exercise 5.3   Use backwards induction to determine the optimal strategies for the two bidders in the dollar auction described in Exercise 4.3. Assume that if a bidder is indifferent between bidding and passing, then she bids.

Exercises 5.4, 5.5, and 5.6 are based on the Stackleberg duopoly game between Clearwater and Sparkling Water, in which Sparkling Water is the Stackleberg leader and Clearwater is the Stackleberg follower.

Exercise 5.4   Suppose that Clearwater has a marginal cost of $0.50 and Sparkling Water has a marginal cost of $1.00. Derive equations for isoprofit curves for both firms at profit levels of $0, $2, and $4.

Exercise 5.5   Suppose the demand for bottled water is given by:

$$P = a - b \cdot (Q_1 + Q_2), \tag{5.12}$$

where a and b are positive constants. The marginal cost of production for both Clearwater and Sparkling Water is constant and equal to c. Find the Nash equilibrium output levels of both firms as functions of the three parameters a, b, and c.

Exercise 5.6   Suppose Sparkling Water and Clearwater can independently set the prices of their bottled water. The marginal cost of production at both firms is $1. At least some consumers are willing to pay more than $1 for bottled water, and they will buy from the firm charging the lowest price. Sparkling Water must choose its price before Clearwater does. This price is revealed to Clearwater before it makes its pricing decision. Find a Nash equilibrium pricing strategy for each firm that involves only credible threats. (*Hint*: The number of consumers who are willing to pay more than $1 for the water is irrelevant.)

• CHAPTER 6 •

Bargaining

6.1 • Introduction

In a market in which there are a large number of small suppliers and demanders, it has proved fruitful to assume that every trader is a price taker and does not engage in any real bargaining. Even in a market where there is a monopolistic seller and a large number of buyers, it is generally assumed that the monopolist sets a single, profit-maximizing price, and that the buyers take the price as given. In those situations where neither side of the market can be thought of as a price-taker, such as the case of a monopolist selling to a monopsonist, economists have not been able to say much about the price and output that will likely result from their bargaining with each other. At least, this was the case prior to recent advancements in game theory.

When a monopolist sells to a monopsonist, there is often a significant difference between the maximum price the monopsonist is willing to pay for a product or service and the minimum price the monopolist must receive to supply that product or service. Although such a gap can also exist between two buyers and sellers in a competitive market, there is a practical inability on the part of buyers to affect the decision of sellers and vice versa. For example, if any of us were to go to a grocery store and complain to the manager about the high price of spaghetti, the manager would be unlikely to do anything other than apologize. The manager knows that, as long as the price is a market-clearing price, if we do not buy the spaghetti, someone else will. She might take our complaint as a signal that the price is *not* a market-clearing price, but that is all our complaining might accomplish. Our strategic options are limited to "take it or leave it." In the case of a monopolist selling to a monopsonist, however, there will be no exchange unless the parties can find mutually acceptable conditions for exchange. And this search is exactly what we mean by **bargaining**.

6.2 · A general bargaining problem

Suppose there are two individuals, both of whom are endowed with some money (that is, the means to purchase goods and services) and some spare time. Amy and Betty live near each other but far from anyone else. Each person has a total of 16 waking hours per day, some portion of which is already committed to certain uses. Amy is endowed with $30 and 4 spare hours per day, and Betty is endowed with $10 and 12 spare hours per day. There exist other combinations of income and spare time that are equally desirable to these people and can be represented by indifference curves, shown in Figures 6.1 and 6.2.

Because we are interested only in Amy and Betty, it would be convenient to summarize the information in Figures 6.1 and 6.2 into a single diagram. This can be

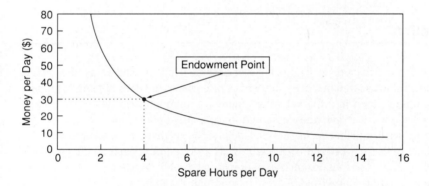

FIGURE 6.1 · Amy's preferences over income and spare time.

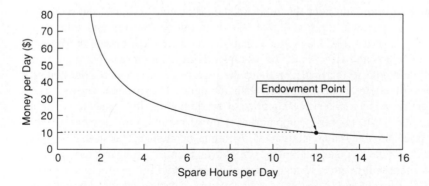

FIGURE 6.2 · Betty's preferences over income and spare time.

done by constructing an **Edgeworth box**, as shown in Figure 6.3. The important elements of this diagram are these: A point in the box represents the income and spare time of *both* Amy and Betty. The origin for Amy is in the lower left-hand corner of the box, and the origin for Betty is in the upper right-hand corner. If Amy were to move from her initial endowment on the indifference curve, labeled IC-Amy, to any point lying on an indifference curve to the northeast of IC-Amy, then she would be better off.

The situation for Betty requires you to stand on your head. Betty would be better off if she could move from her initial endowment on the indifference curve labeled IC-Betty to a point on an indifference curve to the southwest of IC-Betty.

This diagram is useful for revealing the region of possible combinations of income and spare time that make *both* Amy and Betty better off. Any point in the football-shaped region that lies between the two indifference curves IC-Amy and IC-Betty will bring higher levels of utility to both people. Notice that all of the points within this football shaped region are to the southeast of the endowment point. Hence, for both women to be made better off, Betty must give up some of her spare time in return for more income,[1] and Amy must give up some of her income in return for more spare

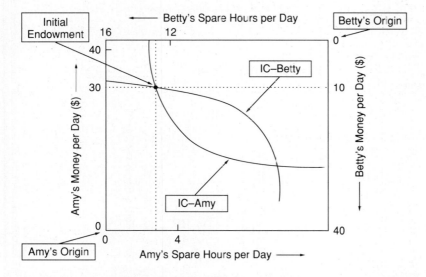

FIGURE 6.3 • An Edgeworth box diagram showing potential outcomes of bargaining between Amy and Betty and their preferences over these different outcomes.

---

[1] Of course this does not imply that Amy is willing to give up any amount of money to get more spare time or that Betty is willing to sell her time for any amount of money. It just means that there exists some set of transactions that will make them both better off.

time. In other words, Betty must sell some of her spare time to Amy (i.e., perform chores for Amy) in return for money.

Without the tools of game theory, about all that economists have been able to say about the precise nature of this exchange is that, if negotiating costs are negligible, then all potential gains from trade will be exhausted. Because potential gains from trade are exhausted only when the "football" is eliminated, this will occur only when the two women have moved to a point in the Edgeworth box at which their indifference curves are tangent to each other. Such points are displayed in Figure 6.4. Notice that these "efficient" points constitute a curve stretching from the point labeled "Amy's Best" to the point "Betty's Best." This is known as the **contract curve**. At this stage economists have tended to assert that if Betty is a better poker player than Amy (that is, more adept at strategic behavior) then the outcome will be closer to the point on the contract curve labeled "Betty's Best"; but if Amy is the better player, then the outcome will be closer to the point labeled "Amy's Best."

All economists find this explanation wanting, but game theorists find this solution of the bargaining problem particularly unacceptable because game theory presumes that all game players are equally intelligent bargainers. A more acceptable solution has been found using the theory of sequential games. This game-theoretic analysis suggests that bargaining power depends on a player's *patience* relative to other players, not on relative poker-playing ability.

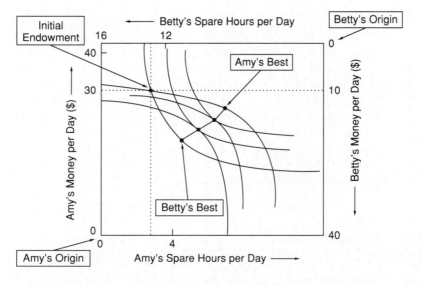

FIGURE 6.4 • The curve going from southwest to northeast is the contract curve: the bargaining outcomes that exploit all gains from trade.

The following analysis of the bargaining problem is far from complete; in particular, it ignores differences in information between the two players. But it does shed some light on the question of which points on the contract curve are the most likely outcome. In Part Four, we will reexamine the bargaining problem in the more realistic setting in which one player has an informational advantage over the other. In such situations it may be rational for the players not to move to a point on the contract curve! This more sophisticated model will allow us to assess the likelihood that this will occur.

6.3 • Bargaining without impatience

Consider a negotiating process whereby two parties are deciding what the price will be for some service. It is common knowledge between them that the buyer (Bill) is willing to pay up to $300 for the service, and that the seller (Sally) will accept anything above $200. The $300 maximum price the buyer is willing to pay is the **buyer's reservation price**, and the $200 minimum price the seller is willing to accept is the **seller's reservation price.** The difference between the negotiated price and the reservation price is each trader's gain from trade. It follows that, as long as trade takes place, Bill's and Sally's gains from trade will sum to $100. It might be helpful to think of this $100 as a pie to be divided between two parties.

We will model the negotiations between these two parties as a sequential game in which Bill makes the first move and offers a price for the service. Sally can then either accept or reject the offer. If Sally accepts, the game is over and the deal is consummated at the offered price. If, however, Sally rejects the first offer, then she will make a counteroffer. Bill can then either accept or reject this offer. The negotiations then end. A game tree for this game is shown in Figure 6.5 under the unrealistic assumption that both players can only offer $201 or $299 and each makes only one offer. This assumption will *not* be used in our analysis. Instead, we will assume that any positive number can be offered and that the number of rounds of offers is very large. The reason for limiting the offering prices and the number of rounds of offers at this point is to keep the game tree from becoming impossibly complicated. The game tree at least makes clear the players in the game, the order of play, and the informational structure of the game.

When one player accepts the other's offer, the payoff to each player equals that player's gains from trade. If neither accepts any offer made by the other, then trade does not take place and the payoff to both players equals $0. In this game something needs to be said about how a player will behave when he or she is indifferent between accepting and rejecting an offer. Our assumption will be that in this situation he or she *accepts* the offer.

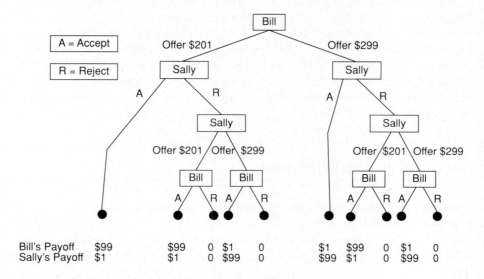

FIGURE 6.5 · The game tree for bargaining between Bill and Sally, with alternating offers.

As the game tree in Figure 6.5 shows, Bill is assumed to have the last move. As long as Sally's last offer is less than $300—even if it is only infinitesimally less than $300—Bill will accept the offer made by Sally. That is, getting something (a gain from trade above zero) is better than getting nothing (no gain from trade). Therefore, Sally's best move at this stage of the game is to offer a shade under $300 for her services. In fact, since we have assumed that Bill will accept an offer that makes him indifferent between accepting and rejecting, Sally might as well offer exactly $300 for her services. If we move up the game tree one more node, it is also clear that Sally will reject any offer made by Bill that is anything less than $300. To accept any other offer would be to ignore her ability to make a more lucrative counteroffer at the next round. This means that Bill, depressing as this might seem to him, might as well offer to buy her services for $300 at the start of the game because he is going to end up paying $300 anyway.

In this example, we see the existence of a "last-mover's advantage." Being able to make the last offer gives Sally the ability to extract the entire surplus—or, in other words, "to eat up all the pie."[2]

---

[2] Strictly speaking, Bill actually has the last move, namely to accept or reject the offer. Nevertheless, it is usually asserted that Sally has the last "real" move.

As you can see, this game is very sensitive to the number of rounds of offers and to who moves first. For example, if there were only one round to this game, so that Sally did not have the chance to present a counteroffer, then the best strategy for Bill would be to offer to buy Sally's services for $200. Sally would accept this because she would be just indifferent between accepting and rejecting the offer. In this case Bill would be able to extract the entire $100 surplus.

We leave it as an exercise to show that if Bill makes the first offer and the number of rounds of offers is an odd number, then Bill will get a payoff equal to the entire surplus; but if the number of rounds of offers is an even number, then Sally will receive all of the surplus. If this strikes you as an odd and unrealistic result, we agree with you.[3] Read on.

6.4 • Bargaining with symmetric impatience

Suppose that instead of only one or two rounds of offers, there are 100 rounds of offers. Furthermore, suppose that a delay in reaching an agreement imposes a cost on the negotiators. It is plausible to believe that this cost might be related to the discounting of future earnings relative to present earnings. When there exists a large opportunity cost to a trader's time, even a few days worth of negotiating delays can generate large time costs. For many people in many circumstances, this cost might just be the annoyance of having to deal with an unsettled and potentially pressure-filled situation. Who, for example, would not heavily discount time spent haggling with a used car salesperson?

To make things concrete, suppose the cost from delaying agreement by one round reduces the gains from trade to both players by 3%. It is in this sense that the players have symmetric impatience. As before, we will continue to assume that Bill and Sally will accept any offer that they are indifferent between accepting and rejecting.

With 100 rounds of offers it is ridiculous to think of drawing a complete game tree, but we can still use backwards induction to figure out Bill's and Sally's rational strategies. Suppose that Sally makes the 100th and final offer. Just as in the previous section, Sally will offer to perform the service for $300 and Bill will accept this offer. As before, Bill knows this when he has to decide on the 99th round what offer to make to Sally. Unlike the previous situation, however, he will offer to buy the service from Sally for $297, and Sally will accept this. This number is derived from calculating the cost to Sally of delaying agreement for one round. Recall that the surplus to be divided has a value of $100, but a delay of one round costs the recipient of the offer 3% of its share of the surplus. By waiting until the 100th round, Sally can receive the entire surplus, but because of her impatience she would be willing to accept 3% less

---

[3] Notice we have begged the question of how the number of rounds in the game is determined.

TABLE 6.1   Nash equilibrium outcome of bargaining game with alternating offers and symmetric impatience

Round	Who Offers	Seller's Share	Buyer's Share	Present Value of Surplus at Round 1
100	Seller	100.0%	0.0%	$5.36
99	Buyer	97.0%	3.0%	$5.52
98	Seller	97.1%	2.9%	$5.69
97	Buyer	94.2%	5.8%	$5.86
96	Seller	94.4%	5.6%	$6.03
95	Buyer	91.5%	8.5%	$6.21
.		.	.	.
.		.	.	.
.		.	.	.
5	Buyer	52.0%	48.0%	$88.85
4	Seller	53.4%	46.6%	$91.51
3	Buyer	51.8%	48.2%	$94.26
2	Seller	53.2%	46.8%	$97.09
1	Buyer	51.7%	48.3%	$100.00

in order to have the bargaining end in the 99th round. Therefore, Sally will reject any 99th round offer less than $297 but accept any 99th round offer greater than or equal to $297. From Bill's perspective, something today ($3) is better than nothing tomorrow, so Bill offers $297.

But Sally knows that Bill is impatient as well. Because Bill receives a payoff in the 99th round of $3, Bill ought to be just indifferent to that outcome and to accepting an offer to buy Sally's services for $202.91 in the 98th round.[4] At this stage the surplus going to Sally is $97.09. Again, Bill knows Sally would be willing to receive 3% less than this in order to obtain the surplus one round earlier. Therefore, Sally ought to be willing to accept an offer by Bill of $294.16 in the 97th round (leaving a surplus of $5.84 for Bill.)

It should be clear by now that each round of the negotiating process imposes a cost on both parties. This cost can be avoided only by making the split of the surplus attractive enough to the other player in the previous round. Some of the optimal offers to make in each round are shown in Table 6.1. By using backwards induction, we

---

[4]In the 99th round Bill received $3.00 from the surplus. But, avoiding the 99th round would have saved Bill 3% of this amount in time and trouble (or $.09). Therefore, Bill would be willing to accept $2.91 in the 98th round.

eventually find that Bill's best initial move is to offer Sally $251.65 for her services and that Sally should accept this offer. Therefore, Bill will end up with a gain from trade of $48.35 and Sally will get a gain from trade of $51.65. Notice that the surplus is split nearly 50/50, but that the last mover, Sally, continues to get a small advantage over Bill.

6.5 · Bargaining with asymmetric impatience

The exact sharing of the surplus using this analysis depends on the number of rounds of offers and the magnitude of the transaction costs. A 50/50 split will occur if the cost of delay is the same for the two parties, the number of rounds is large, and the cost of a one-period delay is small. Although casual empiricism suggests that a 50/50 split is often chosen, this is not always the case.[5]

Suppose delay is more costly to Sally than to Bill, perhaps because she is more impatient to receive the income than he is to receive her services. In particular, suppose delay reduces Sally's gains from trade by 6% but reduces Bill's by only 3%. It remains optimal for Sally to offer a price of $300 in the 100th round because she knows that Bill will accept it, but now Bill's optimal offer to Sally in the 99th round is $294, not $297. This is because should Sally reject the 100th-round offer, she is assured of receiving a price of $300 on the round—but at a time cost of $6. On the 98th round, Sally knows that Bill will accept a gain from trade of $5.82 (97% of $6), so she will offer to supply her services to him for $294.18. And so on. Some of the optimal offers for each player in each round are given in Table 6.2.

We see that Bill's optimal initial offer is now $239.80, which Sally accepts rather than needlessly delay settlement. Notice that the split of the surplus is approximately 2:1 in Bill's favor, which matches the ratio between their delay costs (6:3). This is no coincidence, as we will show.

The impatience we have been talking about is sometimes converted to a **discount factor**. To say that it costs someone x percent of his or her portion of the surplus to wait one more period is equivalent to saying that the gains from a deal that is struck in round t + 1 should be discounted 100 − x percent from the previous round to account for the delay. The 100 − x percent is that player's discount factor. The greater the impatience (the higher the value of x) the lower will be the discount factor (the more the future is discounted.) We will denote the buyer's discount factor by δ_B and the seller's discount factor by δ_S. In the preceding bargaining example, $\delta_B = 97\%$ and $\delta_S = 94\%$.

---

[5]You should go back and review what some of the conditions were that generated this result.

TABLE 6.2   Nash equilibrium outcome of the bargaining game with alternating offers but asymmetric impatience

Round	Who Offers	Seller's Share	Buyer's Share	Present Value of Surplus to Buyer	Present Value of Surplus to Seller
100	Seller	100.0%	0.0%	$5.36	$0.31
99	Buyer	94.0%	6.0%	$5.52	$0.33
98	Seller	94.2%	5.8%	$5.69	$0.35
97	Buyer	88.5%	11.5%	$5.86	$0.37
96	Seller	88.9%	11.1%	$6.03	$0.39
95	Buyer	86.2%	13.8%	$6.21	$0.42
.		.	.	.	.
.		.	.	.	.
.		.	.	.	.
5	Buyer	40.0%	60.0%	$88.85	$79.21
4	Seller	41.8%	58.2%	$91.51	$83.96
3	Buyer	40.5%	59.5%	$94.26	$89.00
2	Seller	42.3%	57.7%	$97.09	$94.34
1	Buyer	39.8%	60.2%	$100.00	$100.00

Each of the previous examples assumed the number of rounds was fixed. In most bargaining circumstances, however, the number of rounds of offers and counteroffers is essentially unbounded. An important result in modern bargaining theory, due to Ariel Rubenstein, is that this type of game has a unique subgame-perfect Nash equilibrium. The proof of Rubenstein's theorem is a testimony to the value of clear and logical thought when thinking about strategic circumstances.

As in the previous section, the buyer's and seller's discount rates will be denoted by δ_B and δ_S. The buyer moves first and proposes that a fixed sum of money be split in the proportions (W_B, W_S), where W_B is the proportion retained by the buyer and W_S is the proportion offered to the seller. For simplicity, we will suppose this sum is $1. The seller then accepts or rejects the split, and the round ends. If the seller rejects the split, she makes a subsequent counteroffer, which the buyer can accept or reject. So far, this sounds identical to the models we have already discussed. What is different, however, is that the game continues as long as the players keep rejecting offers. In theory, the game could last forever.

This game has an infinite number of subgames. As we learned earlier, one of those subgames is the game itself. Denote this game by G_1. Suppose this game has a subgame-perfect equilibrium. It is possible there is more than one such equilibrium. Among the subgame-perfect equilibria of G_1, let Q_B denote the largest payoff for the buyer and let q_B denote the smallest payoff for the buyer. Another subgame of the entire game begins at the subroot where the seller makes her first counteroffer to the buyer. Call this game G_2. Let Q_S denote the highest payoff the seller can obtain among all the subgame-perfect equilibria of G_2, and let q_S denote the smallest payoff the seller obtains among these equilibria.

Consider some constraints on the buyer at the first round of G_1. In order for the offer to have any chance of acceptance (for it to be subgame–perfect), the seller must receive at least $\delta_S \cdot q_S$. This is because the seller can be guaranteed a payoff of q_S once the game reaches the subgame G_2, but since this game is one round in the future, the payoff attained then has to be discounted by δ_S to make it comparable to an immediate payoff. Of course, if the seller gets at least $\delta_S \cdot q_S$, and the total pie to be split is \$1, then the most the buyer can receive equals $1 - \delta_S \cdot q_S$. This means

$$Q_B \leq 1 - \delta_S \cdot q_S. \qquad (6.1)$$

Using similar logic we can find a bound for q_B. If the buyer offers the seller anything greater than or equal to $\delta_S \cdot Q_S$, she will take it, because she knows she can receive at most Q_S once the subgame G_2 is reached. Hence, it makes no sense for the buyer to offer more than $\delta_S \cdot Q_S$ when the game is G_1. This means the buyer can get at least $1 - \delta_S \cdot Q_S$ immediately, or

$$q_B \geq 1 - \delta_S \cdot Q_S. \qquad (6.2)$$

If the buyer rejects the seller's counteroffer, then the game continues on to subgame G_3, where the buyer makes his second offer. We leave it as an exercise for the reader to show that, by reversing the position of the buyer and the seller in the earlier logic, two further constraints can be placed on the payoffs Q_B, Q_S, q_B, and q_S. These constraints are

$$Q_S \leq 1 - \delta_B \cdot q_B, \qquad (6.3)$$

and

$$q_S \geq 1 - \delta_B \cdot Q_B. \qquad (6.4)$$

From equation (6.4) we see that $\delta_B \cdot Q_B - 1 \geq -q_S$. Substituting this inequality into equation (6.1) gives the new inequality

$$Q_B \leq 1 + \delta_S \cdot (\delta_B \cdot Q_B - 1). \qquad (6.5)$$

Solving equation (6.5) for Q_B gives

$$Q_B \leq (1 - \delta_S)/(1 - \delta_S \cdot \delta_B). \tag{6.6}$$

Similarly, from equation (6.3) we know that $\delta_B \cdot q_B - 1 \leq -Q_S$. By substituting this inequality into equation (6.2) and solving for q_B, we get

$$q_B \geq (1 - \delta_S)/(1 - \delta_S \cdot \delta_B). \tag{6.7}$$

Putting equations (6.6) and (6.7) together implies

$$Q_B \leq (1 - \delta_S)/(1 - \delta_S \cdot \delta_B) \leq q_B. \tag{6.8}$$

But Q_B and q_B are the highest and lowest payoffs to the buyer over all the subgame–perfect equilibrium for this game. This means

$$q_B \leq Q_B. \tag{6.9}$$

The inequalities (6.8) and (6.9) imply that

$$q_B = Q_B = (1 - \delta_S)/(1 - \delta_S \cdot \delta_B) \tag{6.10}$$

and, similarly,

$$q_S = Q_S = 1 - (1 - \delta_S)/(1 - \delta_S \cdot \delta_B) \tag{6.11}$$
$$= \delta_S \cdot (1 - \delta_B)/(1 - \delta_S \cdot \delta_B).$$

Thus, when the number of possible rounds is unbounded, the equilibrium payoffs of the two players are determinate and depend only on the discount rates of the two players and on who moves first. Usually the "more patient" player—that is, the player with the largest discount rate—gets more than half of the surplus. This is not always true because the first player to make an offer has a "first–mover advantage." For example, when $\delta_S = 75\%$ and $\delta_B = 70\%$, the buyer is predicted to receive 53% of the pie even though the seller is more patient.

That fact that there is a first–mover advantage in this game poses a problem, because in many situations who goes first is not predetermined but is negotiated between the two parties. If this aspect of the bargaining determines the outcome of the bargaining, then the preliminary negotiations on who goes first are important.

What now determines the outcome of this "prebargaining bargaining"? It is easy to see that we can get into an infinite regress of bargaining stages here.

Fortunately, in most cases, who goes first is not important, because the first mover's advantage goes to zero as the discount rates of the two players go to one. An important determinant of the discount rate is the time between offers. The shorter the time interval between offers, the less costly it is to delay the settlement for one more period. This implies that as the time interval between offers gets small, the discount rates of both players will approach one.

Suppose that the discount factors of the buyer and the seller are decreasing functions of the time interval between offers, t. We will denote the discounts by $\delta_B(t)$ and $\delta_S(t)$. It follows from our theorem that as the maximum number of rounds of bargaining increases without bound, the ratio W_B/W_S converges to

$$(1 - \delta_S(t)) \div (\delta_S(t) \cdot (1 - \delta_B(t))). \qquad (6.12)$$

We want to determine to what W_B/W_S converges as the time interval between offers goes to zero. Clearly, it must be the case that $\delta_B(0) = \delta_S(0) = 1$. Suppose, furthermore, that both discount rate functions are differentiable and $-\delta_B'(0) = r_B > 0$ and $-\delta_S'(0) = r_S > 0$. The numbers r_B and r_S are the buyer's and seller's **instantaneous delay costs.** Then it follows from calculus (l'Hôpital's rule) that as t goes to zero, the ratio (6.1.2) converges to r_S/r_B. That is, the players will agree to divide up the surplus in a ratio that exactly equals the inverse of the ratio of the instantaneous delay costs. Who goes first no longer matters.

6.6 • A bargaining example: Sharing sunk costs

Suppose the new Siberia Gas Company, a privately owned gas producer and distributor in Russia that is considering building a pipeline to Tomsk, a city in central Russia, which is currently not serviced by a gas producer. Residents of the community are collectively willing to pay up to 90 rubles per acre-foot of gas. In any given year they would demand a total of 10,000 acre-feet, implying an annual willingness to pay for gas of 900,000 rubles. At an interest rate of 10%, the present value of the residents' collective willingness to pay for the gas is 9 million rubles.

The Siberia Gas Company can build a pipeline to Tomsk for 3 million rubles. Once it is built, the pipeline lasts forever and can provide gas to Tomsk at a marginal cost of 50 rubles per acre-foot. Satisfying the demand for gas in Tomsk would generate an annual operating cost of 500,000 rubles. At an interest rate of 10% the present value of the stream of operating costs over the lifetime of the pipeline will be 5 million rubles. Therefore, the cost of building the pipeline and providing gas through it to the residents of Tomsk has a present value of 8 million rubles. Building the pipeline and shipping gas to the residents of Tomsk results in a net gain of 1 million rubles. Clearly we are in a situation in which mutually beneficial exchange is possible. In terms of an Edgeworth box, there is a football, perhaps a big one, waiting to be reduced in size through mutually advantageous exchange.

Certain characteristics of the pipeline investment are noteworthy. First, the pipeline must be built before any natural gas can be delivered. Second, the Siberia Gas Company and citizens of Tomsk cannot reach a binding agreement about the price of the delivered gas before the pipeline is built. Third, should the residents of the community decide in the future to buy their gas from some other source, the pipeline will have essentially no salvage value. In the jargon used by economists, the delivery of gas to this community has a large **fixed cost** (cost that does vary with the magnitude of the output), which is also a **sunk cost** (a cost that is largely unrecoverable should the gas producer decide to shut down operations because of low demand).

We have here a sequential-move game. The players in the game are the citizens of Tomsk and the Siberia Gas Company. The order of play is as follows: The Siberia Gas Company moves first and decides whether or not to build a pipeline to Tomsk; the citizens of Tomsk and the Siberia Gas Company then bargain over the price of the gas. We will suppose that the bargaining game is itself a sequential game, much as we discussed in the previous sections of this application.

As we saw in the beginning of this application, when two parties present each other with alternating offers in quick succession, and when they know each other's instantaneous delay costs, they will agree to divide the surplus in a ratio that is the inverse of the ratio of these costs. In this case, let us assume that these costs of delay are the same and that this is common knowledge. Then we know that the citizens of Tomsk and the Siberia Gas Company will agree to divide any surplus equally between them.

The implications of this bargaining process are profound. In order to break even on the construction of the pipeline, the Siberia Gas Company must be certain of receiving a price of 80 rubles per acre-foot. By receiving this price, the firm can be assured of 800,000 rubles per year in revenues, which has a present value of 8 million rubles. Because this exactly matches the present cost of laying the pipeline and providing the gas to Tomsk, the Siberia Gas Company will just break even.

Once the pipeline is built, though, the company will be willing to accept a price equal to the marginal cost of production or 50 rubles per acre-foot rather than the average cost of production (inclusive of the pipeline costs) or 90 rubles per acre-foot. The difference between the marginal and average cost is due to the large sunk costs of the pipeline. As a result, the residents of Tomsk will try to "hold up" the producer; that is, pay the producer only a price equal to the marginal cost of production.[6]

---

[6]Ironically, the customers will probably try to rationalize their position by citing evidence that the gas company is making an "abnormal" profit or "holding up" the consumers.

Because the residents of Tomsk are still willing to pay 90 rubles per acre-foot, the surplus has a present value of 40 rubles per acre-foot • 10,000 acre-feet per year ÷ 10% = 4 million rubles. The gas company can expect a price which splits this 4 million surplus equally between Tomsk and itself. This means the price that Siberia Gas Company *can rationally expect* to negotiate with Tomsk is 70 rubles per acre-foot. Because this is 10 rubles per acre-foot below their break-even price (calculated prior to building the pipeline), they will choose not to build the pipeline.

Even though both parties can be made better off through the construction of a pipeline, their inability to negotiate a binding contract before the pipeline is laid results in the pipeline not being built. We are left with a big football of unexploited gains from trade. Had it been possible to negotiate a contract successfully *prior* to the investment decision, the minimum price that the Siberia Gas Company would have required to provide gas would have been 80 rubles per acre-foot. The maximum amount the citizens of Tomsk would have been willing to pay would still have been 90 rubles per acre-foot, and the resulting negotiated price would have been 85 rubles per acre-foot. In these circumstances, the pipeline would have been built, and the football would have deflated to nothing.

Some of the more clever and wide-awake readers will undoubtedly be wondering if the community can simply build the pipeline itself and thereby avoid the "hold-up" problem. There are many reasons that this is unlikely to occur, among them the following: Although the community as a whole might be willing to pay a great deal for the pipeline, no individual is likely to have the inclination or the means to carry out such a major investment. Someone with a public-spirited bent might serve as an instigator to get the community together to ante up to make the investment, but the sad (and realistic) fact is that many individuals will prefer not to be included in the group. They would rather take a "free ride" off the ones who do join up. The result is that this approach is almost certain to fail.

6.7 • Summary

A great many decisions we make include bargaining in one form or another. How much we pay for a car, how much you will get paid by an employer, how much a firm that produces electricity will pay for coal from another producer, how much the Pentagon will pay for military equipment—these are all examples. Economists historically have said a great deal about the welfare gains from trade but very little about how those gains are shared between the transactors. Game theory applied to bargaining begins to provide a mechanism for understanding better the deals that will be struck.

In this application we have developed a theory of bargaining from a very simple model, in which there is no time discounting, to a relatively complex model. This model predicts that how two bargainers will split the gains from trade depends on who makes the first offer, the number of rounds of offers, and the relative impatience of the two bargainers. Although there is a great deal more to be said about bargaining, we now have a framework with which to structure the future reasoning, and we have developed empirically testable hypotheses.

Understanding how the gains from trade are split has a wide variety of applications. We have highlighted what has become known as the hold-up problem: When an investment generates benefits to a specific demander such as a gas pipeline, the costs of the investment are unrecoverable, and the costs of contracting prior to the investment taking place are high, then that investment may not take place even when everyone could benefit from it.

6.8 • Further reading

Ariel Rubinstein presented the first model of bargaining as a sequential game in "Perfect Equilibrium in a Bargaining Model," *Econometrica* 50(1) (1982), pp. 97-109. This paper is very difficult. Fortunately, the results are presented in a much more readable form in Martin Osborne and Ariel Rubinstein, *Bargaining and Markets* (New York: Academic Press, 1990). Our proof of Rubinstein's bargaining result is due to Ken Binmore, *Fun and Games: A Text on Game Theory* (Lexington, MA: D. C. Heath, 1992), pp. 209-211.

6.9 • Exercises

Exercise 6.1   Suppose that Bill and Sally are bargaining over the division of a $100 surplus. They make alternating offers and do not discount the future at all; that is, they consider the receipt of a dollar at any time in the future equivalent to the receipt of a dollar today. The number of offers is fixed in advance. Show that the last person to make an offer gets all of the surplus.

Exercise 6.2   Suppose Bill, a buyer, and Sally, a seller, are bargaining over the price at which Sally will perform a service for Bill. It is common knowledge that the maximum price Bill will pay is $300 and the minimum price Sally will accept is $200. They bargain over the price in the following manner: Bill offers a price to Sally, who can either accept or reject it. If she accepts Bill's first offer, the game ends and they exchange at this price, P_1. Bill's payoff is $300 - P_1 and Sally's payoff is P_1 - $200. If Sally rejects the offer, then Bill offers *another* price, P_2, which Sally can again accept or reject, and so on. Both players discount future income by 50% per period. So, if Sally accepts Bill's Nth offer, P_N, then Bill's payoff is $(\$300 - P_N)/2^{N-1}$ and Sally's payoff is $(P_N - \$200)/2^{N-1}$. Sally will accept an offer if she is indifferent between accepting and rejecting it.

   (a) Draw the game tree for this bargaining under the simplifying assumption that Bill's only possible offers are $200, $250, or $300, and that they bargain for only two rounds. That is, if Sally rejects Bill's second offer, then they do not trade, and each receives a payoff of $0. Be careful to label the action taken along each branch, to label who moves at each decision node (Bill or Sally), and to label the payoff of both players at each terminal node.

   (b) Use backwards induction to determine the equilibrium strategies for both players if the game ends after four rounds and f Bill can offer Sally anything.

   (c) Use backwards induction to determine the equilibrium strategies for both players if the game ends after *four hundred* rounds and if Bill can offer any number to Sally.

Exercise 6.3 This is a continuation of Exercise 6.2. Suppose it is common knowledge that both Bill and Sally do not discount the future *at all*; that is, their discount rates are exactly equal to one. They know that under a system of alternating offers, the last one to make an offer will get the entire trading surplus of $100 (see Exercise 6.1). Not surprisingly, they cannot agree on who will go last. Sally tries to break the impasse by suggesting that at each round, they flip a fair coin to decide who makes the offer on that round. If the coin comes up heads, Bill gets to make the offer on that round, which Sally can either accept or reject. If the coin comes up tails, then Sally gets to make the offer on that round, which Bill can either accept or reject. If on any round either accepts the other's offer, say P, then Bill's payoff is $300 - P and Sally's payoff is P - $200.

   (a) Draw the game tree under the assumption that they stop the bargaining after two rounds.

   (b) Use backwards induction to find the optimal strategy for the players if there are only two rounds of offers and it is common knowledge that both players have the following von Neumann-Morgenstern utility function over final payoffs:

$$U(x) = \sqrt{x}.$$

   (c) Find optimal strategies if it is common knowledge that Sally is risk-neutral ($U(x) = x$), but Bill is risk-averse ($U(x) = \sqrt{x}$).

• CHAPTER 7 •

Involuntary Unemployment

7.1 • Moral hazard and principal–agent games

Many important economic transactions have the following feature: After an agreement is reached between the buyer and the seller, one of them can take an action that affects the payoff of the other—and this action cannot be perfectly observed by the affected party. Such a transaction is said to expose the affected party to **moral hazard.** An example is auto insurance. Once an insurance company sells a policy to a driver, it cannot monitor that driver's subsequent driving care except at very high cost. The insurance company could stipulate in the insurance contract that the driver must "not act recklessly." But when an accident occurs, how will the company be able to tell whether it was due to "recklessness" or simply to "bad luck"? Because such a clause is virtually unenforceable, the insurance company faces *moral hazard* in the auto insurance market.

Moral hazard appears in many other markets. For example, when a lender makes a loan, she faces the risk that the borrower will act "recklessly" with the money lent and find himself unable to pay back the loan. If the borrower can plausibly argue that a default is due to bad luck rather than bad judgment, then the lender faces moral hazard. Likewise, an employer faces moral hazard when she hires a salesperson, since the new employee could put in a low selling effort but then plausibly blame the resulting low sales on "bad market conditions."

Moral hazard can be modeled as a **principal–agent game**. The game tree for a prototypical principal–agent game is shown in Figure 7.1. In such a game, a **principal** offers a contract to an **agent,** who can accept or reject it. The contract states what the principal and the agent will pay each other at some point in time depending on what both can then observe about the state-of-the-world. *A valid contract cannot*

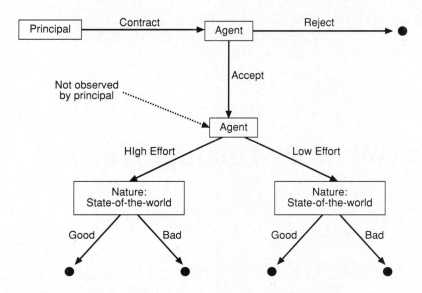

FIGURE 7.1 · The game tree for a prototypical principal-agent game with moral hazard.

commit either party to transfer money under conditions that cannot be independently verified by both. If the agent rejects the contract, then the game ends and both the principal and the agent receive a **reservation payoff** (usually zero). If the agent accepts the contract, then he gets to choose actions that affect the state-of-the-world. After the agent moves, Nature takes other actions that also determine the state-of-the-world. At this point the terms of the contract are carried out and payoffs are earned. The problem for the principal is to design a contract that maximizes her payoff, *taking into account* the rational response of the agent to the terms of the contract.

The principal is exposed to moral hazard in this game if she can neither observe the agent's action directly nor logically determine what the agent's action was from the state-of-the-world at the end of the game. The latter will not be possible if the principal cannot observe Nature's move or does not know the probability with which Nature will take a given action. Nature's role is critical in that it provides the agent with a plausible excuse for a poor outcome. Without this "complication," the principal could deduce the agent's action from the outcome and design the contract so as to eliminate the agent's potential for mischief.

Notice that buyers and sellers can be either principals or agents, depending on whether they move after the contract is negotiated or not. In the application we will develop in this chapter, the principal is an employer or labor buyer, and the agent is a worker or labor seller. In the following chapter, the principal is an insurance company selling unemployment insurance, and the agent is a potentially unemployed worker who might want to buy unemployment insurance.

7.2 • Moral hazard in the labor market

At the heart of Keynesian macroeconomic theory is the notion of **involuntary unemployment**. A worker is said to be involuntarily unemployed if employers will not hire him or her at the current market wage rate while the worker is willing and able to work at that wage. In the standard competitive model of wage determination, involuntary unemployment is inconsistent with market equilibrium.

In this application we will present a model of the labor market in which there is involuntary unemployment *in equilibrium*. This model has two central features. First, labor productivity is determined partly by the firm's technology and partly by the "intensity" with which its workers *choose* to work. Second, it is very costly for the firm to monitor continually the intensity with which its workers work. The result is that each firm and its workers play a principal–agent game with moral hazard. The firm is the principal, the workers are the agents, and the unobservable action is work "intensity."

In the type of labor market we will consider, a market-clearing wage is not a stable equilibrium. If every firm were paying a market-clearing wage, then any one of them could increase its profits by unilaterally increasing the wage it pays and simultaneously reducing the frequency with which it monitors its workers. These two changes can be done in such a way that worker productivity at the firm does not fall. It does not fall because the higher wage makes it more costly for any worker to reduce the intensity with which she works and thereby increase the likelihood of being fired. This offsets the incentive for workers to work less when they are monitored less frequently. The savings from the reduced monitoring compensates the firm for the higher wage bill. The firm is said to be paying an **efficiency wage** because it is using its wage as a strategic variable to affect its labor productivity.

If all firms adopt the strategy of paying an efficiency wage, then the market wage will rise above the market-clearing level and involuntary unemployment will appear in the labor market. In the new equilibrium all firms pay the same wage. But the threat of being fired continues to motivate the workers to work hard, because when a worker loses her current job, she risks a spell of unemployment.

Consider an example. Smartshop, a warehouse and trucking firm in Cleveland, employs workers at its distribution warehouse. These workers load and unload delivery trucks, move pallets around the warehouse, keep inventory records, check for spoilage and vermin infestation, and more generally do whatever needs to be done.

Because the workers are constantly changing job tasks, they have the opportunity to shirk. The fraction of the time that a worker is not shirking will be denoted by E ("effort"). By definition, E lies between 0 and 1. If there are L workers, all of whom are the same; if each work day constitutes one unit of work service; and if every worker's effort level equals E, then $L \cdot E = L_E$ is the amount of "true" work performed. The firm's revenue V depends on the2 output produced by its work force, which is a function of L_E, not L. The revenue function V is strictly increasing in L_E, but at a decreasing rate. We also assume that $V(0) = 0$.

The workers have an identical von Neumann-Morgenstern utility function U, which depends on the wage W and the work effort E. For the sake of simplicity suppose the utility function takes the form

$$W \cdot (1 - E). \tag{7.1}$$

If a worker leaves the firm, she obtains a reservation utility of $\underline{W}$ There is no reason for a worker to accept employment from a firm that generates a utility less than the reservation utility. We will assume that $\underline{W}$ is positive.

Smartshop disciplines workers by firing them if they are found to be shirking "too often." How often is "too often" is set by law. The probability that a worker is caught shirking too often and is fired is a decreasing function of E. This probability will be denoted $\pi(E)$ and is the same for every worker. For simplicity, we will assume that

$$\pi(E) = 1 - E. \tag{7.2}$$

More generally, we could have modeled the probability of being caught shirking as a function of the resources the firm devotes to catching shirkers. That is an extension we leave to another book.

The strategic interaction between Smartshop and each of its workers can be modeled as a principal-agent game with moral hazard. The game tree is shown in Figure 7.2. The firm moves first and selects the wage it will pay its workers, W, and the number of workers it will hire. The workers move next, each making her decision independently. Because the workers are assumed to be identical, Figure 7.2 depicts the situation facing one representative worker, whom we will call Cynthia. Cynthia first decides whether or not to work for the firm. If she rejects the firm's wage offer, then the game ends. If she accepts it, then she moves a second time and chooses her level of work effort E. This move is not observed by the firm. Nature now moves and decides whether or not Cynthia is caught shirking too often and is fired.

Because Cynthia's work effort is not directly observable, Smartshop cannot write a contract in which Cynthia's wage depends on her choice of E. This means that Smartshop's strategy consists simply of the selection of the wage, W, and the number of laborers hired, L. Cynthia's strategy is more complicated. It consists of a rule for

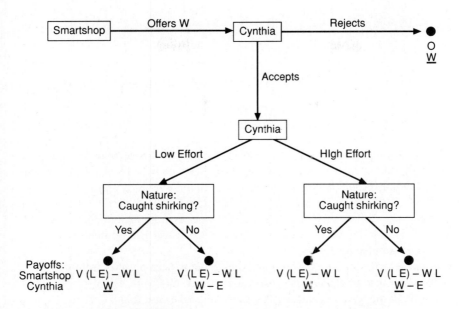

FIGURE 7.2 • The game tree for the principal–agent game with moral hazard played between Cynthia and the Smartshop warehouse and trucking firm.

rejecting or accepting the firm's wage and a rule for determining the intensity with which she works depending on the wage she is paid. The relationship between her wage and her effort is denoted $E(W)$.

This game has three possible outcomes. The first outcome is that the firm makes a contract offer that is rejected by Cynthia. The firm's payoff is assumed to equal 0 and Cynthia's payoff is assumed to equal $\underline{W}$ The value of $\underline{W}$ depends on Cynthia's employment opportunities outside the firm. This reservation utility is treated by both Cynthia and the firm as exogenous. We will consider its determination later.

The second possible outcome is that Cynthia accepts the firm's offer and is not fired for excessive shirking. In this case, the firm's payoff equals $V(L \cdot E) - W \cdot L$ and Cynthia's payoff equals $W \cdot (1 - E)$. The third outcome is that Cynthia accepts the firm's offer but is found to be shirking too often and is fired. We will assume the firm can immediately replace her with an identical worker. As a result, the firm is unaffected by her firing. The firm's payoff is, therefore, $V(L \cdot E) - W \cdot L$, and Cynthia's payoff is her reservation utility, $\underline{W}$

We can solve this game using backwards induction—that is, starting at the end of the game tree and working toward the beginning. Once Cynthia accepts the firm's offer, she chooses her work effort E so as to maximize her expected utility, which is given by:

$$EU(W,E) = \pi(E) \cdot \underline{W} + (1 - \pi(E)) \cdot W \cdot (1 - E) \qquad (7.3)$$
$$= \pi(E) \cdot \underline{W} + W \cdot (1 - E) \cdot (1 - \pi(E))$$

When we substitute our assumed expression for $\pi(E)$ into equation (7.3), we get

$$EU(W,E) = (1 - E) \cdot \underline{W} + E \cdot W \cdot (1 - E). \qquad (7.4)$$

Because Cynthia moves last, it would be rational for her to treat W and $\underline{W}$ as given, and to maximize her expected utility through her choice of E. This is a straightforward calculus problem, and generates an optimum level of E equal to $(W - \underline{W})/(2 \cdot W)$. You should recognize this as her reaction function, which tells her how much effort to expend at any wage. Of course, by our assumption of common knowledge, the firm also knows how she will react to any wage. Her optimal work effort level will be denoted by $E^*(W)$.

Cynthia accepts the firm's offer if and only if her expected utility from the firm's offer is greater than or equal to her reservation utility, or $EU(W, E^*(W)) \geq \underline{W}$. Using equation (7.4), the reader can verify that this will be the case if and only if

$$(1 - E^*(W)) \cdot W \geq \underline{W}. \qquad (7.5)$$

Because E^* is between 0 and 1, it follows that $\underline{W}$ is the lowest wage the firm can offer and still attract any workers. Furthermore, if the firm offers $\underline{W}$ and the worker accepts it, then $E^*(\underline{W}) = 0$. That is, the worker will refuse to do any work! The firm is unequivocally better off offering a wage of 0 than a wage of $\underline{W}$.

Suppose the firm offers a wage W above $\underline{W}$ and the worker accepts it. Because W is greater than $\underline{W}$, her reaction function tells us that her optimal response is to put forward some positive effort. So some work effort is better than no work effort, meaning that $E^*(W) > 0$ and $EU(W, E^*(W)) > \underline{W}$.

When Cynthia uses her optimal strategy, Smartshop's profits, denoted $R(W,L)$, equal

$$R(W,L) = \begin{cases} 0 & \text{if } W \leq \underline{W} \\ \\ V(L \cdot E^*(W)) - W \cdot L & \text{if } W > \underline{W} \end{cases} \qquad (7.6)$$

Let $L_E = L \cdot E^*(W)$. L_E measures the amount of actual work performed by the firm's workers when they all rationally shirk. The firm's profit function can be rewritten in terms of W and L_E as follows:

$$R(W,L_E) = \begin{cases} 0 & \text{if } W \leq \underline{W} \\[2em] V(L_E) - W/E^*(W) \cdot L_E & \text{if } W > \underline{W} \end{cases} \tag{7.7}$$

You may recall that $V(L_E)$ stands for the firm's revenues, which depend on the level of effort the collection of workers put forth. We would expect V to be increasing at a decreasing rate as a result of diminishing marginal product. One functional form that captures this property is $V(L_E) = \sqrt{L_E}$.

The expression $W/E^*(W)$ is the wage paid per unit of actual work performed (rather than hours on the job). Notice that the denominator of this ratio is nonzero as long as W is greater than $\underline{W}$. Smartshop's decision problem is quite simple. First, for a given value of L_E, the firm chooses W so as to minimize $W/E^*(W)$. Because $\underline{W}/E^*(\underline{W}) = +\infty$, this ratio reaches a minimum at some wage strictly greater than $\underline{W}$. We will denote this optimal wage by W^*. This wage is the firm's optimal efficiency wage. This means that

$$W^*/E^*(W^*) \leq W/E^*(W) \text{ for any } W > \cdot \underline{W} . \tag{7.8}$$

For example, if $V(L_E) = \sqrt{L_E}$, then $W^* = 2 \cdot \underline{W}$. Notice that the firm is paying "more than it has to" (that is, more than $\underline{W}$) in order to get the workers to work harder. Second, the firm chooses L_E so as to maximize $R(L_E, W^*)$. We will denote this optimal labor input by L_E^*. In our specific example, L_E will equal $(16 \cdot \underline{W})^2$. It follows from calculus that

$$V'(L_E^*) = W^*/E^*(W^*).^1 \tag{7.9}$$

Equation (7.9) is simply a variant of the familiar profit-maximization condition: Equate the marginal value product with the wage. It follows from the definition of L_E that the firm's optimal level of employment, denoted L^*, equals $L_E^*/E^*(W^*)$.

In equilibrium, all the firms must be paying the same wage, W^*, because they are assumed to be identical to Smartshop. If this wage clears the market, then any worker who is fired from one job can obtain immediate employment at another job. This is what the term *market-clearing wage* means. But then the workers are always employed and the reservation utility $\underline{W}$ must equal W^*. Since we know that $W^* > \underline{W}$, we have a contradiction. This contradiction shows that the equilibrium wage must be *above* the market-clearing wage.

It remains to be shown that no firm will be tempted to hire one of the unemployed workers at a wage below what it is paying its current workers. The reason the firm is

---

[1]Of course, this ignores the possibility that the optimal amount of labor to employ is 0. This will be the case if and only if $V'(0) \leq W^*/E^*(W^*)$. We will assume that this is not the case.

not tempted is that it can predict that the new worker will shirk more often than its current workers do. As a result, this new hire will be less productive. The worker shirks more often because she has less to lose by being fired. But we must show more. We must show that the worker's marginal value product is less than the wage she is paid, whatever that wage is—as long as it is above the reservation wage $\underline{W}$.

Suppose that Smartshop hires Tom at the wage W_T. W_T may be different from the wage W^* the firm is paying its L^* workers. Tom will reject the offer unless $W_T \geq \underline{W}$. Assuming Tom accepts the offer, he will provide $E^*(W_T)$ units of actual work. The firm's marginal profit equals

$$V(L_E^* + E^*(W_T)) - V(L_E^*) - W_T. \tag{7.10}$$

Declining marginal productivity implies that

$$V(L_E^* + E^*(W_T)) - V(L_E^*) - W_T < V'(L_E^*) \cdot E^*(W_T) - W_T. \tag{7.11}$$

It follows from the profit-maximization condition (7.9) that

$$V'(L_E^*) \cdot E^*(W_T) - W_T = W^*/E^*(W^*) \cdot {}^*W_T) - W_T, \tag{7.12}$$

and it follows from the profit–maximization condition (7.8) that

$$W^*/E^*(W^*) \cdot E^*(W_T) - W_T \leq 0. \tag{7.13}$$

Equations (7.11), (7.12), and (7.13) imply

$$V(L_E^* + E^*(W_T)) - V(L_E^*) - W_T < 0. \tag{7.14}$$

But (7.14) means that Smartshop cannot make a profit from hiring Tom no matter *how little or how much it pays him*. This is because the less the firm pays him, the less productive Tom will be. Tom's problem is that he is unable to commit himself to being as productive as the firm's current workers.

Figure 7.3 provides a graphic illustration of our analysis. The heavy bowed line shows the firm's revenue as a function of labor effort (*not* the number of workers). Smartshop's revenue at the optimal effort level is labeled A, and Smartshop's total wage bill at this level of effort, $W^* \cdot L^* = W^*/E^*(W^*) \cdot L_E^*$, is labeled B. The distance between A and B equals the firm's profit.

If the firm hires Tom and pays him the wage W_T, then the effort level goes up by $E^*(W_T)$ and the firm's revenue rises to C. The firm's labor costs increase by W_T to F. The distance between C and F represents the firm's profits after hiring Tom. Because the distance between D and E equals $W^*/E^*(W^*) \cdot E^*(W_T)$ and (7.8) implies that $W^*/E^*(W^*) \cdot E^*(W_T) < W_T$, the point F lies above the point E. By construction, however,

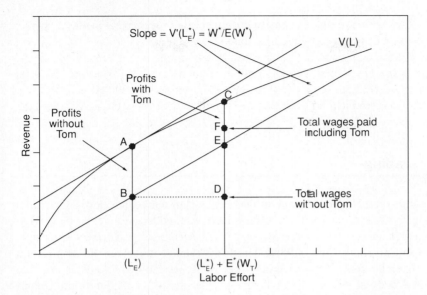

FIGURE 7.3 · Smartshop will make a loss from hiring Tom, no matter how much or how little they pay him.

the distance between C and F is less than the distance between A and B, meaning the firm's profits fall if it hires Tom.

7.3 · Summary

A recurring theme in game theory is the importance of information in determining how rational players behave. Information is at the heart of the problem of moral hazard and principal–agent games in general. A principal-agent game is one in which two strategic players try to contract with each other regarding some mutually advantageous exchange. The principal offers a contract to an agent, who can reject or accept the offer. If the contract is accepted, the payoffs specified in the contract depend on subsequent actions taken by the agent and actions taken by Nature, but they cannot be conditioned on these actions. The reason is that the principal is unable to unravel the independent effect on the payoffs of the agent's action and Nature's action.

In the unemployment game considered in this application, the principal, a representative firm, begins the game by offering a wage contract to an employee. The employee (the agent) accepts or rejects the contract and then decides how much effort to put into the job. The firm cannot directly observe the level of effort, and Nature determines whether the worker is caught shirking. In these circumstances we showed that voluntary unemployment is consistent with an equilibrium wage. This, of course, flies in the face of traditional economic thinking.

Games of moral hazard are characterized by commitment problems. In the unemployment game, the worker cannot credibly commit to a level of effort. Thus, to ensure a relatively high level of effort the firm pays a wage, called an efficiency wage, that is higher than the wage that would equate the supply of workers with the demand.

7.4 • Further reading

The literature on the effect of moral hazard in the labor market has now grown quite large. Many of the seminal journal articles have been collected together by George Akerlof and Janet Yellen in *Efficiency Wage Models of the Labor Market* (Cambridge: Cambridge University Press, 1986). The labor market model in this application borrows liberally from the pioneering work of Robert Solow, "Another Possible Source of Wage Stickiness"; Carl Shapiro and Joseph Stiglitz, "Equilibrium Unemployment as a Worker Discipline Device"; and James Foster and Henry Wan, "Involuntary Unemployment as a Principal–Agent Equilibrium." All three articles are in Akerlof and Yellen's collection.

7.5 • Exercises

Exercise 7.1   Consider the unemployment game played between Smartshop and Cynthia. Suppose the probability of getting caught shirking is equal to $1 - E^2$.

  (a) Find an expression for the expected utility of Cynthia.
  (b) Find an expression for Cynthia's reaction function.
  (c) Find an expression for the optimum wage paid to Cynthia by the firm.
  (d) Find an expression for the optimum level of effort by Cynthia at the optimum wage.
  (e) Show that the optimum wage is greater than $\underline{W}$.

Exercise 7.2   uppose $V(L_E) = \sqrt{L_E}$. What does the model predict will happen to W^*, L^*, and Cynthia's expected utility $EU(W^*, E^*)$ if her reservation wage, $\underline{W}$, increases?

Exercise 7.3   What unilateral actions could an unemployed worker take that would convince the firm it could pay this worker less than its current workers, yet not experience a higher rate of shirking? (*Hint*: How could Tom make it very costly for him to be caught shirking?)

• CHAPTER 8 •

Insurance

8.2 • An introduction to the insurance market

Because the future is inherently uncertain, all people find themselves faced with risk. Most families risk having their house destroyed by a fire or other natural catastrophe and having the income of the main wage earner destroyed by death or disability. On a brighter note, many families risk winning their state lottery. All farmers face the risk that the price of their newly planted crops will be low when they harvest and try to sell them.

Insurance markets consist of buyers and sellers of risk. An insurance policy is a contract with which a household or firm "sells" all or part of some risk it faces to someone else. For example, life insurance is an exchange in which the purchaser of the insurance gives up a certain dollar amount in return for the promise that the life insurance company will replace some fraction of the income lost as a result of the untimely death of a household's breadwinner. A life insurance policy allows a family to reduce the uncertainty surrounding its future income Similarly, a futures contract allows a farmer to reduce his uncertainty about the price he will be paid for his crops. The seller of the futures contract commits herself to buying the farmer's crop at a predetermined price. This commitment transfers the price risk from the farmer to the investor who sells him the futures contract.[1]

A household whose only source of income is that earned by one of its members will likely be willing to pay a high price, relative to the income at risk, to protect itself against the sudden loss of this income. Such a household is said to be poorly **diversi-**

---

[1]This does not mean that the farmer may not eventually be unhappy he purchased this contract. It just means that he can be certain of the price he will receive.

fied. In contrast, an insurance company that already owns a large collection of similar risks—only a few of which will eventually result in a claim—will be willing to sell one more insurance policy for a relatively low price. The insurance company is said to be highly diversified. As a result, a deal can be struck between them. This suggests that there should be mutually acceptable terms under which large insurance companies will buy all the risks facing households.

Casual empiricism suggests, however, that many types of insurance coverage are not provided at all by private insurers, even though we would expect the buyers of such insurance to be willing to pay more for the coverage than the sellers would need to be compensated in order to provide it. For example, workers cannot purchase insurance against the risk that they will be laid off. College students cannot insure themselves against the risk that they will fail their college courses and will have to leave school.

Furthermore, where privately provided insurance protection does exist, it is often incomplete. For example, almost all insurance policies against the risk of an auto collision limit the extent of coverage through the use of deductible clauses or expenditure limits. The purpose of this application is to understand why insurance coverage is so incomplete. That is, why are so many apparently mutually beneficial exchanges not consummated?

One reason for the lack of complete insurance protection is the existence of moral hazard:[2] the ability of insurance buyers to take actions unobservable to the insurance company (but not necessarily unpredictable by the insurance company) that alter the amount of risk they have transferred to the insurance companies.[3] To see what we have in mind, consider the risk to a student from failing his college courses. The probability that this will happen depends, in part, on how hard the student tries to prevent this from happening. Unfortunately, monitoring the student's study effort is prohibitively expensive, if not outright impossible. As a result, any insurance company that agrees to compensate the student in the event of failure will have to provide the same compensation whether the student works a lot or a little. Since a contract of this form shields the student from some of the adverse consequences of failure, the insurance reduces the marginal benefit from working hard. As a result we would expect the student to reduce her effort as the amount of insurance protection pur-

---

[2]If, for some reason, you have skipped Chapter 7, you should go back to it and read the introduction to moral hazard which is contained in the first section.

[3]Another reason is adverse selection: a market situation in which the insurance buyer is better informed of the likelihood and magnitude of the loss than is the insurer. When there is adverse selection, the buyer's willingness to buy an insurance policy on some terms, but not others, allows the company to infer some of the buyer's private information. The problem of adverse selection will be examined in Part Four.

chased increases. The insurance company must take the moral hazard it faces into account in determining whether to offer insurance, what price to charge for it, and whether to restrict the amount of insurance the student can buy.

8.2 · Insurance in the absence of moral hazard

Consider Cynthia, a hypothetical stockroom worker for a grocery store. Whenever she is not laid off, Cynthia earns $400 per week. Every Monday morning, the store decides how many people it will employ that week and which workers it will lay off. Because of Cynthia's low seniority at the store, she faces a 25% chance of being laid off in any week. Layoffs last only one week because the firm has a policy of calling back any laid-off worker the following week. We know from Chapter 7 and our earlier discussion of involuntary unemployment that if Cynthia is laid off, there is some probability that she will not be able to find another job immediately. For the time being we will suppose that no other job opportunities exist.

Because the number of workers laid off varies randomly, Cynthia's income during any week that does not immediately follow a layoff is very uncertain. There is a 75% chance it will be $400 and a 25% chance it will be $0. For the moment, we will assume the probability of a layoff is a fixed number outside Cynthia's control and known to everyone. We will also assume there are no government-provided unemployment insurance benefits, since our goal is to understand why this kind of insurance is provided by the government rather than by private insurers.

Cynthia has a von Neumann-Morgenstern utility function (VNMU), which depends on her weekly income Y, denoted $U(Y)$. We will assume that U is increasing but at a decreasing rate. This means that the higher her weekly income the happier she is, and that she is risk-averse. Without insurance, her expected utility equals $0.25 \cdot U(0) + 0.75 \cdot U(400)$. We will refer to this expected utility as her reservation utility and denote it by U_0. This is the expected utility she can obtain without trading away any of her income uncertainty. Because she is assumed to maximize expected utility, she will never enter into any trades that result in an expected utility that is lower than U_0.

Every Friday, Cynthia can buy an "unemployment insurance" policy from the Allcounty Insurance Company. This insurance policy reimburses her some fraction of her weekly income if she is unemployed the following week. The size of the reimbursement, denoted by I, is called the policy's **indemnity**. In return for the commitment by the insurance company to pay Cynthia I in the event she is unemployed, the company requires Cynthia to pay it a nonrefundable **premium**, denoted P. An unemployment insurance policy is, therefore, completely specified by two numbers: the premium P and the indemnity I. We will denote these two numbers as the ordered pair, (P,I). For example, the policy ($50,$300) written between Cynthia and Allcounty requires a premium from Cynthia of $50. In return, Allcounty promises to pay $300 in the event that Cynthia is unemployed the following week.

If Cynthia purchases the policy (P,I), then her expected utility for the following week at the time of the purchase, denoted EU(P,I), equals

$$EU(P,I) = 0.25 \cdot U(I - P) + 0.75 \cdot U(\$400 - P). \tag{8.1}$$

Cynthia will buy the policy (P,I) only if the expected utility from this policy is greater than or equal to her reservation utility: $EU(P,I) \geq U_0$. Any policy that promises to pay Cynthia her full week's wages if she is laid off, a policy in which I = $400, is said to provide Cynthia with **full insurance** against the risk of unemployment. Such a policy guarantees that Cynthia's income in the coming week will equal $400 – P, regardless of whether she is unemployed or not. If $400 > I, then the policy **underinsures** Cynthia against the risk of unemployment; and if $400 < I, then the policy **overinsures** her against the risk of unemployment.[4]

If Cynthia buys the policy (P,I) from Allcounty, then—assuming no administrative costs[5]—the company's expected profit from the policy, denoted R(P,I), equals

$$R(P,I) = P - 0.25 \cdot I. \tag{8.2}$$

If R(P,I) = 0, then the policy is **actuarially fair**. If R(P,I) > 0, then the policy is actuarially **unfair**; and if R(P,I) < 0, the policy is actuarially **superfair**. Clearly, a policy is actuarially fair if and only if P = 0.25 · I. The constant 0.25 can be thought of as the "price" for actuarially fair insurance, and the indemnity can be considered to be the "quantity" of insurance purchased. For example, if Cynthia wants to buy a policy with an indemnity of $10, the fair premium for that policy would be $2.50. There are an infinite number of fair insurance policies, all of which, in this example, lie on a line between I and P with a slope of 0.25.[6]

Price competition between insurance companies, coupled with their ability to diversify away fully all risk, will cause them to offer only actuarially fair policies. Because we do not yet have the machinery in place to model price competition, we

---

[4]At this stage of the analysis you should not apply a pejorative meaning to the terms *underinsurance* and *overinsurance*. Perhaps better terms would be "less-than-full-insurance" and "more-than-full-insurance." Later on, however, there will be a normative sense to these terms, which will make them well chosen.

[5]There are three possible sources of administrative costs: the cost of writing a new policy, the cost of processing a claim, and the cost of paying a validated claim by selling the asset bought initially with the premium income. Insurance companies refer to this as their **load factor**.

[6]Assuming P is on the vertical axis.

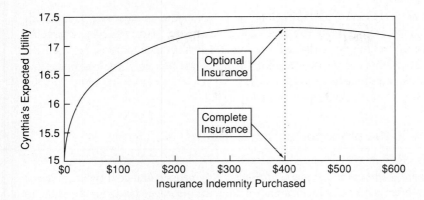

FIGURE 8.1 · Cynthia's expected utility after purchasing fair insurance as a function of the level of indemnity.

will simply assume that Allcounty is a regulated monopoly that is required to offer only actuarially fair policies.

Cynthia's expected utility after buying an actuarially fair policy $(0.25 \cdot I, I)$ equals

$$EU(I) = 0.25 \cdot U(0.75 \cdot I) + 0.75 \cdot U(\$400 - 0.25 \cdot I). \qquad (8.3)$$

Figure 8.1 shows the graph of $EU(I)$ when $U(Y) = \sqrt{Y}$. From this plot it is clear that, if Cynthia is offered the entire set of actuarially fair insurance policies, her optimal decision is to purchase a policy with an indemnity of \$400 and a premium $0.25 \cdot \$400 = \$100$. That is, Cynthia will choose to insure herself fully against the risk of unemployment. Cynthia's decision to insure herself fully does not depend on the presumed functional form of VNMU. It only depends on the fact that she is being offered actuarially fair insurance and that she is risk-averse. For future reference, we will state the general result as a formal proposition.

Theorem 8.1   Suppose a risk-averse decision maker faces the loss of a fixed amount of wealth X with a fixed probability π. Suppose further that this decision maker can purchase an insurance policy with an indemnity of I for the actuarially fair premium of $P(I) = \pi \cdot I$. Then the decision maker's best decision is to fully insure herself and choose an indemnity level of X.[7]

---

[7]This proposition can be extended to situations where the size of the loss is itself random. In such cases, the level of reimbursement will, in general, depend on the size of the loss. If the insurance premium charged is actuarially fair, then the insurance buyer will choose a policy that reimburses her fully for her loss, whatever its size.

In this model, as a risk-averse person, Cynthia is willing to pay more than the fair premium to buy full insurance. The insurance company, being forced to charge an actuarially fair premium, is also willing to sell her insurance at a fair rate. An exchange that benefits her and does not hurt the insurance company will take place, and there is no market failure.

8.3 · Insurance in the presence of moral hazard

Moral hazard is present in the market for unemployment insurance if two conditions hold. First, after purchasing an insurance policy, the insurance buyer must be able to take actions that alter the probability of the loss or the size of the loss. Second, it must be so costly to observe these actions that monitoring the buyer's actions is economically infeasible. Because of these high monitoring costs, the insurance company cannot condition the terms of the policy on the buyer's subsequent actions.

Both these conditions hold in the market for unemployment insurance. First, when Cynthia learns that she has been laid off from her current job, she does not have to wait passively until she is recalled by the grocery store. She can, instead, search for another job. The more effort she puts into her search, the higher will be the probability of finding another job. Second, although Allcounty can costlessly verify Cynthia's employment status, the company cannot monitor her search effort at all. Cynthia knows this information, of course, but the insurance company cannot trust her report. As a result, Allcounty's unemployment insurance policies must indemnify Cynthia if she is unemployed regardless of the amount of effort she spends on Monday finding another job.

We will denote her job search effort by E and will denote by $\pi(E)$ the probability that she does not find another job after she is laid off. The probability $\pi(E)$ decreases as E increases, and she will not find another job if she does not search at all. This means $\pi(0) = 1$.

For the sake of simplicity, we will assume that *all* stores, not just the grocery store, make their employment decisions on Monday morning. If Cynthia does not find another job the morning she is laid off, she will remain unemployed the rest of the week. This assumption allows us to ignore the length of her bout of unemployment. Either she is employed all week and earns $400 or she is unemployed all week and earns nothing.

Because searching for a job is costly, Cynthia must balance the marginal cost of additional search with the marginal expected net benefit. This means that her von Neumann–Morgenstern utility function no longer depends solely on her income, Y, but also depends on the level of effort E she puts into her search. To simplify our later calculations, we will assume this utility function takes the form $U(Y) - E$, where U increases in Y at a decreasing rate.[8] The net benefit of a successful search equals the difference between her income if she finds another comparable job ($400) and the indemnity, I, paid by her policy. The higher the indemnity, the smaller the net benefit from finding another job. Hence, Cynthia will search less the higher the indemnity paid by her policy.

Full unemployment insurance, which provides Cynthia the same income if she is unemployed as she would get if she found another job, reduces the net benefit of another job to zero. If Cynthia has full unemployment insurance, then she will not search for another job when she is laid off. As a result, the probability she is unemployed during the week will be 25%. On the other hand, if Cynthia's policy only offers her partial indemnity against the loss of income, she may find it worthwhile to engage in some search. This will reduce the probability of being unemployed that week to 25% · $\pi(E)$. Since the probability of being unemployed affects the insurance company's expected profit or loss on any policy, the insurance company must look ahead and foresee how Cynthia will behave after she buys one of its policies, before it knows how to price it.

Cynthia and Allcounty are playing a principal–agent game in which the company is the "principal" and Cynthia is the "agent." The game tree is shown in Figure 8.2.

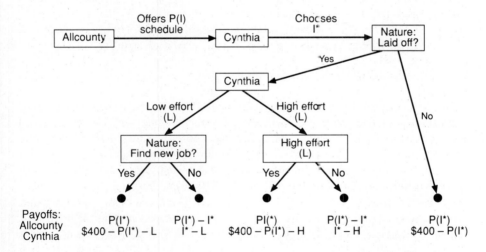

FIGURE 8.2 · Game tree for the principal–agent game played between Allcounty Insurance Company and Cynthia.

---

[8]At the cost of added complexity, we could have made her utility function depend on income and leisure and measured her job search effort by the amount of leisure she has to give up to search for another job.

There are five moves in this game. Allcounty has the first move, in which it announces the premium it will charge for each level of indemnity. We will denote this premium schedule as a function P(I). Cynthia moves second and decides how much insurance to buy. Nature moves third and chooses whether Cynthia is laid off or not. If she is not laid off, the game ends. Otherwise, Cynthia moves again and chooses how hard to search for a job. Nature moves last and determines whether she finds another job or not.

A strategy for Allcounty consists of a premium schedule P(I). In order to avoid modeling price competition, we will continue to assume that Allcounty is a regulated monopolist that is required to offer actuarially fair policies. As we already mentioned, this assumption mimics the effects of price competition. Because the firm's profits depend on a variable outside the firm's direct control, namely search effort E, we will have to modify the definition of *actuarially fair*. A strategy for Cynthia consists of a choice of indemnity level given any premium schedule and a choice of job search effort E(P,I) for every policy.

If Cynthia buys the policy (P,I) but is not laid off, then her payoff is U($400 – P). If she is laid off and puts in an effort of E in searching for a job and finds another job, her payoff is U($400 – P) – E. If she does not find another job after being laid off, then her insurance policy comes into force and her payoff equals U(I – P) – E. If she purchases the policy (P,I) and is laid off, then the expected utility from searching for another job with effort E equals

$$EU(P,I,E) = \pi(E) \cdot (U(I - P) - E) + (1 - \pi(E)) \cdot U(\$400 - P) - E \qquad (8.4)$$

$$= U(\$400 - P) - (\pi(E) \cdot N(P,I) + E),$$

where $N(P,I) = U(\$400 - P) - U(I - P)$. The function $N(P,I)$ is the net benefit to Cynthia from finding another job if she is laid off and owns the policy (P,I). As either P or I increases, the value of N will decrease. Cynthia chooses her job search effort so as to maximize EU(P,I,E). The optimal search effort level will be denoted $E^*(P,I)$. Notice that if the policy (P,I) provides full insurance against income loss (I = $400), then $N(P,I) = 0$ and Cynthia will not search if laid off ($E^*(P,I) = 0$).

Because Cynthia's expected utility function, EU(P,I,E), is common knowledge, Allcounty will expect Cynthia to choose her optimal search strategy, $E^*(P,I)$. As a result, if Allcounty sells the policy (P,I) to Cynthia, the firm's expected profit equals

$$R(P,I) = P - 0.25 \cdot \pi(E^*(P,I)) \cdot I. \qquad (8.5)$$

It follows that the actuarially fair premium to charge for a policy with an indemnity level of I, denoted $P^*(I)$, satisfies the equation

$$P^*(I) = 0.25 \cdot \pi(E^*(P^*(I),I)) \cdot I. \tag{8.6}$$

The expected utility of buying the insurance policy (P,I), given that Cynthia can foresee that, when laid off, she will search for another job with an intensity of $E^*(P,I)$, is given by

$$EU(P,I) = 0.75 \cdot U(\$400 - P) + 0.25 \cdot \pi(E^*(P,I)) \cdot (U(I - P) - E^*(P,I)) \tag{8.7}$$
$$+ 0.25 \cdot (1 - \pi(E^*(P,I))) \cdot (U(\$400 - P) - E^*(P,I))$$
$$= U(\$400 - P) - 0.25 \cdot (\pi(E^*(P,I)) \cdot N(P,I + E^*(P,I)).$$

To help you visualize what is going on, let us assume that $U(Y) = \sqrt{Y}$ and $\pi(E) = e^{-E/4}$. It is a straightforward calculus exercise to show that $EU(P,I,E)$ is maximized at

$$E^*(P,I) = \begin{cases} 4 \cdot \ln(N(P,I)/4) & \text{if } N(P,I) > 4 \\ \\ 0 & \text{if } N(P,I) \le 4 \end{cases} \tag{8.8}$$

The reader can also verify that equations (8.6) and (3.8) imply that the fair premium schedule satisfies the equation

$$P^*(I) = \begin{cases} I/N(P^*(I),I) & \text{if } I < \$270 \\ \\ 0.25 \cdot I & \text{if } I \ge \$270, \end{cases} \tag{8.9}$$

where the constant \$270 is the solution to the equation

$$N(0.25 \cdot I, I) = 4. \tag{8.10}$$

$P^*(I)/I$ is the actuarially fair "price" of insurance at the indemnity level I. The graph of this price function, $P^*(I)/I$, is plotted in Figure 8.3. When the indemnity is near zero, the price is \$0.05 per dollar of indemnity. The price is low because, when she has little or no insurance, Cynthia searches so hard for a job whenever she is laid off that the chance of being unemployed is only 5%. As the indemnity level increases, the price increases, reflecting the reduced effort Cynthia applies to her search for another job. Once the indemnity level rises above \$270, Cynthia no longer bothers to

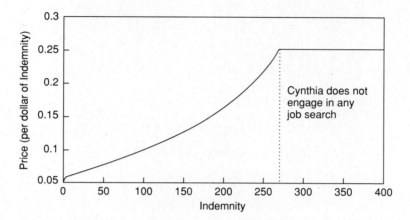

FIGURE 8.3 · The actuarially fair price of insurance as a function of the amount of insurance purchased, taking into account the moral hazard caused by Cynthia's ability to alter the effort she puts into searching for another job when she is laid off.

search for a job when she is laid off and the price of insurance reaches its maximum of $0.25 per dollar of indemnity. The price is high because the probability she will be unemployed, and therefore use her insurance, is high.

Equations (8.8) and (8.9) imply that when Allcounty offers her the actuarially fair premium schedule $P^*(I)$, Cynthia chooses the indemnity level that maximizes

$$EU^*(I) = \begin{cases} \sqrt{(\$400 - P^*(I))} \; - \; 1 \; - \; \ln(N(P^*(I),I)\,/\,4) & \text{if } I < \$270 \\[3em] \sqrt{(\$400 - P^*(I))} \; - \; N(P^*(I)I),\,/\,4 & \text{if } I \geq \$270 \end{cases} \qquad (8.11)$$

The function EU^* is plotted in Figure 8.4. The graph has two "hills." The larger hill reaches its peak at the indemnity level of $134 (incomplete insurance), and the smaller hill reaches its peak at the indemnity level of $400 (complete insurance).

Even though she is being offered actuarially fair insurance, Cynthia will buy $134 of insurance for $15 or $0.11 per dollar of indemnity. If she could buy more insurance at this price, she would. The reason she cannot obtain more insurance at this price is that it is common knowledge that if Cynthia bought more insurance, her behavior would change. Specifically, she would no longer search as hard for a job.

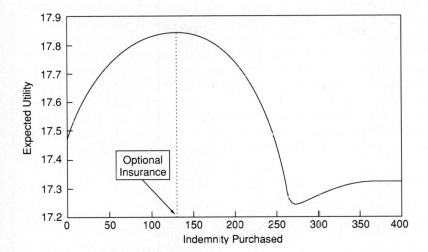

FIGURE 8.4 · An equilibrium for the unemployment insurance market in which Cynthia underinsures herself against unemployment risk.

With only $134 of unemployment insurance protection, she willingly searches so hard for another job whenever she is laid off that the probability of finding one is 55%. Nevertheless, 11% of the time she will find herself unemployed and suffer a week with no income.

8.4 · Welfare effects of moral hazard

We have just seen that moral hazard can cause Cynthia to choose incomplete insurance. But she does this in order to get the benefit of a lower price. As a result, it is not immediately clear whether Cynthia is hurt by moral hazard or not. We will now show that, in general, she is hurt.

Suppose Allcounty could observe Cynthia's job search efforts at no cost. In this case, Allcounty could make its premium P depend on *both* E and I. If Allcounty is constrained to offering only actuarially fair insurance contracts, then the premium P(I,E) must satisfy the equation

$$P(I,E) = 0.25 \cdot \pi(E) \cdot I. \tag{8.12}$$

This collection of actuarially fair contracts includes all the contracts Allcounty offered Cynthia when E was not observable. This is apparent by comparing equation

(8.12) with equation (8.6). As long as insurance companies are always restricted to offering actuarially fair insurance contracts—whether this is due to regulation or market competition—Cynthia will have a strictly larger set of contracts to choose from when moral hazard is absent than when it is present. Because Cynthia moves last, reducing the set of contracts over which she can choose never makes her better off and will usually make her worse off. In general, Allcounty's inability to monitor Cynthia's job search efforts *hurts her*.

We can say more. If Allcounty offers the entire schedule of actuarially fair insurance contracts, then Cynthia chooses the level of indemnity I and the search effort E that maximizes her expected utility. Her expected utility is now given by

$$EU(P(I,E),I,E) = 0.75 \cdot U(\$400 - P(E,I)) + 0.25 \cdot \pi(E) \cdot (U(I - P(I,E) - E) \qquad (8.13)$$

$$+ 0.25 \cdot (1 - \pi(E)) \cdot U(\$400 - P(I,E)) - E)$$

$$= U(\$400 - 0.25 \cdot \pi(E) \cdot I) \cdot (1 - 0.25 \cdot \pi(E))$$

$$+ 0.25 \cdot \pi(E) \cdot U(I \cdot (1 - 0.25 \cdot \pi(E))) - 0.25 \cdot E.$$

We leave it as an exercise for the reader to show that Cynthia's best strategy is to insure herself fully and to choose the effort level that maximizes

$$EU^{**}(E) = U(\$400 \cdot (1 - 0.25 \cdot \pi(E))) - E. \qquad (8.14)$$

Either Cynthia purchases less insurance and searches more when her job search effort is unobservable than when it is, or she fully insures herself in both situations but does not search for a job when her effort is unobservable and does search when her effort is observable.

The problem of moral hazard exists in a variety of risky situations. Life and medical insurance providers, for example, cannot easily observe the efforts taken by its policy holders to reduce their risk from various costly diseases such as stroke, heart attack, cancer, or diabetes. As a result, they cannot reward policy holders for changing their diets, increasing the amount of exercise they do, or breaking their smoking habits.

8.5 · Government responses to market failure in the unemployment insurance market

It is tempting to conclude that we have identified an instance of market failure: that is, a market equilibrium in which there is an inefficient allocation of resources. The resources are job search effort and income risk. But this is a mistake. The market allocation is "inefficient" only if some *feasible* reallocation can produce a Pareto superior outcome. Unless the government can observe Cynthia's job search effort at much lower cost than can a private insurance company, the government cannot get out of the moral hazard game.

There does not appear to be any efficiency gains from having unemployment insurance provided by a government agency rather than by private firms through a competitive insurance market.

8.6 • Summary

In the insurance game, the principal, the insurance company, offers a policy to the agent, the consumer. The policy is completely defined by the premium and the indemnity value. The consumer can accept or reject the policy. The consumer can also, however, behave in a manner that affects the probability of the insurance company's having to pay the indemnity value. Nature also makes a move that affects the probability of a claim. Because it is too costly for the insurance company to distinguish between the agent's actions and Nature's actions, the insurance company finds itself in a delicate position. By offering a full-insurance policy, something that the consumer might desire, the firm will typically end up offering a policy that inspires the consumer to behave in such a risky manner that the insurance company will lose money. Therefore, the consumer will end up being underinsured.

Both these games are characterized by commitment problems. In the unemployment game, the worker cannot credibly commit to a level of effort. Thus, to insure a relatively high level of effort, the firm pays a relatively high wage, called an efficiency wage, and hires fewer workers. In the insurance game, the consumer cannot credibly commit to behaving in a safe manner. Hence, to keep the incentives of choosing relatively safe actions relatively high, the insurance company only offers policies that result in underinsurance.

8.7 • Further reading

The fact that insurers are exposed to moral hazard has been known by economists for some time. Excellent non-game-theoretic discussions are Mark Pauly, "Overinsurance and Public Provision of Insurance: The Roles of Moral Hazard and Adverse Selection," *Quarterly Journal of Economics* 87 (1974), pp. 44–54; Michael Spence and Richard Zeckhauser, "Insurance, Information, and Individual Action," *American Economic Review* 61 (1971), pp. 380–387, and Kenneth Arrow, "Uncertainty and the Welfare Economics of Health Care," *American Economic Review* 53 (1963), pp. 941–969.

These three articles can be found in the collection of readings by Peter Diamond and Michael Rothschild, *Uncertainty in Economics* (New York: Academic Press, 1978).

8.8 • Exercises

Exercise 8.1 Assuming that $U(Y) = \sqrt{Y}$ and $\pi(E) = e^{-E/4}$, show that EU(P,I,E) is maximized at

$$E^*(P,I) = \begin{cases} 4 \cdot \ln(N(P,I)/4) & \text{if } N(P,I) > 4 \\[2ex] 0 & \text{if } N(P,I) \leq 4 \end{cases}$$

Exercise 8.2 Continuation of Exercise 8.1. Prove that the fair premium schedule satisfies the equation

$$P^*(I) = \begin{cases} I/N(P^*(I),I) & \text{if } I < \$270 \\[2ex] 0.25 \cdot I & \text{if } I \geq \$270. \end{cases}$$

Exercise 8.3 Suppose Cynthia's effort E can be costlessly observed by Allcounty; therefore, the firm can offer her the premium schedule: $P(I, E) = e^{-E/4} \cdot I$. Show that Cynthia's best strategy is to insure herself fully and to choose the effort level that maximizes

$$EU^{**}(E) = U(\$400 \cdot (1 - 0.25 \cdot \pi(E))) - E.$$

Exercise 8.4 Suppose that Joe has a VNMU utility function that depends on his income for the term and the number of his waking hours he spends studying. He has 1,250 waking hours in the term. Specifically, $U = y - S^2/1250 -$, where S is the number of hours he spends studying and Y is his income. Joe currently has a term income of $2,000. As an incentive for him to study, Joe's parents have made a deal: If Joe passes his economics course, he will be given $1000; if he fails he will be given nothing. Joe has no other income. The probability of his passing is equal to S/1,250. An insurance company is considering offering Joe income insurance. The insurance company cannot observe S.

(a) If Joe cannot buy insurance against the possibility of failing, how much time will he spend studying and what is his expected utility?

(b) If the insurance company were to offer Joe complete insurance, what is the most Joe will pay for this insurance and how much time will he spend studying?

(c) If the insurance company offers Joe every fair insurance policy, what policies, if any, will Joe be willing to buy?

Exercise 8.5   Suppose a worker can either wear safety goggles or not. The goggles are not 100% effective against the loss of an eye, and the worker works alone so that no one knows whether he is wearing goggles or not. An eye, from the perspective of the worker, has a present value of $1 million. The probability of losing an eye if safety goggles are worn is 10%, whereas if goggles are not worn it is 15%. An insurance company is considering offering insurance for an eye injury. It cannot observe whether goggles are worn or not. Wearing goggles costs the worker (in present value) $10,000 in psychic income. The worker has a utility function given by: $U = \sqrt{Y}$ and currently has a dollar income of $2 million in present value.

(a) Draw a game tree for this game.

(b) Consider an insurance policy that has a premium (in present value) of $100,000 and an indemnity of $1 million. What are the rational decisions for the worker to make? Is this a fair policy? Explain.

(c) Find what, if any, insurance policy would be written if an insurance company could only sell fair policies.

• CHAPTER 9 •

Patents and Product Variety

9.1 • Introduction

One of the more important forms of government regulation is the issuing of patents. A **patent** grants the recipient a legal monopoly in the production of the patented good for the life of the patent. The arguments for and against patents involve a straightforward application of concepts learned in a principles of economics course.

In a competitive market, where information is relatively costless and patents do not exist, new innovations or new products will earn their developers profits only in the short run. In the long run, a particularly good idea or valuable product or service will induce imitators to enter the market, thereby reducing the developer's economic profits to zero. Because the developer is unable to capture the entire stream of profits from her innovation, the private expected benefits from developing a new product will be less than society's expected benefits. The predictable result is that there will be less product innovation and development than is socially desirable.[1]

One way to allow the developer of a new product or production process to capture a larger fraction of the rewards for her brilliance is to give her a legal right to the dollar value of the benefits her insights provide. This can be done by granting inventors a legal monopoly in the production of the good or service they have invented. Essentially, this is what a patent is intended to do.

Of course, as you know, monopolies tend to set their prices above the marginal cost of production and distribution. As a result, they produce and sell fewer products

---

[1] In essence the entrepreneurs in a competitive market are in a prisoner's dilemma. If you already know what that is, then you can appreciate their problem. If you do not, you will learn more about it later in the book.

than is socially efficient. Therefore, in solving one problem (too little innovation), the patent creates a second problem (not enough output of the newly created good). As a compromise, a time limit is typically put on the life span of a patent. In the United States it is typically 17 years. After that time the special information that was used to create the good or service becomes public knowledge.

In this chapter we are not so much interested in the question of whether patents are good or bad, but in how they affect the *variety* of goods and services produced. When we think of the type of products for which patents are an important issue, we frequently have something like the pharmaceutical industry in mind. For example, there might be only one chemical compound that is known to relieve migraine headaches. A patent for the drug will state its precise chemical features. It is fairly straightforward to tell if another firm is infringing on the patent just by looking at the chemical structure of the new drug and comparing it with the patent. More commonly, however, there will exist a variety of drugs that accomplish the same ends through somewhat different means. For example, there are several antibiotics commonly used in treating ear infections. Some require that the patient take the medication twice a day, others require three times a day; some entail a fairly high risk of intestinal disorders, others cause drowsiness. Still, each specific drug is easily characterized by a precise chemical formula, and it is this chemical formula that can be patented.

Contrast the previous case with the example of a car seat for children. Whereas a particular car seat *design* may be patentable, the *concept* of a car seat is not patentable (at least, in the United States). Even after a patent is granted for a specific car seat design, a subsequent developer has a fair amount of scope to imitate many of the features of that design without legally violating the original patent. If the patent owner feels the patent is being violated, the onus is on the patent owner to bring suit against the imitator. Once the suit is levied, it is up to the courts to decide if there is, in fact, a patent infringement. Therefore, the owner of the patent must be reasonably certain that the courts will find the imitator guilty of a patent infringement before it makes sense to file a lawsuit.

It is this last type of situation we are interested in modeling in this application. Although there is no doubt that patents act as a deterrent to entry into a market, they are typically not a perfect deterrent. Therefore, a firm that is granted a patent may not be immune from entry. In this application, we will present and then analyze a game that makes some predictions about when a firm will patent its product and what degree of product variety is likely to ensue.

9.2 · The patent game

Consider a product that is found in over half of American homes: the video cassette recorder (VCR). VCRs have many features. Beyond simply recording and playing back tapes, they can be programmed to record programs when the owner is not at home or is watching a show on another channel; they can be used to edit tapes and to dub a new soundtrack over the original; they are capable of displaying more than one program on the screen at the same time; and they can be tied into the owner's stereo equipment to produce high-fidelity, stereo sound.

To access these features, the owner must use the control knobs and buttons on the front of the machine and follow the instructions given in the owner's manuals or printed on the television screen. These controls can be configured by the manufacturer in a variety of ways. At one extreme, the VCR can be designed so that the only button on the machine itself is an on/off switch and a yes/no button, the user is guided through all functions by answering detailed yes/no questions that appear directly on the TV screen, and many of the machine's most advanced features are deliberately hidden from the novice user. Such a VCR we will refer to as *simple,* because this is how it appears to the novice user. At the other extreme, the VCR can be built with dozens of buttons and controls in plain view on the front of the machine, which the user can use to access all the machine's functions directly, including the most advanced. Such a VCR we will refer to as *complex,* because this is how it appears to a novice user.

We can represent the complexity of any VCR by a number between 0 and 1. A 0 represents the simplest control design, and a 1 represents the most complex control design. Each VCR manufacturer must choose what type of VCR to produce. We can recast the firm's problem as one of choosing where to "locate" on the interval [0, 1] depicted in Figure 9.1. Models of this type are known as **location models,** even when the "location" is something like complexity or reliability rather than a geographic location. A firm that produces a VCR whose complexity equals 0.3 will be said to "lie at 0.3."

Households buy VCRs for many different reasons: They want to rent and watch movies at home; they want to watch and edit video tapes made with their video cameras; they want to record TV programs during the day when they are at work and to record TV programs at night when they are out. Furthermore, people have different levels of comfort with electronic devices and different capacities for successfully

FIGURE 9.1 • The VCR complexity interval in which 0 represents the easiest-to-use model and 1 represents the hardest-to-use model.

following complex instructions. As a result, different households can have very different tastes for the level of complexity in their VCR. Whereas a very complex VCR might drive someone with a fear of dials and buttons batty, it might be just what the aspiring young home video director is looking for. We will suppose that each household has an ideal VCR complexity, say x^*. A household whose ideal VCR complexity equals 0.3 will be said to be "located at 0.3." For such a household, increasing complexity is good as long as the level of complexity is below 0.3; but above 0.3, increasing complexity becomes bad.

These ideal complexity levels are assumed to be uniformly distributed. Informally, this implies that the same number of households are located at every point between 0 and 1. Formally, it implies that the proportion of households whose ideal complexity levels lie between x_A and x_B equals $x_B - x_A$.

9.2.1   The players and game tree

Two firms are assumed to be potentially active in the VCR market. One firm develops the technology to produce a VCR prior to the second firm. The innovating firm moves first. The technology is such that both firms can produce only one type of VCR. It is common to call the first firm into a market the *incumbent firm* and to call the second firm the *entrant*.

At the time the incumbent firm enters the market with its VCR, it has the option to patent its product. The patent gives the firm some legal protection against imitation, but there is enough vagueness in the patent's description that legal imitation by the second firm cannot be ruled out.

Regardless of whether the incumbent firm patents the product or not, the entrant now has the option to enter the VCR industry. If the incumbent has chosen not to patent its VCR, then the entrant can choose any VCR design it wants with impunity and the incumbent will have to battle the entrant in the marketplace rather than the courtroom. If the incumbent chooses to patent its VCR, then the entrant faces the risk of a lawsuit by the incumbent if it enters the industry. Nevertheless, because the success of the lawsuit cannot be ensured, the entrant may find entry worth the risk.

If entry occurs in spite of the incumbent's patent, the incumbent must decide whether or not to sue the entrant. Because lawsuits are expensive, the incumbent may rationally choose not to sue the entrant. Of course, in the event of a lawsuit, both the incumbent and the entrant will incur legal fees.

After all the maneuvering over location, patent filings, and lawsuits, either the entrant stays out of the market (whether voluntarily or involuntarily) or the entrant successfully enters. In the first instance, the incumbent ends up with a monopoly. In the second instance, the incumbent must share the market with the entrant, and the two firms engage in a contest over price and market share.

The game tree is displayed in Figure 9.2. The incumbent begins the game by simultaneously choosing a location and deciding whether or not to patent its product. Subsequently, the entrant chooses whether to enter the market and, if so, where to locate itself. If the incumbent decides not to patent the product, then the game ends. The game also ends if the incumbent patents the product and this deters the entrant from producing VCRs. If the incumbent patents the product and entry occurs, then the incumbent has the option of sueing the entrant. If the incumbent does not sue, then the game ends. If the incumbent sues, then the court ("Nature") makes a random decision about the entrant's guilt and awards damages, which brings the game to an end.

Conspicuously absent from the game tree in Figure 9.2 is the determination of VCR prices. Price setting is simple if the incumbent ends up with a monopoly: The firm charges the monopoly price. But if the entrant successfully enters, then the incumbent must share the market with the entrant and the two firms must play a price-setting game. The outcome of this subgame is a nontrivial part of any complete analysis of our patent game. As you will see, the game is already surprisingly complex without adding the strategic issues of price setting and market sharing. Furthermore, at this stage of the book we lack the tools with which to analyze any reasonable model of the pricing subgame coherently.[2]

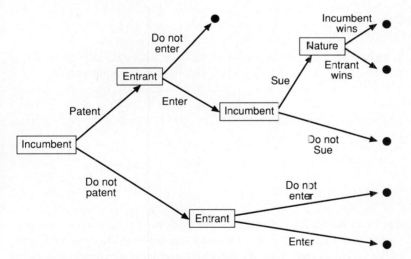

FIGURE 9.2 • The game tree for the patent game. Payoffs have not yet been specified.

---

[2]The problem is that the most reasonable model of price setting is that both firms set their prices *simultaneously* rather than sequentially.

We will assume the incumbent and the entrant charge the same price for the VCR they each produce. In a more advanced treatment of this topic, equal prices would be shown to be the outcome of optimal strategic decision making. In the present case, however, we will simply assume this is the case. One implication of this assumption is that consumers who want a VCR at the single market price will buy a VCR from the firm that is located closest to them (in terms of complexity, not geographic distance). For example, if the entrant lies at 0.30 and the incumbent lies at 0.50, then every consumer willing to buy a VCR at the market price who is located between 0 and 0.40 will buy from the entrant, and every consumer located between 0.40 and 1 will buy from the incumbent.

9.2.2   Payoffs

To calculate the payoffs for each firm, we need to be more specific about the nature of the demand for VCRs. To simplify our calculations, we will assume there are exactly one million potential consumers of VCRs per year. Because we are assuming both firms charge the same price for the VCR, consumers choose between the two firms solely on the basis of their location on the complexity interval. We will assume each consumer buys at most one VCR. The *proportion* of the population with the same preferences for complexity (that is, at the same location) who actually buy a VCR will be denoted by Q_d. By definition, Q_d is a number between 0 and 1. This implies that even households at the same location can value a given VCR design differently. Some households at a given location will be willing to pay more for a VCR than others will, but every household at that location will give the same *ordinal* ranking to every VCR design. They may give different cardinal rankings because of other differences between them, such as income. Q_d depends on the price, P, and the distance these consumers are from the closest firm, denoted t. The specific functional relationship is assumed to be:

$$Q_d(P,t) = \begin{cases} 1 - P/200 - t/2 & \text{if } 1 - P/200 - t/2 \geq 0, \\ 0 & \text{otherwise.} \end{cases} \qquad (9.1)$$

As the price of VCRs rise, *ceteris paribus*, the proportion of the population at a given location that buy VCRs will fall. As the distance between the ideal VCR and the nearest VCR increases, *ceteris paribus*, the proportion of the population at a given location that buy VCRs will also fall. Notice that every consumer would buy a VCR if the price were zero and its design matched the consumer's ideal. But some consumers would not buy a VCR, even if it were free, if its controls were too complex or too simple. Solving for P, the demand function can be rewritten as an inverse demand function:

$$P = 200 - (200 \cdot Q_d) - (100 \cdot t). \tag{9.2}$$

The coefficient "100" in front of the distance parameter t can be interpreted as the dollar cost to the consumer of using a VCR whose complexity differs from the consumer's ideal level by one unit. In other words, if the closest VCR is at 0.50 on the complexity scale and a consumer's preferred VCR complexity is at 0.70, then the closest VCR complexity would be 0.20 units away (t = 0.20). Multiplying 0.20 by 100 equals 20, so the store must charge this consumer $20 less than one located at 0.70 in order that both consumers be equally likely to buy a VCR.

A firm's location affects the demand for its product in two ways. First, the location choice will determine the proportion of the entire population that will buy a VCR from the firm—if they buy a VCR at all. Second, the location choice (as well as the price charged) will determine the proportion of the population at a given location that will buy a VCR because demand at every location falls with the distance to the firm.

Total revenue depends on whether the market is a monopoly or a duopoly. Consider first what happens if there is a single provider of VCRs. Suppose the firm locates at L. The average distance from the firm of those consumers located to the right of L, between L and 1, is $(1 - L)/2$. For these people the average value of Q_d equals $1 - P/200 - (1 - L)/4$. Because $(1 - L)$ of the population lies to the right of the firm, there will be a demand from this segment of the consumer population (in millions) of

$$(1 - L) \cdot (1 - P/200 - (1 - L)/4). \tag{9.3}$$

A similar story holds for the left-hand side. The average value of Q_d for the consumers to the left of the firm's chosen location equals $1 - P/200 - L/4$ and the proportion of the entire population to the left of the firm equals L. So the demand from this segment of the consumer population equals (in millions)

$$L \cdot (1 - P/200 - L/4). \tag{9.4}$$

Adding together the demand from the two groups we get:

$$S_M(L,P) = 3/4 - P/200 + L \cdot (1 - L)/2, \tag{9.5}$$

where $S_M(L,P)$ denotes the quantity demanded (S for sales) from a VCR producer with a monopoly that locates at L and charges a price P.

If the market is a duopoly, then each firm's sales depend on the location of both firms, as well as on their common price. Because the consumers are uniformly distributed between 0 and 1, sales when the incumbent locates at L and the entrant locates at E will be identical to sales when the incumbent locates at

1 – L and the entrant locates at 1 – E. Therefore, there is no loss of generality in supposing that the incumbent only considers locations between 0.5 and 1 (inclusive). Using this assumption about the incumbent, it is now clear that the entrant will always prefer to locate itself to the left of the incumbent rather than to the right. So there is also no loss of generality in restricting the entrant to locations that lie to the left of the incumbent. We will henceforth assume that $1 \geq L \geq 0.5$ and $0 \leq E \leq L$.

Suppose the incumbent locates at L and the entrant then locates D units to the left of the incumbent at L – D. Then the incumbent will sell to those consumers located between L – D/2 (the midpoint between the two firms' locations) and 1, and the entrant will sell to those consumers located between 0 and L – D/2. We will refer to these two subintervals as the incumbent's and the entrant's **market areas** (see Figure 9.3).

To find the number of VCRs that the incumbent firm sells, we once again consider consumers located to the right and to the left of the incumbent's location at L. We have already derived the demand on the right hand side in equation (9.3), but we now have to reconsider the left-hand side demand to account for the entrant. The average distance between the incumbent and any consumer to the left of L who would buy a VCR from it equals D/4. This implies the average value of Q_d equals $1 - P/200 - D/8$. The proportion of the total population that is located to the left of the incumbent and that would buy from it equals D/2. Therefore, sales on the left-hand side of the incumbent will equal (in millions)

$$D/2 \cdot (1 - P/200 - D/8). \tag{9.6}$$

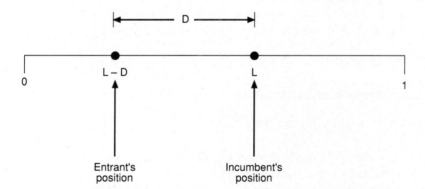

FIGURE 9.3 • The positioning of the two players. The incumbent's VCR is located at L, and the entrant's VCR is located D units to left of the incumbent at L – D.

Adding (9.3) to (9.6) gives sales to the incumbent of

$$S_I(L,D,P) = (1 - P/200) \cdot (1 - L + D/2)$$
$$- D^2/16 - (1 - L)^2/4.$$

(9.7)

In a similar fashion you can verify that the sales of the entrant are given by

$$S_E(L,D,P) = (1 - P/200) \cdot (L - D/2)$$
$$- D^2/16 - (L - D)^2/4.$$

(9.8)

Costs are far easier to calculate. We will assume that both firms face unrecoverable costs of $5 million when they enter the market and constant marginal production and distribution costs of $50 per unit. This implies that total operating costs of each firm (in millions of dollars) once it is in the market equals

$$C(S) = 5 + 50 \cdot S,$$

(9.9)

where S represents sales.

The payoffs for the two firms will be determined in two steps. We will begin by ignoring the costs of patents and lawsuits and calculate the operating profit of the incumbent and entrant. We will then take the other costs into account and determine the net profits of both firms under each possible sequence of actions.

First consider the case where the incumbent has successfully established a monopoly. Using equations (9.5) and (9.9), we find that its operating profits are:

$$\pi_M(L,P) = (3/4 - P/200 + L \cdot (1 - L)/2) \cdot (P - 50) - 5.$$

(9.10)

The monopolist will set the price so as to maximize equation (9.10). The profit-maximizing unit price P_m^* equals

$$P_m^* = \$100 - \$100 \cdot L \cdot (1 - L).^3$$

(9.11)

The monopolist will also choose a location so as to maximize equation (9.10). The profit-maximizing location equals

$$L_m^* = 1/2 \cdot (P - 25)/(P - 50).$$

(9.12)

---

[3] This is found by maximizing the profit function with respect to the price of VCRs. This means that the partial derivative of $\pi_M(L,P)$ with respect to P is found and then set equal to zero.

Equation (9.11) tells us that when the firm has chosen a location of 0.5, the optimal price is \$112.50, while equation (9.12) says that when the price is \$112.50, the optimal location is 0.5. The upshot is that $P_m^* = \$112.50$ and $L_m^* = 0.50$. Define π_M as $\pi_M(L_m^*, P_m^*)$. Hence, when the incumbent firm is a monopoly, π_m^* is \$14.531 million.

Now consider the case where the market is a duopoly. Using equations (9.7), (9.8), and (9.9), we can calculate the profits of both firms as a function of their location and their common price:

$$\pi_I(L,D,P) = [(1 - P/200) \cdot (1 - L + D/2) \tag{9.13}$$
$$- D^2/16 - (1 - L)^2/4] \cdot [P - 50] - 5.$$

$$\pi_E(L,D,P) = [(1 - P/200) \cdot (L - D/2) \tag{9.14}$$
$$- D^2/16 - (L - D)^2/4] \cdot [P - 50] - 5.$$

Because we are deliberately ignoring strategic pricing in this application, we will assume the two firms charge the joint-profit-maximizing price, P_d^*:[4]

$$P_d^* = 100 - 50 \cdot (0.75 \cdot D^2 + L^2 - L - L \cdot D). \tag{9.15}$$

If we substitute equation (9.15) into equations (9.13) and (9.14), we obtain the operating profit of the two firms when they share a duopoly:

$$\pi_I(L,D) = [(2 + 0.75 \cdot D^2 + L^2 - L - L \cdot D)/4 \tag{9.16}$$
$$\cdot (1 - L + D/2) - D^2/16 - (1 - L)^2/4]$$
$$\cdot 50 \cdot (1 - 0.75 \cdot D^2 - L^2 + L + L \cdot D) - 5.$$

$$\pi_E(L,D) = [(2 + 0.75 \cdot D^2 + L^2 - L - L \cdot D)/4 \tag{9.17}$$
$$\cdot (L - D/2) - D^2/16 - (L - D)^2/4]$$
$$\cdot 50 \cdot (1 - 0.75 \cdot D^2 - L^2 + L + L \cdot D) - 5,$$

---

[4]That is, the price that maximizes $\pi_I + \pi_E$. As we will see in Part Three this price is higher— sometimes much higher— than the price predicted under the assumption that the firms cannot cooperate and choose their prices simultaneously. Our pricing rule ignores the incentive that exists for each firm to increase its market area (at the expense of the other firm) by lowering its price.

where $\pi_I(L,D)$ and $\pi_E(L,D)$ represent operating profits for the incumbent firm and the entrant, respectively. Assume it costs the incumbent $0.5 million to patent its design. If the incumbent sues the entrant for patent infringement and the entrant fights the suit, then each firm will incur $1 million in legal expenses.

If the incumbent wins the suit, then the entrant must pay damages to the incumbent. We will assume these damages equal the entrant's operating profits from entry, $\pi_E(L,D)$. If the incumbent loses its suit, then the entrant can keep its profits. We will treat the case where the entrant enters, is sued by the incumbent, and then immediately leaves the market without a fight as if the entrant had not entered the market at all.

Because the patent description is somewhat vague, the court outcome is uncertain. But the closer the entrant's design is to the incumbent's, the higher the likelihood of a decision in the incumbent's favor. We will assume the probability of the incumbent winning, $p(D)$, is given by

$$p(D) = \begin{cases} 1 - 2 \cdot D & \text{if } D \le 0.5 \\ 0 & \text{if } D > 0.5 \end{cases} \qquad (9.18)$$

Equation (9.18) implies that if the entrant were to introduce a VCR design identical to that of the incumbent, meaning that D equals zero, then the incumbent would win any court action with certainty. Conversely, whenever the entrant locates itself more than 0.5 units from the incumbent, then the incumbent will certainly lose a lawsuit for patent infringement. For distances between 0 and 0.5, the probability of winning the lawsuit decreases linearly with the distance between the two firms.

As you can see from Figure 9.2, the game tree has six terminal nodes. These nodes can be reached by the following sequences of actions:

1. The incumbent does not patent its design but the entrant stays out anyway.
2. The incumbent does not patent its design and the entrant enters with a second design.
3. The incumbent patents its design and the entrant stays out of the market.
4. The incumbent patents its design, the entrant enters, but the incumbent does not sue for patent infringement.
5. The incumbent obtains a patent, the entrant enters, the incumbent sues for infringement, and the courts uphold the incumbent's claim.
6. The incumbent obtains a patent, the entrant enters, the incumbent sues for infringement, but the courts decide there is no infringement.

The payoffs (in millions) for each firm in each instance are shown in Table 9.1.

TABLE 9.1   Payoff for the two firms

Outcome	Incumbent	Entrant
(1)	$\pi_m(L)$	0
(2)	$\pi_I(L,D)$	$\pi_E(L,D)$
(3)	$\pi_m(L) - 0.5$	0
(4)	$\pi_I(L,D) - 0.5$	$\pi_E(L,D)$
(5)	$\pi_I(L,D) + \pi_E(L,D) - 1.5$	-1
(6)	$\pi_I(L,D) - 1.5$	$\pi_E(L,D) - 1$

9.2.3   Strategies

A strategy for the incumbent consists of (1) a patent/no patent decision, (2) a location for its design when it patents the design, (3) a location for its design when it does not patent the design, and (4) a decision rule for suing the entrant for patent infringement as a function of the incumbent's design location and the entrant's distance from the incumbent.

A strategy for the entrant consists of an entry/stay out decision and a location for its design as a function of the incumbent's location.

9.2.4   Equilibrium strategies

We will begin by determining the rational location of both firms should the incumbent decide *not* to patent its VCR design. Because the entrant moves last, the method of backwards induction requires us first to determine the entrant's optimal distance from the incumbent firm, $D_{np}^*(L)$, should the firm choose to enter the market. $D_{np}^*(L)$ is simply the value of D that maximizes $\pi_E(L,D)$, holding L fixed. This is the entrant's **no-patent reaction function**. This reaction function is graphed in Figure 9.4, with the distance between the two firms, D, measured along the vertical axis, and the location of the incumbent, L, measured along the horizontal axis.

The entrant will enter the market if and only if the maximum profit from entry, $\pi_E(L,D_{np}^*(L))$, is greater than zero. In this example, the demand is so high that the entrant will enter regardless of where the incumbent chooses to locate. As a result, an incumbent firm that does not patent its product will share the market with the entrant and earn profits of $\pi_I(L,D_{np}^*(L))$.

In Figure 9.5, both the incumbent's and the entrant's profits have been plotted versus the incumbent's location, *assuming an optimal location response by the entrant*. As can be seen, the optimal location of the incumbent is in the middle of the

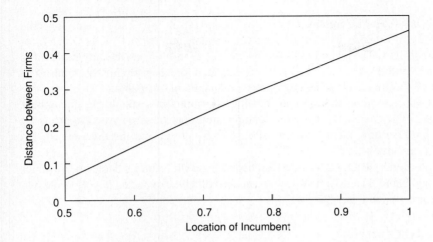

FIGURE 9.4 • No-patent reaction curve of the entrant. ¯he rational response of the entrant to any locational choice by the incumbent is captured by this reaction curve.

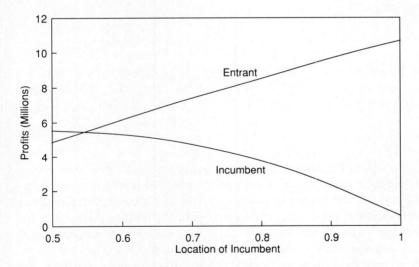

FIGURE 9.5 • The profits for the entrant rise as the incumbent locates farther from the midpoint of the interval, whereas the profits for the incumbent fall.

interval (L = 0.5). The entrant responds by locating itself 0.057 units away from the incumbent (D = 0.057). This means the entrant and incumbent sell VCRs with almost identical designs. The incumbent's profits are $5.533 million and the entrant's profits are $4.822 million. These profits, even when added together, are in stark contrast to the $14.531 million a classical monopolist could earn in this market.

Next we determine the optimal location for both firms should the incumbent patent its VCR design. This is more complicated than the case where there is no patent, because now there is the possibility of a lawsuit and the outcome of this lawsuit is uncertain.

We proceed by backwards induction beginning with Nature's choice of a winner in the legal battle. From Table 9.1, you can verify that the expected payoff to the two firms from a lawsuit are:

Incumbent's net profit:

$$p(D) \cdot (\pi_I(L,D) + \pi_E(L,D) - 1.5) + (1 - p(D)) \cdot (\pi_I(L,D) - 1.5) \qquad (9.19)$$
$$= \pi_I(L,D) + p(D) \cdot \pi_E(L,D) - 1.5.$$

Entrant's net profit:

$$p(D) \cdot (-1) + (1 - p(D)) \cdot (\pi_E(L,D) - 1) = (1 - p(D)) \cdot \pi_E(L,D) - 1. \qquad (9.20)$$

The incumbent will sue the entrant if and only if the expected payoff from the lawsuit is greater than the expected payoff if it does not sue, $\pi_I(L,D) - 0.5$.[5] It follows that the incumbent will sue if and only if

$$p(D) \cdot \pi_E(L,D) > 1. \qquad (9.21)$$

The left-hand side of equation (9.21) is the expected marginal benefit from sueing the entrant and the right-hand side is the expected marginal cost of the lawsuit. So equation (9.21) says the incumbent should sue if and only if the expected marginal benefit of a lawsuit exceeds its expected marginal cost. The function $p(D) \cdot \pi_E(L,D) - 1$ is plotted against D in Figure 9.6 *for the case where L equals 0.5*. As you can see, there exists a threshold distance such that the incumbent will sue if and only if the entrant locates itself closer than this. Such a threshold exists for every value of L and will be denoted as $D_{sue}(L)$.

---

[5]We are assuming that both firms are risk-neutral. You may recall that risk neutrality implies that expected profit maximization is equivalent to expected utility maximization.

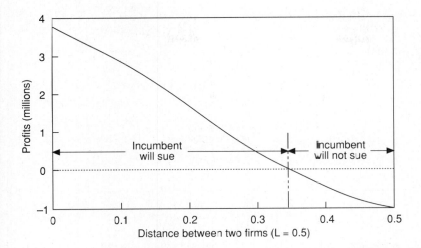

FIGURE 9.6 • Assuming the incumbent locates at 0.5, f the distance between the two firms is less than 0.344, then the incumbent's expected profits are higher by sueing than by not sueing. Otherwise, the incumbent will not sue.

The graph of $D_{sue}(L)$ is plotted in Figure 9.7. It is increasing in L, but at a decreasing rate. If the incumbent locates itself in the middle, it will sue any entrant that comes closer than 0.344, whereas if the incumbent locates itself all the way to the right at 1, then it sues any entrant that comes closer than 0.453.

If the incumbent locates itself at L and the entrant enters and locates itself at L – D, then the entrant's expected profit is given by

$$E\pi_E(L,D) = \begin{cases} (1 - p(D)) \cdot \pi_E(L,D) - 1 & \text{if } D < D_{sue}(L) \\ \\ \pi_E(L,D) & \text{otherwise} \end{cases}$$ (9.22)

The function $E\pi_E$ is graphed against D in Figure 9.8 for the case where L equals 0.5. To the left of the lawsuit threshold, $E\pi_E$ is increasing in D, and to the right it is decreasing in D, and the graph has a discontinuity at the threshold itself. The optimal location for the entrant is right at the threshold, where it is making positive profits. Given our assumed values, this holds for every value of L. So the optimal response of the entrant to the incumbent's patent is to enter the market anyway and locate itself as close to the incumbent as it can without inducing a suit for patent infringement. Because of the high cost of litigation, it is rational for the incumbent to concede some of its market share rather than fight entry, as long as the entrant does not get too close.

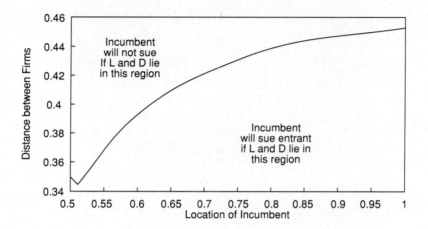

FIGURE 9.7 · For values of L and D to the northwest of the curve the incumbent will not sue; otherwise it will.

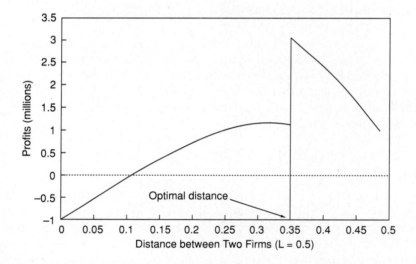

FIGURE 9.8 · The optimal distance for the entrant is 0.344 units from the incumbent, assuming the incumbent locates at 0.5. At this distance the entrant will avoid being sued.

The incumbent's net profits will equal $\pi_1(L, D_{sue}(L)) - 0.5$. The relationship between net profits and L is shown in Figure 9.9. Notice that the incumbent's profits decrease as L increases. Hence, the incumbent's optimal location is at 0.5. At this location the payoff to the incumbent is $8.509 million.

In Figure 9.10 we have redrawn the original game tree from Figure 9.2, but we have added the payoffs we have worked so hard to derive.

The rational behavior behind the payoffs shown in Figure 9.10 are as follows: If the entrant chooses not to enter (regardless of the patent decision), then the incumbent will locate at 0.5 and the price of the VCR it produces will be $112.50. If the entrant chooses to enter and the incumbent firm does not patent its product, then the incumbent firm will locate at 0.5, and the entrant will locate 0.047 units away, and the price of a VCR will be $113.59. If the entrant enters after the incumbent firm establishes a patent, then the incumbent firm will locate at 0.5 while the entrant will locate 0.344 units away. In this case the price of a VCR will be $116.66.

Now, we can completely solve the game by backwards induction. If the incumbent firm patents its design and the entrant enters, it will locate just far enough away from the incumbent to keep the incumbent from sueing. Therefore, the subgame that begins at the incumbent's decision to sue or not sue will result in no suit and payoffs of $8.509 million for the incumbent and $3.212 million for the entrant. As a result, the entrant enters regardless of whether or not the incumbent patents its design. The

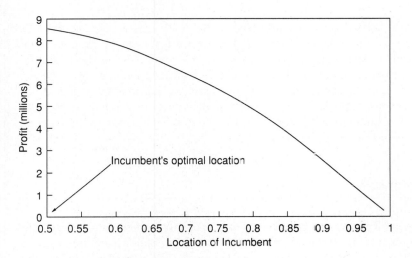

FIGURE 9.9 • After having decided to patent, the incumbent will maximize profits by locating at 0.5.

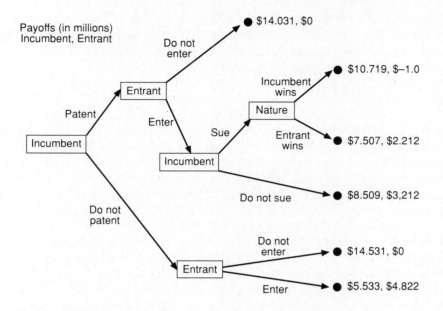

FIGURE 9.10 · The game tree for the patent game is redrawn with payoffs included. The payoffs are derived under the assumption that the players locate optimally.

incumbent can rationally expect a payoff of $8.509 if it patents its product and only $5.533 if it does not. So the incumbent will obtain a patent even though doing so is very costly and it can anticipate that the patent *will not prevent entry*. The incumbent obtains the patent in order to keep the entrant from locating too close to it, thereby increasing its market share. Against a forward-looking and rational opponent, the incumbent never actually has to carry out its implicit threat to sue. Indeed, against a forward-looking and rational opponent, any threat to sue will not be credible, *given the entrant's rational choice of location.*

9.3 · Other equilibria

The equilibrium we have exhibited here is not the only type of equilibrium possible. By altering some of the parameters of this model—the distribution of consumer tastes, the cost of the patent, the cost of fighting the lawsuit, and the cost of production—we could have generated an equilibrium in which the incumbent firm patents its product and *does* bring a suit against the entrant. There are also parameter values for which the equilibrium is one in which the patent successfully deters entry.

9.4 • Summary

We have presented a game with perfect information for which the number of strategies formed a continuum, and have shown how to analyze it using reaction functions and backwards induction. The game, which is an example of a **location game**, shows that it may be rational to patent products even though it can be foreseen that the patent will not deter entry and that the incumbent firm will not necessarily file an infringement suit against an entrant. The patent exists to keep the entrant from copying the incumbent's design too closely. In this way, the incumbent limits the impact of entry on its profits.

Patent protection does not necessarily result in a pure monopoly but can be consistent with some amount of product variety and design copying. It is an open question whether patent protection is the most efficient way to achieve the ultimate objective of efficient resource use in both innovation and production.

9.5 • Further reading

This application was taken largely from an article by Michael Waterson, "The Economics of Product Patents," *American Economic Review* 80 (1990), pp. 860–869.

For a traditional discussion of patents see F. Scherer, *Industrial Market Structure and Economic Performance*, 2nd. Ed. (Chicago: Rand McNally, 1980). Much of the discussion on patents has centered around how patents affect the speed of development. Some of this work has been built from a game-theoretic perspective. For a review of this literature see Kamien and Schwartz, *Market Structure and Innovation* (Cambridge: Cambridge University Press, 1982).

There is a growing literature of spatial economic models. Two of the best articles are Dixit and Stiglitz, "Monopolistic Competition and Optimal Product Diversity," *American Economic Review* 67 (1977), pp. 297–308, and Eaton and Wooders, "Sophisticated Entry in a Model of Spatial Competition," *Rand Journal of Economics* 16 (1985), pp. 282–297.

9.6 • Exercises

Exercise 9.1 Two new franchises in the Shoe Universe chain of shoe stores are choosing where to locate along the highway between two cities, Lorain and Oberlin. The highway between the two cities is a mile long, and there are no other customers or competing stores along this stretch of highway. Let t_i denote the distance of store i from Lorain and $1 - t_i$ is the distance from Oberlin. The two stores are independently owned and operated but are required by Shoe Universe to charge the same prices.

Customers, therefore, choose where to shop solely on the basis of location. The firms choose their location so as to maximize their sales. Total sales to residents in the two cities and each store's share of these sales are given in the table below:

Store sales

From	Total Sales	Shares	
		Store 1	Store 2
Oberlin	$110 \cdot (t_1 + t_2)$	$(1 + t_1 - t_2)/2$	$(1 - t_1 + t_2)/2$
Lorain	$150 \cdot (2 - t_1 - t_2)$	$(3 - t_1 + t_2)/6$	$(3 + t_1 - t_2)/6$

(a) What locations for the two stores maximize their combined total sales?

(b) Suppose the two stores are playing a Stackleberg location game in which store 1 is the leader and store 2 is the follower. Show that the locations you calculated in (a) are *not* Nash equilibria of this game. (*Hint*: Show that if store 1 locates at the location you calculated in (a), then store 2 will want to locate somewhere else.)

(c) Calculate the follower's reaction function.

(d) Find the subgame-perfect Nash equilibrium of this sequential location game.

Exercise 9.2 Denise and Pasha have agreed to "share" a job at the First National Bank of Tallahasee. One of them must work the morning shift, from 9:00 A.M. until "X"; the other must work the afternoon shift, from "X" until 5:00 p.m. Unfortunately, they cannot agree on X. Denise prefers to work in the mornings so that she can be at home with her children in the afternoon. She can be made indifferent between the two shifts only by setting X to 2:00 P.M. Pasha does not have children, and he is indifferent between the two shifts only if X equals 1:00 P.M. These preferences are common knowledge. Their boss suggests the following method for choosing X: One of them is chosen at random. We will call him or her "person 1." Person 1 chooses X. Then person 2 chooses the shift. If person 2 is exactly indifferent between the two shifts, person 1 chooses the shift. In the event both of them are indifferent, the shifts are assigned randomly.

(a) Suppose Pasha is chosen to go first. What is his optimal choice of X?

(b) Suppose Denise is chosen to go first. What is her optimal choice of X?

(c) Is there a first-mover advantage in this game?

Exercise 9.3 The patent game studied in Section 9.2 ignores the following "preemptive legal move" by the incumbent firm should it choose to patent its VCR design: It immediately pays its law firm $1 million to sue the entrant should it enter the market. The law firm gets to keep the $1 million *even if the entrant decides to stay out*.

(a) Redraw the game tree given in Figure 9.2 to incorporate this new possibility.

(b) Suppose the incumbent firm plays its "preemptive legal move" and the entrant enters. Show that the incumbent should sue the entrant if it enters regardless of where it locates itself.

(c) Suppose the incumbent firm patents its design and plays its "preemptive legal move." If the entrant enters the market, where should the entrant locate itself? (*Hint*: Locating far from the incumbent will no longer save it from a lawsuit.)

(d) Use your answer in (c) to determine the circumstances under which the entrant should enter the market if the incumbent patents the product and plays its "preemptive legal move."

(e) Use your answer in (d) to determine where the incumbent should locate itself assuming it plans to patent its design and play its "preemptive legal move."

(f) We already know that the incumbent should patent its design. Use your answers to (a) – (e) to determine whether or not the firm should play its "preemptive legal move."

• CHAPTER 10 •

Time-Consistent
Macroeconomic Policy

10.1 • Introduction

You have undoubtedly learned in your principles of economics class or your intermediate macroeconomics class that monetary policy determines the inflation rate in the
long run. By *monetary policy* we mean the growth rate of the money supply. But the
inflation rate can also affect the growth of output and employment. It is reasonable to
suppose that a country's central bank would like to establish a monetary growth rule
that leads, as far as possible, to price stability and output stability with full employment.

Workers and employers tend to write long-term labor contracts that are expressed
in nominal values rather than real values. This means that workers, when establishing
a nominal wage contract, must predict the behavior of the central bank in order to
predict the subsequent rate of inflation and the real value of their wages. In a model of
perfect information and rational behavior, one in which Nash equilibrium strategies
are chosen, workers should be able to predict the behavior of the central bank even
though the bank chooses a money growth rule after the workers agree on their
nominal wage.

In this chapter we will present a model in which the central bank chooses a
monetary growth rule that results in a level of inflation and employment that is less
desirable from everyone's perspective than an alternative monetary growth rule. The
inability of the central bank to credibly commit to a preferable monetary growth rule
is at the heart of the anomaly. The question then arises as to how the central bank
might possibly precommit to a rate of growth of the money supply that is preferred
by all.

10.2 • Inflation

One of the most commonly used economic terms in the popular press is *inflation*. Unfortunately, it is often used in conflicting ways, a practice that sometimes leads to confused analysis and ridiculous policy prescriptions. To economists, **inflation** consists of a *persistent* increase in the *general* price level. A one-time jump in the price level is not inflation, nor is an increase in the price of a single commodity, even one as important as oil. Whether an unexpected increase in the price of one commodity, such as oil, will be followed by inflation depends on how employers, households, and the government respond to the increase.

During the late 1960s, most of the 1970s, and the early 1980s, many industrialized countries experienced historically high rates of inflation. Figure 10.1 displays the so-called core inflation rate in the United States for the period 1955–1990. The **core inflation** rate is the average percentage increase in prices of all consumer commodities *other than* food and energy. The elimination of these two classes of goods reduces the distortion caused by the large one-time changes in world energy and food prices in 1973, 1974, 1979, and 1986.

Figure 10.1 has some striking features. The first is the steady acceleration in the inflation rate over this period. Starting in 1955 with a core inflation rate of under 2%, the inflation rate began accelerating in the late 1960s until by 1981 it was over 12%. The second feature of Figure 10.1 is the sudden deceleration in the inflation rate between 1981 and 1983 from 12% to less than 5%.

The accelerating inflation of the 1960s and 1970s led many economists during this period to hypothesize that modern economies possessed an "inflationary bias." It was

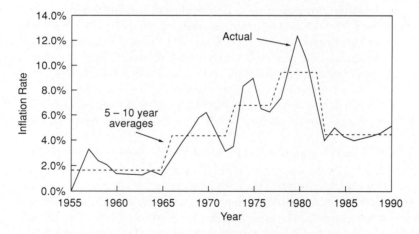

FIGURE 10.1 • The core inflation rate for the United States during the period 1955–1990. The core inflation rate excludes energy and food prices.

argued that central banks are under great political pressure to use inflationary monetary policies to stimulate economic growth and reduce unemployment. We will demonstrate that such a policy will stimulate economic activity only if the public does not anticipate the resulting inflation. But persistent underestimation of persistent inflation is inconsistent with rational behavior. Once the public catches on to what the central bank is doing, the policy will not be stimulative.

It has also been argued that oligopolistic firms can pass on to consumers, in the form of higher output prices, any wage increases demanded by their unionized workers. This, it is claimed, will result in a vicious cycle of wage and price escalation. This explanation, too, has a serious flaw. Although market power can explain why the wages of unionized workers in oligopolistic industries are *relatively* higher than the wages of other workers, market power can account for *persistent increases* in the wages of unionized workers only if there is a *persistent* increase in their market power. Over the last forty years the unionized sector of the American labor force has been *declining* in relative size and importance, not growing. And the largest oligopolistic industries, notably steel and automobiles, have experienced a steady increase in foreign competition.

10.3 • A simple macroeconomic model

Wages are negotiated in terms of money even though workers and employers are ultimately interested in the wage level measured in terms of purchasing power. This has two important implications. First, the money wage that clears the labor market will depend on the rate of inflation expected over the period covered by the contract. Second, if the inflation rate turns out to differ from what was expected when the money wage was negotiated, then workers will be forced by their contracts to supply either more or less labor than they would have supplied had the inflation rate been correctly foreseen.

The inflation rate workers and employers are trying to forecast is not completely random, like the weather, but is influenced by the rate of growth of the money supply, which is under the control of the central bank. So the wage and employment decisions of workers and employers depend on the bank's money growth decision. But the bank's performance, in turn, depends on the wage and employment decisions of the workers and employers. This interdependence means the three groups are embroiled in a game.

Under very general conditions, this game has a Nash equilibrium in which the central bank chooses a money supply growth rate that leads to a higher inflation rate than it would choose if it could move first and set its monetary policy before the workers set the money wage. Unfortunately for the central bank, in our sequential game a low-inflation monetary policy is not **time-consistent**: When the time comes for the central bank to choose the rate of inflation, it will no longer find it optimal to follow a low-inflation policy. A high-inflation policy will be optimal instead.

Macroeconomic modeling emphasizes the aggregate behavior of the economy and ignores the behavior of individual markets. The model we will present below involves the following aggregates: the real output level (y_t), the level of employment (l_t), the price level (p_t), the money supply (m_t), the money wage (w_t), the real wage (r_t), and the expected price level (p_t^e).

10.3.1   Identities

We will measure all price and quantity aggregates in natural logarithms. Variables measured in natural logarithms have some very useful properties. First, the difference in the natural logarithm of two numbers is approximately equal to their percentage difference. That is, $\ln(X) - \ln(Y) \approx (X - Y) \div Y$. Second, the logarithm of the ratio between two numbers equals the difference in their logarithms. That is, $\ln(X/Y) = \ln(X) - \ln(Y)$. Third, the logarithm of one equals zero. This last property of logarithms means the choice of a unit for the original variable X determines the zero point for the transformed variable $\ln(X)$.

In what follows we will make use of the following definitions:

$$\pi_t = p_t - p_{t-1} \qquad \text{rate of price inflation} \tag{10.1}$$

$$g_t = m_t - m_{t-1} \qquad \text{rate of growth of the money supply}$$

$$\pi_t^e = p_t^e - p_{t-1} \qquad \text{expected rate of price inflation;}$$

the following identity:

$$r_t = w_t - p_t, \qquad \text{the real wage (in logarithms);} \tag{10.2}$$

and the following normalizations:

$$m_1 = 0, \tag{10.3}$$

$$p_1 = 0.$$

From equations (10.1) and (10.3) it follows that

$$\pi_2 = p_2, \tag{10.4}$$

$$g_2 = m_2,$$

$$\pi_2^e = p_2^e.$$

Finally, we will assume that the production of output depends only on the quantity of labor input and that there are constant returns to scale in production: a 1% increase in labor leads to a 1% increase in output. By normalizing employment correctly, this implies

$$y_2 = l_2,$$
(10.5)

which will allow us to substitute output for labor freely in later equations.

10.3.2   Actions and order of play

To avoid inessential technical details, we will model the economy using a highly stylized sequential game played out over two time periods. During the first time period, the workers choose the money wage at which they will work in the second period, w_2. They make this decision without knowing what the price level will be in the second period. At the beginning of the second period, the central bank chooses the rate of growth for the money supply, g_2. Employers then choose the level of employment and the level of real output, y_2. The game tree is shown in Figure 10.2.

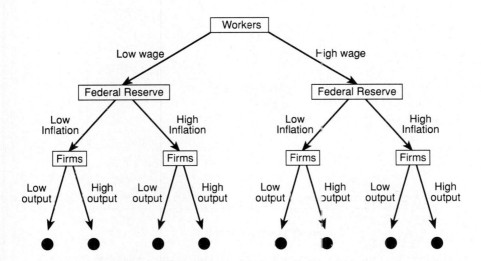

FIGURE 10.2 • The game tree for the macroeconomic policy game played between workers, employers, and the central bank.

The central bank controls the inflation rate indirectly through its control of the growth in the money supply. Although the causal linkage between money growth and inflation is not yet settled among economists, we will take an extreme monetarist position and assume all price inflation is caused by money growth. That is,

$$\pi_2 = I(g_2),$$ (10.6)

where $I(\bullet)$ is a strictly increasing function.

Evidence in favor of a causal relationship between money growth and inflation can be found in the cross-national survey data graphed in Figure 10.3. Because of the presumed causal link, we will hereafter assume the central bank chooses the inflation rate π_2 directly.

10.3.3 Strategies

A strategy for the workers consists of a money wage w_2. A strategy for the central bank consists of an inflation policy of the form $\pi_2(w_2)$. The fact that the rate of inflation can depend on the wage selected by the workers turns out to be an important reason for the central bank's poor performance in this game. A strategy for employers consists of a

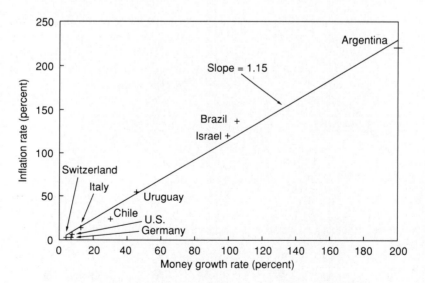

FIGURE 10.3 • Average rates of inflation during the period 1977-1987 plotted against the average rate of growth of the money supply over the same period.

real output rule of the form $y_2(w_2, \pi_2)$. The graph of y_2 versus π_2 for a fixed money wage w_2 is often referred to as an **aggregate supply curve**.

10.3.4 Payoffs

Workers are utility maximizers who value both real income and leisure. For a given real wage, increasing employment leads to increasing real worker income but decreasing leisure. Decreasing marginal utility from both income and leisure implies that for any real wage r there is a utility-maximizing level of employment, $l^S(r)$. This is just a labor supply curve (in logarithms). For simplicity, we will assume that

$$l^S(r) = \alpha \cdot r, \tag{10.7}$$

where α is simply a constant.

We assume the labor market is perfectly competitive and that both workers and employers are price takers. As a result, the workers collectively can be assumed to behave *as if* their goal is to minimize

$$(l_2 - \alpha \cdot r_2)^2. \tag{10.8}$$

Equation (10.8) says that, for a given real wage, the workers want to minimize the difference between the level of employment eventually chosen by employers (l_2) and the utility-maximizing level of employment ($\alpha \cdot r_2$). Equation (10.8) also implies that the marginal loss in utility from a deviation in actual and desired employment rises as the deviation rises.

If we substitute equations (10.2), (10.4) and (10.5) into equation (10.8), we get the worker payoff function

$$U_W(w_2, y_2, \pi_2) = -(y_2 - \alpha \cdot (w_2 - \pi_2))^2. \tag{10.9}$$

The central bank's goal is simple. It has target values for real output and inflation, denoted y^* and π^*, and wants to steer y_2 and π_2 toward its two targets using its one policy instrument: π_2. Assume the central bank's goal is to maximize the payoff function

$$U_{FR}(y_2, w_2, \pi_2) = -(y_2 - y^*)^2 - \mu \cdot (\pi_2 - \pi^*)^2, \tag{10.10}$$

where the constant μ in (10.10) measures the relative importance placed by the central bank on its output target versus its inflation target. The larger μ is, the more weight is given to price stabilization and the less weight is given to output stabilization. The fact that we have squared the two terms in equation (10.10) implies that as y_2 or π_2 get farther away from the target values, there are increasing marginal losses in utility. Big misses are proportionately more painful than small misses.

Employers are profit-maximizing price takers. At the profit-maximizing level of employment, $l^D(r)$, the marginal physical product of labor equals the real wage. For simplicity we will assume the demand for labor (in logarithms) can be written as:

$$l^D(r) = -\theta \cdot r_2 \tag{10.11}$$
$$= -\theta \cdot (w_2 - p_2)$$
$$= \theta \cdot (\pi_2 - w_2),$$

where we have made use of identity (10.4). When interpreting the parameter θ, it is important to recall that the variables are in logarithmic form. For example, if θ equals 1, then labor demand equals the inverse of the real wage rate.

Since the labor market is assumed to be perfectly competitive, we can assume that employers collectively act *as if* their goal were to minimize

$$(l_2 - \theta \cdot (\pi_2 - w_2))^2. \tag{10.12}$$

That is, for a given wage rate employers want to minimize the difference between the actual level of employment and their profit-maximizing level of employment. Once again, there is increasing marginal dissatisfaction as the difference increases. If we substitute equation (10.5) into equation (10.12), we get the employer payoff function

$$U_E(w_2, y_2, \pi_2) = -(y_2 - \theta \cdot (\pi_2 - w_2))^2. \tag{10.13}$$

10.3.5 Equilibrium

Since this is a sequential game, we can determine the perfect Nash equilibrium using backwards induction.

Employers move last. Given the money wage chosen by the workers (w_2) and the rate of inflation chosen by the central bank (π_2), the employer's profit-maximizing strategy is to maximize U_E. The only variable in their payoff function over which they have discretion is the output (or employment) level. The absolute best employers can do is to set y_2 so that U_E is equal to zero. This means that the economy's aggregate supply curve, y_2^E, is given by

$$y_2^E(w_2, \pi_2) = \theta \cdot (\pi_2 - w_2). \tag{10.14}$$

The central bank moves second. Being rational and well informed, it knows how employers will react to different inflation rates. namely through equation (10.14). Its optimal strategy is to maximize U_{FR} subject to (10.14). That is, it chooses π_2 so as to minimize

$$(\theta \cdot (\pi_2 - w_2) - y^*)^2 + \mu \cdot (\pi_2 - \pi^*)^2. \tag{10.15}$$

Differentiating equation (10.15) with respect to π_2, setting the resulting expression equal to zero, and solving for π_2 yields the optimal inflation policy

$$\pi_2^E(w_2) = (\mu \cdot \pi^* + \theta^2 \cdot w_2 + \theta \cdot y^*) \div (\mu + \theta^2). \tag{10.16}$$

The workers move first. The optimal wage depends on the worker's forecasts about the future output and inflation rate. The inflation forecasts are called **inflationary expectations** in the macroeconomic literature and will be denoted π_2^e. Given π_2^e, the worker's maximize U_W subject to equation (10.14). That is, they choose w_2 so as to minimize

$$U_W(w_2, y_2^E(w_2, \pi_2^e), \pi_2^e) \tag{10.17}$$

$$= (y_2^E(w_2, \pi_2^e) - \alpha \cdot (w_2 - \pi_2^e))^2$$
$$= (\theta \cdot (\pi_2^e - w_2) + \alpha \cdot (\pi_2^e - w_2))^2$$
$$= (\theta + \alpha)^2 \cdot (\pi_2^e - w_2)^2.$$

The wage that minimizes (10.17) is

$$w_2^E = \pi_2^e. \tag{10.18}$$

What inflation forecast should workers use? Rationality dictates that workers form their expectations by looking ahead and foreseeing the inflation rate that will be generated by the central bank's optimal inflation policy. This means

$$\pi_2^e = \pi_2^E(w_2). \tag{10.19}$$

If the workers behave in this way, they are said to have **rational expectations.**
    Equations (10.16), (10.18) and (10.19) yield the recursive relation

$$w_2^E = (\mu \cdot \pi^* + \theta^2 \cdot w_2^E + \theta \cdot y^*) \div (\mu + \theta^2) \tag{10.20}$$

which simplifies to

$$w_2^E = \pi^* + (\theta \div \mu) \cdot y^*. \tag{10.21}$$

If the workers select this money wage, then the central bank will choose an inflation rate that results in a logarithmic real wage, r_2^E, of zero. Equations (10.7), (10.11), and (10.14) now imply

$$y_2^E(w_2^E) = l^D(r_2^E) = l^S(r_2^E) = 0. \tag{10.22}$$

The resulting equilibrium is one of full employment, regardless of the central bank's output target, y^*. Because the workers' inflationary expectations turn out to be correct, this equilibrium is also said to be characterized by **perfect foresight**. Perfect foresight is a consequence of our assumption that there is no uncertainty. We will show next that this last characteristic can be easily dispensed with and replaced with imperfect but **unbiased foresight**.

Equations (10.18), (10.21), and (10.22) imply that the central bank can reach its inflation and output targets if and only if $y^* = 0$. But there are many reasons that the central bank might consider the full-employment level of output to be socially suboptimal: distortions in labor supply caused by income taxes and unemployment compensation, distortions in labor demand caused by corporate income taxes, and distortions in the labor market caused by the exercise of market power by monopolistic unions or monopsonistic employers. Whenever y^* is strictly positive, the equilibrium level of inflation will be above the target level.

10.3.6   A numerical example

Suppose the central bank sets a target inflation rate of 2% and a target output level 2% above the full employment level of output, and that both goals have equal weight. This means $\pi^* = 0.02$, $y^* = 0.02$, and $\mu = 1$. Suppose also that θ equals 1.

Suppose the central bank were to announce both targets to the national media. If the workers believe the bank's announcement, then they will set the logarithm of the money wage, w_2, to 0.02. If the central bank keeps its promise and holds the inflation rate to 2%, employers will then produce the full employment level of output.

This outcome is represented by the point labeled A in Figure 10.4. Inflation is measured on the vertical axis and output is measured (in logarithms) on the horizontal axis. The central bank's inflation and output targets correspond to the point labeled B. The upward-sloping line through A is the aggregate supply curve derived for employers given the money wage (in logarithms) of 0.02.

The problem with this outcome is that although it is rational for the central bank to promise to keep inflation to 2%, once the workers set the nominal wage to 0.02, it is not rational for the bank to keep its promise. The central bank's promise is **time-**

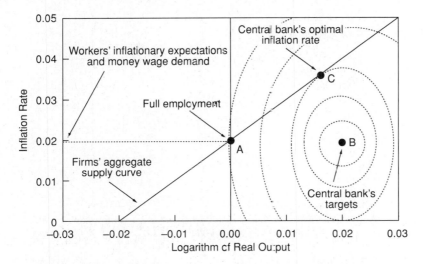

FIGURE 10.4 · If workers naively believe the central bank's promise to keep inflation to 2%, then the bank will renege on its promise and choose a higher inflation in order to boost output above the full-employment level.

inconsistent. Instead, the bank will choose the inflation rate associated with the point on the aggregate supply curve labeled C. As a result, the bank will break its promise and allow the inflation rate to rise about 4%. This means that the real wage in period 2 will be lower than either workers or employers thought it would be when they initially set the money wage. Employers will respond to the lower real wage by producing an output level above the "full-employment" rate of output.

An output level above "full employment" sounds contradictory until we make the distinction between the demand and supply of labor before the inflation rate next year is known (**ex ante** demand and supply) and the demand and supply of labor after the inflation rate is known (**ex post** demand and supply). At the "full-employment" level of employment and equilibrium wage, the workers are maximizing their utility and employers are maximizing their profits based on their *ex ante* forecasts about the price level. Once the money wage is fixed, though, the employer is free to alter the level of employment, and the workers have to acquiesce and provide this level of employment. Those are the contractual terms. When output is above the full-employment level, the workers are providing *more* labor at a lower real wage than they initially expected. Conversely, when output is below the full-employment level of output, workers are providing *less* labor at a higher real wage than they initially expected. In both instances, the workers regret the contract they voluntarily entered into with employers in period 1.

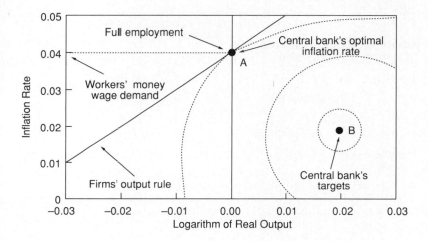

FIGURE 10.5 · At a Nash equilibrium for the macroeconomic policy game, output is at the full-employment level and workers' forecasts about the rate of inflation turn out to be correct.

Because the central bank's promise that inflation will be held to 2% is not binding and it is in the Fed's interests to stimulate a higher inflation rate than this, the workers should not believe the bank's announcements. The only promises they should believe are those that the bank will actually carry out. One credible inflation promise the bank could make is represented by the point labeled A in Figure 10.5. If the central bank were to promise to set an inflation rate of 4% and the workers were to believe this, then the nominal wage would be set at 0.04. As a result, the point A, which corresponds to full employment, would end up being the bank's preferred point on the resulting aggregate supply curve. Consequently, the bank would find it in its best interest to carry through on its promise and set the inflation rate at 4%.

The bank's promise to hold inflation to 4% is, therefore, *credible*. Unfortunately for the bank, this is the *only* credible promise the bank can make, so it must resign itself to missing *both* its inflation target and its output target by 2%. This outcome is the only one that is consistent with rational behavior on the part of all the players.

10.4 · The effect of supply and demand shocks[1]

The game we have modeled so far is one of perfect information and certainty. In reality, however, the economy is buffeted by many random shocks: changes in labor produc-

---

[1]The reader need not follow the mathematics in this section in order to understand the remaining sections. The essence of the section is its conclusions.

tivity, the demand for money, investment, exports and imports, savings rates, and so on. We can introduce shocks like these into our simple macroeconomic model simply by adding some randomness to the relationship between money growth and inflation. That is, we will replace equation (10.6) by

$$\pi_2 = I(g_2) + e_2, \tag{10.6'}$$

where e_2 is a random variable with a mean of zero and a positive variance. One interpretation of e_2 is that it represents random fluctuations in the demand for money. If money demand increases, then a given increase in the money supply will result in less inflation because some of the new money will be hoarded rather than spent; conversely, if there is a decrease in money demand, then any given increase in the money supply will result in more inflation. The quantity $I(g_2)$ will hereafter be called the central bank's inflation policy and will be denoted π_2^D. This is the bank's choice variable, not the inflation rate actually observed, π_2.

In order to complete the specification of our new game, we need to state when the workers, employers, and central bank officials learn of the value of e_2, as well as their attitudes toward risk. We will suppose that actual money demand is not revealed to any of the three players until after they have made their moves. In other words, we will consider a model with perfect information and *uncertainty* about the payoffs.

Suppose the utility functions U_W, U_{FR}, and U_E specified earlier are also the players' von Neumann-Morgenstern utility (VNMU) functions. Then it can be shown that, on average, the outcome of the new game is identical to that of our original game with certainty. In our derivation of the equilibrium strategies we will make use of the following result from advanced calculus:

Theorem 10.1   (maximization with expected values) Let $f(x,e)$ be differentiable function of the two arguments x and e, and let e be a random variable such that $E(f(x,e)) < M$ for some constant M and all values of x. Then the value of x that maximizes $E(f(x,e))$, denoted x^*, must satisfy the equation $E(f_x(x^*,e)) = 0$, where f_x denotes the partial derivative of f with respect to x.

We begin with employers, who choose y_2 so as to maximize

$$E(U_E(w_2, y_2, \pi_2^D)) = - E(y_2 - \theta \cdot (\pi_2^D + e_2 - w_2))^2. \tag{10.23}$$

Theorem 10.1 implies that the optimal output rule for an employer satisfies

$$E(y_2^E - \theta \cdot (\pi_2^D + e_2 - w_2)) = 0 \tag{10.24}$$

or

$$y_2^E = E(\theta \cdot (\pi_2^D + e_2 - w_2)) \tag{10.25}$$
$$= \theta \cdot E(\pi_2^D + e_2 - w_2)$$
$$= \theta \cdot (\pi_2^D - w_2 + E(e_2))$$
$$= \theta \cdot (\pi_2^D - w_2),$$

where the last equality follows from our assumption that e_2 has a mean of zero. Notice that the aggregate supply rule (10.25) is the same as that in equation (10.14), which is the aggregate supply curve when employers have no uncertainty about the rate of inflation.

The central bank now chooses its inflation policy π_2^D so as to maximize

$$E(U_{FR}(y_2, w_2, \pi_2^D)) = - E((y_2 - y^*)^2 + \mu \cdot (\pi_2^D + e_2 - \pi^*)^2 \tag{10.26}$$

subject to equation (10.25). That is, it maximizes

$$E(U_{FR}(y_2, w_2, \pi_2^D)) = - E[(\theta \cdot (\pi_2^D - w_2) - y^*)^2 + \mu \cdot (\pi_{2+}^D e_2 - \pi^*)^2]. \tag{10.27}$$

Theorem 10.1 implies that optimal inflation policy, π_2^{DE}, satisfies the equation

$$E(\theta^2 \cdot (\pi_2^{DE} - w_2) - \theta \cdot y^* + \mu \cdot (\pi_2^{DE} + e_2 - \pi^*)) = 0 \tag{10.28}$$

or, using the rules of probability theory,

$$\theta \cdot (\pi_2^{DE} - w_2) - y^* + \mu \cdot (\pi_2^{DE} - \pi^*) = 0, \tag{10.29}$$

which implies

$$\pi_2^{DE}(w_2) = (\mu \cdot \pi^* + \theta^2 \cdot w_2 + \theta \cdot y^*) \div (\mu + \theta^2). \tag{10.30}$$

Notice that right-hand side of equation (10.30) is identical to the right-hand side of equation (10.16), which is the central bank's optimal inflation policy when there are no demand or supply shocks.

Finally, the worker's optimal wage maximizes

$$E(U_W(w_2, y_2, \pi_2^D)) = - E(y_2 - \alpha \cdot (w_2 - \pi_2^D))^2 \tag{10.31}$$

subject to (10.30) and (10.25). That is, the workers maximize

$$- E((\theta + \alpha) \cdot (w_2 - \pi_2^{DE}(w_2)))^2. \tag{10.32}$$

But the expression inside the expectation signs in (10.32) does not contain the random variable e_2. So the workers maximize (10.32) simply by choosing the wage w_2^E that satisfies

$$w_2^E = \pi_2^{DE}(w_2^E). \qquad (10.33)$$

Substituting (10.30) and solving for w_2^E, we obtain

$$w_2^E = \pi^* + (\theta \div \mu) \cdot y^*, \qquad (10.34)$$

which is the same expression as (10.21), the optimal wage when there were no shocks. Since e_2 has a mean of zero, (10.33) can be rewritten as

$$\begin{aligned} w_2^E &= \pi_2^{DE}(w_2^E) + E(e_2) \\ &= E(\pi_2^{DE}(w_2^E) + e_2) \\ &= E(\pi_2^E), \end{aligned} \qquad (10.35)$$

so that, *on average,* the equilibrium nominal wage equals the equilibrium rate of inflation. As a result, *on average*, the equilibrium real wage will equal zero and output will equal the full employment level of output.

10.5 • One solution to the central bank's problem: Precommitment

The inflationary outcome of the simple policy game discussed above results in part from the inability of the central bank to fix its money growth policy *before* the workers and employers settle on the money wage. The bank could reach its inflation target (though not its output target) if the workers could be sure that such a choice were in the bank's own best interests. This means that the game's payoffs would have to be altered so that choosing the low-inflation policy would be an equilibrium strategy of the game.

For example, suppose the head of the central bank offered to resign if the inflation rate exceeded the announced target value. This would make it in the bank's interest not to exceed this target. However, because the bank does not have perfect control over the rate of inflation, the head of the bank might find such a promise very risky. As an empirical matter, no central bankers are known to have made such a promise either in the United States or elsewhere. This suggests that the degree of control over the inflation rate may simply be too low.

As a result, penalties probably need to be imposed on the central bank from the outside. Once again, governments seem to be unwilling to impose such penalties.

One reason may be that, in many countries (the United States being an important exception), the head of the central bank is a member of the government in power (and usually a member of the executive cabinet). In such cases, the central bank's "preferences" over output and inflation are simply those of the government of which it is a part. This means no outside authority exists to discipline the bank.

10.6 • Summary

The establishment of central banks by most governments during the last century has been for the express purpose of achieving rates of inflation and employment that are set by the politicians in power rather than by the marketplace. This application calls into question the ability of the central bank to achieve such goals. Workers and employers who anticipate the behavior of the central bank may undermine its best laid plans. Under a reasonable set of conditions, the central bank may be led to a monetary growth policy that results in its missing *both* its inflation and its output targets. This is not because central bankers are stupid or foolish but because the banks' actions are constrained by their strategic interaction with their workers and employers. The strategic behavior of workers and employers simply makes the bank's targets unobtainable. This may explain why inflation persists in many countries despite cries from all sides for a lower rate.

10.7 • Further reading

The macropolicy model in this application is based on a paper by Matthew Canzoneri, "Monetary Policy Games and the Role of Private Information," *American Economic Review* 75 (1985), pp. 1056-1070. The first part of this paper is very readable, but the second half is quite difficult. A more general model (and more difficult paper) is that of Robert Barro and David Gordon, "A Positive Theory of Monetary Policy in a Natural Rate Model," *Journal of Political Economy* 91 (1983), pp. 589-601. The more empirically minded are encouraged to read William Poole's analysis of the 1970–1980 period from a game-theoretic perspective, "Monetary Policy Lessons of Recent Inflation and Disinflation," *Journal of Economic Perspectives* 2 (1988), pp. 90–98.

One of the first discussions of the problem of "time consistency" in dynamic games was by Finn Kydland and Edward Prescott, "Rules Rather Than Discretion: The Inconsistency of Optimal Plans," *Journal of Political Economy* 85 (1977), pp. 473–480. Although this paper looks at the problem abstractly, it is not that mathematically advanced.

10.8 · Exercises

Exercise 10.1   Suppose the central bank sets a target inflation rate of 0% and a target output level 1% above the full employment level of output, and suppose the inflation target is twice as important as the output target. Find the subgame-perfect Nash equilibrium.

Exercise 10.2   Consider a two-player sequential-move game with perfect information and certainty. One player is the government, which has a utility function given by $y - (m - 1)^2$, where y is the logarithm of output and m is the logarithm of the money supply. The government has discretion over m. The other player is a "price setter," whom we will refer to as the "agent," with a utility function given by $p - p^2/2m$, where p is the logarithm of price and is set by the agent. Suppose that y equals $m - p$ as long as m - p is nonnegative, and equals 0 otherwise. Assume the government makes the first move.

  (a) Find the reaction function for the agent.
  (b) Find the subgame-perfect equilibrium strategeies.
  (c) Find the equilibrium value of y.

Exercise 10.3   Suppose all the conditions of Exercse 10.2 hold except that the agent makes the first move.

  (a) Find the reaction function for the government.
  (b) Is an announcement that m will equal 1 credible? Explain!
  (c) Find the subgame-perfect equilibrium strategies.
  (d) Find the equilibrium value of y.

• CHAPTER 11 •

Nash Equilibrium II

11.1 • Introduction

There are many situations in which players in a game must make decisions without perfect information of the decisions made by the other players. For example, Ford Motor Company must decide how much money to spend on research and development (R & D) during the coming year without complete knowledge of how much General Motors will spend. Similarly, in an election using secret ballots, when you vote you cannot know for certain how other people will vote.

In the previous chapter you were introduced to strategic decisions in situations where the players moved in sequence and knew all the previous moves that had been made.[1] This meant players knew exactly where they were on the game tree. In this chapter you will be introduced to games in which knowledge of how a player either has behaved in the past or will behave in the future is simply unknown to some of the players. These are called games of **imperfect information**. While there are many ways in which information can be obscured, in this chapter we will restrict ourselves to situations in which players make their decisions "simultaneously."

11.2 • Chronological time and game time

When we talk about simultaneous moves by players in a game, we have in mind something like the following. Two kids are out on a sidewalk playing "rocks, paper,

---

[1]Recall that in Chapter 3 you considered decision problems in which the decision maker moved after Nature, yet did not observe Nature's moves.

scissors." As you probably know, the players in this game recite the words "rocks, paper, scissors," in unison. When they come to the word "scissors," each player simultaneously makes a hand signal indicating she has chosen a rock (a fist), paper (an open hand), or scissors (index and middle fingers extended). The winner of the game depends on the signals chosen by the two players. A rock "smashes" scissors, scissors "cuts" paper, and paper "covers" rock. Therefore, a player who chooses the hand signal for a rock will beat a player who chooses the hand signal for scissors but lose to a player who chooses the hand signal for paper, and so on. The important aspect of this game is that neither player learns what the other has chosen until after both of them have moved. Indeed, there exists a strong incentive to wait just a fraction of a second in order to learn the sign chosen by the other player. Frequently, such cheating causes the game (not to mention the friendship) to disintegrate, but we will not get into this here.

Now consider a slightly different version of this game. Suppose a third child is present and plays the role of a referee. Instead of the childern reciting the three words in unison and then simultaneously flashing a hand signal, the referee takes one child out of sight of the other and asks her to reveal a hand signal. The referee then goes back to the second child and, without revealing what hand signal the first child selected, asks the second child to reveal a hand signal. After this, the referee announces the winner. Although the hand signals were chosen in *chronological* sequence, the difference between the two versions of the game is totally inconsequential. In both versions, the players have exactly the same information at the time they make their decision. There is no reason to think either child will play differently when there is a referee than when there isn't one (although this ignores the possibility of cheating). In this chapter, *chronological* time is important only insofar as it affects the time when information becomes available to the players of the game.[2]

Interesting economic games are seldom characterized by perfect chronological simultaneity, and we will not waste any time trying to cook up examples. But there are many games in which the players move "simultaneously" in our extended sense of the term.

For example, consider a small town with only two car dealerships, Trusty Rusty and Honest Ava. The town also has a weekly newspaper in which both dealers advertise the prices of their cars. Neither dealer knows what prices the other dealer will advertise in the newspaper, but each knows that the advertised price of cars at one dealership will affect the number of car buyers at the other. We will suppose it always makes sense to advertise. The decision problem faced by each dealer is,

[2]Chronological time does become important in dynamic games where future payoffs must be "discounted." This will be examined in more detail in Part Five.

therefore, very simple: Select the price to advertise in the newspaper. As a result, the dealers find themselves playing a "pricing game."

Both owners must place their newspaper ads *before* they know the prices the other owner will advertise that week. The newspaper's weekly deadline for ads is noon on Monday. Any ad received after the deadline will not appear in that week's edition. There is no reason for both dealers to make their pricing decisions at exactly the same time. One dealer might turn in her ad to the newspaper on Thursday, while the other dealer might turn in his ad on Friday. As long as the newspaper employees are discreet and do not talk about submitted ads, both dealers have made simultaneous moves from a game-theoretic perspective.

11.3 · Modeling simultaneous-move games

Even though the game between the two car dealerships is not a sequential game, we can depict it by the game tree in Figure 11.1. Although we will not make much use of game trees in this chapter, a reason for displaying the game tree is to prepare for the analysis of games that consist of both simultaneous and sequential moves.

Figure 11.1 shows a game tree that depicts the pricing game between Trusty Rusty and Honest Ava. The initial node, labeled A, shows Honest Ava moving first and Trusty Rusty moving second. This seems to contradict our assumption that the moves are made simultaneously. The reason there is no inconsistency is that Trusty Rusty's two decision nodes are in the same **information set**. This means Trusty Rusty does not know whether he is at node B or node C when he is called upon to make his pricing decision. Following the convention we established for game trees in Chapter 4, we show two or more decision nodes in a game tree in the same information set by

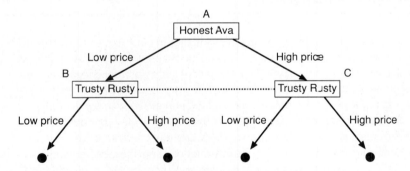

FIGURE 11.1 Game tree for the pricing game between Trusty Rusty and Honest Ava.

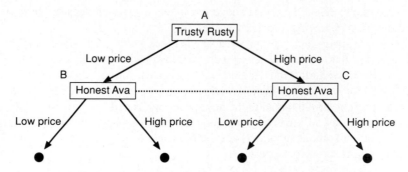

FIGURE 11.2 An equivalent game tree for the pricing game showing Trusty Rusty moving first.

connecting them with a dotted line. Although at first glance the tree diagram suggests that Honest Ava moves before Trusty Rusty in chronological time, the fact that nodes C and B are in the same information set means that no information about Honest Ava's "earlier" move reaches Trusty Rusty before he must decide what price to advertise. Therefore, the "second" move is made simultaneously with the first move in "game time."

The game tree can also be described by Figure 11.2. Now, Trusty Rusty is shown as moving first chronologically, but his move is not revealed to Honest Ava until after she moves; that is, Honest Ava's information set consists of the two nodes B and C. Again, the two moves are simultaneous in game time.

11.4 • Dominant and dominated strategies

When you were first introduced to optimal decision making in Chapter 1, you had to answer questions of the form: "Given a set of exogenous constraints, which sequence of actions will lead to the highest payoff?" In Chapters 4 and 5, interdependence among decisionmakers was introduced. To underscore this interdependence, the term *decision-maker* was replaced by the term *player,* and the phrase *sequence of actions* was replaced by the term *strategy.* In order to predict the strategies players would choose, we asked a different question: "Given a set of exogenous constraints, *and* a set of players in a game who are rational, *and* all the information about these decisionmakers' objectives, payoffs, and previous actions, which strategy is the best for each of them?"

Probably the most remarkable of the results in Chapter 5 was our demonstration that a player in a game with perfect information, even one with a large number of decision nodes, could use backwards induction to predict perfectly how everyone would rationally behave at every decision node. That is, the future, though not yet acted out, could be predicted with certainty. Unfortunately, backwards induction cannot be employed in simultaneous-move games to predict how the other players will move. Nevertheless, under certain conditions, good predictions can still be made. We will use the pricing game described previously to show how this can be done.

To simplify things, we will assume each of the two car dealers has only two choices: Either advertise a high price ("high") or advertise a low price ("low").[3] The payoffs to Honest Ava are shown in Table 11.1.

Although the numerical values listed in the table are hypothetical, their relative magnitudes make economic sense.[4] Whatever the price advertised by Honest Ava, her sales and profits will be higher, the higher the price advertised by Trusty Rusty. Conversely, whatever the price advertised by Trusty Rusty, Honest Ava's sales and profits will be lower, the higher the price she advertises. The best outcome for Honest Ava occurs when she advertises a low price and Trusty Rusty advertises a high price, and she, therefore, steals most of his potential customers. The worst outcome for Honest Ava occurs when she advertises a high price and Trusty Rusty advertises a low price, and he steals most of her potential customers. If both advertise a high price, then neither is "stealing" customers from the other and the profit margin will be relatively high on each car sold. On the other hand, if both advertise a low price, they also are not "stealing" customers from each other, but the profit margin is relatively low on each car sold.

Because the outcome of her pricing decision is not entirely in her own hands but depends on what Trusty Rusty chooses to do, and she has no way to know with certainty what Trusty Rusty will do, it makes sense to begin by asking some relatively

TABLE 11.1 Payoffs to Honest Ava in the pricing game

		Trusty Rusty's Strategy	
		Low	High
Honest Ava's Strategy	Low	$100	$200
	High	$50	$150

Low = Advertise a low price.
High = Advertise a high price.

---

[3]Clearly this is unrealistic in that there are a very large number of prices that might be chosen.
[4]As you will see, other possible relative magnitudes also make economic sense.

simple questions. If Honest Ava believes Trusty Rusty will advertise a low price, then what is her best strategy? The answer from Table 11.1 is clear: Advertise a low price. But because we cannot be certain Trusty Rusty will advertise a low price, we must also ask a second question. What is her best strategy if she believes Trusty Rusty will advertise a high price? The answer is again clear: Advertise a low price. Putting these two answers together gives us an interesting result. No matter *what* Honest Ava believes Trusty Rusty will do, she does strictly better if she advertises a low price than if she advertises a high price. We say that the strategy "advertise a high price" is **dominated** by the strategy "advertise a low price."

Only one of Honest Ava's strategies is left when we eliminate the dominated strategy: Advertise a low price. We will call such a strategy a **dominant strategy.** Therefore, even without knowing what Trusty Rusty will do, in this simple game we can predict what Honest Ava will do: She will advertise a low price.

Let us now make our simple example just a little more complex. Suppose the two dealers can choose among three possible prices: a high price, a low price, and a medium price. The payoff matrix for this new game is shown in Table 11.2. Once again, Honest Ava's payoffs are higher the higher the price advertised by her rival. But her payoff no longer decreases monotonically as she increases her advertised price. The reason is that although Honest Ava's sales will be lower the higher her price, her profit per car will be higher. Because her total profit is the product of her sales and her profit per car, her total profit may go up or down.

If Trusty Rusty advertises a low price, then Honest Ava's best strategy is to advertise a high price. But if Trusty Rusty advertises a medium or high price, then Honest Ava's best strategy is to advertise a medium price. Honest Ava has no dominant strategy given that under some circumstances it is best to advertise a medium price and under others it is best to advertise a high price. But she should never

TABLE 11.2   Payoffs to Honest Ava in the modified pricing game

		Trusty Rusty's Strategy		
		Low	Medium	High
Honest	Low	$90	$120	$150
Ava's	Medium	$100	$150	$200
Strategy	High	$110	$140	$170

Low = Advertise a low price.
Medium = Advertised a medium price.
High = Advertised a high price.

advertise a low price because that strategy is dominated. Although we cannot (yet) predict in this instance what strategy Honest Ava will choose, we can predict which strategy she will *not* choose; she will *not* advertise a low price.

DEFINITION: A **dominant strategy** for a player is one that is always strictly better than *every other* strategy for that player regardless of the strategies chosen by the other players. A **dominated strategy** for a player is one that is always strictly worse than *some other* strategy for that player regardless of the strategies chosen by the other players.

Very careful readers will recognize that these definitions use the terms strictly better than and strictly worse than rather than equal to or better than and equal to or worse than. The difference between the phrases involves ties. It may be the case that against some particular strategy of an opponent, two different strategies generate the same payoff to a player. To take account of this possibility, we introduce two new definitions.

DEFINITION: A **weakly dominant strategy** for a player is one that is always equal to or better than *every other* alternative strategy for that player regardless of the strategies chosen by the other players. A **weakly dominated strategy** for a player is one that is always equal to or worse than *some other* strategy for that player regardless of the strategies chosen by the other players.

Later on, you will see examples where the difference between dominant and weakly dominant strategies is important.

11.5 • Dominant strategy equilibrium

Let us return to our original simple game in which each car dealer has only two strategies. Honest Ava's payoffs are those in Table 11.1 and Trusty Rusty's payoffs are those in Table 11.3. The payoffs to Trusty Rusty are symmetrical to those assumed earlier for Honest Ava.

To get an indication of how Trusty Rusty will behave, we ask the same questions we asked of Honest Ava:

TABLE 11.3   Payoffs to Trusty Rusty in the car pricing game

		Trusty Rusty's Strategy	
		Low	High
Honest Ava's Strategy	Low	$100	$50
	High	$200	$150

> If Trusty Rusty believes Honest Ava will advertise a high price, then what is his best strategy?

and

> If Trusty Rusty believes Honest Ava will advertise a low price, then what is his best strategy?

The answer to both questions is the same: Advertise a low price. So advertising a low price is a dominant strategy for Trusty Rusty.

Table 11.4, which combines Tables 11.1 and 11.3, is called a **payoff matrix**. It displays the payoffs to each player for every possible combination of strategies the players could choose. For example, if Trusty Rusty advertises a low price (corresponding to the left column) and Honest Ava advertises a high price (corresponding to the bottom row), then the table entry ($50, $200) tells us that Honest Ava's payoff will be $50 and Trusty Rusty's payoff will be $200.

In this game, each player has an unambiguous "best strategy" regardless of what he or she believes the other player will do. It is generally accepted that when each player in a game has a dominant strategy, then those strategies are the ones chosen.

TABLE 11.4   Payoff matrix for the car-pricing game

		Trusty Rusty's Strategy	
		Low	High
Honest Ava's Strategy	Low	($100, $100)	($200, $50)
	High	($50, $200)	($150, $150)
		Payoffs: (Honest Ava, Trusty Rusty)	

This collection of dominant strategies, when they exist, is called a **dominant strategy equilibrium** for the game.

Recall from Chapter 5 that a pair of strategies with the property that each is best given the strategy chosen by the other player constitutes a Nash equilibrium for the game. Whenever a game possesses a dominant strategy equilibrium, the collection of dominant strategies constitutes the *only* Nash equilibrium for the game. Take a moment to convince yourself that the dominant strategy equilibrium (low, low) is the only Nash equilibrium for the pricing game. We leave a rigorous proof of this as an exercise.

The equilibrium in this game is somewhat surprising. If *both* players were to advertise a high price instead of a low price, they would *both* be better off. Another way of saying this is that the outcome of the combination of strategies (high, high) is **Pareto superior** to the outcome of the combination of strategies (low, low). The term *Pareto superior* simply means *both* parties are better off at the first outcome than at the second.[5] The problem with the combination of strategies (high, high) is that these strategies are "strategically unstable": Each dealer has an incentive to switch over to advertising a low price if he or she thinks the opponent will advertise a high price.

If somehow both parties could agree to advertise a high price and absolutely commit to that action, then it is conceivable the strategy combination (high, high) might be chosen. Economists have considered strategic situations in which those sorts of binding agreements and commitments can take place. Such games are the province of **cooperative game theory.** As we already stated in Chapter 5, in this book we will deal only with noncooperative games and assume these sorts of agreements and commitments cannot be enforced.

The game just described is an example of a **prisoner's dilemma,** and it has far-reaching applications in all the social sciences, not just economics. You will see economic variations of the prisoner's dilemma game in later applications. One important noneconomic application of the prisoner's dilemma is as a model of an arms race between two belligerent nations.

These two countries—call them A and B—begin the game with military parity. That is, neither can initiate a successful preemptive attack on the other. Should it ever become common knowledge that one of them had obtained such decisive military superiority over the other, then the inferior country would be forced immediately to

---

[5]Pareto superiority is related to the notion of *Pareto optimality* but is not quite the same. A resource allocation is Pareto optimal if and only if it is Pareto superior to every other feasible resource allocation. Pareto optimality is a property of a particular resource allocation, whereas Pareto superiority is a ranking among pairs of resource allocations. If an outcome is Pareto optimal, then it is impossible to rearrange resources without harming someone. The perspective taken is global, encompassing *all* affected parties and *all* possible resource allocations.

TABLE 11.5   Payoff matrix for an arms race between two countries

		Country B's Military Expenditure	
		Spend 0	Spend X
Country A's	Spend 0	(0, 0)	(100, −100)
Military	Spend X	(−100, 100)	(−10, −10)
Expenditure			
		Payoffs: (Country A, Country B)	

capitulate. Either country can gain military superiority by spending X dollars more on military preparedness than its rival does during the coming year. If both countries spend the same amount, then parity between them is maintained. Assuming both countries can keep their expenditures a secret from the other until after they are spent, we have a simultaneous-move game whose game matrix is given in Table 11.5. The exact payoff numbers given are not important, only their relative magnitude.

The reader should verify that both countries have a dominant strategy: Spend X. The outcome of this dominant strategy equilibrium is that parity is maintained, yet both countries are worse off by the resources diverted into armaments rather than into more productive public and private investment. The interested reader will find references to the very large literature on arms race models in Section 11.11.

11.6 • Iterated dominant strategy equilibrium

The assumption that rational players will choose dominant strategies is quite powerful and not terribly controversial. In many instances, however, the players may not have dominant strategies. We saw this earlier when Honest Ava's payoffs conformed to Table 11.2. We have reproduced these payoffs in Table 11.6, along with the symmetric payoffs of Trusty Rusty.

The same information embedded in Table 11.6 is also displayed in the form of a game tree in Figure 11.3. Notice that all of Trusty Rusty's decision nodes are connected by dotted lines, implying they are all within the same information set. The payoffs to the two players are shown on the right-hand side of the tree.

Although no strategy is dominant, advertising a low price is *dominated* by both of Honest Ava's alternative strategies. That is, she can do strictly better by advertising a medium or a high price than by advertising a low price, regardless of what Trusty

TABLE 11.6   Payoff matrix of modified car-pricing game

		Trusty Rusty's Strategy		
		Low	Medium	High
Honest	Low	($90, $90)	($120, $100)	($150, $110)
Ava's	Medium	($100, $110)	($150, $150)	($200, $140)
Strategy	High	($110, $150)	($140, $200)	($170, $170)

Payoffs: (Honest Ava, Trusty Rusty)

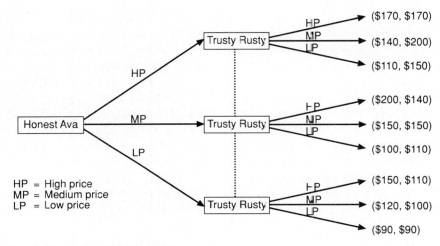

HP = High price
MP = Medium price
LP = Low price

Payoffs: (Honest Ava, Trusty Rusty)

FIGURE 11.3 • A game tree for the pricing game in which Trusty Rusty and Honest Ava have three pricing options and move simultaneously.

Rusty does. Depending on what she thinks Trusty Rusty will do, Honest Ava will choose to advertise either a medium price or a high price. Because Trusty Rusty's payoffs are symmetric to those of Honest Ava, advertising a low price is also a dominated strategy for him. Because both players know the other's payoffs, it makes sense for each to believe the other will not advertise a low price. This means both players can simplify the payoff matrix by eliminating the first row and column, as is done in Table 11.7.

TABLE 11.7 Payoff matrix for the modified car-pricing game tree after eliminating all dominated strategies

| | | Trusty Rusty's Strategy | |
		Medium	High
	Medium	($150, $150)	($200, $140)
Honest Ava's Strategy			
	High	($140, $200)	($170, $170)
	Payoffs: (Honest Ava, Trusty Rusty)		

In terms of the game tree, the elimination of this particular dominated strategy can be thought of as pruning away every path on the game tree that corresponds to the action "advertise a low price." The new game tree is shown in Figure 11.4.

If Honest Ava believes Trusty Rusty will advertise a medium price, then her best strategy is to advertise a medium price as well. This remains her best strategy if she believes Trusty Rusty will advertise a high price. That is, in the new simplified game, advertising a medium price is a *dominant strategy* for Honest Ava. Because of the symmetry in the payoffs for the two players, advertising a medium price is also a dominant strategy for Trusty Rusty. Therefore, we conclude that each player will advertise a medium price.

Advertising a medium price is an *iterated dominant strategy* for both players because it is selected by sequentially eliminating both players' dominated strategies.

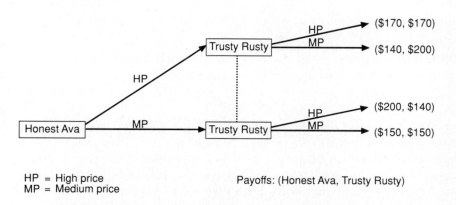

HP = High price
MP = Medium price   Payoffs: (Honest Ava, Trusty Rusty)

FIGURE 11.4 A game tree for the pricing game in which each player's dominated strategy has been pruned away.

In the modified car-pricing game, two iterations are needed before we are left with one strategy for each player: In the first iteration, we eliminate advertising a low price. In the second iteration, we eliminate advertising a high price. In games with a large number of strategies and players, many iterations may be required to find the iterated dominant strategies for every player—assuming these exist. As a result, iterated dominant strategies are more difficult to find than dominant strategies. Here is a formal definition.

DEFINITION: S_i^1 consists of all of player i's strategies that are *not* dominated. S_i^2 consists of all the strategies in S_i^1 that are not dominated *if we restrict the other players to the strategies in S_j^1*. The sets S_i^3, S_i^4, and so on are defined in the same recursive fashion. Let S_i^∞ denote the intersection of this infinite sequence of nested sets of strategies. A strategy is an **iterated dominant strategy** for player i if it is the only strategy in S_i^∞.

Not surprisingly, whenever every player has an iterated dominant strategy, this collection of strategies is called an **iterated dominant strategy equilibrium**. We leave it as an exercise to show that if a simultaneous-move game has an iterated dominant strategy equilibrium, then the collection of iterated dominant strategies is the only Nash equilibrium for the game.

11.7 • Nash equilibrium

Unfortunately, there are many games for which there is neither a dominant strategy nor an iterated dominant strategy equilibrium. An example of such a game is shown in Table 11.8.

TABLE 11.8   A third possible payoff matrix for the pricing game that has no dominant or iterative dominant equilibria

		Trusty Rusty's Strategy		
		Low	Medium	High
Honest	Low	($100, $75)	($120, $70)	($140, $60)
Ava's	Medium	($95, $90)	($130, $95)	($150, $100)
Strategy	High	($90, $110)	($120, $120)	($160, $110)
		Payoffs: (Honest Ava, Trusty Rusty)		

The payoffs in Table 11.8 need some explaining. Whereas in earlier examples the two dealerships were essentially identical, now they are different. The reason for the asymmetry is that Honest Ava has a reputation for haggling with customers and reducing her prices below those she advertised in the paper, whereas Trusty Rusty has a reputation for not haggling and sticking to his advertised prices. Given these payoffs, Honest Ava always does best by advertising the same price she expects Trusty Rusty to advertise. The reader can verify this by finding Honest Ava's highest payoff in each column of Table 11.8.

Trusty Rusty, on the other hand, often does best by *not* advertising the same price as Honest Ava does. The reader can verify this by finding Trusty's highest payoff in each row of Table 11.8. Trusty does best to advertise a low price when Honest Ava does, to advertise a medium price when she advertises a high one, and to advertise a high price when she advertises a medium one. The reason for this last result is that there are many car buyers who do not like to haggle and so prefer to buy from Trusty Rusty unless they expect a very large price break from Honest Ava.

The reader can verify that neither player has any dominated strategies. The optimal strategy for each player now depends critically on what strategy the player believes his or her opponent will adopt. What belief(s) can we identify as "rational," given that it is common knowledge that both players are intelligent payoff maximizers?

Because Honest Ava is rational, she will choose the strategy that is best, given her belief as to the strategy Trusty Rusty will choose. Because she knows Trusty Rusty is rational, she knows Trusty Rusty will choose the strategy that is best, given his belief as to the strategy she will choose. So Honest Ava's optimal strategy depends on what she believes Trusty Rusty believes she will do. Carefully consider the possibilities.

If Honest Ava believes that Trusty Rusty believes she will advertise a high price, then she must also believe Trusty Rusty will advertise a medium price, because that is his best strategy *given his hypothetical belief*. As a result, her best strategy is to advertise a medium price, *not* a high price, and Trusty Rusty's hypothesized belief will turn out to be wrong. Her conjecture about Trusty Rusty is inconsistent with optimal behavior for each player and thus is not rational. Read the previous two sentences again, because they get at the heart of how to find a "rational strategy."

The result is similar if we hypothesize that Honest Ava believes Trusty Rusty believes she will advertise a medium price. This belief implies she also believes Trusty Rusty will advertise a medium price, because that is his best strategy *given his hypothetical belief*. As a result, Honest Ava's best strategy is to advertise a high price, *not* a medium price. Again, her conjecture is not consistent with rational behavior on the part of each player.

But now suppose Honest Ava believes Trusty Rusty believes she will advertise a low price. This means she believes Trusty Rusty will also advertise a low price, because that is his best strategy *given his hypothesized belief*. As a result, Honest

Ava's best strategy is to advertise a low price—which is precisely what Honest Ava believes Trusty Rusty believes she will do. This conjecture is consistent with optimal behavior. Our conclusions are summarized in Table 11.9. The table should be read from left to right, one row at a time.

In Table 11.10, we have constructed a similar table for Trusty Rusty. You should take the time to confirm the entries in this table before you go on. This table shows that when Trusty Rusty believes Honest Ava believes he will advertise a low price, then his best strategy is, in fact, to advertise a low price. Any other strategy choice by Trusty Rusty requires him to believe he can "out-fox" his rival and do something his rival doesn't expect.

So what is likely to happen? The best prediction is that both players will advertise a low price. This is the only pair of strategies that are best for each player given "rational beliefs" about what the opponent will do (and "rational beliefs" about what

TABLE 11.9 Honest Ava's best strategy for each belief she could have about Trusty Rusty

Honest Ava's Belief about Trusty Rusty's Belief about Her Strategy	Honest Ava's Belief about Trusty Rusty's Strategy	Honest Ava's Best Strategy
Low price	**Low price**	**Low price**
Medium price	High price	High price
High price	Medium price	Medium price

Note: The self-confirming belief is shown in **boldface**.

Table 11.10 Trusty Rusty's best strategy for each belief he could have about honest Ava

Trusty Rusty's Belief about Honest Ava's Belief about His Strategy	Trusty Rusty's Belief about Honest Ava's Strategy	Trusty Rusty's Strategy
Low price	Low price	**Low price**
Medium price	Medium price	High price
High price	High price	Medium price

Note: The self-confirming belief is shown in **boldface**.

the opponent believes the player will do, and so on). Put another way, this pair of strategies/beliefs are *mutually consistent* with each other.

The strategy pair we have found—(low, low)—is a *Nash equilibrium*. The way we found this equilibrium is similar to the way one can find an equilibrium price and quantity for a competitive market. To find a market equilibrium you start from some quantity, say 100 bushels of corn, and ask: At what market price will this exact amount be supplied? Suppose the answer to this question is $5 per bushel. You then ask: If the market price is $5 per bushel, how much corn will be demanded by consumers? If the answer is 100 bushels—the quantity you started with—then you have found an equilibrium. Otherwise, you must select some other quantity and test to see if it is an equilibrium.

We have already seen that if every player in a game has either a dominant or an iterated dominant strategy, then these strategies constitute the only Nash equilibrium for the game. But, as we have just seen, Nash equilibrium strategies need not be either dominant or even iterated dominant. There is more controversy over the assumption that rational players will play Nash equilibrium strategies than there is over the assumption that such players will play their dominant strategies or iterated dominant strategies. Nevertheless, it carries a virtual monopoly position as a solution concept for noncooperative games.

Ever since it was discovered that a competitive market equilibrium, under certain rather general circumstances, yields an outcome that is Pareto optimal (no one can be made better off without making someone worse off), it has become traditional (and useful) among economists to ask if other equilibria also have this property. The prisoner's dilemma game exemplified by the payoff matrices in Tables 11.4 and 11.5 show Nash equilibria are not necessarily Pareto optimal. In fact, the prisoner's dilemma game proves that even a dominant strategy equilibrium can fail to be Pareto optimal.

11.8 · Focal point equilibrium

One of the reasons game theory is so interesting and so frustrating is that very frequently games have more than one equilibrium. Consider the following famous game called the **Battle of the Sexes.** In this game it is assumed there is a couple, say Chuck and Di, making a decision about how to spend an evening. Let us suppose Chuck would prefer to spend an evening watching a videotape of famous polo matches at home. Di would prefer to spend the evening at a local rock and roll club. Obviously, they could go their separate ways, but this is not as appealing to either of them as being

Table 11.11 Payoff matrix for battle of the sexes

		Chuck's Strategy	
		Polo	Music
Di's Strategy	Polo	**(−5,10)**	(−30,−20)
	Music	(−2,−5)	**(12,2)**
		Payoffs: (Di, Chuck)	

together. A possible payoff matrix is shown in Table 11.11. The numbers in the table reflect an ordinal utility ranking for the four outcomes.

This game has two Nash equilibria. In Table 11.11 we have printed the payoffs associated with these two Nash equilibrium strategies in **boldface**. You should confirm this before going further. Since there are two Nash equilibria, how are the players to choose between them? Thomas Schelling suggested that in **coordination games** such as this one, one of the many Nash equilibria might stand out from the others because of some asymmetry that is common knowledge to the players. Such a Nash equilibrium he called a **focal point equilibrium**.

Although Schelling did not provide a formal theory of such equilibria—indeed, the concept of a *focal point* has eluded formalization—he convincingly showed the pervasiveness of such equilibria, usually in the guise of "social conventions." For example, consider the following six coordination games devised by Schelling:

(1) Name "heads" or "tails." If you and your partner name the same, you both win a prize; otherwise, you win nothing.

(2) Circle one of the following numbers: 7, 100, 13, 261, 99, 555. You win if both you and your partner circle the same number.

(3) You are to meet someone in New York City. You have not been instructed where to meet; you have no prior understanding with the other person of where to meet; and you cannot communicate with each other. You are simply told that you will have to guess where to meet, that she is being told the same thing, and that you will have to try to make your guesses coincide.

(4) You are told the date but not the hour of the meeting in game number (3); the two of you must guess the exact minute of the day for the meeting.

(5) Write some positive number. You win if your number matches that of your partner.

(6) On the first ballot, candidates polled as follows:

Smith	19%
Jones	28%
Brown	15%
Robinson	29%
White	9%

The second ballot is about to be taken. You have no interest in the outcome except that you will be rewarded if someone gets a majority on the second ballot and you voted for that person. The same is true for every other voter, and this is common knowledge. For whom do you vote on the second ballot?

In all of these coordination games, there are many Nash equilibria. Yet, Schelling found that in every case most people zeroed in on a few of these equilibria. For example, 86% of his sample chose "heads" in (1), 87% chose one of the first three numbers in (2), more than half proposed meeting at the information booth in Grand Central Station at 12:00 noon in (3) and (4), 40% guessed "1" in (5), and over 80% voted for Robinson in (6).

Furthermore, Schelling found that people chose focal points even when such an equilibrium selection process discriminated against them. For example, consider the following variation of (1) above:

(1')   A and B are to choose heads and tails without communicating. If both choose heads, A gets \$3 and B gets \$2; if both choose tails, A gets \$2 and B gets \$3. If they choose differently, neither gets anything. You are A (or B). What do you choose? Notice that if you both choose at random, there is only a 50% chance of successful coordination and an expected value of \$1.25 each, which is less than either \$2 or \$3.

Schelling found that 73% of those given the role of player A and 68% of those given the role of player B chose heads—substantially better coordination than would occur by chance—despite the bias against B. Notice that if both A and B try to get the \$3, they end up with nothing.

11.9   Mixed strategy equilibrium

Up to this point we have been entirely concerned with a specific type of strategy called a **pure strategy**. A pure strategy is one that calls for the selection of exactly one action at each decision node. Unfortunately, many simultaneous-move games do not have a Nash equilibrium when the players are restricted to a finite set of pure strategies.

An example of a game with no pure-strategy Nash equilibrium is shown in Table 11.12. This is another variation of the pricing game. With the payoffs given, Honest Ava wants to match Trusty Rusty's price, but Trusty Rusty *does not* want to match Honest Ava. It is not a Nash equilibrium for both of them to advertise a low price, because if Trusty Rusty believes Honest Ava will advertise a low price, his best strategy is to advertise a high price. Nor is it a Nash equilibrium for Ava to advertise a low price and for Rusty to advertise a high price, because if Honest Ava believes Trusty Rusty will advertise a high price, her best strategy is to advertise a high price also. The reader can verify that neither of the other two strategy pairs are Nash equilibria either. Because there is no Nash equilibrium, there is neither a dominant strategy equilibrium or an iterated dominant strategy equilibrium.

If we demand of any acceptable solution for a game that it be a Nash equilibrium, but no Nash equilibrium for that game exists, then we are unable to predict how the players will behave. The resolution to this impasse is to expand the set of possible strategies so as to allow players to choose actions randomly. Such a strategy is called a **mixed strategy**.

Poker players will have no problem understanding the importance of mixed strategies. *Poker* is the name given to a group of card games that involve betting. One simple version of this game begins with the players being dealt five cards. Play proceeds clockwise around the table. On every round, every player still in the game has the choice to drop out of the game ("fold"), increase the amount of money all players must put in the pot in order to stay in the game ("raise"), or place in the pot the amount of money announced by the last person who raised ("see"). Play continues around the table until either everyone but one person folds, or no one raises. Once betting stops, the players still in the game reveal their cards to one another. The player with the best hand wins all the money that has been placed in the pot.

Poker players know that "bluffing"—that is, betting a lot of money when one's cards are unlikely to win—can be very helpful in keeping one's opponents off bal-

TABLE 11.12   Payoff matrix for the car-pricing game that has no Nash equilibrium in pure strategies

		Trusty Rusty's Strategy	
		Low	High
Honest Ava's Strategy	Low	($100, $50)	($75, $100)
	High	($50, $220)	($200, $200)
	Payoffs: (Honest Ava, Trusty Rusty)		

ance. If you only raise when you have a very good hand, then your opponents will soon figure this out. Armed with this information, their optimal strategy is to fold the minute you start raising the stakes. Because very little money will be in the pot if everyone folds quickly, you will win only a small amount of money. On the other hand, if you occasionally bet on a lousy hand, your opponents can no longer be sure of the quality of your hand from the way you bet. As a result, you can lure them into betting against you when you have a good hand, thereby winning more money.

Good tennis players are also aware of the power of mixed strategies. If your opponent runs up to the net, your best response is either to hit the ball hard to one side of her ("passing shot") or to hit the ball softly over her head ("lob"). The best defense against a passing shot is to intercept the ball right at the net and hit it where the opponent cannot reach it (a "volley"). The best defense against a lob is to halt well short of the net and hit an "overhead smash" that the opponent cannot return. Well-executed volleys and overhead smashes are almost always winning shots.

The aggressiveness with which your opponent rushes to the net depends on how confident she is that she can anticipate your response. If you always hit passing shots or always hit lobs, then your opponent will be able to adjust her strategy accordingly and win the game. Even if you are very good at hitting passing shots and not very good at hitting lobs, hitting an occasional lob will make your passing shots more effective by keeping your opponent away from the net.

Let us return to the game described by the payoff matrix of Table 11.12 and see whether we can make sense of mixed strategies in an economic setting. Let P_A denote the probability that Honest Ava advertises a low price, and let P_R denote the probability Trusty Rusty advertises a low price. Recall from Chapter 2 that if the two players' random choices are made independently, then the probability that both will advertise a low price equals $P_A \cdot P_R$; the probability that both advertise a high price equals $(1 - P_A) \cdot (1 - P_R)$; and so forth.

It follows that Honest Ava's **expected payoff**, denoted $E(\pi_A)$, equals

$$E(\pi_A) = P_A \cdot P_R \cdot \$100 + P_A \cdot (1 - P_R) \cdot \$75 \tag{11.1}$$
$$+ (1 - P_A) \cdot P_R \cdot \$50 + (1 - P_A) \cdot (1 - P_R) \cdot \$200$$
$$= (\$200 - \$150 \cdot P_R) - (\$125 - \$175 \cdot P_R) \cdot P_A.$$

Similarly, Trusty Rusty's expected payoff, denoted $E(\pi_R)$, equals

$$E(\pi_R) = P_A \cdot P_R \cdot \$50 + P_A \cdot (1 - P_R) \cdot \$100 \tag{11.2}$$
$$+ (1 - P_A) \cdot P_R \cdot \$220 + (1 - P_A) \cdot (1 - P_R) \cdot \$200.$$
$$= (\$200 - \$100 \cdot P_A) + (\$20 - \$70 \cdot P_A) \cdot P_R$$

We know that in order for Honest Ava to determine her best strategy, she must first form a belief about what Trusty Rusty believes she will do. Suppose Honest Ava believes Trusty Rusty believes she will choose a low price with a probability P_A^e. If P_A^e < 2/7, then $20 – $70 • P_A^e > 0 and equation (11.2) implies that Trusty Rusty should set P_R = 1; that is, always choose a low price. But then Honest Ava should advertise a low price with certainty also—which is not consistent with Honest Ava's conjecture about what Trusty Rusty believes she will do. Likewise, if P_A^e > 2/7, then $20 – $70 • P_A^e < 0 and equation (11.2) implies that Trusty Rusty should set P_R = 0; that is, never choose a low price. In that case, however, Honest Ava should also never select a low price—and not with a probability greater than 2/7 as she has conjectured Trusty Rusty believes she will do. Only when P_A^e = 2/7 is Trusty Rusty indifferent between advertising a low and a high price and, therefore, is unpredictable. And only when Trusty Rusty is unpredictable is it optimal for Honest Ava to be unpredictable as well.

What have we learned? We have seen that it is rational for Honest Ava to believe Trusty Rusty finds Honest Ava unpredictable only if Trusty Rusty's belief about Honest Ava makes *him* unpredictable. And Trusty Rusty will be unpredictable only if he is *exactly indifferent between advertising a low price and a high price*. This will happen if and only if 0 = $20 – $70 • P_A or P_A = 2/7. Table 11.13 summarizes what we know so far.

A similar argument applies to Trusty Rusty. It is rational for Honest Ava to find him unpredictable only if Honest Ava's belief about him makes *her* unpredictable. And she will be unpredictable only if she is exactly indifferent between advertising a low price and advertising a high price. It follows from (11.1) that she is unpredictable if and only if $125 – $175 • P_R = 0, or P_R = 5/7. Table 11.14 summarizes our conclusions.

The only pair of mixed strategies that can constitute a Nash equilibrium is the one in which Honest Ava advertises a low price with a probability of 2/7 and Trusty Rusty advertises a low price with a probability of 5/7. Given what each believes the other player will do, and what each believes its rival believes it will do, neither has an incentive to modify its beliefs, and so each will be unpredictable. This, of course, is what makes it a Nash equilibrium.

TABLE 11.13 Trusty Rusty's best strategy given his belief about Honest Ava

If Trusty Rusty believes this about Honest Ava …	Then Trusty Rusty will choose …
$0 \leq P_A < 2/7$	High price with certainty
$2/7 < P_A \leq 1$	Low price with certainty
$P_A = 2/7$	Unpredictable

TABLE 11.14   Honest Ava's 's best strategy given her belief about Trusty Rusty

If Honest Ava believes this about Trusty Rusty ...	Then Honest Ava will choose ...
$0 \leq P_R < 5/7$	High price with certainty
$5/7 < P_R \leq 0$	Low price with certainty
$P_R = 5/7$	Unpredictable

Some economists feel uneasy about assuming players use mixed strategies. They claim it is fairly rare for people actually to randomize over their pure strategies. A counterargument is that it is not necessary for anyone actually to randomize. It is only necessary that they appear unpredictable to their opponents. For example, suppose Honest Ava advertises a low price if the current month begins on a Monday or Thursday. If Trusty Rusty does not know she is using this decision rule, then her choice will *appear* unpredictable to him.

Mixed strategies are necessary to ensure the existence of a Nash equilibrium for some games. But is this enough? Are there games for which there is no Nash equilibrium even when mixed strategies are allowed for? Happily, under very general conditions a Nash equilibrium is known to exist as long as the players have mixed strategies at their disposal. We conclude with the simplest of the known Nash equilibrium existence theorems.

Theorem (Existence of a Nash equilibrium)   Every game with a finite number of players, each of whom has a finite number of pure strategies, possesses at least one Nash equilibrium, possibly in mixed strategies.

The proof of this important theorem is beyond the level of this book. The interested reader will find references to the proof as well as more general Nash equilibrium existence theorems in Section 11.12.

11.10 · Games with continuous strategies

When players have a continuous array of choices, **reaction functions** can be used to find any pure strategy Nash equilibria that exist. Recall from Chapter 5 that in a game with n players, player's i's reaction function $R_i(s_1, \ldots, s_{i-1}, s_i, \ldots, s_n)$ gives that player's best strategy *given* that Player 1 chooses strategy s_1, Player 2 chooses strategy s_2, and so on. It follows that the collection of pure strategies $(s_1{}^*, \ldots, s_n{}^*)$ is a Nash equilibrium if and only if

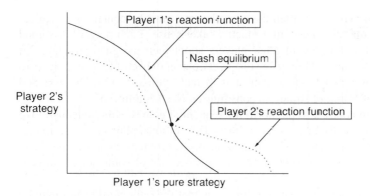

Figure 11.5 • The reaction functions of two players along with all the pure strategy Nash equilibria.

$$s_i^* = R_i(s_1^*, \ldots, s_{i-1}^*, s_i^*, \ldots, s_n^*), \text{ for every } i. \tag{11.3}$$

If there are only two players, equation (11.3) simplifies to

$$s_1^* = R_1(s_2^*) \tag{11.4}$$
$$s_2^* = R_2(s_1^*).$$

Diagrammatically, equation (11.4) means that if the reaction functions R_1 and R_2 are graphed together with s_1 on the x-axis and s_2 on the y-axis, then the two graphs intersect at the point (s_1^*, s_2^*). Such an intersection is shown in Figure 11.5.

11.11 • Summary

We have examined games in which every player is ignorant of the actions her opponents have taken. In such games, the player's optimal strategy depends on what she thinks her opponents will do. These beliefs, in turn, depend on what she believes all her opponents believe the other players, including herself, will do. The infinite regress makes it impossible to use the method of backwards induction to determine the players' optimal strategies.

Fortunately, sometimes players can determine that some strategies are inferior regardless of what the other players do. The sequential elimination of such dominated strategies sometimes leads to a single optimal strategy for each player. Such a collection of strategies constitutes an iterated dominant strategy equilibrium. When such an

Exercise 11.8   The San Francisco Forty-niners and the New York Jets are in the Super Bowl. It is fourth down with 10 seconds left in the game. The score is New York 10, San Francisco 7, and San Francisco has possession of the ball 8 yards from the goal line. Neither team has any time-outs left, so, barring some very unlikely events, this will be the last play of the game. San Francisco has two options: (1) kick a field goal (worth 3 points) and tie the game; or (2) go for the touchdown (worth 6 points) and either win or lose the game. Should San Francisco go for the touchdown, they will end up playing a simultaneous-move "touchdown game" with New York. The objective of each team is to maximize the probability of winning the game. The resulting payoff matrix is given in Table 11.17. Notice that New York wants to match its defense against San Francisco's offense, whereas San Francisco wants to avoid such a match.

(a) Show that the touchdown game has no Nash equilibrium in pure strategies.
(b) Find the unique Nash equilibrium in mixed strategies for the touchdown game.
(c) Assuming both teams play the Nash equilibrium strategies you found in part (b), calculate the probability San Francisco will win the game.
(d) This game has three possible outcomes for San Francisco: win, lose, and tie. San Francisco's von Neumann-Morgenstern utility function U over these outcomes is U(win) = 1, U(lose) = 0, U(tie) = 0.3. Use your answer to part (c) to determine whether San Francisco should kick the field goal and tie the game or go for the touchdown and victory. A field goal has a 95% chance of being successful.

Exercise 11.9   Prove that if a simultaneous-move game has a dominant strategy equilibrium, then this is the only Nash equilibrium for the game.

Exercise 11.10.   Prove that if a simultaneous-move game has an iterated dominant strategy equilibrium, then this is the only Nash equilibrium for the game.

TABLE 11.17   Payoff matrix for the touchdown game

		San Francisco	
		Pass	Run
New York	Defend against the Pass	(50, 50)	(60, 40)
	Defend against the Run	(90, 10)	(20, 80)
		Payoffs: (San Francisco, New York)	

• CHAPTER 12 •

The Coase Theorem

12.1 • Introduction

In 1991 the Nobel Prize in economics was awarded to Ronald Coase of the University of Chicago. Professor Coase has made many contributions to economics, but the greatest derive from an article written in 1960 entitled *The Problem of Social Cost*. Over the last thirty years this has become one of the most cited academic articles ever written.[1] In this paper Coase discusses the role of property rights and civil liability rules in determining alternative resource allocations. The article cuts to the quick of the interaction between the public and private sectors. Various insights that Coase presented in this article have come to be known as the **Coase theorem**. Surprisingly, economists have tended to dwell on one portion of this article that was alluded to 186 years earlier in Adam Smith's *Wealth of Nations* and is based on a set of assumptions that are frequently unrealistic. Simply put, this part of the article says that if there are no legal or strategic barriers to efficient bargaining, then people can always negotiate themselves to a Pareto optimal outcome. Furthermore, civil liability rules will have no effect on the allocation of economic resources. These rules will only affect the distribution of income.

The Coase theorem is an example of what Joseph Farrell calls a **decentralization result**. A decentralization result is a claim that if certain conditions hold, then self-

---

[1]One should be careful about jumping to conclusions about the relative value of an article based on the number of times it is cited. Although Coase's article is frequently referenced by lawyers, the article is also of great importance to economists.

ishly optimizing individuals will behave in such a way that the aggregate outcome is **Pareto efficient.** *Pareto efficient* means that no one can be made better off without making someone else worse off. One decentralization result with which you may be familiar is the "first welfare theorem" of economics: Any market equilibrium for an economy in which there exists a perfectly competitive market for every good will be socially efficient. Notice that the conditions of the welfare theorem are very strong. Perfectly competitive markets in every good do not exist because of such things as increasing returns to scale and **externalities**. An externality is any cost or benefit that is imposed involuntarily on someone.

What makes Coase's decentralization result very surprising in comparison to the first welfare theorem is that it has almost no assumptions. It claims to hold in the presence of monopoly, incomplete markets, and externalities. It appears to say that the benefits of perfect competition and complete markets can be achieved without the existence of these conditions. The Coase theorem also appears to eliminate any role for government policy in enhancing economic efficiency. As is usually the case with bold claims, skepticism is in order. The Coase theorem has two critical requirements: (1) Citizens and firms must be legally free to negotiate any agreements they wish, and (2) all bargaining must be efficient.

The requirement of efficient bargaining is anything but innocuous. Indeed, lawyers have from the very beginning recognized that the power of Coase's original article lies in its discussion of the role of the law when bargaining is inefficient. Inefficiency can arise either through explicit bargaining costs or through imperfect information about the gains from bargaining. If bargaining is inefficient, then people may not be able to negotiate themselves to a Pareto optimal outcome, and the rules of civil liability can be important. This version of the "Coase theorem" has become a cornerstone of tort law.

We saw in Chapter 6 that when bargaining is costless and the bargainers are perfectly informed, then not only is the bargaining outcome efficient, but agreement is reached almost immediately. The fact that most bargaining is protracted is indirect proof that the conditions for efficiency are seldom satisfied in the real world. One of the primary sources for inefficiency is imperfect information. In Part Four we will show how uncertainty about the opponent's payoffs can lead to impasses and a willingness on the part of the bargainers to walk away from situations in which both sides would gain from a deal.

In this application we will examine the validity of the Coase theorem under the assumption that bargaining is very costly. The purpose of this assumption is to mimic the effect of imperfect information on the bargaining outcome without requiring the complicated machinery of Part Four. Until then you must accept our claim that the results in this chapter also hold under the more realistic assumption that the bargainers are uncertain about whom they are bargaining with.

12.2 • A brief history of the topic

Ever since the creation of Adam Smith's "invisible hard," one of the most important questions in economics has been the conditions under which free markets lead to the efficient use of scarce resources. This area of economics is often called **welfare analysis.** The most commonly used notion of efficiency used by welfare analysts is that of Pareto optimality. Recall from Chapter 9 that a resource allocation is Pareto optimal if no other resource allocation can make one person better off without making another person worse off. Alternatively, a resource allocation is Pareto optimal if all the possibilities for mutually advantageous exchange have been exhausted.

Having defined Pareto optimality, the next question is to describe the conditions under which it exists. The answer to this question was greatly advanced by the development of marginal analysis in the late nineteenth century. Perhaps the greatest expositor of the uses of marginal analysis was Alfred Marshall at Cambridge University. His *Principles of Economics*, first published in 1890, stood as the standard text in economics for two generations. One of Marshall's students and his successor at Cambridge was Arthur Pigou. Although Pigou never possessed the international stature of Marshall, among his most important contributions was a very clear presentation of the distinction between **private costs** and **social costs**.

To see what Pigou meant by these two terms, consider a paper mill that is located along the banks of a river. The mill uses lumber, labor, and the power provided by the river's current to produce paper. In the process, the mill also produces chemical wastes, which are dumped into the river and carried downstream. In deciding how much paper to produce, the mill will take into account the cost of the lumber and the labor, but will ignore the use of the river for power and waste disposal. That is, it treats the river as a "free" resource. The use of the river may be "free" to the mill's owners in the sense that there is no explicit charge, but to the households located downstream the mill's use of the river may impose large costs. For example, the discharge from the paper mill may kill a significant number of fish, thereby making fishing a less productive and enjoyable activity. Or it may create an unpleasant aroma that makes life less enjoyable for those households located near the river. Or it may make the water poisonous, thereby making it dangerous for children to play in the water. The point is that somebody other than the owners of the paper mill bears a cost from the paper mill's use of the river. This cost is called an **externality.** Because the paper mill does not bear this cost, it cannot be expected to take the externality into account when choosing its output or its production process. In fact, if the paper industry is very competitive, then the only way the paper mill can stay in business in the long run is to ignore the cost of any resources for which the firm is not explicitly charged.

Pigou correctly noted that an important distinction needed to be made between the *private* costs to the firm of producing paper and the *social* costs of producing paper. He recalled from his tutelage at the hands of Marshall that freely competitive markets led firms to choose outputs where *marginal private benefits* equaled *marginal private costs*, because this is where private benefits to the firm (profits) are maximized. What Pigou made clear was that if the objective was to maximize net social benefits, then outputs should be chosen where *marginal social benefits* equaled *marginal social costs*. As long as private costs and social costs were the same, competitive markets and voluntary exchange would result in Pareto optimality. But when there was a divergence—at least, at the margin—then competitive markets might fail to achieve the necessary conditions for Pareto optimality, namely the production of outputs where marginal *social* benefit equaled marginal *social* cost.

This problem led Pigou to search for policies that would force markets in which externalities existed to equate marginal social cost with marginal social benefit. Pigou suggested taxing the polluting firm an amount equal to the cost it imposed on its downstream neighbors. In the words of more modern economists, this tax would force the firm to **internalize** the externality. Once this was done, competitive market discipline would generate a market equilibrium in which marginal social benefits equaled marginal social costs.

The economics profession treated the Pigouvian solution to the problem of externalities as being insightful, accurate, and the last word on the subject—at least until Coase wrote his 1960 article. In essence, Coase cast into doubt the value of Pigouvian taxes for remedying externalities. What follows is the most interesting and important of Coase's examples with which he challenged Pigou's analysis.

12.3.1   The Coase example: Setting the stage

Imagine a railroad that owns a pair of tracks running through the middle of a farmer's land. The railroad must decide each day how many trains to run along these tracks. Unfortunately, the trains sometimes produce sparks as they travel. If crops are planted too close to the tracks, then the sparks from the trains may set the crops on fire and destroy them.

The problem, stated in a Pigouvian manner, is that the railroad's activities impose an externality on the farmer. The Pigouvian response is to tax the railroad so as to internalize this externality. The result, according to Pigou, would be to equate the marginal social benefit from running each train with its marginal social costs. With such a tax, it was believed, the number of trains run would be socially efficient.

12.3.2   It takes two to tango

Coase is justly famous for his thoughts on social cost in part because of his insights about the essence of an externality. An externality can be thought of as an *involuntary exchange*. But any exchange requires two parties. In the railroad–farmer example there are *two* ways to reduce the externality. The first and most obvious way is for the railroad to run fewer trains. The second way, which is just as effective, is for the farmer to plant his crops farther away from the tracks. If the objective is to reduce the amount of burned crops in the most efficient way, then it is unclear whether fewer trains should be run or fewer acres of land should be planted. More facts are needed to determine which solution is more efficient.

What is important at this stage is that you not naively jump to the conclusion that the "trains cause the damage." The trains cause damage only if there are crops near the railroad tracks. The crops "cause the damage" just as much as the trains do. As with any exchange, voluntary or not, "it takes two to tango."

12.3.3   Some more facts

If it runs one train per day, the railroad will produce transportation services with a market value of $150 per year.[2] If it runs two trains per day, the resulting services are worth $250 per year. Adding a third train per day will increase the total value of its services to $280. The marginal cost of running each train is constant and equals $50 per year. If the railroad were not liable for any damage it caused, then it would choose to run two trains per day. The reason is simple: Adding a third train per day generates additional revenue of $30 while imposing an additional cost of $50. By contrast, the second train adds $100 to the firm's revenues while only adding $50 to its costs. Even before we consider external costs, it is clearly both privately and socially inefficient to run more than two trains per day. For this reason, we will hereafter ignore these other options.

The farmer owns two plots of land, which are identical except for their physical location. One plot runs along one side of the tracks, and the other runs along the other side. If no fire damage is inflicted, the market value of the crops grown on each plot equals $500. The marginal production costs of putting the first plot into cultivation equal $350, and the marginal costs of putting the second plot into cultivation equal $490. These numbers imply that if the farmer were fully compensated for any dam-

---

[2]We apologize for the absurdity of the numbers. Should the reader be interested in looking at the original Coase article, however, she will see that the numbers we use are nearly the same as the numbers Coase uses. Perhaps this will make an otherwise dense article a little less dense.

The railroad's profits, however, *do* depend now on the number of plots under cultivation. If the farmer plants crops on only one plot, then the railroad incurs expected damages of $60 for each train run; if the farmer cultivates both plots, then the railroad incurs expected fire damages of $120 per train run. The railroad's expected profits are shown in Table 12.3. The entries in columns 2 and 3 are obtained by subtracting the expected damages from the entries in the first column.

If the farmer places no plots under cultivation, then the railroad will run two trains and earn an expected profit of $150. If one plot is planted, then the railroad will run only one train and earn an expected profit of $40. And if both plots are put into cultivation, then the railroad will run no trains and earn a profit of zero. These choices by the railroad have been highlighted in Table 12.3.

Let us take a moment to put Tables 12.2 and 12.3 together. The farmer values the marginal output of a second plot at $10. The railroad would be willing to pay the farmer up to $40 to get the farmer to take the second plot out of production. Our analysis of bargaining in Part Two predicts that as long as both players are impatient and bargaining is costless, a bargain will be struck. The farmer values the output of the first plot at $150. Because the railroad is willing to pay the farmer only $150 − $40 = $110 to take it out of production, no bargain will be struck with regard to the first plot. Our prediction is that after all the bargaining is done, one train will be run per day and one plot will be cultivated. *This is exactly the outcome that the benevolent dictator would have chosen.*

An alternative legal arrangement is that the railroad is not liable for any crop damages caused by its trains. Instead, the farmer is held fully liable for any damage caused by planting next to the train tracks. Under these circumstances, the railroad is guaranteed to earn $100 in net revenue from the first train and $50 from the second train. As a result, the railroad must be paid at least $50 in order to agree voluntarily not to run the second train, and must be paid $100 in order to agree not to run any trains.

The farmer's expected profits now depend on both the number of trains run and the number of plots planted. These profits are shown in Table 12.4. The entries in

TABLE 12.3   The railroad's net profit if the railroad is fully liable for fire damage

| | | Farmer | | |
		0 Plots	1 Plot	2 Plots
	0 Trains	$0	$0	**$0**
Railroad	1 Train	$100	**$40**	−$20
	2 Trains	**$150**	$30	−$90

TABLE 12.4   Farmer's net profit if the farmer is fully liable for fire damage

		Farmer		
		0 Plots	*1 Plot*	*2 Plots*
	0 Trains	$0	$150	**$160**
Railroad	*1 Train*	$0	**$90**	$40
	2 Trains	$0	**$30**	−$80

Table 12.4 differ from those in Table 12.2 because of the expected crop damage due to fire. Recall that the expected damage equals $60 per train run on and per plot planted.

If no trains are run, then the farmer will plant on both plots and earn a net revenue of $160. On the other hand, if one or two trains are run, then he will cultivate only one plot and earn, respectively, $90 or $30. Therefore, the farmer would be willing to pay up to $90 – $30 = $60 to get the railroad to cut back from two trains to one train per day. Because the railroad values the second train at only $50, as long as bargaining is costless, we predict a deal will be struck. On the other hand, the farmer is willing to pay the railroad only $160 – $90 = $70 to reduce the number of trains from 1 to 0. Because the railroad will only accept a payment of $100 to do this, we predict no deal will be struck. The predicted outcome of the bargaining is that one train will be run and one plot will be cultivated. *Once again, this is the same result that the benevolent dictator would have chosen.*

What this example tells us is that as long as the property rights are well defined—that is, either the farmer gets compensation from the railroad for damage that occurs to his crops or the farmer must suffer the fire damage himself without any compensation—and as long as bargaining costs are zero and the benefits to both parties from any agreement are common knowledge, then the second plot will not be planted and one train will run per day.[3] This is exactly the Pareto optimal outcome.

12.3.6   What have we learned?

After working with such a special example, let us generalize what we have discovered: As long as bargaining costs are very low, information is perfect, and property rights for

---

[3]The Coase theorem is often lazily stated as follows: "It makes no difference to the outcome how the property rights are assigned." This is not true. The distribution of income and wealth *will* depend on the placement of property rights. For example, the farmer will be wealthier if he must be compensated for crop damage than if he is not compensated for crop damage.

all resources have been defined, then bargaining will take place until no more mutually advantageous exchanges are possible. But if no more mutually beneficial exchanges are possible, then the economy must be at a point of Pareto optimality, because no one can be made better off without making someone worse off. In 1960, when Coase was writing up his thoughts, Adam Smith had already revealed in *The Wealth of Nations* that a laissez-faire economy with no externalities would be led by an invisible hand to produce greater wealth. Coase's contribution was to clarify the important role of bargaining and property rights in ensuring Pareto optimality in the presence of externalities. Where property rights are not well defined—as in the famous example of a common fishery—it will be impossible for people to bargain over the property rights to the fish in the fishery. As a result, excess fishing may take place even if bargaining is very cheap. We will have more to say about the problem of common resources in Chapter 15.

This, of course, has a number of important policy implications. Among them is that as long as the assumptions of the Coase theorem are met, no policymaker need worry herself about the existence of external costs or benefits, because mutually advantageous exchanges will result in a Pareto optimal outcome for the economy. In essence, the Pigouvian solution was wrong, or at least not necessary. Furthermore, if we are interested only in efficiency and not in distribution, then how property rights are allocated is unimportant. The production decisions of firms will be unaffected.

12.4 • The effect of bargaining costs

One of the crucial assumptions of the previous analysis was that bargaining costs were zero and information was perfect. Keeping all the specifics of the previous example intact, we will now assume bargaining costs are high enough that it never pays the railroad and the farmer to negotiate. Although this assumption is extreme, weakening it does not alter our conclusions but does greatly complicate our analysis. Our assumption means that the two producers simply take the legal rules as given and make their production decisions independently of each other. Because the decisions made by the railroad may affect the farmer and the decisions by the farmer may affect the railroad, the two firms are playing a noncooperative game.

There are two other players in this game besides the railroad and the farmer. One of these players, whom we will call the "legislator," determines how crop damage will be apportioned between the railroad and the farmer. Her objective is to maximize expected net social welfare. The other player, Nature, determines whether or not a fire occurs.

The order of moves in this game is fairly simple. The legislator decides what fraction of crop damage due to fire will be paid by the railroad, α, and what fraction will be paid by the farmer, β. For simplicity we will constrain the legislator to values of α and β that sum to 1. That is, the legislator cannot subsidize the two parties by setting $\alpha + \beta$ less than 1, nor can she impose a tax by having $\alpha + \beta$ sum to more than 1. We will examine the effect of a tax later.

At one extreme, the legislator could have the railroad pay all damages ($\alpha = 1$, $\beta = 0$); at the other extreme, she could have the farmer pay for any damages ($\alpha = 0$, $\beta = 1$); or she could have the railroad and the farmer share the cost of the crop damage (for example, $\alpha = 2/3$, $\beta = 1/3$). Subsequently, the railroad decides how many trains to run each day, and, simultaneously, the farmer decides how many plots of land to farm. After these production decisions are made, Nature decides whether or not the crops catch on fire. The game then ends. For the sake of convenience, a summary of the relevant numerical information is given in Table 12.5.

The game begins with the legislator, who selects α and β, the fraction of crop damages paid for by the railroad and the farmer. The railroad, the farmer, and Nature then play the game displayed in Figure 12.1. Recall that the dashed lines between the farmer's three decision nodes mean they are in the same information set. That is, the farmer does not know the railroad's decision when he has to make his own decision. The three payoffs shown at each of the 12 terminal nodes are those of (in order) the railroad, the farmer, and the legislator.

To solve the game, we begin at the end of the game tree with Nature's move. Nature, as you know, acts randomly according to probabilities that are common

Table 12.5   Summary of relevant information

TRAIN INFORMATION

Number of Trains Run	Operating Cost	Revenue
1	$50	$150
2	$100	$250

CROP INFORMATION

Number of Plots Planted	Operating Cost	Revenue
1	$350	$500
2	$840	$1,000

EXPECTED CROP DAMAGE

Railroad	Farmer	
	1 Plot	2 Plots
1 Train	$60	$120
2 Trains	$120	$240

head. Although the farmer and the train company can not attain Pareto optimality on their own, they can be steered there by the proper actions of the all-knowing legislator. Long live bureaucracy.

12.5 • Bureaucracy versus the market

At the beginning of this chapter we argued that the claims of some Coase theorem advocates should be treated with skepticism. You should be equally skeptical of the conclusion just reached that the legislator can attain Pareto optimality when the market fails. The legislator can determine the best liability rule only if she can determine how the parties will behave under every possible rule. This requires a lot of information, much of which may be known only to the affected parties. For example, our hypothetical legislator would have to know the marginal costs of both the farmer and the railroad, the demand for their goods and services (in order to determine marginal revenue), and their von Neumann–Morgenstern utility function over income. The latter, in particular, may be very difficult to determine.

But if the legislator is privy to all this information, then the two affected parties should be as well. But then bargaining is likely to be efficient and the Coase theorem will hold. Precisely when we look to the legislator to repair the damage caused by inefficient bargaining, we find that the legislator may not know enough to choose the optimal liability rule.

If the payoffs are not known with certainty to the legislator, she may be able to devise a way for the farmer and the railroad to truthfully provide this information to her. They will be truthful only if she makes it in their own interests to be truthful. But this limits what the legislator can do with the payoff information provided by the railroad and the farmer. She may have to convince the two parties that this information will be kept secret and used in only a limited way. Now we have a much more complicated game than any we have considered so far. We cannot begin to unravel it until we have learned how to analyze games in which information and knowledge play central roles. This is the subject of Part Four.

12.6 • A modified view of Pigouvian taxes

For fifty years the Pigouvian view of appropriate policy measures monopolized the economics profession. Pigou's solution to the railroad–farmer problem would be to tax the railroad an amount equal to the expected cost that its trains will impose on the farmer.

If the farmer receives this tax as compensation, then we have created a situation that is identical to holding the railroad liable for all damage and holding the farmer liable for none. Assuming the farmer and the railroad cannot bargain with each other, the railroad will choose not to operate any trains and the farmer will choose to plant on both plots. This is a worse outcome (by $20) than what would occur if no taxes were imposed at all.

But suppose the tax is collected from the railroad and then used to reduce the tax burden of the general population. Now the situation is quite different.[4] Now the farmer *and* the railroad pay for the damages. Suppose the tax equals $60 per train if the farmer plants only on one plot and equals $120 per train if the farmer plants on both plots. This is equivalent to holding *both* the farmer and the railroad fully liable for the damages ($\alpha = 1$, $\beta = 1$). Assuming the farmer and the railroad cannot cooperate with each other, they play a noncooperative, simultaneous-move game whose payoff matrix is displayed in Table 12.9.

Neither player has a dominant strategy, although the strategy of running two trains is dominated by the strategy of running one train. Once we delete this dominated strategy, no other strategies are dominated for either player. If the farmer cultivates one plot, then the railroad will want to run one train; otherwise it would prefer to shut down. If the railroad runs one train, then the farmer prefers to plant on only one plot. But if the railroad runs two trains, he prefers to plant on both plots. Therefore, the game does not have an iterated dominant strategy equilibrium. But there are two Nash equilibria in pure strategies and one in mixed strategies. One of the pure strategy equilibria has the railroad running one train per day and the farmer planting on only one plot. The other equilibrium has the railroad running no trains and the farmer planting on both plots. We leave it as an exercise to determine the mixed strategy equilibrium.

TABLE 12.9   Expected payoff matrix when the railroad is taxed but the farmer receives no compensation for crop damage

		Farmer	
		1 Plot	*2 Plots*
	0 Trains	($0, $150, $150)	($0, $160, $160)
Railroad	*1 Train*	($40, $90, $190)	(−$20, $40, $140)
	2 Trains	($30, $30, $180)	(−$90, −$80, $70)
	Expected payoffs: (Railroad, Farmer, Legislator)		

[4]Because the taxes collected will be a very small proportion of total taxes, we can assume the reduction in tax burden to any individual from the imposition of these taxes on the railroad is negligible.

The Nash equilibrium in which one train runs and only one plot is cultivated is the Pareto optimal outcome that would be chosen by a benevolent dictator. Thus, the legislator can attain the Pareto optimal outcome through Pigouvian taxes so long as she is careful about what she does with the revenue collected. This result is a modest vindication of Pigou.

12.7 • Summary

This application has analyzed one of the most important theorems in the economics of the public sector. We have seen that the outcome of a situation in which one party engages in activities that inadvertently affect another party depends on many factors. Among these are the legal rules on property rights and the potential for efficient bargaining. The role of the legislator in determining which games are played out between firms and consumers is both subtle and important. To quote Coase, from his famous article:

> It would clearly be desirable if the only actions performed were those in which what was gained was worth more than what was lost. But in choosing between social arrangements within the context of which individual decisions are made, we have to bear in mind that a change in the existing system [that] will lead to an improvement in some decisions may well lead to a worsening of others. . . . In devising and choosing between social arrangements we should have regard for the total effect. This, above all, is the change in approach which I am advocating.

Sounds like a pitch for game theory to us!

12.8 • Further reading

The reader is strongly encouraged to read Ronald Coase, "The Problem of Social Cost," *Journal of Law and Economics* 3 (1960), pp. 1–45. Aside from its relevance to this application, it should simply be part of your general education. Coase's ideas have received a great deal of attention. Other articles that clarify or extend the notion of property rights and resource allocation include R. Turvey, "On Divergences between Private and Social Costs," *Economica* 30 (1963), and Harold Demsetz, "The Exchange and Enforcement of Property Rights," *Journal of Law and Economics* 7 (1964). For a more modern view of the Coase theorem, see the compilation of articles in Ronald

Coase, *The Firm, the Market, and the Law* (Chicago: University of Chicago Press, 1988). The effect of imperfect information on the conclusions of the Coase theorem are clearly set forth in Joseph Farrell, "Information and the Coase Theorem," *Journal of Economic Perspectives* 2 (1987), pp. 113–144.

Two articles that have shown the relevance of the cooperative results embedded in the Coase theorem are Steven Cheung, "The Fable of the Bees: An Economic Investigation," *Journal of Law and Economics* 16 (1973), pp. 11–34, and Ronald Coase, "The Lighthouse in Economics," *Journal of Law and Economics* 17 (1974).

Arthur Pigou set out his ideas most clearly in *The Economics of Welfare* (London: Macmillan, 1920). Pay particular attention to Part II.

12.9 • Exercises

Exercise 12.1   Suppose the farmer and the railroad cannot coordinate their actions, but the farmer must move before the railroad. Draw the game tree for this case and use backwards induction to find the Nash equilibrium under the assumption:

    (a) The farmer is liable for all damages.
    (b) The railroad is liable for all damages.
    (c) The railroad is liable for five-sixths of the damages and the farmer is liable for one-sixth.

In each case, compare the equilibrium outcome with that of the corresponding simultaneous-move game analyzed in the text.

Exercise 12.2   Confirm the entries in the third row of Table 12.1.

Exercise 12.3   Use the expected payoffs given in Figure 12.2 to construct the entries for the payoff matrix of the farmer–railroad game in the case where α is unspecified.

Exercise 12.4   Use the payoff matrix you constructed in Exercise 12.3 to show that the farmer–railroad game has an iterated dominant strategy equilibrium if $\alpha < 5/12$ or $\alpha > 11/12$.

Exercise 12.5   Use the payoff matrix you constructed in Exercise 12.3 to show that if $\alpha > 5/6$, then the farmer–railroad game has a unique Nash equilibrium in which no trains are run and the farmer plants on both plots.

Exercise 12.6   Use the payoff matrix you constructed in Exercise 12.3 to show that if $\alpha < 5/6$, then the farmer–railroad game has a unique Nash equilibrium in which two trains are run and the farmer plants on only one plot.

Exercise 12.7   Find the other Nash equilibrium in pure strategies for the farmer–railroad game when the payoff matrix is that in Table 12.8. Show that each of the mixed strategy equilibria is a randomization over the two pure strategy equilibria.

Exercise 12.8   Find the mixed strategy equilibrium for the farmer–railroad game when the payoff matrix is given by Table 12.9. (*Hint*: Simplify the game first by eliminating all dominated strategies.)

• CHAPTER 13 •

Cournot and Bertrand Duopoly

13.1 • Introduction

In Chapter 5 we analyzed a Stackleberg duopoly in which two firms in an industry chose output sequentially. In this application we will consider models that seem similar except that the firms move simultaneously. The first model, attributable to Auguste Cournot, assumes that firms choose their outputs simultaneously. This joint output is dumped onto a market and price adjusts so as to clear the market. The second model, attributable to Joseph Bertrand, assumes the firms choose their prices simultaneously. Because market price and industry sales are linked through the demand curve, it might seem to make little difference whether the simultaneous decisions are made with respect to output or price. As we will see, however, there is a dramatic difference.

13.2 • The Cournot model

In 1838 Augustin Cournot, one of the first mathematical economists, developed a model designed to explain how firms in industry structures ranging from duopoly to perfect competition would choose their output in an attempt to maximize profits. Two aspects of Cournot's model set it apart from much of the work in economics that was going on at the time. First, his thoughts were presented in the form of a rigorous model in which assumptions were clearly laid out and explicit functional relations were specified. Second, each firm's profits depended on what the other firms chose to do.

Although Cournot's model preceded game theory per se, it was a very important predecessor to subsequent developments by von Neumann and Morgenstern, Nash, and others. In this section we will present Cournot's original model in order to compare it with the game-theoretic variation on it that follows.

In Cournot's model, the market price is determined by the aggregate output put on the market by all the firms in an industry. No individual firm directly controls the market price, and all firms receive for their products exactly the same market price. In short (although Cournot would not have put it this way), price is not a strategic variable. Cournot also assumed that the products produced by all the firms are identical (homogeneous), and that all outputs appear on the market simultaneously. The price for the product equals the market-clearing price. Finally, the market price P received by all firms is assumed to be a decreasing function of the total output produced by all firms, Q_T. That is,

$$P = P(Q_T). \tag{13.1}$$

An implication of this specification of the demand function is that as one firm increases output, it not only reduces the price for its own product but simultaneously reduces the price received by all other firms, thereby affecting their profits as well.

Not having the notion of Nash equilibrium with which to predict firm behavior, Cournot assumed each firm would choose its output in the belief that the other firms would hold their outputs constant. This assumption is called the **Cournot conjecture**.

To see how this assumption completes the Cournot model, consider a (near-) duopoly: the worldwide market for large (400+ passenger) commercial airplanes. The two dominant firms are Airbus Industries (Firm A) and the Boeing Corporation (Firm B).[1] For simplicity, we will assume that these two firms are the only two in the industry.

We will suppose the demand for large commercial airplanes is given by

$$P = 13 - (Q_B + Q_A), \tag{13.2}$$

where P is the price in millions of dollars per plane, and Q_i is the rate of output for firm i in planes per year.[2]

The marginal production cost of a plane is assumed to be an increasing function of the rate of output. Specifically, the marginal cost of a plane for firm i is given by

---

[1] The other major manufacturer is McDonnell Douglas.

[2] Any linear demand function is likely to be a very unrealistic representation of the true demand equation, particularly toward its end points. To the extent we ascribe any realism to this equation, it is over "the relevant range.".

$$MC_i(Q_i) = 3 + 0.42 \cdot Q_i^{1.1}, \tag{13.3}$$

and thus total cost is given by

$$TC_i(Q_i) = 3 \cdot Q_i + 0.2 \cdot Q_i^{2.1}. \tag{13.4}$$

For simplicity, we will assume both firms can produce an unlimited quantity of planes. It follows that Airbus's and Boeing's profits, denoted π_A and π_B, are given by

$$\pi_i(Q_A, Q_B) = (10 - (Q_A + Q_B)) \cdot Q_i - 0.2 \cdot Q_i^{2.1}. \tag{13.5}$$

Tables 13.1 and 13.2 display the profits for each firm as a function of the output of both. The profit entries in these tables are obtained as follows: Each column corresponds to an output level for Boeing, and each row corresponds to an output level for Airbus. For example, $Q_A = 2$ and $Q_B = 3$ correspond to the third row and the fourth column of each table. At this particular pair of output levels, the market price equals $13 - (3 + 2) = \$8$ million per plane. Boeing's profit of $(8 - 3) \cdot 3 - 0.2 \cdot 3^{2.1} = \$13$ million, rounded to the nearest million dollars, provides the entry in Table 13.1, and Airbus's profit of $(8 - 3) \cdot 2 - 0.2 \cdot 2^{2.1} = \$9$ million, rounded to the nearest million dollars, provides the entry in Table 13.2.

An examination of the first row of Table 13.1 and the first column of Table 13.2 reveals that the maximum profit either firm can earn is \$20 million. To obtain this profit, the firm must be a monopolist and must produce four planes per year.

To predict firm behavior, we need to specify the belief each firm has about how the other will behave. The Cournot conjecture is one such specification. According to

TABLE 13.1 Boeing Corporation profit in Cournot model (to the nearest \$ million)

		Boeing Corporation Output							
		0	1	2	3	4	5	6	7
	0	0	8	15	18	20	19	15	9
	1	0	7	13	15	17	14	9	2
	2	0	6	11	13	12	9	3	−4
Airbus	3	0	5	9	10	8	4	−2	−11
Industries	4	0	4	8	6	4	−0	−8	−18
Output	5	0	3	5	3	0	−5	−14	−25
	6	0	3	2	1	−3	−10	−20	−32
	7	0	2	1	−2	−7	−15	−26	−39

Table 13.2   Airbus Industries profit in Cournot model (to the nearest $1 million)

		Boeing Corporation Output							
		0	1	2	3	4	5	6	7
	0	0	0	0	0	0	0	0	0
	1	8	7	6	5	4	3	3	2
	2	15	13	11	9	8	5	2	1
Airbus	3	18	15	13	10	6	3	0	−2
Industries	4	20	17	12	8	4	0	−3	−7
Output	5	19	14	9	4	−0	−5	−10	−15
	6	15	9	3	−2	−8	−14	−20	−26
	7	9	2	−4	−11	−18	−25	−32	−39

this conjecture, Airbus chooses its output under the assumption that Boeing will continue to produce at its current level. Boeing chooses its output similarly.

Back up temporarily to Chapter 5 and recall the Stackleberg game. In this game a "leader" moved first and chose an output level. This move was observed by the "follower," who responded by choosing the output that maximized its profits given the output decision of the leader. The market price was determined by their joint output decisions. The follower's decision-making process was rational *because of the sequential nature of the game.* In Cournot's model, each firm is assumed to act *as if* it were the follower in a Stackleberg output-setting game.

If Airbus is currently producing two planes per year, for example, then Cournot's conjecture implies that Boeing will choose an output of three planes per year, because that corresponds to the largest entry in the third row of Table 13.1. Airbus is assumed to behave in the same way. If Boeing is currently producing four planes per year, for example, then Airbus will choose an output of two planes per year, corresponding to the largest entry in the fifth column of Table 13.2.

Because the firms are acting as Stackleberg followers, we know from Chapter 4 that their behavior can be summarized by a **reaction function**. The reaction function for a Stackleberg follower gives the output level that maximizes the firm's profit for each possible output level of the leader. The reaction functions of both firms are graphed in Figure 13.1.

So, what outputs will Boeing and Airbus choose? Cournot argued the two firms would choose the pair of outputs that correspond to the intersection of the two reaction curves. Such a pair of outputs is commonly called a **Cournot equilibrium** and is labeled A in Figure 13.1. At this point both firms are producing three planes and earning $10 million in profits. It is an "equilibrium" in the following sense: If the two firms choose to produce this pair of outputs, and if each firm behaves according

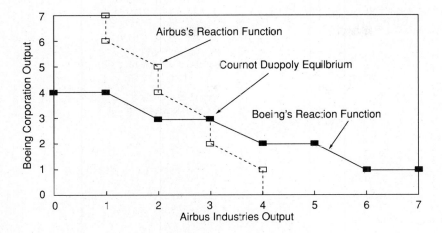

FIGURE 13.1 • Reaction functions for Boeing and Airbus.

to the Cournot conjecture, then neither firm will unilaterally change its output the next time the two firms must choose their outputs.

If you have been paying careful attention to the game-theoretic material so far and you have followed our example carefully, you must be a little bit queasy. In Cournot's model, firms are assumed to believe their rivals will hold output constant as they change their own output. That is, each acts as a Stackleberg follower. But if Boeing really expects Airbus to act in this manner, then it would only be *rational* to act as a Stackleberg leader and choose the point on Airbus's reaction curve that maximizes its profit. This point is labeled A in Figure 13.2. At this point Boeing produces four planes per year, Airbus responds by producing two planes per year, and Boeing makes a profit of $12 million. Notice that this is $2 million more than it earns at the Cournot duopoly equilibrium. Of course, Airbus can make the same calculation and will arrive at the same conclusion: It should act as a Stackleberg leader and choose the point labeled B on Boeing's reaction curve at which its profit is maximized.

If the Cournot conjecture is valid, then both firms will act as Stackleberg followers. But if each firm expects the other to act in this way, then each one will prefer to act instead as a Stackleberg leader. And so the Cournot conjecture will turn out to be invalid. Game theory, as you know, takes as a central premise that players behave in

Table 13.3   Cournot duopoly equilibrium of Boeing-Airbus Cournot model

| Output (Planes) | | Profits ($ millions) | | Market Price |
Boeing	Airbus	Boeing	Airbus	($ million/plane)
3	3	10	10	7

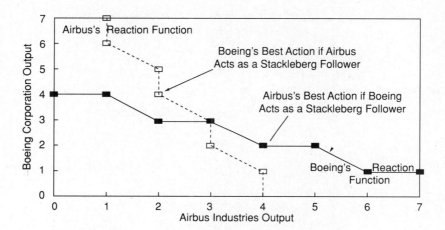

FIGURE 13.2 · The best output levels for Boeing and Airbus if each believes the other will behave as a Stackleberg follower.

a rational manner. The Cournot conjecture is at odds with the game-theoretic assumption that the managers of the two firms are rational and—and here is the rub—believe their opponents to be rational as well.

13.3 · The Cournot game

Let us try to recast the interaction between Airbus and Boeing in a more satisfying way. The game we will now describe we will refer to as the *Cournot output game*. Our game differs from Cournot's model in two important ways. First, instead of Cournot's multiperiod framework, we will assume the firms interact exactly once and then never meet again. Equivalently, we could assume the firms meet repeatedly, but each time, the managers are concerned only with that period's profits and completely ignore the future. Second, we will assume the two firms move *simultaneously*, rather than sequentially.

We will continue to use all of Cournot's other assumptions. Specifically, the two firms are assumed to have discretion only over their output and to be unable to collude with each other. So a pure strategy for each firm consists of a single output level. Once the two firms choose their strategies, the market price immediately adjusts so as to clear the market. The payoffs to each firm are the profits displayed previously in Tables 13.1 and 13.2.

Now that we have reformulated the Cournot problem as a simultaneous-move game, we need to find the game's Nash equilibria. We claim the only pure strategy Nash equilibrium is the Cournot duopoly equilibrium shown in Figure 13.1. The proof of this assertion is simple. The pair of outputs (Q_A, Q_B) is a Nash equilibrium if and only if each output level is profit-maximizing *given* the output of the other firm. But this is possible if and only if the point (Q_A, Q_B) lies on both firms' reaction curves. This, however, means that (Q_A, Q_B) is the Cournot duopoly equilibrium.

13.4 · Adding dynamics to the Cournot game

Recall that Cournot's original model is a multiperiod model based on non-game-theoretic behavioral "conjectures." Unfortunately, these conjectures are not rational. We have provided a game-theoretic rationalization of Cournot's duopoly equilibria, but only by abandoning the Cournot's dynamic framework and modeling the strategic interaction of the firms as a static, simultaneous-move game. Is it possible to provide a game-theoretic rationalization of the Cournot duopoly equilibrium in a dynamic framework?

The answer is: Yes and no. In Chapter 24 we will examine a game that consists of infinite repetitions of our static Cournot game. We will show that the strategy of choosing the Cournot duopoly equilibrium output levels each period is a Nash equilibrium of this repeated Cournot game. In this sense, Cournot's duopoly equilibrium can be rationalized using a dynamic model.

But the repeated Cournot game has other Nash equilibria as well, some of which are preferred by both firms to the Cournot duopoly equilibrium outcome. These new equilibria can be interpreted as forms of "self-enforcing collusion" between the duopolists. As a result, it is doubtful the Cournot duopoly equilibrium will always be observed. We must defer further discussion of the repeated Cournot game until Part Five.

13.5 · Analytical derivation of reaction functions[3]

Boeing's reaction function, $R_B(Q_A)$, is the output level that maximizes Boeing's profits holding Airbus's output at Q_A, namely:

$$\pi_B(Q_A, Q_B) = (10 - (Q_A + Q_B)) \cdot Q_B - 0.2 \cdot Q_B^{2.1}. \tag{13.6}$$

---

[3]This section is optional. It uses calculus to solve for reaction functions and the Nash equilibrium of the Cournot game.

TABLE 13.8   Nash equilibria of Boeing–Airbus Bertrand pricing game

| Price (millions/plane) | | Profits ($ millions) | | Industry Output |
Boeing	Airbus	Boeing	Airbus	(Planes)
4	4	0	0	9
5	5	4	4	8

13.8 • Contestable monopoly

Until recently, there was near unanimity that monopolized markets were inefficient. A profit-maximizing monopolist will set price above marginal cost. As a result, the price will be greater than the minimum required to induce the monopoly to voluntarily supply the good. In economic jargon, the monopolist earns economic rents. At the output chosen by the monopolist, the marginal benefit of an additional unit (the height of the demand curve) will exceed the marginal cost of producing that unit (the height of the marginal cost curve). The divergence between marginal benefit and marginal cost results in the inefficiency.

Over the last decade a group of economists led by William Baumol have argued that the firms in what they call *contestable markets* are unable to earn economic rents because of the threat of entry from *potential competitors*. Furthermore, should the government institute policies that artificially increased the number firms in the industry, the result would be higher costs and prices and lower consumer welfare.

A **contestable market** is one for which: (1) an unlimited number of potential firms exist who can produce the (homogeneous) product with a common technology, (2) entry into the market does not involve a **sunk cost**—that is, an expenditure that cannot be completely recovered should the firm decide to leave the market, and (3) firms are price-setting Bertrand competitors. A **contestable monopoly** is a contestable market with a Nash equilibrium in which exactly one firm supplies the entire market. In a contestable monopoly, since the threat of entry drives monopoly rents to zero, the firm will produce the greatest output at which the firm remains financially viable. This is referred to as a **second-best** output. This means that although marginal benefit does not equal marginal cost, it is as close as is possible without government subsidies to the monopoly.

For an example of a contestable market, consider the provision of scheduled passenger airline service between Cleveland and Kansas City. The inputs for providing this service are gates at both the Cleveland and Kansas City airports, a flight crew, fuel, and an airplane. Although the capital rental cost of the plane is a fixed cost to the firm, it is not a sunk cost. Should an airline decide to leave this market, it can either use its planes on other routes or it can lease the planes to other airlines through a well-developed airplane leasing market.

We will suppose there are two firms currently capable of providing regular service on this route, Midwest Airlines and Air Express. Q_M will denote the number of passengers carried on Midwest's planes (in thousands per month) and P_M will be Midwest's ticket price (in dollars per person); Q_X will denote the number of passengers carried on Air Express's planes, and P_X will be the airline's ticket price. The cost of carrying Q passengers (in thousands per month) is the same on both airlines and equals (in thousands of dollars per month)

$$C(Q) = 25 + 100\ Q. \tag{13.20}$$

The market demand curve is given by:

$$P = 155 - 10\ Q. \tag{13.21}$$

The average cost curve and the market demand curve are plotted in Figure 13.5. The average cost curve is declining and intersects the demand curve at an output level of 5,000 passengers per month. This volume of airline service is demanded when the market price equals $105 per ticket.

Consumers want to buy a ticket from the airline offering the lowest price. If both airlines offer the same price, then consumers initially choose between the two airlines randomly. Both airlines have the option of limiting the number of seats they sell. A customer turned away from the first airline it tries to buy from can immediately try to

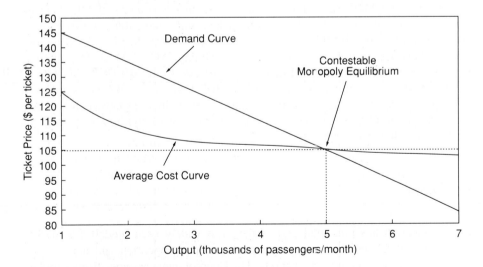

FIGURE 13.5 • Hypothetical average cost and market demand for passenger airline travel between Cleveland and Kansas City.

majoring in economics. The second option is to require one term of univariate calculus. The third option is to require two terms of calculus: one of univariate calculus and one of multivariate calculus. We will denote the first option as L (low requirement), the second option as M (medium requirement), and the third option as H (high requirement).

Each member of the committee has a preference ranking over the three options that is common knowledge to everyone on the committee. In a small department like this it would seem likely that these views would be known by others in the department. Concerns over curriculum are a common lunch topic, and faculty members are rarely shy about expressing their opinions on issues of pedagogy. In short, over the years each of the committee members' views about the importance of mathematics in an economics curriculum have been expressed, and these views are not likely to be changed by a committee discussion.

Pat is very sympathetic with those students who are math-phobic and would prefer to have no math requirement. He argues that the math required for rigorous theoretical analysis can be taught at graduate school to those few students who choose that route and has only a limited role in an undergraduate curriculum. In fact, Pat would always rather have fewer math courses required than more math courses. We can express Pat's rankings of the options as follows:

$$U_{Pat}(L) > U_{Pat}(M) > U_{Pat}(H).$$ (14.1)

Equation (14.1) can be read in a manner more appealing to people like Pat, as Pat gets greater satisfaction (utility) from the adoption of option L than from the adoption of either of the other options, and he prefers option M to H.[2]

In contrast, were multivariate calculus required for an economics major, Sue would make good use of it in the upper-level courses she teaches. It is her sense that virtually all interesting economic relationships are multivariate and therefore one term of univariate calculus alone is not of much use to her. As a result, she prefers the H option, followed by the L option, followed by the M option. Or,

$$U_{Sue}(H) > U_{Sue}(L) > U_{Sue}(M).$$ (14.2)

Mary is not as strident as either of her colleagues. She certainly recognizes the value of calculus in economics, but she is also aware that many students might be dissuaded from choosing economics as a major if they must take two terms of calculus. It is her view that a simple version of multivariate calculus can be added to an

---

[2]That is, if you know that L is preferred to M and that M is preferred to H, then you can *infer* from transitivity that L is preferred to H.

upper-level economics class at little cost, at least as long as the students have already had some univariate calculus training. She prefers option M. If she were asked to choose between H and L, she would reluctantly choose H. Therefore,

$$U_{Mary}(M) > U_{Mary}(H) > U_{Mary}(L) \tag{14.3}$$

Because of his seniority in the department, Pat is chosen to chair the committee. Each member of the committee hopes that a consensus will develop, making a vote unnecessary, but, knowing the past history of each of the other members, realizes that such a consensus is unlikely. Indeed, we will assume a consensus does not emerge.

Instead, the matter is put to a vote. There are, of course, many voting procedures the committee could use, but we will suppose this vote takes place using secret ballots. Furthermore, all three options are voted on simultaneously. Each committee member is allowed to vote for only one option, and the option that receives the greatest number of votes wins. This selection method, called **plurality voting**, is a fairly common voting procedure. In the event of a tie between two or more options, the chair's vote will break the tie. With only three voters, a tie will occur only if all three voters vote for different options, thereby creating a three-way tie. When this happens, the option chosen by the chair will be the one reported out by the committee.

To summarize: There are three members of a committee who are trying to choose between three options. There is a decided lack of agreement about which option is best for the department. One of the committee members, Pat, has been designated the chair of the committee. The chair carries with it the ability to cast a tie-breaking vote. It would seem that by virtue of the extra voting power, it is more likely that Pat's preferred outcome will be chosen. This intuition is confirmed by the naive voting model presented below.

14.3 • Naive voting

The members of the committee vote "naively" if they ignore the fact that they are playing a game and simply vote for their most preferred outcome. If all three members of the committee act in this way, then the outcome of the vote is very straightforward and intuitive: Pat will vote for L, Mary will vote for H, and Sue will vote for M. By virtue of being chair, Pat's vote will break the deadlock. Therefore, L is chosen by the committee and the economics majors will not be required to take any math courses. Furthermore, Pat ends up with the option that he thinks is the best of the three. The power to be chair brings with it desirable outcomes (from the perspective of the chair). There are no surprises.

14.4 · Strategic voting

Aside from the moral conviction to "tell the truth," there is no obvious reason that each person should vote with his or her heart. The members of the committee are really interested in the outcome of the vote, not whether their vote accurately reflects their view of the way the economics major ought to be structured. From this perspective, we can be sure that the three committee members will vote from their hearts if and only if it is rational for them to do so. A voter who votes so as to maximize the expected utility of the election outcome is a **strategic voter**.

Because the voting is by secret ballot, each committee member votes without knowing how anyone else voted. This means the vote can be modeled as a simultaneous-move game. A game tree for this voting game is shown in Figure 14.1. Notice that each player has only one information set.

The equilibrium concept we will employ to make predictions about strategic voting behavior is Nash equilibrium. Finding the Nash equilibria is made much easier if we first eliminate any dominated strategies. This will allow us to prune the game

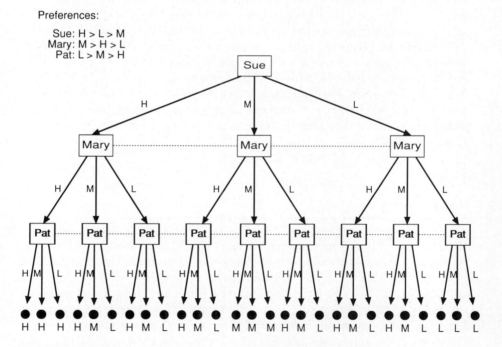

FIGURE 14.1 · Game tree for the committee voting game with tie breaking by the chair.

tree and greatly simplify the analysis. Because Pat gets to vote twice, it is most likely that he has dominated strategies that can be pruned from the decision tree.

Consider Pat's best voting strategy for every possible pair of votes by Mary and Sue. These optimal strategies are displayed in boldface in Table 14.1, but you should verify them.

Notice in Table 14.1 that all the entries in the last column are printed in boldface. This means that no matter what Sue or Mary chooses to do, Pat can never do better than he does when he votes for option L. Either Pat's vote has no effect on the outcome—as occurs when Mary and Sue both vote for the same option—or he can ensure the adoption of his preferred option, L. This means that voting for L *weakly dominates* voting for either of the other two options. So voting for either H or M is a weakly dominated strategy for Pat, and voting for L is a weakly dominant strategy. Voting for L is not a dominant strategy because under three circumstances (Mary and Sue both vote for M, or both vote for H, or both vote for L) Pat is indifferent between voting for L and voting for either of the other two options.

If we prune from the game tree Pat's two weakly dominated strategies, we obtain the simpler game tree shown in Figure 14.2.

Knowing that Pat will rationally vote for L may allow us to make some further predictions about the voting behavior of Mary and Sue. Because Mary is the voter who most vehemently dislikes L, it makes some sense to see what we can say about her vote. Mary, you may recall, prefers M to H and H to L. Table 14.2 shows her best strategy for each possible vote by Sue, assuming Pat chooses his weakly dominant strategy and votes for L.

Table 14.1 Voting outcomes

Sue's Vote	Mary's Vote	Pat's Vote		
		H	M	L
H	H	**H**	**H**	**H**
H	M	H	M	**L**
H	L	H	M	**L**
M	H	H	M	**L**
M	M	**M**	**M**	**M**
M	L	H	M	**L**
L	H	H	M	**L**
L	M	H	M	**L**
L	L	**L**	**L**	**L**

Pat's preferences: $U_{Pat}(L) > U_{Pat}(M) > U_{Pat}(H)$.
Pat's best outcomes are shown in **boldface**.

Preferences:

Sue: H > L > M
Mary: M > H > L
Pat: L > M > H

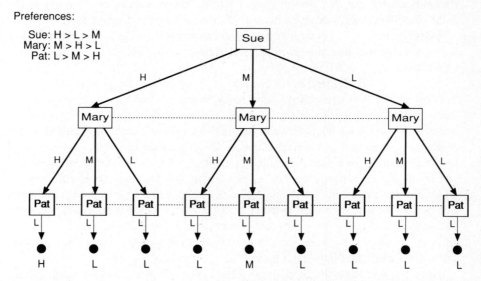

Figure 14.2 • The game tree after pruning away Pat's weakly dominated strategies.

Table 14.2   Voting outcomes

		Mary's Vote		
Pat's vote	Sue's Vote	H	M	L
L	H	**H**	L	L
L	M	L	**M**	L
L	L	**L**	**L**	**L**

Mary's preferences: $U_{Mary}(M) > U_{Mary}(H) > U_{Mary}(L)$.
Mary's best outcomes are shown in **boldface**.

Because none of the last three columns is entirely in boldface, no voting strategy is weakly dominant over the other two. But voting for L is weakly dominated by the strategy of voting for H. Voting for H is strictly better than voting for L if Sue votes for H or M, and is no worse than L if Sue votes for L. Because the domination of H over L assumes that Pat will play his weakly dominant strategy, voting for L is an *iterated weakly dominant strategy* for Mary. Although it is still unclear how Mary rationally ought to vote, it makes sense for her *not* to vote for L. Once again, we can prune Mary's iterated dominated strategy from the game tree to arrive at the still simpler game tree shown in Figure 14.3.

Preferences:

Sue: H > L > M
Mary: M > H > L
Pat: L > M > H

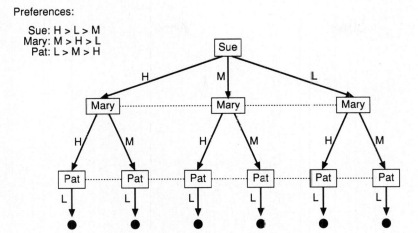

FIGURE 14.3 The game tree after pruning away Mary's iterated dominated strategy.

We now consider Sue's decision. Sue prefers H to L and L to M. Table 14.3 shows her best strategy for each possible strategy by Mary, assuming Pat chooses his weakly dominant strategy and votes for L and Mary does not choose her iterated weakly dominated strategy and votes for either H or M.

If Sue expects Mary to vote for H then Sue's best strategy is to vote for H; if Sue expects Mary to vote for M, then Sue's best strategy is to vote for either H or L. In no circumstances does it make sense for Sue to vote for M. Therefore, voting for M is an iterated weakly dominated strategy for Sue. But voting for H also weakly dominates voting for L. So voting for H is an iterated weakly dominant strategy for Sue. Time to pick up the axe again and prune the game tree. The result is shown in Figure 14.4.

Table 14.3 Voting outcomes

Pat's Vote	Mary's Vote	Sue's Vote		
		H	*M*	*L*
L	H	**H**	L	L
L	M	L	M	**L**

Sue's preferences: $U_{Sue}(H) > U_{Sue}(L) > U_{Sue}(M)$.
Sue's best outcomes are shown in **boldface**.

Preferences:

Sue: H > L > M
Mary: M > H > L
Pat: L > M > H

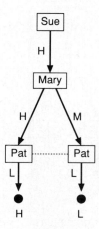

FIGURE 14.4 • The game tree after pruning away Sue's iterated weakly dominated strategies.

Figure 14.4 assumes Sue will adopt her iterated weakly dominant strategy and vote for H, Pat will adopt her weakly dominant strategy and vote for L, and Mary will *not* adopt her iterated weakly dominated strategy of voting for L. As Figure 14.4 shows, if Mary votes for H, then H is chosen, and if she votes for M, then L is chosen. Beause she prefers H to L, voting for H is an iterated weakly dominant strategy. The completely pruned tree is shown in Figure 14.5.

If you feel breathless we are sympathetic. Take a moment to come to grips with *the bottom line*. We can, after all the going back and forth, predict the outcome of the voting. Pat will vote for L, Mary will vote for H, and Sue will vote for H. Remarkably, H wins, even though the chair of the committee, Pat, considers this his *worst outcome*. The "power" to break ties turns out to be a bad thing for the person who is unlucky enough to be saddled with it. Oddly enough, once the committee is assigned, there should be a fight among the members *not* to be chosen as chair, even though the chair brings with it extra voting "privileges."

Of course, what drives the result is that Mary does not vote "naively." She recognizes that if she were to do so, then she would end up with what she considers to be the worst outcome. Therefore, she behaves strategically.[3]

---

[3]To single out Mary as acting strategically is unfair. We have assumed that all three committee members vote strategically. It happens that Mary's strategic vote differs from her naive vote, whereas the strategic votes for the other two members of the committee coincide with their naive votes.

Preferences:

    Sue: H > L > M
   Mary: M > H > L
    Pat: L > M > H

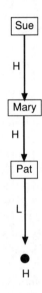

FIGURE 14.5 • The game tree after all the iterated weakly dominated strategies have been eliminated.

14.5 • Other equilibria

We are not done with our analysis of this game. Although the "paradoxical" equilibrium is the only iterated weakly dominant equilibrium of this game, there are four other pure-strategy Nash equilibria, in addition to many mixed-strategy Nash equilibria.

First, there are the three "unanimity" Nash equilibria in which all three committee members vote for the same outcome. These are clearly equilibria, in that no member can alter the outcome by unilaterally changing his or her vote. But we dismissed these equilibria at the very beginning of this application as very unlikely. Each equilibrium requires that one of the players vote for his or her worst option, and this action is weakly dominated by voting for either of the other options. If it were possible for the committee to arrive at a unanimous decision when their preferences are so disparate, then there would be no need for undertaking a game-theoretic analysis. The problem here is precisely that a consensus decision seems so unlikely.

The fourth pure-strategy Nash equilibrium has Pat voting for L (his preferred option), Mary voting for H (her preferred option), Sue voting for L (her second most preferred option), and the committee selecting option L. We leave it as an exercise to verify that this is a Nash equilibrium. The problem with this equilibrium is that *both*

Sue and Mary are worse off at this equilibrium than at the "paradoxical" equilibrium. The only player who gains is Pat, even though he behaves the same in both instances. Assuming the equilibrium of the game is common knowledge, this knowledge should lead Sue and Mary to focus on the paradoxical equilibrium rather than this one. Although the outcome is consistent with rational behavior, it would seem to be less likely than the "paradoxical" equilibrium.

14.6 • A concern

Predicting the voting patterns in the previous scenario was not a straightforward task. Not many people would look at the preference orderings and immediately conclude that Mary and Sue would end up voting for H while Pat votes for L. Indeed, if it were obvious, it probably would not be considered a paradox!

Part of the reason for the subtlety of the outcome is that the dominant strategies for Mary and Sue require a fairly large number of iterations. As you were (painfully) aware, our analysis kept bouncing back and forth until we finally arrived at iterated dominant strategies.

Do people actually go through these iterations to find their rational strategies? It is hard to imagine that this sort of thinking occurs (consciously) in the heat of a committee meeting. Unfortunately, the analysis of games under the assumption of limited rational ability is still in its infancy. We cannot answer the question we raised, but it is certainly a concern.

14.7 • Pat's counter-strategy: Precommitment

Suppose Pat is stuck being chair of the committee and knows Sue's and Mary's preferences. What can he do to avoid the disaster he can see looming? Clearly, he wants to change the game. One way to do this is to precommit as to how he will vote in the event of a tie. For example, suppose Pat committed himself to voting for M (his second most preferred outcome) in the event of a tie. He might do this by publicly promising to act in this way before the vote so as to make it too embarrassing or dishonorable to act differently should a tie occur. If Sue and Mary consider Pat's precommitment to be credible, and this belief is common knowledge, then the outcomes expected by the three participants are given in Table 14.4.

It remains a weakly dominant strategy for Pat to vote for option L. But now it is iterated weakly dominant for Mary to vote for M and for Sue to vote for L. We leave the verification of this claim to the reader. The outcome of the unique iterated weakly dominant strategy equilibrium is that option L is adopted, which is Pat's preferred outcome.

Table 14.4   Voting outcomes

		Pat's Vote		
Sue's vote	Mary's Vote	H	M	L
H	H	**H**	**H**	**H**
H	M	H	M	**M**
H	L	H	M	**L**
M	H	H	M	**M**
M	M	**M**	**M**	**M**
M	L	**M**	**M**	**L**
L	H	H	M	**L**
L	M	**M**	M	**L**
L	L	**L**	**L**	**L**

Pat's preferences: $U_{Pat}(L) > U_{Pat}(M) > U_{Pat}(H)$.
Pat's best outcomes are shown in **boldface**.

The second way Pat can alter the game is to announce his vote publicly before Sue and Mary vote. Now the game is partly sequential and partly simultaneous. Because Pat moves first, Mary and Sue can condition their vote on Pat's. We leave it to the reader to show that one Nash equilibrium outcome of this new game is the unanimous adoption of option M, which is Pat's second most preferred outcome.

14.8 • Summary

Economists are interested in the allocation of resources in a variety of settings. Frequently, those settings are characterized by markets, but not always. In this application we were concerned with a decision made by a small committee using a common voting procedure: plurality voting with special dispensation given to the chair of a committee. Even though the chair is granted the power to break a tie with his vote, in some circumstances that power can work against the chair, perhaps dramatically. In the example in this application, the outcome that the chair views as being the least desirable is the one that eventually gets voted into place. This is true even though the chair's preferred outcome would be chosen if all participants naively voted for their true preferred option.

How frequently might this paradox arise?[4] If we think of any possible set of preference rankings between three people and three alternatives as being equally

---

[4]We have refrained from referring to the paradox as an economic problem becuase it is unclear which of the three options is the most "efficient."

likely, then there are 216 distinct sets of preference orderings. Of these, 48 orderings result in the potential for some form of the chair's paradox. So, in small committees using plurality voting with tie breaking by the chair, the paradox could be expected to occur about 20% of the time.

14.9 • Further reading

In the last twenty years there has developed a very large literature on strategic voting. Some good surveys of this literature at the undergraduate level are Dennis Mueller, *Public Choice* (New York: Cambridge University Press, 1979); Peter Ordeshook, *Game Theory and Political Theory: An Introduction* (New York: Cambridge University Press, 1986); and Steve Brams *Rational Politics* (Washington, DC: CQ Press, 1985). A sophisticated treatment of preference revelation can be found in J. Green and J. J. Laffont, *Individual Incentives in Public Decision-Making* (Amsterdam: North Holland, 1979). The journal *Public Choice* carries many articles in this area as well, many of them nontechnical enough for an undergraduate reader.

14.10 • Exercises

Exercise 14.1 Find Sue's optimal strategy for each possible choice of strategy by Mary and Pat by constructing an outcome table similar to Table 14.1 in the text and circling Sue's best outcome(s) for each row of the table.

Exercise 14.2 Suppose Sue's preferences change so that she prefers H to M and M to L. That is, Sue likes Pat's preferred option, L, *less* than she did before. Show there no longer exists an iterated weakly dominant strategy equilibrium, but there does exist a pure-strategy Nash equilibrium in which option M, Pat's second most preferred outcome, is adopted. That is, Pat can do better if he can get Sue to like his preferred option, L, *less*.

Exercise 14.3 Verify that if Pat alters the game by credibly precommitting himself to voting for option M in the event of a tie, then the unique iterated weakly dominant strategy equilibrium is for Pat and Sue to vote for option L and for Mary to vote for option M.

Exercise 14.4 Suppose Pat changes the game by publicly announcing his vote before Mary and Sue cast their secret ballots. Draw the new game tree and find all the pure-strategy Nash equilibria for the new game.

Exercise 14.5.   Suppose the committee uses the tie-breaking procedure used in the U.S. Senate. The chair (Pat) does not get to vote unless there is a tie on the basis of the votes cast by the other committee members (Mary and Sue). The chair can break the tie only by voting for one of the two options that are tied. For example, if Mary votes for M and Sue votes for H, then Pat gets to break the tie by voting for *either M or H, but he cannot now vote for L*. Draw the game tree and find all the pure-strategy Nash equilibria of the resulting game.

• CHAPTER 15 •

The Use of Common Resources

15.1 • Introduction

Most of us have been in the following situation: We are at a social setting with a group of friends, just about to watch a movie, when the host brings out a big bowl of popcorn. The popcorn is put down on a central table and everyone is invited to share in this communal offering. Although we are normally civilized human beings, the ravenous manner in which we devour the popcorn is Neanderthal. The popcorn is gone before the plot even begins to thicken. Contrast that scenario with this one: You are spending a quiet evening alone, just you and a bowl of popcorn and a favorite movie. You eat the popcorn a fluffy kernel or two at a time, and a small bowl lasts throughout the movie.

Different social scientists would undoubtedly offer a variety of explanations for the contrast between the gluttonous behavior we evidence when sharing popcorn with friends and the relaxed way we eat it by ourselves. Most economists, however, would argue that the gluttony in the earlier setting was caused by a lack of well-defined property rights for the bowl of popcorn. In an earlier application in which we discussed the Coase theorem, we saw how the establishment of property rights either induced a Pareto optimal resource allocation—if transaction costs were low—or could be used by policymakers to bring the allocation of resources closer to a Pareto optimal allocation—if transaction costs were high. In this application we will present a model that predicts behavior when property rights cannot be established. The spirit behind sharing a communal bowl of popcorn—namely the fostering of a sense of community and friendship—is probably laudable. The sad fact seems to be that as people "compete" for the fixed amount of popcorn, they tend to shove as much as they can into their mouths as fast as they can lest someone else deprive them of their "just" allocation. Of course, while eating popcorn alone one need not have such concerns and can eat at a more leisurely pace.

The problems associated with undefined property rights extend to a wide variety of economic applications. In this example we will suppose that two firms require the use of a common input: a pond containing fish. Neither firm owns the pond. Instead, the pond is community property. Our objectives are to make some predictions of how the two firms will behave and to determine whether the resulting resource allocation is Pareto optimal.

Any fisherman knows the problems with overfishing. Although more fishing effort will result in more fish being caught, the stock of fish may be so diminished by the extra effort that the future catch is substantially reduced, if not eliminated. If one fisherman owned the pond, we would expect him to take into account the future cost of pulling one more fish out of the water today when deciding whether that extra fish was worth the effort. When more than one fisherman have the right to fish the pond, each of them will only bear a fraction of the future costs of pulling a fish out today. Because they do not bear the full cost, they will overfish.

Although the intuition seems fairly straightforward, we seek in this application to formalize the logic. As we noted earlier, the analysis and conclusions found in this application apply to a wide variety of important economic situations. You should therefore think of this application as a metaphor for the general problem of sharing a common resource.

15.2 • Some simple fish biology

Although we ultimately want to ask how fishing affects the stock of fish, we will begin by presenting a model of how nature alone determines the stock of fish. As with all models we will simplify a great deal, while trying not to lose the essence of the problem.

In this model it is important to distinguish carefully between stocks and flows. We will compare the stock of fish—that is, the number of fish *at a point in time*—with fish births and deaths, which are additions and subtractions to the fish stock *per unit of time*. Births and deaths are flows into and out of the fish stock. To simplify matters, we will combine the births and deaths into a variable called the *net births,* which is the net addition to the fish stock per unit of time. If net births are positive, then the fish stock will grow; conversely, if the net births are negative, then the stock of fish will decline.

Suppose, for whatever reasons, the stock of fish in a pond is very low. A lusty fish looking for a mate will have a difficult time finding one. Although the net birth rate in these circumstances may be positive, it will probably be low. This means the stock of fish will grow, but slowly. As the stock of fish gets bigger, however, it becomes easier to find a mate, and the increase in net births means the stock of fish starts to grow faster and faster. Once the fish stock becomes large enough, finding a mate will no longer be such a problem, but the competition for food starts becoming fierce. As a result, the number of deaths will rise. Once this happens, net births, though still positive, will start to fall, and the stock of fish will grow more slowly. Deaths will continue to climb until net births equal zero, at which point the stock of fish will stop growing. This point of zero population growth is an **ecological equilibrium.** In this equilibrium, the flow of fish into the stock (births) matches the flow of fish out of the stock (deaths); that is, net births are zero. This equilibrium stock of fish is called the **carrying capacity** of the pond. Our biological story can be captured in the three diagrams shown in Figures 15.1, 15.2, and 15.3.

The three figures show there are two equilibrium stocks of fish. One equilibrium stock is zero, and the other is 100,000. What distinguished these two stocks as equilibria is that in both cases net births are zero.

A mathematical equation which describes the relationships in Figures 15.1, 15.2, and 15.3 is given by:

$$B = g \cdot N \cdot (1 - (N/K)) \qquad (15.1)$$

where B is net births, N is the stock of fish, K is the carrying capacity of the pond, and g is the growth rate of the stock of fish when the stock is near zero. Figures 15.1, 15.2, and 15.3 assumed (15.1) holds, g equals 1, and the carrying capacity of the pond is

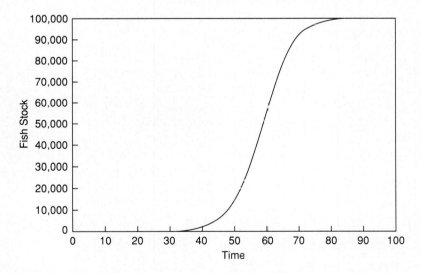

FIGURE 15.1 • This diagram depicts how a small initial stock of fish grows over time.

100,000 fish. You might find it useful to try different growth rates and carrying capacities to see how the relationship between fish stock and carrying capacity changes with changes in g and K. Computer spreadsheets are very helpful in performing a large number of "what if" questions quickly.

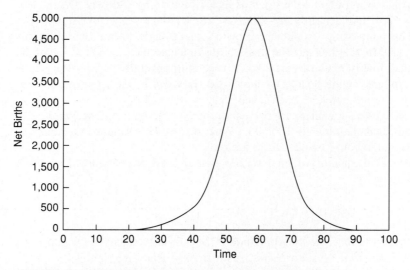

FIGURE 15.2 • This diagram depicts how, starting from a small stock of fish, the net birth rate changes over time.

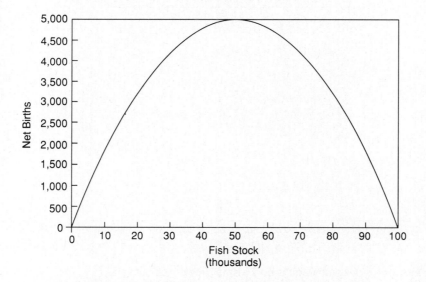

FIGURE 15.3 • Figures 15.1 and 15.2 are combined to relate the net birth rate to the fish stock.

15.3 • Fishing and carrying capacity

Fishing, of course, upsets the natural equilibrium by increasing the death rate. We will continue to define B as natural births of fish minus natural deaths. Although fishing does not affect the biological relationship between B and N, it will affect the equilibrium values of B and N.

If B is zero and some number of fish, say C, begin to be caught on a regular basis, then the stock of fish will fall. A crucial question is: If C fish are caught per time period, then what will be the long-run ecological equilibrium fish stock? As we saw earlier, an equilibrium stock of fish exists when there is neither growth nor decay in the stock of fish. This will occur when the net birth rate exactly equals C, the rate of fishing. In Figure 15.4 we see that if the number of fish caught per unit of time equals C, then the equilibrium stock of fish must by either N_1 or N_2. At these two stocks the net birth rate equals C.

15.4 • Technical efficiency in fishing

Technical efficiency is defined as getting the largest output possible for given levels of inputs. If ten workers and one machine can repave a one-mile stretch of road in one week, but a firm hires 20 workers and one machine to repave the road in one week, then the firm is being technically inefficient.

In terms of the fishing example, we can define a variable E that denotes *fishing effort*. The higher the value of E, the greater are the resources devoted to fishing. E incorporates, among other things, the number of boats and the amount of time each

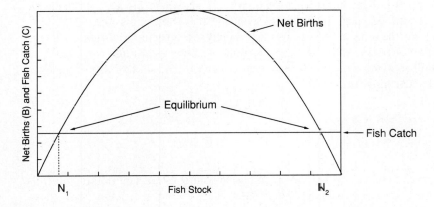

FIGURE 15. 4 • If the rate of fishing equals C, then the equilibrium stock of fish will be either N_1 or N_2.

boat is on the water. In simplistic terms, you can think of E as boat-hours per unit of time (notice that E is a flow variable). Everything else being equal, including the stock of fish, the more effort that goes into catching fish, the greater the catch. Furthermore, everything equal, including the effort put into fishing, the larger the stock of fish, the larger the catch. These last two sentences imply that as fishing effort increases, ce*teris paribus*, the catch will increase, and as the stock of fish increases, *ceteris paribus*, the catch will increase. We can capture these assertions in the following equation:

$$C = a \cdot E \cdot N. \tag{15.2}$$

Recall that C is the catch of fish per time period and N is the fish stock. In equation (15.2), a is some constant that measures the technical ability to convert effort into a *catch rate*, C/N.

Recall that in equilibrium, net births just offset the number of fish caught, or B = C. Algebraically, this means the stock of fish will adjust naturally to the point where the right-hand side of equation (15.1) equals the right-hand side of equation (15.2):

$$g \cdot N \cdot (1 - (N/K)) = a \cdot E \cdot N. \tag{15.3}$$

Solving this equation for N yields the functional relationship between the *equilibrium* stock of fish and the level of fishing effort:

$$N = K - (a\,K/g)\,E. \tag{15.4}$$

Equation (15.4) says that if E goes up by 1 unit, then the equilibrium stock of fish goes down by (aK/g) units. This relationship is shown in Figure 15.5 under the assumption that K equals 100,000 fish, g equals 20%, and a equals 0.2.

Assuming the stock of fish adjusts fairly rapidly toward equilibrium to any changes in the level of fishing effort, we can substitute equation (15.4) into equation (15.2) and obtain an expression for the size of the catch of fish as a function of the effort devoted to catching fish:

$$\begin{aligned} C &= a \cdot E \cdot [K - (a\,K/g) \cdot E] \\ &= (a\,K) \cdot E - (a^2\,K/g) \cdot E^2. \end{aligned} \tag{15.5}$$

Equation (15.5) relates the fish catch (output) to fishing effort (input). It is simply the production function for fishing the pond. The shape of the production function is shown in Figure 15.6.

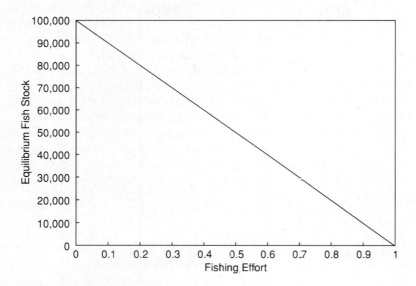

FIGURE 15.5 • Fishing effort is plotted against the equilibrium stock of fish, assuming that K = 100,000, g = 20%, and a = 0.2.

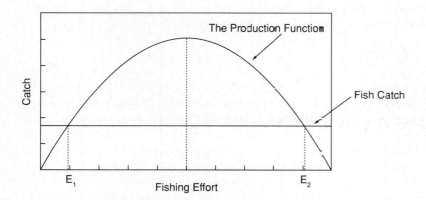

FIGURE 15.6 • The production function for fishing the pond.

The slope of the production function is the marginal productivity of effort. As you can see from Figure 15.6, as effort increases, the slope of the production function declines, implying a diminishing marginal product throughout. But what is particularly interesting is that there is negative marginal product once effort exceeds Eδ. A catch of C_1 can be achieved by employing an effort of E_1 or E_2, but the employment of E_2 is *technically inefficient*. Any amount of effort beyond Eδ is technically inefficient because the same level of output can be achieved with less effort. A reasonable question to ask is: What relevance does the downward-sloping portion of the production function have, since no one would have any incentive to employ a level of effort where there is negative marginal productivity? As you will see, a reasonable *person* would not purposely choose a level of effort that is technically inefficient, but a reasonable *group of people* might be induced to choose collectively a technically inefficient level of output.

15.5 · The fishery game

You have now fought your way through a series of technical and primarily biological relationships. In the end, you were presented with a production function for catching fish. Here is where the game theory begins.

Suppose there are two fishing firms who are deciding how much effort to put into fishing for lobsters: Lobsters 'R Us and Lobster World. The fishing effort of the two firms will be represented by the number of boat-hours the two firms employ. Clearly, the equilibrium stock of fish depends on the total effort of the two firms. That is,

$$E = E_1 + E_2, \qquad\qquad (15.6)$$

where E is the total fishing effort, E_1 is the effort employed by Lobsters 'R Us, and E_2 is the effort spent by Lobster World. Since the decision each firm makes about its fishing effort affects the overall fish stock, and this effort in turn affects the other firm's catch, they are embroiled in a game.

We will assume the ratio between the two firm's catches equals the ratio of their fishing efforts. For example, if Lobster World engages in no fishing effort, then Lobsters 'R Us receives the entire catch. If, however, Lobster World engages in 30% of the total effort, then Lobsters 'R Us receives only 70% of the total catch. Algebraically, this means

$$C_1 = (E_1 / (E_1 + E_2)) \cdot C, \qquad\qquad (15.7a)$$

and

$$C_2 = (E_2 / (E_1 + E_2)) \cdot C. \tag{15.7b}$$

Consider the situation from the perspective of Lobsters 'R Us. Equations (15.5), (15.6), and (15.7), when taken together, explain how the catch for Lobsters 'R Us depends on E_1 and E_2. That is,

$$C_1 = (E_1/(E_1 + E_2)) \cdot (a K \cdot (E_1 + E_2) - (a^2 K/g) \cdot (E_1 + E_2)^2) \tag{15.8}$$
$$= (a K - (a^2 K/g) \cdot E_2) \cdot E_1 - (a^2 K/g) \cdot E_1^2.$$

Equation (15.8) is the production function for Lobsters 'R Us. The only variable that Lobsters 'R Us has discretion over on the right-hand side of (15.8) is its level of effort, E_1. If we somewhat arbitrarily select values for the parameters in equation (15.8), such as $a = 0.2$, $K = 100,000$, $g = 20\%$, and $E_2 = 0.3$, we can rewrite equation (15.8) as

$$C_1 = 14,000 \cdot E_1 - 20,000 \cdot E_1^2. \tag{15.9a}$$

In contrast, consider how the total catch for both firms varies with E_1. Combining equations (15.5) and (15.6) with the assumed values of the parameters gives

$$C = 4,200 + 8,000 \cdot E_1 - 20,000 \cdot E_1^2. \tag{15.9b}$$

In Figure 15.7 we have drawn equations (15.9a) and (15.9b). You will probably gain insight into this problem if you take the time to try different parameter values and see how these functions change.

The most interesting aspect of Figure 15.7 is that the level of effort by Lobsters 'R Us that maximizes the total catch, denoted as $E_1\delta$ in Figure 15.7, is different from the level of effort that maximizes the firm's own catch, denoted by $E_2\delta$. The difference is due to the negative effect of Lobsters 'R Us' effort on Lobster World's catch.

So far we have kept the analysis in terms of units of effort and units of fish. Assuming Lobsters ''R Us is a profit-maximizing enterprise, we need to relate fishing effort to firm profit. Suppose a unit of effort costs w dollars. Then total cost as a function of effort is given by:

$$TC_1(E_1) = w \cdot E_1. \tag{15.10}$$

Furthermore, suppose both firms are price takers in the fish market and that the price of a fish equals P_f. Then Lobsters 'R Us' total revenue is given by:

$$TR_1(C_1) = P_f \cdot C_1. \tag{15.11}$$

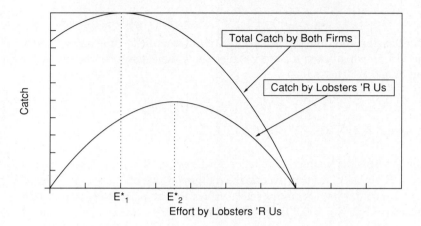

FIGURE 15.7 • Assuming specific parameter values, the relationship between the effort employed by Lobsters 'R Us and both its own catch and total catch is shown.

Equation (15.10) is expressed in terms of Lobsters 'R Us' effort, whereas equation (15.11) is expressed in terms of Lobsters 'R Us' catch. Fortunately, equation (15.9a), the firm's production function, relates the firm's effort to its catch. Using this we can write the profits of Lobsters 'R Us as:

$$\pi_1(E_1, E_2) = P_f \cdot \{(a K - (a^2 K/g) \cdot E_2) \cdot E_1 - (a^2 K/g) \cdot E_1^2\} - w \cdot E_1 \qquad (15.12)$$

Note that Lobsters 'R Us' profit depends on E_1 *and* E_2. Because of the symmetry between the two firms, there is a similar expression for Lobster World:

$$\pi_2(E_1, E_2) = P_f \cdot \{(a K - (a^2 K/g) \cdot E_1) \cdot E_2 - (a^2 K/g) \cdot E_2^2\} - w \cdot E_2 \qquad (15.13)$$

We will suppose that the two firms choose their effort levels simultaneously. Therefore, the game tree has the simple form given in Figure 15.8.

Unfortunately, Figure 15.8 ignores the fact that each firm has a continuum of possible strategies. For simplicity it is assumed in the diagram that each firm can choose between only two strategies, high effort and low effort.

Because any positive level of effort is possible for either firm, the game tree is not useful for finding the equilibrium strategies. But there is hope. Chapter 10 provided us with a method for finding the Nash equilibria of games like these: (1) Find each player's reaction function, and (2) find the point where the graphs of these two functions intersect.

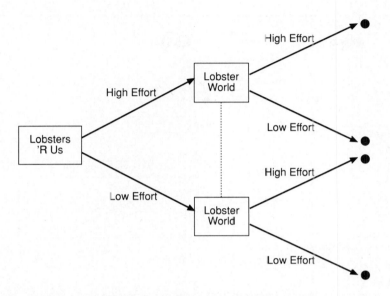

FIGURE 15.8 • The game tree for the fishery game.

Recall that a reaction function simply denotes the optimal action for one firm given different possible actions taken by the other firm. For example, Figure 15.9 displays three isoprofit curves for Lobsters 'R Us under the following conditions:

$$a = 0.2; \qquad\qquad\qquad\qquad\qquad\qquad\qquad (15.14)$$

$$g = 20\%;$$

$$K = 100,000;$$

$$w = \$100;$$

and $P_f = \$0.10$.

The "highest" isoprofit curve Lobsters 'R Us can reach when Lobster World chooses 0.2 units of effort is the one that corresponds to a profit level of $281.25. The firm achieves this maximum profit level by choosing 0.375 units of effort. Alternatively, if Lobster World chooses 0.4 units of effort, then the highest isoprofit curve Lobsters 'R Us can attain is the one corresponding to a profit level of $151.25, which requires 0.275 units of effort by Lobsters 'R Us. Finally, a profit of $61.25 is the best Lobsters 'R Us can attain if Lobster World chooses an effort level of 0.6.

As we showed in Chapters 4 and 10, the reaction curve for Lobsters 'R Us is found by collecting these optimum responses to alternative actions by Lobster World. The

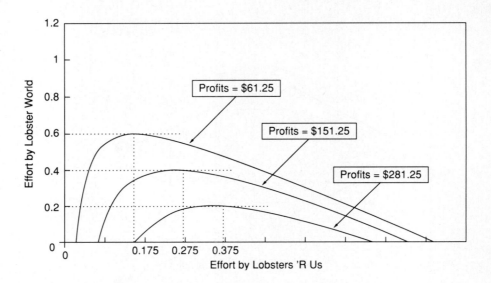

FIGURE 15.9 • Isoprofit curves for Lobsters 'R Us assuming specific parameter values.

same can be done for Lobster World. Under the assumed parameter values in equation (15.17), the reaction curves for each firm are displayed in Figure 15.10.

The optimum level of effort for Lobsters 'R Us *at any given level of effort chosen by Lobster World* can be found by maximizing the profit function, holding Lobster World's level of effort constant. The partial derivative of equation (15.12) with respect to E_1, *treating E_2 as if it were a constant*, is given by:

$$\partial\pi_1/\partial E_1 = P_f \cdot (a\,K - (a^2\,K/g) \cdot E_2) - 2\,P_f \cdot (a^2\,K/g) \cdot E_1 - w. \tag{15.15}$$

We find the profit-maximizing level of effort E_1^* by setting equation (15.15) equal to 0 and solving for E_1 in terms of E_2.

$$E_1^*(E_2) = M - 0.5 \cdot E_2, \tag{15.16}$$

where M is the constant

$$M = g/(2\,a) - w\,g/(2\,P_f\,K\,a^2). \tag{15.17}$$

Equation (15.17) is the reaction function for Lobsters 'R Us. The right-hand side is made up of a set of variables none of which is at the discretion of Lobsters 'R Us. The

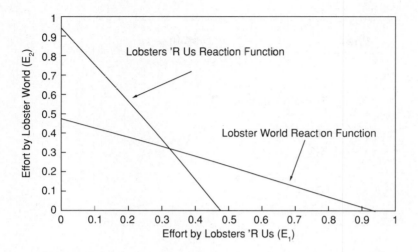

FIGURE 15.10 • The reaction curves for Lobsters 'R Us and Lobster World.

constant M is the profit-maximizing level of effort for either firm if it were the sole owner of the pond. For values of the parameters listed in (15.14), M equals 0.475. At this level of fishing effort, if one firm were to own the pond, then the equilibrium fish stock would be 52,000 fish and the equilibrium catch would be 4,992 fish per period. Similarly, Lobster World's reaction function is given by:

$$E_2^*(E_1) = M - 0.5 \cdot E_1. \tag{15.18}$$

Finding the Nash equilibrium means finding strategies in which no player has an incentive to alter his strategy given the strategy chosen by the other players. That is, if we think of the collection of Nash equilibrium strategies as reflecting a commonly held belief by the players, then this common belief will lead the players to act in accordance with their equilibrium strategy.

The reaction curves of both firms are plotted in Figure 15.11. Only at the intersection of the two reaction functions are the beliefs each player has about the other consistent with the rational behavior of both. At this intersection point, both firms choose an effort level of 0.317 and neither has any incentive to behave differently if each believes the other will choose this level of effort.

Mathematically, it is straightforward to find this intersection. Simply substitute equation (15.18) for E_2 in equation (15.16) and solve the resulting expression for E_1.

$$E_1^* = M - 0.5 \cdot (M - 0.5 \cdot E_1^*) \tag{15.19}$$

or

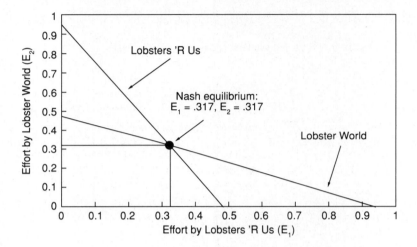

FIGURE 15.11 • The reaction curves for Lobsters 'R Us and Lobster World.

$$E_1^* = E_2^* = (2/3) \cdot M. \tag{15.20}$$

Equation (15.20) predicts the two firms will collectively expend one-third more effort than either would were it the sole owner of the pond.

15.6 • Some efficiency implications

Aside from predictions about firm behavior there are also some important efficiency implications from this analysis. We know that no owner of the pond would ever employ so much effort as to be at a point of negative marginal product, since this would be inconsistent with profit maximization. But consider what happens if there are two firms, neither of which owns the pond.

Once again let us make use of the specific values for g, a, K, w, and P_f listed in equation (15.17). As we saw in the previous section, the Nash equilibrium level of effort for each firm equals 0.317, and each catches 2,322 fish. Therefore, the total level of fishing effort equals 0.634, resulting in a total catch of 4,644 fish. Equation (15.5) tells us, however, that the same number of fish could be caught by expending an effort of only 0.367 units. This means 0.267 units of effort are being wasted. As a result, about 42% of the total cost of harvesting the 4,644 fish brought in by the two firms could be avoided if the strategic interaction between the two firms could be avoided.[1] In this example there is a large technical inefficiency. You should try other parameters and see how responsive the technical inefficiency is to them.

15.7 • Summary

The prediction that competing firms or individuals will "waste" common resources is an important conclusion of game theory. It has implications for dinner party hosts (how to set up a table so that party-goers get maximum enjoyment), city planners (how to reduce rush hour traffic costs), and international lawyers (how to reduce the probability of conflicts when natural resources cross international boundaries).

A similar problem exists when there is a common output. For example, suppose that the output of a good or service can be shared by a number of people. Defense services are a case in point. If an F-14 fighter jet is based near a community, then all members of the community simultaneously get the benefits the F-14 provides. Any single person's consumption of the defense capabilities of the F-14 fighter do not in any way diminish their neighbor's consumption of these services. Defense is said to be a *public good*. There is a serious question as to whether private firms will provide goods in which the output can be shared in this way, because it may be difficult for firms to induce people to buy their product. If you have a choice of whether to buy a public good or wait until one of your neighbors buys it, you might very well choose to wait. Unlike situations in which there is a common input—as with the fishery problem, where there will likely be too many resources devoted to fishing—when there is a common output there will be too few private resources devoted to producing it. You will see more about the problem of providing public goods in Part Four.

The game we studied in this example assumed only two players. Unfortunately, in general, the inefficiencies associated with the use of common resources only become more severe as the number of players increases.

15.8 • Further Reading

An early non-game-theoretic treatment of the fishery problem is Gordon Scott, "Economic Theory of a Common Property Resource: The Fishery," *Journal of Political Economy* 62 (1954), pp.124–142. A more modern dynamic treatment of the same

---

[1]One way in which this strategic behavior could be avoided, at least in the short run, is if the two fishing companies merge into one fishing company. But this would begin to undermine the extent of competition in the fish market.

problem is Gordon Munroe, "Economics of Fishing: An Introduction," in John Butlin, ed., *Economics of Environmental and Natural Resource Policy* (Boulder, CO: Westview Press, 1981).

15.9 • Exercises

Exercise 15.1   Consider two fisheries fishing from the same pond. The fish stock in the pond has a biological growth rate of 20% per month, and the carrying capacity of the pond is 50,000 fish. The technical catch rate per unit of effort for either firm is 0.005 per month. Both firms are price takers in the input and output markets. The market price of fish is $1 per pound, and the price per unit of effort is $125.

(a) Find the amount of fish that will be caught by either firm if the firms employ Nash equilibrium strategies.
(b) Find the magnitude of the technical inefficiency that results if both firms employ Nash equilibrium strategies.

Exercise 15. 2   Suppose that all the conditions in the previous question apply except that one firm has a cost per unit of effort of $150 and the other firm has a cost per unit of effort of $100. How will your answers to parts (a) and (b) change?

Exercise 15.3   Consider two people eating from a communal bowl of popcorn. There are a total of 1,000 kernels in the bowl. Each person must simultaneously decide how many kernels to eat per minute. Call this variable r_1 for one person and r_2 for the other person. The net benefits any person gets from eating popcorn can be written as $B_i = 4 \cdot Q_i + 50 \cdot r_i - r_i^2$, where Q_i is the number of kernels i eats. The proportion of all the kernels that any person gets is equal to the relative speed with which the person eats. So person 1 will get $r_1/(r_1 + r_2)$ percent of all the kernels.

(a) If only one person eats popcorn, how many kernels per minute will maximize net benefits?
(b) Derive the reaction function for each person and find the pure-strategy Nash equilibria. (*Hint*: Use the fact that the players' schedule is symmetric between the two players.)

• CHAPTER 16 •

Strategic Trade Policy

16.1 • Introduction

Subsidization of firms that engage in international trade is a common practice throughout the world. Yet in the standard competitive two-good, two-country model of international trade, such subsidies do not appear to make economic sense. The standard model predicts that an export subsidy will shift the terms of trade against the country imposing it, thereby hurting itself and benefiting overseas consumers. In the standard model, we should readily welcome the exports of any country that is foolish enough actually to subsidize our consumption of its goods.

Why would so many countries in the world adopt policies that appear not to be in their best interests? Before we simply conclude that governments are irrational (or captives of certain industries), we would do well to note that the standard trade theory makes other predictions that are not consistent with the evidence.

One of these predictions is that a country will maximize its national income by specializing in the production of those goods in which it has a **comparative advantage** and importing those goods in which it has a comparative disadvantage.[1] If we assume that countries act so as to maximize their income and wealth, then the theory predicts that most trade will take place between countries that have very different

---

[1] The specialization theorem assumes every country makes up a relatively small proportion of world markets.

endowments, technologies, or preferences, and there will be little intraindustry trade (trade in the same category of goods) between nations. Instead, countries will export those goods in which they have a comparative advantage and will import those in which they have a comparative disadvantage.

Yet, international trade statistics reveal that a large proportion of world trade is carried out by a relatively small number of highly industrialized nations. These countries have similar endowments of factors (particularly human and physical capital), technologies, and consumer preferences, and they ship very similar goods to each other.

Fortunately, classical trade theory can be brought into alignment with the data by relaxing the assumption that all markets are perfectly competitive. In this application we will show how a domestic monopolist may find it profitable to sell in a foreign market against a foreign monopolist even if prices in both countries are the same and the production costs of both firms are the same.

We will then go on to show that export subsidies can allow a country to shift monopoly rents away from the foreign producer toward the domestic producer. If the shift in profits is greater than the cost of the subsidy, then it is rational for the government to grant a subsidy to the domestic firm. Of course, when both countries can do this, the resulting game played between the two governments is a prisoner's dilemma and both countries end up worse off. As a result, negotiated reductions in export subsidies—such as those currently being negotiated under the General Agreement on Tariffs and Trade (GATT)—will make both countries better off.

16.2 · Imperfect competition and intraindustry trade

Suppose two countries, the United States (US) and Great Britain (GB), both produce coal. There is only one coal producer in each country: Americoal (A) and Britcoal (B). For simplicity of exposition, we will assume both firms produce with the same constant returns-to-scale technology. We will consider the case of increasing returns to scale later. We will select our units so the marginal cost of production in both countries equals $1 billion per unit. Unless stated otherwise, the price of coal will be quoted in billions of dollars ($billions) per unit, and firm revenue, cost, and profits will be quoted in billions of dollars.

Again for simplicity, we will assume the domestic demand for coal in the two countries is the same and can be represented by the following linear inverse demand functions:

$$P_{US}(Q_{US}) = 8 - Q_{US.} \tag{16.1a}$$

$$P_{GB}(Q_{GB}) = 8 - Q_{GB}, \tag{16.1b}$$

where P_{US} and P_{GB} are the prices of coal in the US and Britain, measured in dollars per metric ton, and Q_{US} and Q_{GB} are the quantities consumed in the US and Britain.

Suppose there is no trade in coal—say because of extremely high tariffs or transportation costs. Such a situation is referred to as **autarky**. Then each firm will choose its output so as to maximize the following "autarkic profit functions:"

$$\pi^A(Q_{US}) = (8 - Q_{US}) \cdot Q_{US} - Q_{US}, \tag{16.2a}$$

$$\pi^B(Q_{GB}) = (8 - Q_{GB}) \cdot Q_{GB} - Q_{GB}. \tag{16.2b}$$

We leave it to the reader to show that the profit-maximizing output level and price in each country is the same: 3.5 units and $4.5 per unit. Both Americoal and Britcoal earn a profit of $11.25 billion. These monopoly rents are shared by the firm's shareholders, the government (through taxes), and the coal miners.

Now suppose free trade opens up between Britain and the US. We will assume that transportation costs eat up one-third of the coal shipped in either direction. That is, if three units of coal are shipped by Americoal to Britain, then only two units actually reach Britain.[2] Because the pretrade price in both countries is the same, yet transportation costs are so high, it would appear that neither firm would want to export coal to the other. But this is wrong. The marginal cost of producing a unit of coal is $1 billion, but the marginal revenue earned from exporting this coal to the other country equals $3 billion · 2/3 = $2 billion. The first number is the revenue per unit sold in the other country, and the second is the fraction of coal exported that is actually sold. Beause this is more than the marginal cost of $1 billion the firm will earn marginal profits of $1 billion from entering the foreign market.

Marginal revenue in the foreign market is initially greater than the marginal revenue in the domestic market because in the domestic market the monopolist has to cut the price to *all* customers in order to sell any additional coal. In the foreign market no such cost is incurred; this cost is, instead, borne by the foreign monopolist. As a result, there is a strong incentive for each domestic monopolist to enter the other monopolist's market. Of course, if they both do this, they will drive down the prices in both markets.

Before we go further, we will formalize our trade model as a game. For the sake of simplicity, we will assume the two firms cannot enter into binding agreements with

---

[2]We could assume that the "lost coal" has simply been bartered with the shipping firm for its transportation services. Alternatively, we could assume there is a money charge for transportation, but that the marginal cost of getting a unit of coal to the foreign market is higher than the marginal cost of getting a unit of coal to the domestic market. Our results are the same in either case, but the analysis is simplified by assuming the transportation costs are paid for in coal rather than money.

each other and that they choose their domestic sales and exports simultaneously. This means they play a simultaneous-move, quantity-setting ("Cournot") duopoly game. This game is more complicated than the duopoly games studied in Chapter 12 because there are now two markets to consider and each firm has two quantity decisions. Americoal must choose the amount of coal to sell in the domestic American market, Q_{US}^{A}, and the amount to export to Britain, Q_{US}^{A}. Likewise, Britcoal must choose the amount of coal to sell domestically, Q_{GB}^{B}, and the amount to export to the US, Q_{GB}^{B}. The profit functions of the two firms are given as follows:

$$\pi^{A}(Q_{US}^{A}, Q_{GB}^{A}, Q_{US}^{B}, Q_{GB}^{B}) = P_{US}(Q_{US}^{A} + 2/3 \cdot Q_{US}^{B}) \cdot Q_{US}^{A} \tag{16.3a}$$
$$+ P_{GB}(Q_{GB}^{B} + 2/3 \cdot Q_{GB}^{A}) \cdot 2/3 \cdot Q_{GB}^{A} - (Q_{US}^{A} + Q_{GB}^{A}),$$

$$\pi^{B}(Q_{US}^{A}, Q_{GB}^{A}, Q_{US}^{B}, Q_{GB}^{B}) = P_{GB}(Q_{GB}^{B} + 2/3 \cdot Q_{GB}^{A}) \cdot Q_{GB}^{B} \tag{16.3b}$$
$$+ P_{US}(Q_{US}^{A} + 2/3 \cdot Q_{US}^{B}) \cdot 2/3 \cdot Q_{US}^{B} - (Q_{GB}^{B} + Q_{US}^{B}).$$

Inspection of these profit functions reveals that, because marginal costs are constant, the profit earned by Americoal from its US operations, namely $P_{US}(Q_{US}^{A} + 2/3 \cdot Q_{US}^{B}) \cdot Q_{US}^{A} - Q_{US}^{A}$, depends only on its domestic sales, Q_{US}^{A}, and Britcoal's exports, Q_{US}^{B}. And the profit earned by Americoal from its British operations, namely $P_{GB}(Q_{GB}^{B} + 2/3 \cdot Q_{GB}^{A}) \cdot 2/3 \cdot Q_{GB}^{A} - Q_{GB}^{A}$ depends only on its foreign sales, Q_{GB}^{A}, and Britcoal's domestic sales, Q_{GB}^{B}. The same holds true for Britcoal. This implies our trade game can be modeled as two separate Cournot games, one game played in the American market and the other in the British market. We know how to find the Nash equilibria of two-player Cournot games: We calculate each firm's reaction function and find where the graphs of the two functions intersect. The intersection point represents a pure-strategy Nash equilibrium of the game.

We leave it as an exercise to derive the reaction functions for each firm in each market from the profit functions (16.3a) and (16.3b). These reaction functions have been graphed in Figures 16.1. and 16.2.

Because market demand is the same in both countries and both firms have the same marginal costs, these two games are essentially identical. In equilibrium, in each country the domestic firm produces 5.5 units of coal, 2.5 units for domestic consumption and 3 units for export, and the price equals $3.5 billion per unit.

The resulting "cross-hauling" of coal between the United States and Britain seems inefficient. After all, only two-thirds of the exported coal actually reaches consumers. Given that each firm ships 3 units, this means that 2 units are wasted in shipping coal between the two markets. Given the marginal cost of $1 billion per unit, the waste from cross-hauling comes to $2 billion.

Although it appears that free trade results in a reduction of welfare, this conclusion ignores the pro-competitive effects of trade within each country. Under free trade, 4.5

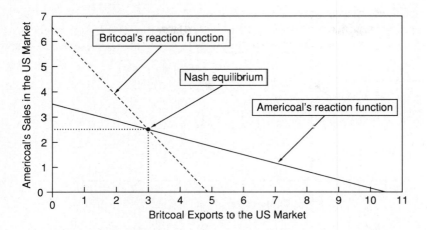

FIGURE 16.1 · Reaction functions for Americoal and Britcoal in the American coal market.

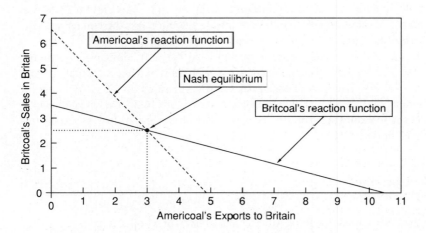

FIGURE 16.2 · Reaction functions for Americoal and Britcoal in the British coal market.

units of coal are consumed in each country (2.5 units provided by the domestic producer and 2 units provided by the foreign producer) at a market price of $3.5 billion per unit, compared to consumption of 3.5 units (provided entirely by the domestic producer) at a price of $4.5 billion per unit under autarky. So more coal is consumed in each country under free trade than under autarky and this coal is sold for

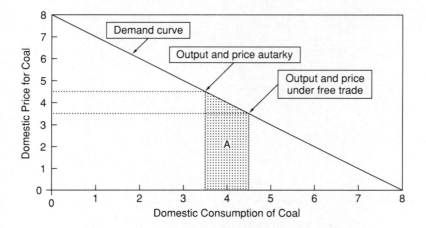

FIGURE 16.3 • Consumer surplus increases by $4 billion when free trade is introduced.

less. Each firm earns a profit of $4 billion from its foreign sales and $6.25 billion from its domestic sales, or $10.25 billion overall—$1 billion less than under autarky. The fall in profits equals the value of the coal lost in transit.

Clearly, the coal consumers gain from trade and the coal company owners and workers lose. Furthermore, the gain in consumer welfare is much greater than the loss in producer welfare. The gain in consumer surplus generated by the introduction of free trade equals the area of the region labeled A in Figure 16.3.[3] This area equals $4 billion, so net welfare (the sum of consumer and producer surplus) has been improved by $4 billion – $1 billion = $3 billion.

16.3 • Export subsidies

Suppose the US government gives Americoal a subsidy of $1 billion for every unit of coal it exports. Because this subsidy will have no effect on Americoal's or Britcoal's profits from their US operations, it will have no effect on the US market. But there is a big effect on the British market. The subsidy is equivalent to a reduction in Americoal's marginal production cost. At every level of domestic sales chosen by Britcoal, Americoal's optimal level of exports is higher than before.

As Figure 16.4 shows, Americoal's reaction curve shifts rightward. Americoal's

---

[3]If coal demand is income neutral, then the market demand curve is identical to the income-compensated demand curve, which is the appropriate tool to use to derive the change in consumer surplus.

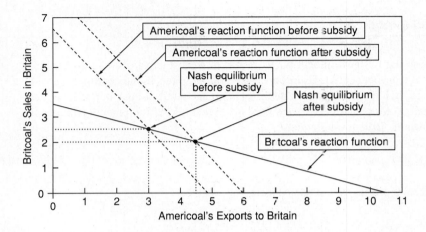

FIGURE 16.4 • An export subsidy shifts Americoal's reaction curve rightward, resulting in an increase in exports to Britain and a decrease in domestic sales by Britcoal.

TABLE 16.1   Market equilibrium in Britain before and after export subsidy

Subsidy	Q^A_{GB}	Q^B_{GB}	P_{GB}	π^A	π^B	Subsidy
No	3	2.5	3.5	4	6.25	0
Yes	4.5	2	3	9	4	4.5
Change	+1.5	−0.5	−0.5	+5	−2.25	+4.5

equilibrium output increases by 50% (from 3 to 4.5 units) and Britcoal's falls 20% (from 2.5 to 2 units). The price falls, but only by 14% (from $3.5 billion per unit to $3 billion per unit). As a result, Americoal's profits go up from $4 billion to $9 billion (inclusive of the subsidy), and Britcoal's profits go down from $6.25 billion to $4 billion. Because the subsidy leaves US coal prices unchanged, it increases Americoal's profits by $5 billion, yet costs the US government only $4.5 billion. Overall, the US is better off by $0.5 billion.[4]

---

[4]This conclusion assumes the subsidy is financed by a lump-sum tax on the American coal industry. If the subsidy is financed in any other way, then it may reduce allocative efficiency within the US and redistribute income. In this case, some Americans could be made worse off by the subsidy. We are also ignoring the possibility of retaliation by Britain, which we will examine in the next section.

16.4 • Optimal export subsidies

Suppose the US government wants to set the export subsidy so as to maximize Americoal's profits net of the subsidy. We will refer to this as the "optimal" subsidy. The subsidy will be denoted by s and is paid on each unit of coal shipped, not each unit actually sold (remember that one-third of the coal is lost in shipment). Americoal's profits from its British sales equals

$$\pi_{GB}^{A}(Q_{GB}^{A}, Q_{GB}^{B}, s) = ((8 - Q_{GB}^{B} - 2/3 \cdot Q_{GB}^{A}) \cdot 2/3 + s - 1) \cdot Q_{GB}^{A}, \qquad (16.4a)$$

and Britcoal's profits from its domestic sales equal

$$\pi_{GB}^{B}(Q_{GB}^{A}, Q_{GB}^{B}) = (8 - Q_{GB}^{B} - 2/3 \cdot Q_{GB}^{A} - 1) \cdot Q_{GB}^{B}. \qquad (16.4b)$$

If we maximize π_{GB}^{A} with respect to Q_{GB}^{A}, we obtain Americoal's reaction function:

$$Q_{GB}^{A*}(Q_{GB}^{B}, s) = 39/8 - 3/4 \cdot Q_{GB}^{B} + 9/8 \cdot s, \qquad (16.5a)$$

and if we maximize π_{GB}^{B} with respect to Q_{GB}^{B}, we obtain Britcoal's reaction function:

$$Q_{GB}^{B*}(Q_{GB}^{A}, s) = 7/2 - 1/3 \cdot Q_{GB}^{A}. \qquad (16.5b)$$

Solving these two linear equations simultaneously for Q_{GB}^{A*} and Q_{GB}^{B*} results in the two expressions:

$$Q_{GB}^{A*}(s) = 3 + 3/2 \cdot s, \qquad (16.6a)$$

$$Q_{GB}^{B*}(s) = 5/2 - 1/2 \cdot s, \qquad (16.6b)$$

which implies an equilibrium price of

$$P_{GB}^{*}(s) = A - Q_{GB}^{B*}(s) - 2/3 \cdot Q_{GB}^{A*}(s) \qquad (16.7)$$
$$= 7/2 - 1/2 \cdot s.$$

The government's objective is to maximize

$$V_{US}(s) = \pi_{GB}^{A}(Q_{GB}^{A*}(s), Q_{GB}^{B*}(s), s) - s \cdot Q_{GB}^{A*}(s) \qquad (16.8)$$
$$= 4 + s - 1/2 \cdot s^2.$$

V_{US} is maximized at s = \$1 billion per unit. So the subsidy assumed in Section 16.3 turns out to be optimal.

16.5 • Subsidy wars

If the US can grant an export subsidy to Americoal, then Great Britain can grant an export subsidy to Britcoal. We can model this as a two-stage game. In the first round the American and British governments choose what subsidy to give their domestic coal producer. In the second round, Americoal and Britcoal choose their domestic sales and exports, treating the export subsidies as givens. Depending on what the governments do in the first round, four possible subgames are played in the second round.

If neither country imposes a subsidy, then we know from Section 16.2 that Americoal and Britcoal will each earn $6.25 billion in profits from their domestic sales and $4 billion from their exports, or $10.25 billion overall. From Section 16.4 we know that the optimal export subsidy is $1 billion per unit. If the US is the only country to adopt this optimal subsidy, then we know from Section 16.3 that Americoal continues to earn $6.25 billion in profit from its domestic sales, but now earns $9 billion in profit from its exports to Britain. Total profits net of the $4.5 billion subsidy equals $10.75 billion. Meanwhile, Britcoal's total profits fall to $8 billion ($4 billion domestically and $4 billion from its exports to the US). Because the two markets are assumed to be symmetric, the numbers are simply reversed if Britain is the only country to adopt an optimal subsidy. That is, net of the subsidy, Britcoal's profits increase to $10.75 billion and Americoal's profits fall to $8 billion. Finally, suppose both countries adopt the optimal subsidy. Now each company earns $4 billion from its domestic sales and $9 billion from its exports, so total profits net of the $4.5 billion subsidy paid equals $8.5 billion.

The payoff matrix for the first stage of this game is given in Table 16.2. The reader can readily verify that each government has a dominant strategy: Adopt an export subsidy. Yet, both countries would be better off if they could make a binding agreement not to impose any export subsidies at all. Simply put, the two governments are caught in a prisoner's dilemma.

Many of the world's trading nations are currently negotiating multilateral reductions in their export subsidies through the General Agreement on Tariffs and Trade

TABLE 16.2 Payoff matrix for subsidy game between the United States and Great Britain

		Great Britain	
		No Subsidy	Subsidy
The US	No Subsidy	(10.25, 10.25)	(8, 10.75)
	Subsidy	(10.75, 8) Payoff: (US, Britain)	(8.5, 8.5)

(GATT). These negotiations are not yet completed and may yet fail. Their existence is evidence in favor of our admittedly simple prisoner's dilemma model: No country will unilaterally reduce its export subsidies, yet all countries would benefit from simultaneous reductions or eliminations.

16.6 • Increasing returns to scale

We have assumed so far that both producers have constant returns to scale. Yet monopoly is more usually associated with increasing returns to scale. Fortunately, increasing returns to scale (declining average cost) only strengthen our results.

Assuming no export subsidies and starting from autarky, each monopoly now has *two* incentives to enter the foreign market. First, even if prices in both markets are the same, marginal revenue in the foreign market will be above marginal revenue in the domestic market. Second, exports, by increasing output, drive down the firm's production costs. The equilibrium of the two Cournot games played between the two monopolists will, therefore, involve cross-hauling. Finding the equilibrium of this game, however, is more complicated because each market cannot be treated in isolation.

Increasing returns also increases the incentives to impose an export subsidy. Now, not only does the subsidy shift monopoly rents away from the foreign producer toward the domestic producer, but, by increasing the domestic firm's output, it also reduces the firm's costs. In the two-stage subsidy game, both governments will award export subsidies to their coal producers.

16.7 • Summary

In this chapter we have sought to account for two apparent empirical refutations of classical trade theory: (1) the general popularity of export subsidies simultaneously with the desire of governments to negotiate bilateral subsidy reductions with their main trading partners, and (2) the extensive cross-hauling of similar goods between countries with very similar factor endowments.

Both puzzles can be explained by the existence of extensive market power in some markets. Three firms control most of the international market for commercial aircraft, one firm dominates the international market for mainframe computers, and so on. Domestic monopolists will find it to their advantage to enter foreign markets even if foreign firms are entering the domestic market. The pro-competitive effect of the resulting competition in all markets may increase consumer welfare enough to compensate for the cost of all the "wasteful" transporting of goods.

Furthermore, export subsidies can provide a strategic tool for shifting monopoly rents away from foreign producers to domestic producers. The size of the shift can be large enough to "pay" for the subsidy, making it a rational strategy for a government to pursue even if its goal is to maximize total national income and not just the welfare of the exporting industry. Unfortunately, all countries have this tool at their disposal. If the countries cannot make binding agreements with each other, then the resulting noncooperative subsidy-setting game played between them resembles a multilateral prisoner's dilemma: although no country benefits from unilaterally reducing its subsidies, all would benefit from simultaneous reductions.

16.8 • Further reading

A good, though advanced, survey of the recent literature on trade theory in the presence of imperfect competition is Paul Krugman's contribution to the *Handbook of Industrial Organization,* Vol II, edited by R. Schmalensee and R. Willig (New York: Elsevier Science Publishers B.V., 1989), Chapter 20. A much simpler summary can be found in Krugman's article "Is Free Trade Passe?," *Journal of Economic Perspectives* 1 (1987), pp.131–144. Our model of trade with export subsidies is based on the work of James Brander and Barbara Spencer, "Export Subsidies and International Market Share Rivalry," *Journal of International Economics* 18 (1985), pp. 83–100.

16.9 • Exercises

The problems are based on the Cournot model of Sections 16.2 through 16.5.

Exercise 16.1   Use the profit functions given in equations (16.3a) and (16.3b) to derive algebraic expressions for Americoal's and Britcoal's reaction functions in both the US and the British markets. Find the equilibrium of the two Cournot games.

Exercise 16.2   Suppose the US government "broke up" Americoal into a large number of price-taking firms with constant marginal production costs of $1 billion per unit. What will happen to the market equilibrium in both the US and Britain?

Exercise 16.3   Suppose initially there is free trade in coal between the US and Britain and there are no export subsidies. Now suppose the US imposes a tax, called a *tariff,* of $1 billion per unit on Britcoal's imports into the US. So if the US price of coal is P_{US}, then Britcoal receives only $P_{US} - 1$. Calculate the new reaction function for Britcoal and the new Cournot equilibrium. By how much do Americoal's profits go up? How much tariff revenue is collected by the government? How much does consumer surplus go down? Assuming that the tariff revenue is rebated to consumers, is national welfare enhanced by the tariff or not?

PART FOUR

Games with Private Information

• CHAPTER 17 •

Bayesian Equilibrium

17.1 • Introduction

One of the most important new ideas in economics is that private information is a valuable resource whose exploitation can affect economic and social welfare as much as the exploitation of labor, land, or technology. By *private information* we mean knowledge about the state-of-the-world that is possessed by some players and is not possessed by other players.[1] Examples of private information include: the financial condition of a company that has not yet been revealed by the firm's executives to its stockholders; the willingness of a new job applicant to work overtime in order voluntarily to meet periodic deadlines; the results of a secret poll of a union's members concerning the provisions in a new labor contract.

Unfortunately, economists cannot analyze the production and consumption of information in the same way that they study physical resources such as labor, steel, or wheat. Among its many anomalies, information tends to be indivisible, simultaneously consumable by many people, and capable of causing discontinuous changes in the behavior of those who come to possess it. Classical price theory, with its reliance on marginal analysis, is not capable of handling these features very well. Fortunately, game theory has proved to be a very powerful tool for modeling information and studying its economic role.

---

[1]Private information does not have to be certain information. Private information also exists when one player has a different set of probabilistic beliefs about Nature's actions than another player.

Private information is generally of two kinds: knowledge about the previous actions taken by the players in a game, and knowledge about the state-of-the-world. The first type of private information you already encountered when we examined simultaneous-move games in Part Three. Recall that such games could be modeled as sequential games in which the player who moved "second" was ignorant of the move made by the player who moved "first." That is, information about the first player's move was private to that player. This was displayed on the game tree by including the second player's decision nodes in a single information set.

Because the selection of the state-of-the-world can be modeled as a random "choice" by a fictitious player we have called Nature, the second kind of private information can also be modeled using information sets. For example, suppose one player, Jill, is ignorant of the payoffs of a second player Jack, whose payoffs are either *high* or *low*. The uncertainty arises because Jack's payoffs depend on the state-of-the world. Jack knows the state-of-the-world when he moves, but Jill does not. This can be modeled as follows: Nature moves first and randomly chooses Jack's payoffs. Nature's move is revealed to Jack before he has to make a move, but is never directly revealed to Jill. In this way, extremely complicated forms of knowledge and ignorance can be captured rigorously .

It is impossible to talk about games in which the players have private information without making some type of inference or assumption about players' *beliefs* about other players. To see why, consider your search for a job when you graduate from college. You will have a better sense of what activities you would like to be engaged in than will any potential employer. In the hopes of securing a job offer with some employer, you might very well find it in your interest to try to convince her that the job she has described to you is exactly what you are looking for. The employer's problem is to determine whether or not to *believe* you, and your problem is to make your claim *believable*. As a result, an equilibrium involves not only a collection of strategies, but also a collection of beliefs about the state-of-the-world.

In the sequential- and simultaneous-move games we considered earlier, the players were always assumed to be symmetrically informed about Nature's moves. That is, Nature's moves were always assumed to be immediately observed by all. In such games, any player's choice of action depends only on information that is already known to everyone. Because all players are aware of the informational structure of the game, no action by a player can reveal anything about the state-of-the-world that is not already known to all ("common knowledge"). In games of this kind, expected utility, backwards induction, and Nash equilibrium are the tools required to find the possible mutually rational strategies and beliefs for the players.

In this chapter, we will concentrate on games in which the players are asymmetrically informed about Nature's moves. This introduces a new element into the game: the possibility that an informed player's actions may reveal her private information.

This possibility adds a new dimension to the task of constructing a rational strategy. Players now have to ask themselves: What does it mean about the state-of-the-world if the other player makes some particular move? And players must determine whether their actions can reveal any of their private information to the opposing players.

To get some idea of how this works, consider the following example. A textile firm and a labor union are negotiating a labor contract. The firm and the union each know what contract terms it will accept, but neither of them knows what the opponent will accept or reject. As a result, both sides have an incentive to pretend their positions are different than they are. The labor union will make strong claims about not accepting less than, say, $8.00 per hour, while knowing full well that most of its membership could earn only $7.50 in alternative employment. The firm will claim that a wage payment in excess of, say, $7.25 per hour will force the firm into bankruptcy when, in fact, the firm could afford to pay up to $7.75 and still break even. For these reasons, both sides must question the truthfulness of the positions taken by the opponent.

Because talk is cheap, it is seldom completely credible. In order for the union to convince the management of the firm that they really do have a high reservation wage, the workers may have to do something painful, such as strike. If it is the case that workers will strike more frequently the higher their reservation wages, then a strike will serve as a credible indicator that management must pay more for labor or risk losing its services. But how can the firm make it too expensive for workers with low reservation wages to strike? The answer is simple. Occasionally, the firm must call the union's bluff and risk a strike even though, in the short run, a strike hurts the firm as much as it does the union.

This chapter will introduce some new tools for studying games with private information. The first tool is a simple result from probability theory called Bayes' theorem, which was introduced in Chapter 3. A second tool is an extension of the notion of Nash equilibrium, called a **Bayesian equilibrium.** This chapter presents some tips for finding Bayesian equilibria. Although these tips fall short of a complete recipe, they are capable of finding the Bayesian equilibria for many interesting games.

17.2 • Modeling private information

Consider the following stylized example: A surgeon, Dr. Elizabeth Kutt, performed an appendectomy on a young wife and mother, Marla Smith. During the operation, Ms. Smith died from a hemorrhage. Her husband, Simon Smith, has hired the attorney Ronald Kahn and filed suit against Dr. Kutt for $1 million, alleging malpractice. Mr.

Kahn has agreed to take the case on a contingent fee basis: He receives one-third of whatever Mr. Smith gets through either an out-of-court settlement or a jury award; Mr. Smith has no other litigation expenses.

Dr. Kutt does not have malpractice insurance. As a result, she will have to pay any jury award or settlement as well as all of her legal expenses out of her own pocket. Her one advantage over Mr. Smith, however, is that she knows whether she has committed malpractice or not. By this we mean that if the doctor knows she is innocent, then she also knows that her lawyer will be able to prove this to a jury and that Mr. Smith will lose the court contest. On the other hand, if the doctor knows she is guilty, then she knows that Mr. Kahn will be able to prove this to a jury and that Mr. Smith will win the $1 million in damages he has claimed.[2] Of course, of the $1 million award, Mr. Kahn will receive one-third ($333,333) and Mr. Smith will receive two-thirds ($666,667).

Although Mr. Smith and Mr. Kahn do not know whether Dr. Kutt is guilty of malpractice or not, they know that she knows, and she knows that they know that she knows, and so forth. That is, it is common knowledge that she knows whether she is guilty or innocent (and can prove it in court). We will also suppose that it is common knowledge that half of all deaths during appendectomy surgery involve malpractice by the surgeon.

If the case goes to trial, Dr. Kutt must hire an attorney and incur a $100,000 legal bill. Should the jury find the doctor innocent of malpractice, however, Mr. Smith must reimburse her for this bill. This implies that the doctor loses nothing (besides her time and her good name) by going to court when she is innocent, but risks losing $1.1 million—$1 million to Mr. Smith and his attorney and $100,000 to her own attorney—when she is guilty. Dr. Kutt can avoid this large expense only by reaching an out-of-court settlement with Mr. Smith. For convenience, we have summarized the relevant facts in Table 17.1.

Let us begin by completely describing the game being played, following the guidelines in Chapter 4.

Players: Dr. Kutt, Mr. Smith, and Nature.

Actions: Dr. Kutt has one action: Offer an out-of-court settlement. This nonnegative offer will be denoted by S.[3] Mr. Smith has one action: Accept or reject Dr. Kutt's

---

[2]What is important is not whether she can truly predict the trial outcome with certainty, but whether she believes she can do this and whether Mr. Smith believes she can do this. Of course, such extreme certainty is unlikely. A more realistic assumption is that if the doctor is guilty of malpractice, then she believes it is very likely that Mr. Smith will win the lawsuit. This assumption complicates the analysis without altering the important characteristics of the resulting equilibrium.

[3]Of course, a negative settlement offer can be made. But since it will be rejected without question, we will eliminate it from further consideration.

TABLE 17.1 The malpractice settlement game

Financial facts:

1. Jury award if Dr. Kutt is found guilty	$1 million
2. Jury award if Dr. Kutt is found innocent	$0
3. Mr. Smith's legal fees if he wins	$333,000
4. Mr. Smith's legal fees if he loses	$100,000
5. Mr. Smith's legal fees if he settles	1/3 of settlement
6. Dr. Kutt's legal fees if there is a trial, and she loses	$100,000
7. Dr. Kutt's legal fees if there is a settlement or she wins	$0

Probabilistic facts:

1. One-half of all appendectomy deaths involve malpractice.
2. Dr. Kutt knows for certain whether she committed malpractice.

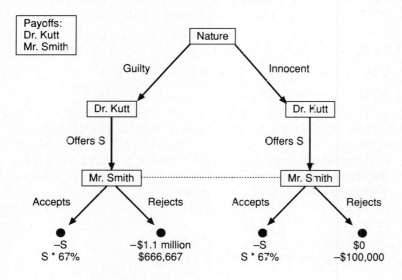

FIGURE 17.1 • The game tree for the settlement game.

offer. This response will be denoted by A. Nature has one action: Choose the surgeon's guilt or innocence. This move will be denoted by G.

Order of play and payoffs: These are shown in the game tree in Figure 17.1. The payoffs assume that both strategic players are selfish and risk-neutral. Therefore each player's von Neumann-Morgenstern utility (VNMU) is captured by the expected dollar payoffs.

Information: Although Nature moves first, this move is observed only by Dr. Kutt; it is not observed by Mr. Smith or his attorney. When a player does not observe some move that occurs before his, he does not know exactly where he is in the game tree. Recall that a players's information set consists of those nodes between which the player cannot distinguish.[4] When Dr. Kutt offers to settle, Mr. Smith does not know whether the doctor is guilty or innocent. This means his two decision nodes lie in the same information set. Using the graphical convention we established in Chapter 3, in Figure 17.1 we have connected Mr. Smith's two decision nodes with a dotted line.

Strategies: A strategy is a rule that tells a player what choice to make at every *information set*. In Mr. Smith's case, this means that his strategy cannot make use of any information other than Dr. Kutt's offer, S. In particular, it cannot make use of Dr. Kutt's guilt or innocence, because Mr. Smith does not know this when he has to decide whether to accept or reject the offer. Mr. Smith has an information set for each of Dr. Kutt's offers. Therefore, a strategy for Mr. Smith can be represented by a function A(S). Here is an example of a possible strategy for Mr. Smith:

$$A(S) = \begin{cases} \text{accept} & \text{if } S \geq \$1 \text{ million.} \\ \text{reject} & \text{if } \$100{,}000 \leq S < \$1 \text{ million.} \\ \text{accept} & \text{if } S < \$100{,}000. \end{cases}$$

Dr. Kutt has two information sets: one corresponding to her being guilty and another corresponding to her being innocent. A strategy for Dr. Kutt, therefore, consists of two offers: one offer when she is guilty, denoted S(guilty), and another offer when she is innocent, denoted S(innocent). These offers need not be different. An example of a possible strategy for Dr. Kutt is:

S(guilty) = $500,000.

S(innocent) = $50,000.

17.3 • Beliefs

Suppose Dr. Kutt offers Mr. Smith $500,000. If Mr. Smith accepts, then he gets two-thirds of the settlement or $333,333 for certain. If he rejects the offer and goes to court, however, he faces a very uncertain outcome because of his ignorance about Dr. Kutt's

---

[4]A reasonable understanding of information sets is crucial to the following analysis. You may want to review the material in Chapter 3 before proceeding.

guilt. That is, going to court is tantamount to playing a lottery. In order to make a rational decision, Mr. Smith must be able to calculate the expected utility of this lottery. This calculation requires him to multiply the VNMU of each outcome by the probability this outcome occurs and add these weighted utilities together. There remains one problem: What is the probability of winning or losing the lawsuit?

The simple (and simple-minded) response to this problem is to argue that since half of all appendectomy deaths are attributable to malpractice, there is a 50% chance that the doctor is guilty. The problem with this approach is that it ignores the possible information embedded in the offer made by Dr. Kutt. It is very naive to believe that there is a 50% chance that Dr. Kutt is guilty of malpractice just because 50% of all appendectomy deaths are due to malpractice. As we will see, a more intelligent method of calculating beliefs is to have them depend on the offer Dr. Kutt makes.

At every information set, the player making the decision forms an assessment of the probability of being at each decision node in the set. We will refer to this collection of probability assessments as the **player's beliefs.** In our settlement game, Dr. Kutt's beliefs are trivial, since the doctor's two information sets each contain only one decision node.[5] Mr. Smith's beliefs, however, are not trivial. He has an information set for every possible settlement offer Dr. Kutt can make to him. Each of these information sets contains two decision nodes—one that corresponds to the doctor being guilty and one that corresponds to her being innocent. At each of these information sets, Mr. Smith must form a probability assessment that the doctor is guilty. The probability that the doctor is guilty given she made an offer of S dollars will be denoted $\pi_g(S)$.

Table 17.2 displays some possible beliefs for Mr. Smith. Suppose Mr. Smith has the "naive" belief given in Table 17.2: He believes the doctor has a 50% probability of being guilty regardless of what Dr. Kutt offers him. The expected payoff to Mr. Smith of going to court, based on this belief, equals the legal compensation he must pay Dr. Kutt if Dr. Kutt is innocent times the probability Dr. Kutt is innocent, plus the jury award (after legal fees) if Dr. Kutt is guilty times the probability of Dr. Kutt being guilty, or $-\$100,000 \cdot 50\% + \$666,666 \cdot 50\% = \$283,333$. Mr. Smith's optimal decision is now easy to determine: He should reject any offer that nets him less than $283,333 and accept any offer that nets him more than $283,333. Since Mr. Smith's lawyer takes one-third of any settlement, this means that he should reject a settlement offer less than $425,000 and accept a settlement offer greater than $425,000. Mr. Smith is indifferent between accepting and rejecting an offer of $425,000; for the moment, we will assume he accepts the offer. Assuming this is the strategy chosen by Mr. Smith, we can now use backwards induction to obtain a simpler game tree

---

[5]Because Dr. Kutt knows where she is on the game tree, the probability of being at any decision node is either 1 or 0.

TABLE 17.2   Possible beliefs for Mr. Smith

Naive belief:
$\pi_g(S) = 50\%$ for every offer S.

More sophisticated belief:

$$\pi_g(S) = \begin{cases} 1 & \text{if } S \geq \$1 \text{ million.} \\ \\ 0 & \text{if } S < \$1 \text{ million.} \end{cases}$$

Very sophisticated belief:

$$\pi_g(S) = \begin{cases} 1 & \text{if } S \geq \$1 \text{ million.} \\ 50\% & \text{if } \$100,000 < S \leq \$1 \text{ million.} \\ 0 & \text{if } S \leq \$100,000. \end{cases}$$

in which the only decision nodes belong to Dr. Kutt. This game tree is shown in Figure 17.2.

If Dr. Kutt is guilty, then any settlement offer of less than $425,000 will be rejected and she will end up in court, which will cost her $1.1 million. On the other hand, a settlement offer greater than or equal to $425,000 will be accepted and the case will never come to trial. Thus, the payoff to Dr. Kutt if she is guilty can be

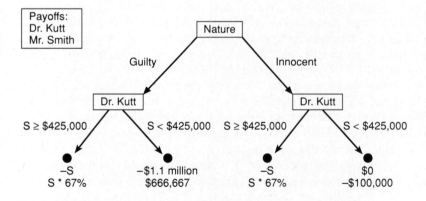

FIGURE 17.2 • The game tree, properly pruned, for the settlement game assuming naive beliefs on the part of Mr. Smith.

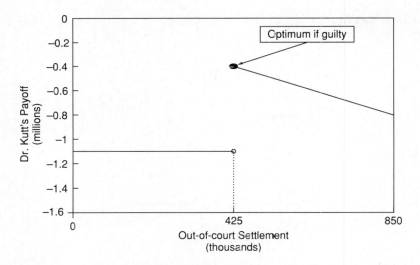

FIGURE 17.3 · Dr. Kutt's payoffs for different settlement offers, assuming she is guilty and Mr. Smith is naive.

expressed as follows:

$-$ \$1.1 million   if S < \$425,000.

$-$ S   if S ≥ \$425,000.

In Figure 17.3 we have plotted Dr. Kutt's payoff as a function of her offer under the assumption that she is guilty. As can be readily seen, Dr. Kutt's optimal action is to offer Mr. Smith \$425,000.

If Dr. Kutt is innocent, then a settlement offer of less than \$425,000 will be rejected but the doctor will win in court. The payoff in this case is \$0. A settlement offer of greater than or equal to \$425,000 will be accepted. The payoff to Dr. Kutt if she is innocent can be expressed as follows:

         \$0   if S < \$425,000.

        $-$ S   if S ≥ \$425,000.

Figure 17.4 contains the payoffs to Dr. Kutt if she is innocent. Clearly, the optimal action is to offer less than \$425,000 (it makes no difference how much the offer is).

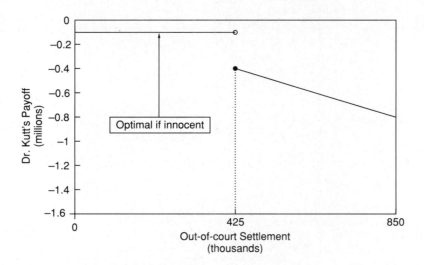

FIGURE 17.4 • Dr. Kutt's payoffs for different settlement offers, assuming she is not guilty and Mr. Smith is naive.

17.4 • Forming rational beliefs using Bayesian updating

As you may have already noticed, the analysis we just performed has a disturbing feature: Mr. Smith's "naive" belief about the doctor's guilt ignores the information contained in Dr. Kutt's offer. Mr. Smith can see that Dr. Kutt's optimal response to his strategy is to make a different settlement offer when the doctor knows she is innocent than when she knows she is guilty. As a result, Mr. Smith can reason that *the doctor's offer reveals her guilt or innocence.*

But if Mr. Smith can deduce the doctor's guilt or innocence, then he can deduce the outcome of a court contest. On the basis of this information, it is rational for Mr. Smith to change his strategy: He will reject an offer of $425,000 or any offer between $425,000 and $1,000,000, and will accept any offer below $425,000 or above $1,000,000. Unfortunately (for Mr. Smith), the doctor's optimal response to this new strategy by Mr. Smith is always to offer him $0. Now, however, the doctor's offer contains no information about her guilt or innocence. We seem to be caught in a vicious circle. Although it is relatively easy to see that the naive belief is a poor one, it is much harder to see with what Mr. Smith should replace it.

Consider how the naive strategy was devised. Although Mr. Smith cannot be sure of Dr. Kutt's guilt or innocence, he is not totally ignorant of his chances of winning a juried trial either. He is aware that, when an appendectomy has resulted in death, 50% of the time the surgeon has been guilty of malpractice. We will refer to this probability as Mr. Smith's **prior belief** about the doctor's guilt. In the previous discussion this prior belief served as the basis behind the naive strategy. We need a method for Mr. Smith to form "rational beliefs" based solely on his knowledge of the game, his prior beliefs about the doctor's guilt, and his belief about the strategy the doctor will adopt. The method we will use is called **Bayesian updating.**

Bayesian updating involves the use of Bayes' theorem, which is an identity concerning conditional probabilities. As you saw in Chapter 3, Bayes' theorem can be stated as follows:

$$P(A \mid B) = \frac{P(B \mid A) \cdot P(A)}{P(B \mid A) \cdot P(A) + P(B \mid \text{not } A) \cdot P(\text{not } A),} \qquad (17.1)$$

where A and B represent any two arbitrary events and $P(\text{not } A) = 1 - P(A)$. $P(A)$ is called the **prior probability** that the event A will occur and $P(A \mid B)$ is called the **posterior probability** that the event A will occur, given that the event B has occurred.

Let A be the event "the doctor is guilty" and let B(S) be the event "the doctor offered S to Mr. Smith." Then the term on the left-hand side of equation (17.1), $P(A \mid B(S))$, is the probability the doctor is guilty given she offered S to Mr. Smith. More to the point, $P(A \mid B(S))$ is Mr. Smith's **rational belief** about the doctor's guilt based on an offer of S. We propose that $\pi_g(S) = P(A \mid B(S))$. In order to calculate $P(A \mid B(S))$ using Bayes' theorem, we need to know all of the probabilities that appear on the right-hand side of equation (17.1).

$P(A)$ is the probability the doctor is guilty before she makes her offer, and $P(\text{not } A)$ is the probability the doctor is innocent before she makes her offer. The obvious values to use for $P(A)$ and $P(\text{not } A)$ are Mr. Smith's prior beliefs, so $P(A) = P(\text{not } A) = 50\%$. $P(B(S) \mid A)$ is the probability Dr. Kutt will offer S to him when she is guilty; and $P(B(S) \mid \text{not } A)$ is the probability Dr. Kutt will offer S when she is innocent. These two conditional probabilities form part of a (possibly mixed) strategy for Dr. Kutt. To apply Bayes' theorem, Mr. Smith needs only to hypothesize a strategy for Dr. Kutt. In a moment you will see why this is useful, but first consider an example.

Let us suppose Mr. Smith hypothesizes that Dr. Kutt's strategy is to offer him S (with certainty) when she is guilty and to offer \$0 (with certainty) when she is innocent. Given these presumptions, Bayesian updating leads to the following beliefs for Mr. Smith.

$$\pi_g(S) = P(A \mid B(S)) \qquad (17.2)$$

$$= \frac{P(B(S) \mid A) \cdot 0.5}{P(B(S) \mid A) \cdot 0.5 + P(B(S) \mid \text{not } A) \cdot 0.5}$$

$$
= \begin{cases} 1 \cdot 0.5 \div (1 \cdot 0.5 + 0 \cdot 0.5) & \text{if } S = 500,000, \\ 0 \cdot 0.5 \div (0 \cdot 0.5 + 1 \cdot 0.5) & \text{if } S = \$0, \\ \text{undefined} & \text{otherwise} \end{cases}
$$

$$
= \begin{cases} 1 & \text{if } S = \$500,000, \\ 0 & \text{if } S = \$0, \\ \text{undefined} & \text{otherwise.} \end{cases}
$$

Notice that Bayes' theorem cannot be used to determine $\pi_g(S)$ for offers other than $500,000 or $0, because Dr. Kutt's strategy assigns a zero probability to those offers. That is, Bayes' theorem places no constraints on Mr. Smith's beliefs about Dr. Kutt's guilt when the doctor makes a move that is inconsistent with the strategy Mr. Smith believes the doctor is using.[6]

17.5 · Bayesian equilibrium

Nash equilibrium requires that each player's strategy be an optimal response to the equilibrium strategies of all the other players. In games with imperfect information, however, there exists a potential problem when a player has to make a move at a decision node that is contained in an information set with other decision nodes. When the player makes a decision at this point in the game, she cannot be sure how the game will be played out thereafter. As a result, she cannot be sure which move at this node is her "best" one. We can resolve the problem by having every player form a belief about which node in the information set has been reached. If the belief is nonprobabilistic, then we can proceed as before. If the belief is probabilistic, then every action results in a lottery. As long as the von Neumann-Morgenstern axioms hold, these lotteries can be ranked according to their *expected* utility and an optimal action can still be determined.

In games with private information, specifying an equilibrium necessitates specifying every player's strategies and beliefs. First, in order for each player's strategy to be rational, the collection of strategies must constitute a Nash equilibrium. That is, each player's equilibrium strategy must be an optimal response to her opponent's equilibrium strategies, given her knowledge of the game tree, her private information, and her beliefs. Second, these strategies must not involve "incredible" threats. Put another way, the strategies must be subgame perfect.

---

[6]There have been a number of proposals as to what beliefs Mr. Smith should form in situations such as this, but they are beyond the level of this textbook.

In order for the collection of beliefs to be rational, each player's belief must be derivable from the common prior belief and the other players' equilibrium strategies using Bayesian updating. Such mutually consistent strategies and beliefs constitute a **Bayesian equilibrium.**

Definition   A Bayesian equilibrium exists when two conditions are met:

1. The collection of strategies constitute a subgame perfect Nash equilibrium, given the player's beliefs.
2. Every player's beliefs can be derived using Bayesian updating, the equilibrium strategies of the other players, and the common prior beliefs about Nature's moves.

At this point you may be bothered by a certain circularity in the reasoning behind a Bayesian equilibrium: Mr. Smith's optimal strategy depends on his beliefs about Dr. Kutt's guilt or innocence. Dr. Kutt's optimal strategy depends on Mr. Smith's optimal strategy, which implies that it also depends on Mr. Smith's beliefs. But Mr. Smith's beliefs depend on Dr. Kutt's optimal strategy, which implies that it depends on Mr. Smith's beliefs. This circularity is not that different from what we encountered in Chapter 11 when we looked at Nash equilibrium for simultaneous-move games. This should not be surprising given that simultaneous-move games are games with a type of private information. This information consists of the player's move. The concept of Bayesian equilibrium is no more or less circular than the notion of Nash equilibrium itself.

17.6 • A Bayesian equilibrium for the malpractice settlement game

It is one thing to define a Bayesian equilibrium, and quite another to find one. In many instances in economics, finding an equilibrium involves the use of an *algorithm,* that is, a "recipe" or well-defined plan of attack. For example, one algorithm for finding the equilibrium price in a perfectly competitive market is to plot the supply and demand curves and find where the curves intersect. In Chapter 5, to give another example, we presented the algorithm of backwards induction for finding the sub-game perfect equilibrium of a sequential-move game.

Unhappily, there is no well-established algorithm for finding Bayesian equilibria. This, as you might imagine, is extremely frustrating. One crude (i.e., not very helpful) algorithm for finding a Bayesian equilibrium has three steps: (1) propose a possible set of strategies and beliefs; (2) check to see if the proposed strategies satisfy the first condition of the definition; and (3) check to see if the beliefs satisfy the second condition of the definition. Because there are frequently a very large number of possible strategies and beliefs, this algorithm will often take a long time to find an equilibrium. Furthermore, once you have located a Bayesian equilibrium for a game, you cannot be sure it is the *only* Bayesian equilibrium. In general, there will be many equilibria.

All this serves as a warning for what is about to follow. We will now derive one Bayesian equilibrium for the settlement game. The purpose of this detailed derivation is to provide some tips and guides about how to pare down the possible strategies and beliefs in order to arrive at those that constitute an equilibrium. What we propose is *not a complete recipe or algorithm.*

In the settlement game, Mr. Smith must decide between a certain outcome if he accepts the doctor's offer and an uncertain outcome if he rejects it. A belief (any belief) about the outcome of the lottery transforms Mr. Smith's decision from one in which he has incomplete information about the outcome of his actions into a well-defined decision problem with uncertainty. Mr. Smith chooses the lottery with the highest expected utility.

Tip 17.1 Convert the game from one with incomplete information to a decision problem with uncertainty.

If $\pi_g(S)$ is Mr. Smith's assessment of the probability that the doctor is guilty given an offer S, then the expected payoff from going to court equals

$$- \$100{,}000 \cdot (1 - \pi_g(S)) + \$1 \text{ million} \cdot \pi_g(S). \tag{17.3}$$

Because Mr. Smith can avoid going to court by accepting a settlement offer, the preceding equation is very helpful in deciding whether to accept an offer. Mr. Smith's optimal strategy is given in Table 17.3. Now we will eliminate from consideration some of Dr. Kutt's strategies because they are dominated by other strategies.

Tip 17.2 Find and eliminate dominated strategies.

First, Dr. Kutt will never make an out-of-court settlement if she is innocent of malpractice, because she has nothing to lose by going to court. That is, a strategy in

TABLE 17.3 Mr. Smith's optimal strategy

Accept the offer if $S > - \$100{,}000 + \pi_g(S) \cdot \$1.1$ million.
Reject the offer if $S < - \$100{,}000 + \pi_g(S) \cdot \$1.1$ million.
Accept or reject if $S = - \$100{,}000 + \pi_g(S) \cdot \$1.1$ million.

which the doctor makes any settlement with Mr. Smith when she is innocent is dominated by a strategy of offering $0 *regardless of how Mr. Smith responds to the offer*.

Suppose Dr. Kutt always offers $0 when she is innocent. Mr. Smith, using Bayesian updating to calculate $\pi_g(S)$, must believe with certainty that a nonzero settlement offer implies Dr. Kutt is guilty. That is, $\pi_g(S) = 1$ whenever S > $0. It now follows from Table 17.3 that Mr. Smith will *never* accept an offer between $0 and $1 million, will *always* accept an offer above $1 million, and is indifferent between accepting and rejecting an offer of $1 million. We will initially assume that Mr. Smith always accepts $1 million offers. If we did not end up with an equilibrium after making this assumption, we would have to return to this stage of our analysis and drop it.

Tip 17.3 Use whatever you can deduce about the optimal strategy for one player to update the beliefs and strategies of the other players.

If Dr. Kutt is guilty and makes an offer between $0 and $1 million, Mr. Smith will reject the offer, and the doctor will pay $1.1 million—a $1 million judgment plus $100,000 in legal fees. The doctor is better off avoiding court by simply offering $1 million. Likewise, the doctor is better off offering $1 million than offering more than $1 million, because Mr. Smith will accept all such offers. From this we can conclude that the only offers Dr. Kutt will make are either $1 million or $0. The doctor offers $1 million only when she is guilty and offers $0 when she is innocent. But she may sometimes bluff and offer $0 even though she is guilty.

Tip 17.4 Use backwards induction to eliminate sequentially dominated strategies.

The sequential elimination of dominated strategies and the sequential refining of beliefs have taken us a long way. We have been able to narrow down Dr. Kutt's Bayesian equilibrium strategy to one of three:

> *Honest strategy:* Always offer $1 million when guilty and always offer $0 when innocent.
>
> *Dishonest strategy:* Always offer $0 whether guilty or innocent.
>
> *Deception strategy:* Always offer $0 when innocent, but when guilty offer $0 with probability p and offer $1 million with probability 1 − p.

Tips 17.2, 17.3, and 17.4 will get us no further. At this point, we must simply test each of these possible strategies in turn to see if they form part of an equilibrium. The testing is done as follows: Starting from the proposed strategy for Dr. Kutt, we use Bayesian updating to determine Mr. Smith's beliefs. We then use Mr. Smith's beliefs and Table 17.3 to determine his optimal response to the doctor's strategy. Finally, we use backwards induction to determine the doctor's optimal response to Mr. Smith's strategy. If we end up with the strategy we started with, then we have found a Bayesian equilibrium. If not, the proposed equilibrium must be discarded and another one tested.

Tip 17.5   Propose a specific strategy when you get stuck (we are stuck) and check it against the requirements of a Bayesian equilibrium.

Suppose Dr. Kutt adopts the "honest" strategy. Given this strategy, Mr. Smith will conclude that an offer of $0 implies the doctor is innocent and will always accept it. But if Mr. Smith will always accept an offer of $0, then the guilty doctor should exploit this and always offer $0 as well, a contradiction. So the honest strategy cannot be part of a Bayesian equilibrium.

Tip 17.6   Propose another strategy and check it against the requirements of a Bayesian equilibrium.

Now suppose the doctor adopts the "dishonest" strategy and always offers $0. Bayes' theorem implies that the doctor's offer contains no information about her guilt or innocence. As a result, the posterior probability of the doctor being guilty equals the prior probability of 50%. It follows from Table 17.3 that Mr. Smith will reject the offer. But if this is true and the doctor is guilty, then the doctor should always offer $1 million and avoid needlessly incurring legal costs. The contradiction implies that this strategy is not part of a Bayesian equilibrium.

This leaves only the "deception" strategy. This is a mixed strategy in which the doctor randomly chooses between the honest strategy and the dishonest strategy. Under this strategy, the doctor offers $0 when she is innocent. When she is guilty, however, she offers nothing ("bluffs") with probability p and offers $1 million ("admits her guilt") with probability $1 - p$.

Tip 17.7   Learn from your failures!

If Dr. Kutt plays a mixed strategy, then Mr. Smith must play a mixed strategy as well. For if Mr. Smith always accepts an offer of $0, then Dr. Kutt will always want to offer $0 when she is guilty; and if Mr. Smith always rejects an offer of $0, then the doctor will never want to offer $0 when she is guilty. So Mr. Smith's best response to the doctor's deception strategy is to play a mixed strategy himself: He always accepts an offer of $1 million, but he accepts an offer of $0 ("drops his suit") with probability q and rejects it ("calls the doctor's bluff") with probability $1 - q$. He randomizes in order to make bluffing by the doctor costly but not *too* costly.

We have collected our numerous inferences and assumptions about our proposed Bayesian equilibrium into Table 17.4.[7] We have placed question marks where we have not yet deduced the appropriate action or belief.

Tip 17.8   Keep track of what you have learned using a table similar to Table 17.4.

We are almost done. We have narrowed down our search to three numbers: p, q, and $\pi_g(\$0)$. Fortunately, we have three restrictions on these numbers:

1. $\pi_g(\$0)$ must be consistent with Bayes' theorem.
2. The value of p chosen by Dr. Kutt must make Mr. Smith exactly indifferent between accepting and rejecting an offer of $C.
3. The value of q chosen by Mr. Smith must make Dr. Kutt, if guilty, exactly indifferent between offering $0 and $1 million.

TABLE 17.4   A Bayesian equilibrium of settlement game

Dr. Kutt's strategy:
   If guilty, offer:
      $1 million with probability $1 - p$.
      $0 with probability p.
   If innocent, always offer $0

Mr. Smith's strategy:
   Always accept if S ≥ $1 million.
   Always reject if $0 < S < $1 million.
   Accept with probability q if S = $0.

Mr. Smith's belief about Dr. Kutt's guilt:

$$\pi(S) = \begin{cases} 1 & \text{if } S > 0. \\ ? & \text{if } S = \$0. \end{cases}$$

---

[7]There are other Bayesian equilibria that differ from this one in how the doctor behaves when she is innocent.

Tip 17.9 Identify the variables that remain unknown, but that are necessary to determine a Bayesian equilibrium fully and see what restrictions can be placed on their values.

Let A be the event "the doctor is guilty," and let B be the event "the doctor offers $0." Bayes' theorem states

$$\pi_g(\$0) = P(A \mid B) \tag{17.4}$$

$$= \frac{P(B \mid A) \cdot P(A)}{P(B \mid A) \cdot P(A) + P(B) \mid \text{not } A) \cdot P(\text{not } A)}$$

Since $P(B \mid A) = p$, $P(B \mid \text{not } A) = 1$, $P(A) = P(\text{not } A) = 50\%$, we get

$$\pi_g(\$0) = (p \cdot 1/2) \div (p \cdot 1/2 + 1 \cdot 1/2) \tag{17.5}$$

$$= p \div (1 + p).$$

We have already determined that Mr. Smith must randomize whenever Dr. Kutt offers him $0. Such randomization is optimal only if he is indifferent between accepting and rejecting $0. From Table 17.3 we know Mr. Smith is indifferent between accepting and rejecting the settlement offer if and only if

$$\$0 = -\$100,000 + \pi_g(\$0) \cdot \$1.1 \text{ million} \tag{17.6}$$

$$= -\$100,000 + (p \div (1 + p)) \cdot \$1.1 \text{ million},$$

or

$$p = 10\%. \tag{17.7}$$

It now follows from equation (17.4) that $\pi_g(\$0) = 10\% \div 1 + 10\% = 1/11$. Table 17.5 provides an update of our inferences so far.

Tip 17.10 Keep track of where you are.

All that remains is to determine the value of q, the probability that Mr. Smith will accept an offer of $0. Such an action is tantamount to dropping his lawsuit. Because Dr. Kutt is playing a mixed strategy, q must be chosen so that, when guilty, Dr. Kutt will be exactly indifferent between offering $100,000 and $1 million. Her payoff when she offers $1 million is exactly –$1 million. Her payoff when she offers $0 equals

TABLE 17.5   Bayesian equilibrium of settlement game

Dr. Kutt's strategy:
  If guilty, offer:
    $1 million with probability 0.9.
    $0 with probability 0.1.
  If innocent, always offer $0.

Mr. Smith's strategy:
  Always accept if S ≥ $1 million.
  Always reject if $0 < S < $1 million.
  Accept with probability q if S = $0.

Mr. Smith's belief about Dr. Kutt's guilt:

$$\pi(S) = \begin{cases} 1 & \text{if } S > \$1 \text{ million} \\ 1/11 & \text{if } S = \$0. \end{cases}$$

$\$0 \cdot P(\text{Mr. Smith accepts offer of } \$0)$ (17.8)

   $- \$1.1 \text{ million} \cdot P(\text{Mr. Smith rejects offer of } \$0)$

     $= \$0 \cdot q - \$1.1 \text{ million} \cdot (1 - q)$

     $= - \$1.1 \text{ million} + \$1.1 \text{ million} \cdot q.$

The probability q must satisfy the equation

$$- \$1.1 \text{ million} + \$1.1 \text{ million} \cdot q = - \$1 \text{ million} \tag{17.9}$$

or

$$q = 1/11. \tag{17.10}$$

This frequency of acceptance by Mr. Smith will keep the doctor from bluffing more than 10% of the time. If Mr. Smith accepts more frequently than this, then bluffing becomes too tempting to the doctor and she will always bluff. If Smith accepts less frequently than this, then Dr. Kutts will never bluff.

Our final conclusions are summarized in Table 17.6. From our derivations, we know that these beliefs and strategies form a Bayesian equilibrium: Mr. Smith's

---

TABLE 17.6   Bayesian equilibrium of settlement game

Dr. Kutt's strategy:
   If guilty, offer:
      $1 million with probability 0.9.
      $0 with probability 0.1.
   If innocent, always offer $0.

Mr. Smith's strategy:
   Always accept if S ≥ $1 million.
   Always reject if $0 < S < $1 million.
   Accept with probability 1/11 if S = $0.

Mr. Smith's belief about Dr. Kutt's guilt:

$$\pi(S) = \begin{cases} 1 & \text{if } S > \$1 \text{ million} \\ 1/11 & \text{if } S = \$0. \end{cases}$$

---

strategy is optimal given his beliefs, Dr. Kutt's strategy is optimal given Mr. Smith's strategy, and Mr. Smith's beliefs are consistent with Bayes' theorem and the doctor's strategy. This equilibrium will result in one of three observable outcomes:

1. Dr. Kutt offers $1 million and Mr. Smith accepts it.
2. Dr. Kutt offers $0 and Mr. Smith accepts it.
3. Dr. Kutt offers $0 and Mr. Smith rejects it.

The case will end up in court only if outcome 3 occurs. Using the algebra of conditional probabilities, we can calculate the probability Dr. Kutt offers $0, $P(B)$, to be:

$$P(B) = P(B \mid A) \cdot P(A) + P(B \mid \text{not } A) \cdot P(\text{not } A) \tag{17.10}$$

$$= 1/10 \cdot 1/2 + 1 \cdot 1/2$$

$$= 0.55.$$

The probability Mr. Smith will reject an offer of $0 equals $10/11 = 0.909$. So the probability that both events occur and the case ends up in court equals $0.55 \cdot 0.909 = 0.50$.

17.7 • Summary

In this chapter we have shown how to model and analyze games in which some of the players have private information. Information sets provide a concise way of showing what each player knows whenever he or she is called on to move.

When a player reaches a decision node that is contained in an information set along with at least one other node, the outcome of any decision is uncertain. In order to resolve the uncertainty, the player must form a belief, usually probabilistic, of the likelihood that the game has placed him at each possible decision node in the information set. These beliefs allow the player to transform an ill-formed decision with imperfect information into a standard decision with uncertainty.

As a result, the formation of beliefs becomes a central concern. Fortunately, Bayes' theorem places constraints on these beliefs. This leads to the notion of a Bayesian equilibrium as a collection of beliefs with the twin properties:

1. Each player's strategy is an optimal response to the other player's strategies and the player's beliefs about the moves of nature.
2. Each player's beliefs about Nature's moves is consistent with the other player's strategies and Bayes' theorem.

We then found a Bayesian equilibrium of a fairly sophisticated malpractice settlement game. Although we were unable to provide a full-proof algorithm for finding every Bayesian equilibrium of every game, we were able to provide some tips and tricks.

17.8 • Further reading

A slightly more advanced treatment of the material in this chapter can be found in Chapter 5 of *Information and Games* by Eric Rasmusen (New York: Basil-Blackwell, 1989). Many very interesting games involving information are discussed in an informal way in *Thinking Strategically: The Competitive Edge in Business, Politics, and Everyday Life* by Avinash Dixit and Barry Nalebuff (New York: Norton, 1991). An excellent but very advanced treatment analysis of games with private information can be found in Part III of *A Course in Microeconomic Theory* by David Kreps (Princeton, NJ: Princeton University Press, 1990).

The original inspiration for the game between Dr. Kutt and Mr. Smith was the article by Ivan Png, "Strategic Behavior in Suit, Settlement, and Trial," *Bell Journal of Economics* 14 (1983), pp. 539–550.

17.9 • Exercises

The first three exercises all concern the malpractice settlement game discussed in this chapter.

Exercise 17.1   Suppose Doctor Kutt cannot predict the outcome of a court contest with certainty, but she has a better idea than does Mr. Smith of the probability of winning in court. How can the game tree be modified to incorporate this fact?

Exercise 17.2   Suppose the law changes so that Mr. Smith no longer must pay Dr. Kutt's legal expenses if Smith loses in court. How would this affect the game tree?

Exercise 17.3   Continuation of Exercise 17.2. Show that strategies and beliefs in Table 17.6 no longer constitute a Bayesian equilibrium.

Exercise 17.4   Suppose the HAL Corporation is a monopolist in the Cleveland market for mainframe computers. We will suppose that the market is a "natural monopoly," meaning that only one firm can survive in the long run. HAL faces only one potential competitor, DEC. In the first period, HAL moves first and chooses one of two prices for its computers: *high* or *low*. DEC moves second and decides whether to enter the market or not. Here are the first-period profits of the two firms as a function of their decisions:

		HAL	
		High	Low
	Enter	0, 0	0, 0
DEC			
	Stay Out	5, 0	1, 0
		Payoffs are: (HAL, DEC)	

In the second period, three things can occur:

(1) *DEC did not enter in the first period.* Then HAL retains its monopoly forever and earns monopoly profits of $125 - C$, where C is its costs. DEC earns zero profits.

(2) *DEC entered in the first period and has the lower costs.* HAL leaves the market and DEC gets the monopoly forever, earning the monopoly profits of $100 = 125 - 25$, where 25 are its costs, which is common knowledge. HAL earns zero profits.

(3) *DEC entered in the first period and HAL has the lower costs.* In this case, DEC drops out of the market, HAL retains its monopoly forever, and it earns monopoly profits of $125 - C$, where C is its costs. DEC earns zero profits.

DEC's payoff from playing this game equals 0 if it decides to stay out, and it equals the sum of its profits in the two periods minus entry costs of 40 if it decides to enter. HAL's payoff equals the sum of its profits in the two periods. HAL's costs, C, can be either 30 (*high*) or 20 (*low*). This cost information is private information. That is, HAL knows the true value of C when it chooses its first-period price, but DEC does not know this when it decides whether to enter the market or not. DEC's prior belief about C before playing the game is:

Prob(C = 20) = 0.75   (HAL's costs are *low*)

and

Prob(C = 30) = 0.25   (HAL's costs are *high*).

(a) Draw the game tree for this game. Because this is a game with imperfect and asymmetric information, be careful about showing the information sets of both players.
(b) What strategies are available to HAL? What strategies are available to DEC? What beliefs are possible for HAL? What beliefs are possible for DEC?
(c) Show that the following constitutes a Bayesian equilibrium:

HAL's strategy: Choose the low price regardless of cost.

DEC's strategy: Enter if HAL chooses a high price, and stay out if HAL chooses a low price.

DEC's beliefs: P(C = 20 | high) = 0 and P(C = 20 | low) = 0.75.

Exercise 17.5 It is common knowledge that 25% of used 1985 sedans will need extensive repairs in the near future (i.e., they are "lemons") and 75% will need no repairs (i.e., they are "good cars"). It is also common knowledge that: If the car is a lemon, it is worth $1,000 to the buyer and $500 to the seller; if the car is good, it is worth $6,000 to the buyer and $3,000 to the seller; the sellers know the condition of their car but the buyers do not; and buyers and sellers are both risk-neutral. Beverly, who wants to sell her 1985 sedan in order to get cash to pay her college tuition, places a newspaper ad and offers a take-it-or-leave-it price, P. Jim, who wants to buy a 1985 sedan, sees the ad. If he buys the car from Beverly, Jim's payoff equals the difference between the purchase price and the value of the car. Conversely, if she sells the car to Jim, Beverly's payoff equals the difference between the selling price and the value of her car. The game tree is shown in Figure 17.5.

Find the values of p, q, and π that make the following strategies and beliefs a Bayesian equilibrium:

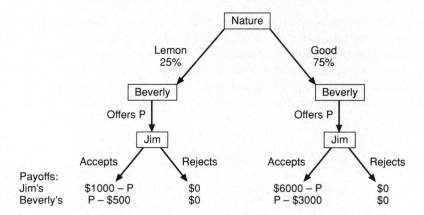

FIGURE 17.5 · Game tree for used car game played between a buyer (Jim) and a seller (Beverly).

> ***Beverly's strategy:*** If the car is good, always offer $5,500; if the car is a lemon, offer $5,500 with probability p and offer $1,000 with probability $1 - p$.
>
> ***Jim's strategy:*** Always reject a price above $5,500; accept a price of $5,500 with probability q; always reject a price between $1000 and $5,500; always accept a price at or below $1000.
>
> ***Jim's beliefs:*** If the price is below $5,500, then the car is a lemon for sure; if the price is $5,500 or higher, then the car is a lemon with probability π.

Proceed as follows:

(a) Given Beverly's strategy, use Bayes' theorem to find an expression for π in terms of p, denoted $\pi(p)$.

(b) If Jim rejects a price of $5,500, his payoff equals $0. If he accepts the price, his expected payoff equals $\$(\$6{,}000-\$5{,}500) \cdot (1-\pi)+(\$3{,}000-\$5{,}500) \cdot \pi$. Because his equilibrium strategy calls for him to randomize when Beverly offers to sell for $5,500, he must be indifferent between these two outcomes. Use this fact to solve for π.

(c) Now use the value for π you found in part (2) and the expression for $\pi(p)$ you found in part (1) to solve for p.

(d) If Beverly's car is a lemon and she offers a price of $1,000, then her payoff equals $\$1{,}000-\$500 = \$500$. If she offers a price of $5,500, then her expected payoff equals $\$0 \cdot (1-q)+q \cdot (\$5{,}500-\$500)$. Because Beverly's equilibrium strategy calls for her to randomize when her car is a lemon, she must be indifferent between these two outcomes. Use this fact to solve for q.

(e) Finally, show: Jim's beliefs are consistent with Bayes' theorem and Beverly's strategy at every price; Jim's strategy is optimal given his beliefs about Beverly; and Beverly's strategy is an optimal response to Jim's strategy.

• CHAPTER 18 •

Limit Pricing

18.1 Introduction

Adam Smith, over two hundred years ago, recognized that the established firms in an industry might try to behave strategically to keep new competitors out of the industry. In the last thirty years, models of increasing precision and rigor have revealed a number of strategies a firm might rationally use to deter or retard entry into the industry. Not surprisingly, most of this theoretical articulation has been game theoretic.

One of the first economists to examine the problem of entry deterrence with the tools of modern price theory was Joe S. Bain. Bain was interested in how a monopolist might use price and output decisions to maintain its monopoly position. His work was soon embellished by Modigliani in 1958 and Sylos-Labini in 1962. A simplified version of Bain's model, which has come to be known as **entry limit pricing**, is presented in this chapter. We will follow with a modern game-theoretic formulation.

Suppose a monopolist faces the industry demand curve shown in Figure 18.1. Because the demand curve is downward-sloping, the marginal revenue curve will lie below it. As you can see, we have assumed that the firm faces a constant marginal cost curve but a downward-sloping average cost curve. These cost curves are consistent with a firm with constant average variable costs and with some fixed costs. The short-run, profit-maximizing output is determined by setting marginal revenue equal to marginal cost. The profit-maximizing price is the highest price at which this output can be sold. The profit-maximizing price and output are labeled P_1 and Q_1 in Figure 18.1.

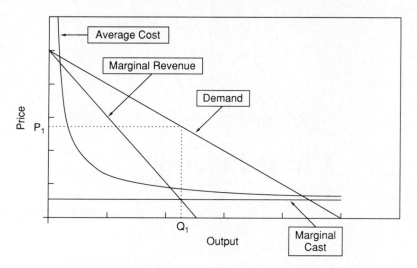

FIGURE 18.1 • A profit-maximizing monopolist in the short run will choose Q_1 and P_1 as its output and price.

Suppose another firm is considering whether or not to enter the industry. It is traditional to refer to the existing firm as the **incumbent** and to its potential competitor as the **entrant**. Assume the entrant can produce an identical product for the same cost as the incumbent. Because both firms produce the same homogeneous product, the market price will be determined by the total quantity both firms produce.

The models developed by Modigliani and Sylos-Labini assume the potential entrant believes the incumbent firm will not alter its output or sales in response to entry. Furthermore, the incumbent firm believes the entrant believes this, and so on. In game-theoretic terms, the entrant's belief is common knowledge. Under this assumption, if prior to entry the incumbent produces Q_1 unit of the good, then the potential entrant believes Q_1 units of the good will continue to be produced by the incumbent after entry. Therefore, the only demand left for the entrant is that which extends to the right of Q_1. If we bring this "leftover" demand, or what is called the **residual demand**, back to the vertical axis, we have the demand that the entrant believes it will face if it enters. This is shown in Figure 18.2. As long as the residual demand curve lies above the average cost curve over some range of prices, the entrant can make positive profits by entering.[1] To be even more specific, associated with the residual

---

[1]Profits equal $Q \cdot (P - AC)$, or quantity times the difference between price and average cost. As long as price exceeds average cost at a positive quantity, there will be positive profits.

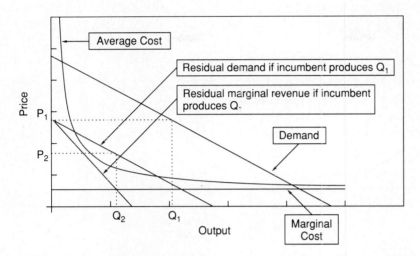

FIGURE 18.2 · If the residual demand curve lies above average cost, then entry is profitable. The output that maximizes profits occurs where the residual marginal revenue curve is equal to marginal cost.

demand curve is a residual marginal revenue curve. The entrant, given its beliefs, will maximize profits by setting the residual marginal revenue equal to marginal cost. As you can see from Figure 18.2, when the incumbent produces Q_1, entry will occur in this model (P > AC) and the entrant's profits will be maximized by producing Q_2 (P = MC). The resulting industry output of $Q_1 + Q_2$ lowers the future profits of the incumbent firm.

As Bain pointed out, however, if the incumbent firm knows the entrant's beliefs, the incumbent firm may have an incentive to produce a preentry output different from Q_1, the output that maximizes short-run profits. Consider Figure 18.3. Suppose the incumbent firm produces an output of Q_1^*, somewhat greater than the short-run, profit-maximizing output of Q_1. Because of the higher level of output by the incumbent, the residual demand facing the entrant is farther to the left than it was in Figure 18.2. At no point is average cost above the residual demand. Therefore, entry will not occur. The highest price (smallest output) at which entry is deterred is referred to as the **limit price**. The strategy of charging the limit price is called the **limit pricing strategy**. This strategy allows the incumbent monopolist to increase its future profits by giving up some short-run profits.

If the present value of the incumbent's profit stream from limit pricing and successfully deterring entry exceeds the present value of the profit stream from maximizing short-run profits and inducing entry, then it is obviously better to charge thelimit price.

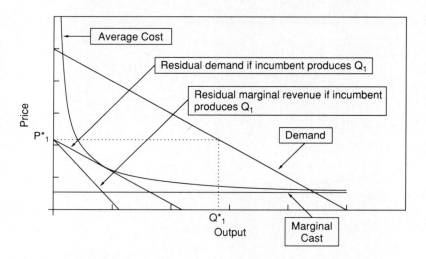

FIGURE 18.3 • When the incumbent firm chooses a limit pricing strategy, it chooses the smallest output at which entry is deterred.

If entry is *accommodated*—that is, the incumbent specifically chooses an output knowing full well that entry will occur—the combined output of both firms in the postentry periods is higher than what is produced by the monopolist engaged in limit pricing. Because the restriction of output is what causes the allocative inefficiency (welfare loss) from monopoly, society seems to be better off in the postentry period by not allowing limit pricing.[2] Before entry occurs, however, the short-run, profit-maximizing incumbent monopolist will produce a smaller output than will an incumbent engaged in limit pricing. Therefore, limit pricing can also have beneficial social welfare effects in the preentry period.

18.2 • A game-theoretic look at limit pricing

The Modigliani-Stylos-Labini model, though a tremendous improvement on what preceded it, leaves a lot to be desired. For example, it is hard to justify the belief that an incumbent firm will not alter its output after entry occurs. Although the incumbent might *threaten* to do so, the threat is simply not credible. It is not hard to see that the incumbent, once entry has taken place, will have an incentive to modify the output chosen.

---

[2]Exactly how this rule can be made operational is a difficult and unanswered question.

The model developed above was substantially improved upon by Michael Spence in 1977 and Avinash Dixit in 1980. Both economists developed models in which the incumbent firm could invest in capacity that *allowed* it to increase output in the face of entry. Therefore, the incumbent need not actually produce a limit pricing output, only credibly threaten to produce that output.

In 1982 important articles on limit pricing and predatory pricing were written by Paul Milgrom, John Roberts, David Kreps, and Robert Wilson. These authors succeeded in presenting a model in which strategic pricing behavior is undertaken by firms who are rational and farsighted. We will present in this section a modified version of the Milgrom-Roberts-Kereps-Wilson model due to Jean Tirole.

Let us suppose that the small town of Oberlin, Ohio, currently has only one pizza parlor, called Joe's. In Cleveland, not very far away, there is a restaurateur named Maria who is considering opening up a pizza restaurant in Oberlin. Her decision will depend on Joe's strategic response to her entry. Following the spirit of Milgrom and Roberts, we will suppose Joe's costs are *unknown to Maria*. Because Joe knows something that Maria does not (namely his costs), this is a game with private information.

In our game, if Joe believes Maria will not enter the Oberlin pizza market when she believes he has relatively low production costs, then he will try to convince her of this. But simply telling her that his costs are low won't work. Maria will be able to see that it is in Joe's interest to keep her out of the Oberlin pizza market, regardless of his costs. Therefore, she will only be persuaded if the information she gets about Joe's costs is *credible*. Herein lies the rub.

One possible way Joe might convince Maria that he has low costs is to *signal* this fact to her through some observable behavior. One such behavior might be to charge a relatively low price for pizza. A lower price for a meal at Joe's might be a credible way to tell Maria that his costs are low. But this signal will be credible only if the price is low enough so that a high-cost operation would be severely punished if it charged such a low price. That is, the signal must be *costly* in order to be persuasive.

As you know, we cannot analyze a game without first defining it. Joe and Maria are the only strategic players in the game, but Nature also plays a role. The game tree for this game is sketched in Figure 18.4. There are two time periods but four rounds of moves. In the first round, Nature makes the first move and chooses whether Joe's costs are high or low. This choice is observed by Joe but not by Maria. In the first time period Joe's is the only pizza parlor in Oberlin. Joe makes the second move in which he decides what price to charge and, therefore, how much pizza to sell.[3] At the *start* of the second time period it is Maria's turn to move. After observing Joe's price and

---

[3] We choose to model the decision Joe makes as one of selecting quantity instead of price for reasons that will become apparent shortly.

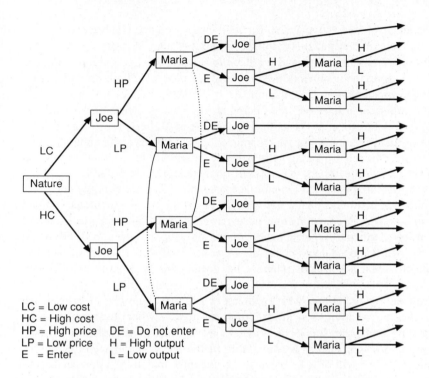

FIGURE 18.4 · The game tree for the limit pricing game.

quantity, but not his costs, she must decide whether or not to enter the Oberlin market. The game then ends. If she decides not to enter, then Joe has to set his price and output in the second period. If she does enter, then Maria and Joe simultaneously choose their outputs and their common price is set "by the market." Maria's production costs are common knowledge. Joe's production costs become common knowledge only after Maria chooses to enter.[4] Although we have omitted the numerical payoffs from the game tree, they are forthcoming.

18.2.1   A specific example

Unfortunately, a general analysis of this game gets rather complex. Since specificity will help us to cut through the notation, let us numerically specify some important relationships.

---

[4]This assumption makes the second period duopoly game much easier to evaluate.

The demand for pizza in Oberlin is given by the inverse demand function:

$$P = 100 - 0.1 \cdot Q, \tag{18.1}$$

where Q is the total quantity of pizza sold in Oberlin and P is the price per pizza. Joe's total costs are either

$$TC_J(Q_J) = 10 \cdot Q_J \tag{18.2}$$

if Joe has low costs, or

$$TC_J(Q_J) = 20 \cdot Q_J, \tag{18.3}$$

if Joe has high costs. Maria's total costs are

$$TC_M(Q_M) = 6{,}300 + 20 \cdot Q_M. \tag{18.4}$$

The \$6,300 term in equation (18.4) represents the entry costs that Maria must incur to produce pizzas in Oberlin. Once the entry decision has been made, these entry costs are unrecoverable, or **sunk costs**. These might represent a one-time license fee from the city of Oberlin or some initial advertising expense to let people know she is in the market. She knows her marginal cost will be \$20 per pizza, which happens to equal the marginal cost of a pizza to Joe if Joe has high costs. But Maria has heard rumors that Joe gets a deal on tomato sauce through his brother-in-law, who operates a tomato sauce plant outside of Toledo. At the beginning of time period 1 she places a 50% probability that Joe has high costs and a 50% probability that he has low costs.[5] Finally, the two time periods are close enough together that we need not worry about discounting future profits.

18.2.2   The second time period if Maria does not enter

It always makes sense to work from the end of the game back toward the beginning. If Maria chooses not to enter, then Joe simply selects a simple monopolistic profit-maximizing output level in the second time period. Because Joe's marginal revenue is given by

$$MR_J(Q) = 100 - 0.2 \cdot Q, \tag{18.5}$$

---

[5]The reason for the clause "At the beginning of time period 1" is that the decision Joe makes at the beginning of period 1 may cause Maria to alter her beliefs about his costs.

setting MR equal to marginal cost gives Joe's optimal output. The solution when costs are either high or low is summarized in Table 18.1. If Joe's costs are high, the optimal output is 400, the optimal price is $60, and his profit is $16,000. If his costs are low, then the optimal output is 450, the optimal price is $55, and his profit is $20,250.

18.2.3   The second time period if Maria enters

If Maria decides to enter the Oberlin pizza market, the payoffs are somewhat more complex to derive. With two firms in the Oberlin pizza market, it is now a duopoly. Recall, however, our assumption that the two firms produce a homogeneous product and that the market price depends only on the sum of their outputs. Therefore, the payoffs in the second time period will be determined in the same way that we solved the Cournot duopoly game in Part Three.

Because the market demand in time period 2 can be written as

$$P = 100 - 0.1 \cdot (Q_J + Q_M), \tag{18.6}$$

Joe's profits are[6]

$$\pi_J(Q_J, Q_M, C_J) = Q_J \cdot ((100 - 0.1 \cdot (Q_J + Q_M)) - C_J), \tag{18.7a}$$

where C_J is either 10 or 20 depending on whether Joe's costs are low or high. Maria's profit function is

$$\pi_M(Q_J, Q_M) = Q_M \cdot (100 - 0.1 \cdot (Q_J + Q_M)) - 20) - \$6{,}200. \tag{18.7b}$$

To find Joe's reaction function—that is, Joe's rational output conditional on the output choice for Maria and his costs—denoted $Q_J^*(Q_M, C_J)$, we maximize equation (18.7a)

TABLE 18.1   Outcome in period 2 if Maria does not enter

Joe's	Joe's Costs	
	High	Low
Quantity	400	450
Price	$60	$55
Profits	$16,000	$20,250

---

[6]Profits are being expressed as output times the difference between price and average cost.

over Q_J. The solution is found analytically by setting the partial derivative of equation (18.7a) with respect to Q_J equal to zero and solving for Q_J^*. This yields

$$Q_J^*(Q_M, C_J) = ((100 - C_J)/0.2) - Q_M/2. \tag{18.8}$$

In the same way we can obtain Maria's reaction function,

$$Q_M^*(Q_J) = 400 - Q_J/2. \tag{18.9}$$

Solving these two expressions simultaneously for Q_M and Q_J yields the Nash equilibrium outputs. The Cournot equilibrium market price and firm profits can now be calculated using equations (18.6), (18.7a) and (18.7b). The equilibrium outcome of the Cournot game is summarized in Table 18.2.

18.2.4 Maria's entry decision

Notice that if Joe's costs are high, then Maria earns a profit of $811.11, but if Joe's costs are low Maria suffers a loss of $855.56. This is an important result. It tells us (and Joe) that Maria will enter if she knows that Joe's costs are high but will not enter if she knows Joe's costs are low. If, somehow, Joe can *signal credibly* to Maria that he has low costs, then he can keep her from entering the market. This is the central feature of any limit pricing model.

In games with asymmetric information there are two types of Bayesian equilibria: **separating equilibria** and **pooling equilibria**. In a separating equilibrium, Joe be-

TABLE 18.2 Equilibrium outcome of Cournot game in period 2 if Maria enters the market

	Joe's Costs	
	High	Low
Joe:		
Quantity	266.67	333.33
Price	$43.33	$46.67
Profits	$7,111.11	$11,111.11
Maria:		
Quantity	266.67	233.33
Price	$46.67	$43.33
Profits	$811.11	−$855.56

haves differently when his costs are low than when his costs are high. In a pooling equilibrium, Joe behaves the same in the two situations. Sometimes the limit pricing game has only separating equilibria, sometimes it has only pooling equilibria, and sometimes the game has both kinds of equilibria. We have designed our game to have both kind of equilibria so we can present techniques for finding both types.

18.2.5 Finding a separating equilibrium

The only means at Joe's disposal with which to signal his costs to Maria is his first period output/price decision. If there is to be a separating equilibrium, when Joe has high costs he must choose a quantity/price combination that makes Maria believe he has high costs. We will show that this consists of a low output and a high price. If, on the other hand, Joe has low costs, then this must also be signaled accurately to Maria through a high output and a low price. Alternatively, *if Joe has low costs, it must not be in Joe's best interest to choose a high price and a low output, and if Joe has high costs, it must not be in Joe's best interest to choose a low price and a high output.*

Let us now examine the implications of that last sentence. Define $\pi_{J1}(P^H, C^H)$ to be Joe's profits in the first time period if he chooses a high price and his costs are high, and define $\pi_{J2}^{\ C}(C^H)$ to be Joe's profits in the second period if his costs are high, Maria enters, and the Cournot game ensues. The sum of $\pi_{J1}(P^H, C^H)$ and $\pi_{J2}^{\ C}(C^H)$ gives Joe's payoff from having high costs and charging a high price in the first time period with all the consequences thereof. Now define $\pi_{J1}(P^L, C^H)$ to be Joe's profits in period 1 if he charges a low price *even though he has high costs*, and define $\pi_{J2}^{\ M}(C^H)$ to be Joe's profits in the second period assuming Maria stays out and he maintains his monopoly (and his high costs). The sum of $\pi_{J1}(P^L, C^H)$ and $\pi_{J2}^{\ M}(C^H)$ is the payoff to Joe from charging a low price in the first time period even though his costs are high with all the consequences thereof. For a separating equilibrium to exist, it must be the case that when Joe's costs are high Joe's earns more by charging a high price in the first time period than by charging a low price in the first time period. Or

$$\pi_{J1}(P^H, C^H) + \pi_{J2}^{\ C}(C^H) \geq \pi_{J1}(P^L, C^H) + \pi_{J2}^{\ M}(C^H) \qquad (18.10)$$

in order for a separating equilibrium to exist. Table 18.3 describes each of the variables in equation (18.10).

Equation (18.10) is a necessary condition for a separating equilibrium to occur, but it is not a sufficient condition. It must also be the case that if Joe's costs are low, then his payoff is higher when he charges a low price than when he charges a high price. In Table 18.4 we have defined four new variables. For Joe to prefer charging a low price in period 1 when his costs are low, the following equation must be satisfied:

$$\pi_{J1}(P^H, C^L) + \pi_{J2}^{\ C}(C^L) \le \pi_{J1}(P^L, C^L) + \pi_{J2}^{\ M}(C^L). \tag{18.11}$$

Equations (18.10) and (18.11) are very important in what follows, and you should take the time to make sure you understand why they must be true for a separating equilibrium.

While equations (18.10) and (18.11) put some boundaries on the price/output choices for Joe that constitute a separating equilibrium, we can say more. If Joe charges a high price in time period 1 (meaning he has high costs), then Maria, believing that Joe has high costs, will enter at the beginning of time period 2. But if Maria is going to enter in time period 2, then Joe might as well charge the short-run monopoly price in time period 1.

We showed earlier that if Joe's costs are high, then the short-run monopoly price is $60; therefore, the separating equilibrium price of pizza in period 1 will be $60 when Joe's costs are high. His profits will be $16,000 in the first time period, Maria will

TABLE 18.3   Variables in equation (18.10)

$\pi_{J1}(P^H, C^H)$	Joe's profits in period 1 if his costs are high and he charges a high price.
$\pi_{J2}^{\ C}(C^H)$	Joe's profits in period 2 if his costs are high and he has not deterred entry and a Cournot game ensues.
$\pi_{J1}(P^L, C^H)$	Joe's profits in period 1 if his costs are high and he charges a low price.
$\pi_{J2}^{\ M}(C^H)$	Joe's profits in period 2 if his costs are high and he has deterred entry and he charges a high price in period 2.

TABLE 18.4   Variables in equation (18.11)

$\pi_{J1}(P^H, C^L)$	Joe's profits in period 1 if his costs are low and he charges a high price.
$\pi_{J2}^{\ C}(C^L)$	Joe's profits in period 2 if his costs are low and he has not deterred entry and a Cournot game ensues.
$\pi_{J1}(P^L, C^L)$	Joe's profits in period 1 if his costs are low and he charges a low price.
$\pi_{J2}^{\ M}(C^L)$	Joe's profits in period 2 if his costs are low and he has deterred entry and he charges a high price in period 2.

enter, and he will earn \$7,111.11 in the second time period. Combining the two profits means that Joe will earn a total of \$23,111.11. Maria will earn \$811.11 in the second time period.

The separating equilibrium price when his costs are low is, unfortunately, more difficult to determine. Take another look at equation (18.10). If Joe's costs were high, then his profits in period 1 from charging the high (monopoly) price are denoted $\pi_{J1}(P^H, C^H)$. But we have already deduced that P^H is the monopoly price and so $\pi_{J1}(P^H, C^H)$ equals $\pi_{J2}{}^M(C^H)$. Since Table 18.2 tells us that $\pi_{J2}{}^C(C^H)$ equals \$7,111.11, we can simplify equation (18.10) to

$$\$7,111.11 \geq \pi_{J1}(P^L, C^H). \tag{18.12}$$

The right-hand side of this equation—that is, Joe's profits when his costs are high—can be written as a function of price

$$\pi_{J1}(P^L, C^H) = (P^L - 20) \cdot (100 - P^L) \cdot 10. \tag{18.13}$$

Combining equations (18.12) and (18.13) yields the necessary condition

$$\$7,111.11 \geq (P^L - 20) \cdot (100 - P^L) \cdot 10. \tag{18.14}$$

In Figure 18.5 we have drawn Joe's first-period profits, when he has high costs, as a function of the price he charges. The diagram shows that in order for P^L to be part of a separating equilibrium, it must be either below \$31 or above \$91.

A similar analysis can be done using the other necessary condition for a separating equilibrium, equation (18.11). Noting that $\pi_{J1}(P^H, C^L)$ equals $\pi_{J2}{}^M(C^L)$, and recalling that the second-period Cournot game will yield profits to Joe of \$11,111.11, allows us to simplify equation (18.11) to

$$\$11,111.11 \leq \pi_{J1}(P^L, C^L). \tag{18.15}$$

Expressing $\pi_{J1}(P^L, C^L)$ explicitly as a function of price gives

$$\$11,111.11 \leq (P^L - 10) \cdot (100 - P^L) \cdot 10. \tag{18.16}$$

Solving this quadratic inequality implies that P^L must lie between \$26 and \$66. For a diagrammatic presentation of equation (18.16), see Figure 18.6.

Constraints (18.14) and (18.16) give the range of low prices that can be part of a separating equilibrium. The low price must fall between \$26 and \$31. Because any of

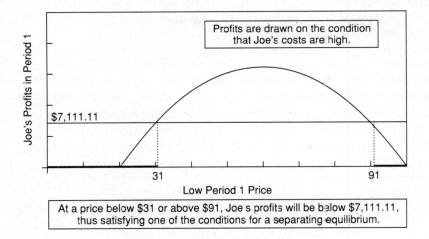

FIGURE 18.5 • Joe's profits as a function of price, when Joe has high costs. For the low price to result in a separating equilibrium, it must be lower than $31 or higher than $91.

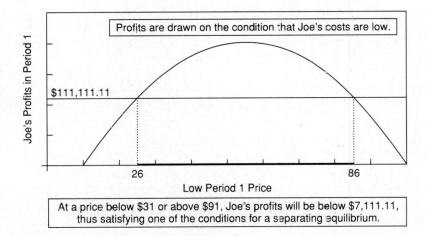

FIGURE 18.6 • Joe's profits as a function of price, when Joe has low costs. For the low price to result in a separating equilibrium, it must fall between $26 and $66.

these prices will form a separating equilibrium, the optimal low price must maximize Joe's profits subject to the constraint that the price lies between $26 and $31. As Figure 18.7 makes clear, the optimal price equals $31.

Therefore, in a separating equilibrium, if Joe has low costs he will charge a first-period price of $31, end up with a profit of $14,490 in the first time period, deter entry, and earn $20,250 in the second time period, for a total payoff of $34,740. Maria, because she does not enter, earns nothing. If, on the other hand, Joe has high costs, he will charge a price of $60 in the first time period, earn a profit of $16,000, induce entry, play a Cournot game in which the market price will equal $46.67, and have profits in the second time period of $7,111.11. The total payoff to Joe will be $23,111.11, and Maria will earn profits of $811.11.

The salient features of the separating equilibrium are detailed in Table 18.5.

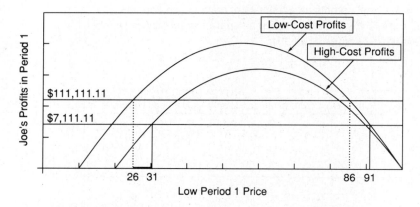

FIGURE 18.7 • In a separating equilibrium, Joe must choose a low price of $31.

TABLE 18.5   The separating equilibrium of the limit pricing game

Costs	Joe's Price in Period 1	Maria's Response in Period 2	Payoffs (Joe, Maria)
Low	$31	No entry	($34,740, $0)
High	$60	Entry	($23,111, $811)

18.2.6 Finding a pooling equilibrium

We now need to consider the possibility that the game has a pooling equilibrium. Recall that a pooling equilibrium implies the informed player's actions reveal nothing about what type of player he is. In this case, it means Joe must choose the same first-period price when his costs are high as when his costs are low. Only then will his prices in the first period not reveal anything about Joe's costs.

Oddly enough, if there exists a pooling equilibrium, then entry must be deterred. To see why this is necessary, suppose that entry were *not* deterred. Under a pooling equilibrium, no information is conveyed to Maria from the price chosen by Joe. Therefore, if she believes prior to Joe's price/output decision that there is a 50% chance that his costs are low, then she must maintain the same beliefs after his price/output decision. For Maria to enter, it must be the case that her expected profits from entering are greater than zero, or

$$0.5 \cdot \pi_M(C^L) + 0.5 \cdot \pi_M(C^H) \geq 0, \tag{18.17}$$

where $\pi_M(C^i)$ is Maria's profit in the second-period Cournot game when Joe's costs are either high ($i = H$) or low ($i = L$).

Recall that Maria's costs are common knowledge. So if Maria will enter in the second period, Joe is aware of this. Since entry is not deterred, Joe can do no better than to charge the short-run, profit-maximizing price in period 1. But this price depends on Joe's costs; the profit-maximizing price is $60 when his costs are high and $55 when they are low. But charging different prices on the basis of different costs is inconsistent with the assumption that the equilibrium is a pooling one. The contradiction shows that in any pooling equilibrium, Maria is deterred from entering.

This means that in order for there to exist an equilibrium pooling price, equation (18.17) must *not* be true, or

$$0.5 \cdot \pi_M(C^L) + 0.5 \cdot \pi_M(C^H) < 0. \tag{18.18}$$

Since $\pi_M(C^L)$ is –$855.55 and $\pi_M(C^H)$ is $811.11, Maria's expected profits are –$22.22, so equation (18.18) is satisfied.

We have not yet established that there exists a pooling equilibrium for our example. All we have shown is that a pooling equilibrium must be one in which Maria does not enter and found the condition necessary to ensure she will not enter. We must still identify under what conditions a pooling price P^* is a rational choice for Joe. For Joe to choose a pooling price, Joe's profits when he charges the pooling price and deters entry must always exceed the profits Joe could get from charging the short-run, profit-maximizing price in the first period, whatever his costs. Suppose Joe's costs are high. Then P^* must satisfy

what will be the equilibrium of the Cournot game? For what values of α will the entrant not enter?

(c) Determine a Bayesian equilibrium for this game. Check that the entrant's beliefs about the incumbent's costs are consistent with the incumbent's strategy and Bayes' theorem.

· CHAPTER 19 ·

Adverse Selection and Credit Rationing

19.1 · Adverse selection

The players in a game are said to be asymmetrically informed if some player cannot directly observe an action taken during the game that another player can. If this unobserved action is made *after* the uninformed player moves, then this player is exposed to moral hazard. In Part Two we showed how traders in the markets for insurance and labor are exposed to moral hazard. One consequence of moral hazard is that some trades that would benefit both parties are not realized.

If the unobserved action is made *before* the uninformed player moves, then this player is exposed to **adverse selection**. A stockbroker is exposed to adverse selection when she trades with a group of traders, some of whom may have inside information. Inside information is any information that affects profitability of a company but is known only to a select few, frequently the management of the company. These privileged few are referred to as *insiders*. Similarly, an insurance company is exposed to adverse selection when it offers to sell life insurance to a group that includes people who know they are at risk for cancer because of their family history. Also, a used car buyer is a player in an adverse selection game when the buyer observes only some of the qualities of a used car after she makes a purchase while the seller has already had a chance to observe the used car's qualities before the sale.

Figure 19.1 displays the prototypic game tree for a two-person game with adverse selection. First, nature moves and determines the informed player's **type**. A player's

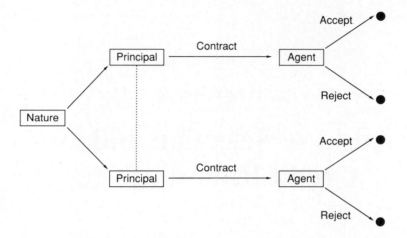

FIGURE 19.1 · A prototypic game tree for a two-player game with adverse selection.

type is anything that affects that player's preferences over the outcomes of the game—for example, the player's degree of risk aversion, discount rate, labor productivity, or exposure to a random loss in wealth. The informed player knows his or her type, but the uninformed player does not. Another way of saying this is that the uninformed player does not know precisely against whom she is playing. The uninformed player offers the informed player a contract, which the informed player can either accept or reject.

In this application we will examine the market for bank loans. Potential borrowers differ in their credit-worthiness—that is, the likelihood they will repay their bank loan. Unless the amount being borrowed is very high, the bank will not be willing to incur the costs to become as well informed about the borrower's credit-worthiness as is the borrower.

The bank's problem is that the interest it charges will affect the types of borrowers who accept its terms. We will show that after some point, *an increase in the bank's interest rate will cause the credit-worthiness of the bank's borrowers to fall*. But because the bank does not know any particular borrower's credit-worthiness, the bank must offer loans to all borrowers at the same interest rate. We will go on to show that although there may exist an excess demand for loans at the current market interest rate, no bank will be willing to increase its rates for fear of reducing the quality of those borrowing from it. The result is a competitive market equilibrium in which credit is "rationed" on the basis of something other than price.

19.2 • Lending in the absence of adverse selection

Consider the hypothetical case of four recent college graduates who have decided to form a printing company, the Obie Printing Company. We will treat the four as a single decision-making entity, which we will call *the firm*. Because the four budding capitalists have no previous business experience, their suppliers to be paid in advance. They need $100,000 in "working capital" simply to get their business off the ground. Because the four founders have almost no funds of their own, they apply to a local bank, the National Savings Bank, for a one-year, $100,000 loan. We will treat the bank as a single decision maker and refer to it hereafter as *the bank*.

It is common knowledge to both the firm and the bank that there is no guarantee the firm will be profitable. There is a 70% chance that Obie Printing's services will be in high demand over the next year, and a 30% chance that the demand for its services will be low. If demand is high, then the firm's revenues will be $160,000. If demand is low, the firm's revenues will be $50,000. Expected revenue equals $160,000 · 0.70 + $50,000 · 0.30 = $127,000.

The bank and the firm must negotiate the interest rate r for this one-year loan. The loan contract requires that all revenues earned by the firm must be used first to repay the bank loan. If the firm's revenue is greater than what it owes the bank, then the bank is paid $100,000 · (1 + r), and the four partners share profits of

$$\$160,000 - \$100,000 \cdot (1 + r) = \$100,000 \cdot (60\% - r). \tag{19.1}$$

The loan payment of $100,000 · (1 + r), however, is not the bank's net profit from this loan. The funds it lent to the firm were themselves borrowed by the bank from depositors. To calculate the bank's profit, we must subtract the principal and interest the bank must pay depositors for the use of the funds lent out. We will suppose the bank can obtain funds at 2%. This means that if the bank obtains $100,000 in funds from its depositors (say, by selling one-year certificates of deposit), then a year from now it has to repay these depositors $102,000.[1] If the loan is repaid, the bank's profits equal

$$\$100,000 \cdot (1 + r) - \$102,000 = \$100,000 \cdot (r - 2\%). \tag{19.2}$$

If the firm's revenue is less than what it owes the bank, then the firm will default on the loan and must declare **bankruptcy**. Bankruptcy is obviously a bad outcome

---

[1]If the supply of funds is perfectly elastic, then the marginal cost of funds to the bank equals the interest rate paid on these funds, that is, 10%. However, if the supply of funds is not perfectly elastic (the bank has some local market power), then the marginal cost of funds will be higher than the interest rate paid. The size of the difference between the marginal costs of funds and the interest rate charged depends on the elasticity of demand.

TABLE 19.1   Profits to Obie Printing and National Savings Bank

	Obie Printing	*National Savings Bank*
Loan repaid	$100,000 • (60% − r)	$100,000 • (r − 2%)
Loan defaulted	−$70,000	−$52,000

for the bank, because it means the firm will not pay back all that the bank is owed.[2] The loss to the bank, when the firm declares bankruptcy, equals $50,000 − $102,000 = −$52,000. The $50,000 is the firm's revenue when it declares bankruptcy, and $102,000 is the amount the bank must repay its depositors. Bankruptcy is also a bad outcome for the firm. Not only will the four former students fail to receive any compensation for their year of hard work, but they will also have to pay legal costs and will incur increased lending costs in the future. We will assume that the total cost of bankruptcy for the firm equals $70,000. The payoffs to the bank and to the firm are summarized in Table 19.1.

The problem for both the firm and the bank is that neither learns whether the demand for the firm's services is low or high until *after* they negotiate the terms of the loan. Figure 19.2 below shows the game tree for this game. The firm moves first and offers to loan $100,000 to the firm at an interest rate of r. There is no bargaining over this rate. It is a take-it-or-leave-it offer. If the firm rejects the loan terms, then the game ends and both the bank and the firm earn zero profits. If the firm accepts the loan terms, then Nature next determines whether the firm's demand is high or low. The game then ends and profits are determined according to Table 19.1. We will assume that both the firm and the bank are risk-neutral wealth maximizers.

A strategy for the bank consists of an interest rate r. A strategy for the firm consists of a rule for deciding which interest rates are acceptable and which are not. If the firm accepts the loan at the interest r, then its expected profit equals

$$0.70 \cdot \$100,000 \cdot (60\% - r) + 0.30 \cdot -\$70,000 = \$70,000 \cdot (30\% - r). \tag{19.3}$$

Clearly, the firm will accept the loan if and only if the interest rate charged by the bank is less than or equal to 30%.

If the bank makes the loan, then its expected profit equals

$$0.7 \cdot \$100,000 \cdot (r - 2\%) + 0.3 \cdot -\$52,000 = \$70,000 \cdot (r - 24.3\%). \tag{19.4}$$

---

[2]Although the firm has assets—the printing equipment, for example—we will assume that if the firm declares bankruptcy, then the sale of these assets will satisfy only the firm's other more senior creditors, and the bank will be left with nothing. The means that the loan, from the perspective of the bank, is unsecured.

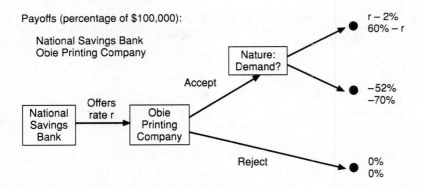

FIGURE 19.2 • Game tree for the lending game played between National Savings Bank and Obie Printing Company when both players are symmetrically informed about the future demand for Obie Printing's services.

This is nonnegative if and only if $r \geq 24.3\%$. If the firm has no other source of funds and the bank refuses to haggle over the interest rate, then the bank will offer an interest rate of 30%, and the firm will accept it.

19.3 • Lending in the presence of adverse selection

In the previous section we assumed that the firm and the bank were symmetrically informed about the likelihood that the loan would be repaid. In most lending situations, however, at the time the loan is negotiated, the borrower has a more accurate estimate of the probability of default than does the lender.

Suppose, as before, that the firm's revenue will be either "high" or "low." Although the four partners do not know what demand will be when they apply for a loan from the bank, informal market surveys have given them an estimate of the probability p that demand will be high. Because they did the survey themselves, there is no way for the four partners to share this information with the bank credibly. The bank knows it is in the firm's interest to claim p is a high number and, therefore, that the loan is very safe, whether or not this statement is true.

Although the bank does not know p, it believes that p is either 0.40 ("poor credit risk"), 0.60 ("moderate credit risk"), or 0.80 ("good credit risk"). From previous experience, the bank has learned that these three types of risk are not equally likely. It is most likely that Obie Printing is a good credit risk, next most likely that Obie Printing is a moderate credit risk, and least likely that the firm is a poor credit risk. The bank's beliefs about the firm's credit-worthiness are given in Table 19.2. These

TABLE 19.2   The bank's beliefs about Obie Printing's credit risk

Credit Risk	Probability
Poor ($p = 0.40$)	0.05
Moderate ($p = 0.60$)	0.45
Good ($p = 0.80$)	0.50
Expected credit risk ($\underline{p}$)	0.69

beliefs about p are common knowledge. Notice that the expected credit risk, denoted $\underline{p}$, is 0.69, almost exactly what we assumed it to be in the previous section.

As before, when demand is low, Obie Printing earns revenues of only $50,000 and must declare bankruptcy. The firm's revenue when demand is high, R_H, is no longer independent of p. Instead, it is the firm's *expected revenue* that is independent of p. We will suppose that $R_H(p)$ is such that the expected revenue for the firm is $127,000. Specifically, $R_H(p)$ satisfies the expression

$$R_H(p) \cdot p + (1 - p) \cdot \$50,000 = \$127,00 \tag{19.5a}$$

or

$$R_H(p) = \$50,000 + (\$77,000 \div p). \tag{19.5b}$$

Risky business ventures differ from less risky ones in having more *variable* revenue for a given cost. The more likely the firm will be successful (high value of p), the lower is the firm's revenue when it is successful (Table 19.3). Whatever the value of p, if demand is high, then the firm will be able to repay the bank loan.

The game tree for the adverse selection game played between Obie Printing and the bank is shown in Figure 19.3. Nature moves first and chooses the firm's credit-worthiness, p. The bank then offers to loan Obie Printing $100,000 at an interest rate r, which the firm can either accept or reject. Because the bank does not know p, its three decision nodes lie in a single information set. Because Obie Printing knows p, each of its decision nodes lies in a separate information set. As before, if the loan is

TABLE 19.3   Obie Printing's revenue if successful and unsuccessful

Credit-worthiness	Revenue		Expected Revenue
	High	Low	
Poor ($p = 0.40$)	$242,500	$50,000	$127,000
Moderate ($p = 0.60$)	$178,333	$50,000	$127,000
Good ($p = 0.80$)	$146,250	$50,000	$127,000

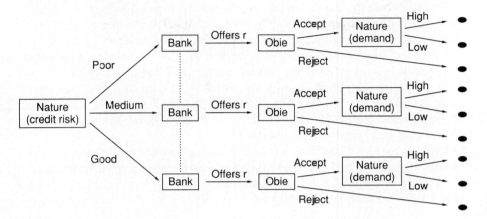

FIGURE 19.3 · The game tree for the bank loan game played between National Savings Bank and Obie Printing Company when the bank faces adverse selection.

rejected, then the game ends and both players get a payoff of zero. If the firm accepts the loan, then Nature chooses demand. If demand is high, the loan is repaid; if demand is low, the firm defaults and is bankrupt. As before, the cost of bankruptcy to Obie Printing is $70,000.

Because the bank does not observe Nature's selection of p, a strategy consists of the selection of a single loan rate r. Because Obie Printing *does* observe p, a strategy consists of the selection of a maximum acceptable interest rate, what we can call a **reservation interest rate**, for each value of p. This strategy will be represented as a function $r^*(p)$.

Obie Printing's optimal strategy is to accept any loan that will result in a nonnegative expected profit. This implies the firm accepts any interest rate below the rate at which its expected profit is exactly zero. This, of course, is the firm's reservation interest rate. It is defined by the expression

$$0 = p \cdot (R_H(p) - \$100,000 \cdot (1 + r^*(p)) + (1 - p) \cdot -\$70,000 \qquad (19.6a)$$

$$= p \cdot (\$50,000 + (\$77,000 \div p) - \$100,000 \cdot (1 + r^*(p)) + (1 - p) \cdot -\$70,000$$

$$= \$100,000 \cdot p \cdot ((7\% \div p) + 20\% - r^*(p)),$$

or

$$r^*(p) = 20\% + (7\% \div p). \qquad (19.6b)$$

The function $r^*(p)$, the maximum interest rate the firm will accept, is plotted in Figure 19.4 and displayed in tabular form in Table 19.4. The disturbing feature of this function is that r^* is a *decreasing* function of p. That is, *bad credit risks are willing to pay a higher interest rate than are good credit risks*. The reason is that a poor credit risk is unlikely to have to pay the interest on the loan. When a poor credit risk does repay the loan, it has high profits with which to do so. In contrast, a good credit risk is not sheltered as much by bankruptcy. When it repays the loan interest, it does so out of more modest profits. The result is that poor credit risks are less sensitive to the interest paid on a loan than are good credit risks.

Let $p^*(r)$ be the probability that Obie Printing repays its loan given that it accepts the loan at an interest rate r. The probability of repayment will depend on the interest rate charged by the bank. If the bank charges an interest rate less than 28.8%, then the firm will always accept the loan, regardless of its credit-worthiness. This means

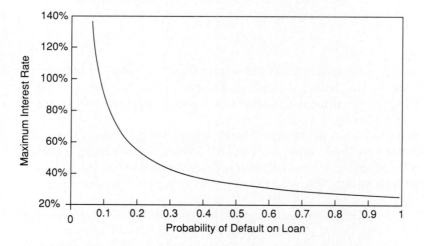

FIGURE 19.4 · The highest interest rate Obie Printing will accept depending on its credit-worthiness.

TABLE 19.4   Maximum interest rate Obie Printing is willing to pay

p	$r^*(p)$
0.4	37.5%
0.6	31.7%
0.8	28.8%

Note: $r^*(p)$ is reported to only three significant digits.

$$p^*(28.8\%) = 0.40 \cdot 0.05 + 0.60 \cdot 0.45 + 0.80 \cdot 0.50 \qquad (19.7)$$

$$= 0.69.$$

If the bank charges between 28.8% and 31.7%, however, Obie Printing will borrow only if it is a medium or bad credit risk. Poor credit risks account for $0.05/0.50 = 0.10$ of this subgroup. As a result,

$$p^*(31.7\%) = 0.40 \cdot 0.10 + 0.60 \cdot 0.90 \qquad (19.8)$$

$$= 0.58.$$

And if the bank charges an interest rate between 31.7% and 37.5%, then the firm will accept the loan only if it is a bad credit risk. So,

$$p^*(37.5\%) = 0.40. \qquad (19.9)$$

Of course, if the bank charges above 37.5%, then Obie Printing will never accept the loan and $p^*(r)$ is undefined.

Since $p^*(r)$ is common knowledge, the bank knows that its expected profit, denoted $\pi(r)$, equals

$$\pi(r) = \begin{cases} p^*(r) \cdot \$100{,}000 \cdot (r - 2\%) = + (1 - p^*(r)) \cdot -\$52{,}000 & \text{if } r \leq 37.5\% \\ \\ 0 & \text{if } r > 37.5\% \end{cases} \qquad (19.10)$$

Inspection of equation (19.10) shows that the bank should charge either 28.8%, 31.7%, 37.5%, or any interest rate above 37.5% (at which it knows there will be no lending). At all other interest rates, the bank can increase the interest rate yet keep the probability of default unchanged. The bank's expected profits at each of these interest rates are shown in Table 19.5. The bank can make a positive profit only if it charges

TABLE 19.5   The consequences for the bank of making a loan at different interest rates

Interest Rate r	Probability of Repayment: $p^*(r)$	Bank's Expected Profit $\pi(r)$
28.8%	69%	$2,337.50
31.7%	58%	−$4,633.33
37.5%	40%	−$17,000.00
Above 37.5%	(undefined)	$0

the relatively low rate of 28.8%. Higher rates cause the probability of default to increase so much that the higher losses on the loans that default more than offset the higher interest income from the loans that are repaid.

19.4 · Market equilibrium with adverse selection

So far we have been concerned only with the relationship between one bank, National Savings Bank, and one potential borrower, Obie Printing Company. We now want to see how the bank and the firm behave when they have alternatives to lending to and borrowing from each other.

Suppose there exists a second bank, the State Bank, and 99 additional new firms that also want to borrow $100,000 in working capital. The State Bank is identical to the National Savings Bank. The 100 firms wanting to borrow from these two banks appear identical to both banks, but they really are not: Five of the firms are poor credit risks ($p = 40\%$), 45 of them are medium credit risks ($p = 60\%$), and 50 of them good credit risks ($p = 80\%$).

The probability of repayment by firm i will be denoted p_i. Each firm knows p_i and acts independently of the other firms. We know from the previous section that firm i will borrow from a bank only if it can obtain a loan rate at or below $r^*(p_i)$. If the firm borrows, it does so from the bank offering the lowest loan rate. For simplicity, we will assume that if both banks offer the same loan rate, exactly half of the borrowers apply for a loan from one bank and exactly half apply for a loan from the other.[3]

As we have already noted, banks are financial intermediaries. This means the funds they loan out to the firms are obtained from depositors by paying these depositors interest. The banking market, therefore, consists of two interrelated submarkets: the market for deposits and the market for loans. The interest rates National Savings Bank pays on deposits and charges for loans will be denoted R_N^D and R_N^L, respectively; State Bank's interest rates will be denoted R_S^D and R_S^L. On every dollar National Savings Bank obtains from its depositors and then lends out, its expected profit equals

$$\pi_N(R_N^L, R_N^D) = p^*(R_N^L) \cdot R_N^L + (1 - p^*(R_N^L)) \cdot -\$0.50 - R_N^D, \qquad (19.11)$$

---

[3]We are implicitly assuming that a firm cannot apply for a loan from both banks. If the firms can apply to both banks without either one knowing this, then there is a strong potential for fraud: If the firm gets both $100,000 loans, then its best strategy is to default, pay each bank the "bad revenue" of $50,000, pay the bankruptcy costs of $70,000, and pocket the remaining $30,000! Now there is moral hazard as well as adverse selection. For a hilarious example of what can happen when such a scheme backfires, see Mel Brooks's movie *The Producers*.

where $p^*(r)$ is defined in Table 19.4. The first term in equation (19.11) equals the interest income per dollar of loan times the probability of repayment; the second term is the loss per dollar of loan that results when the borrower defaults times the probability of default; and the third term is the interest paid per dollar of deposit to the depositor. A similar expression holds for State Bank.

We will assume there are 100 potential depositors, each with $100,000 to deposit with the two banks. As with the firms, although these depositors appear identical to both banks, they are not. Also like the firms, each depositor is characterized by an interest rate, called the depositor's reservation interest rate, and denoted r^D_i. This interest rate is the *lowest* interest rate the depositor will accept before she will deposit her funds in a bank. Depositors have different reservation interest rates in part because they face different alternative investing opportunities and different investing horizons. One depositor will find a 30-day bank CD (certificate of deposit) paying 7.46% attractive, while another depositor will not.

We will assume these reservation interest rates are uniformly distributed between 0% and 10% and that this distribution is common knowledge. That is, 1 depositor will accept an interest rate of 0.1% or lower, 2 depositors will accept an interest rate of 0.2% or lower, 20 depositors will accept an interest rate of 2% or lower, and so on. Each depositor knows her reservation interest rate and acts independently of the other depositors. For simplicity, we will assume that if the two banks offer the same deposit rate, every interested depositor deposits $50,000 with one bank and $50,000 with the other.

Nature moves first and assigns a reservation interest rate, r^D_i, to every depositor, and a probability of repayment, p_i, to every new firm. The two banks then engage in Bertrand competition in the market for loans and deposits. That is, they simultaneously announce a loan and deposit rate. Depositors and borrowers then simultaneously apply to the banks for a loan or a deposit account. Finally, each bank simultaneously decides which loan and deposit applications to accept. A greatly simplified sketch of the game tree is shown in Figure 19.5.

Although the game looks very complicated, we can simplify our search for an equilibrium by restricting ourselves to **symmetric equilibria**: those in which both banks are charging the same loan and deposit rates. We will denote the deposit and loan rates at such an equilibrium by R^{D*} and R^{L*}. One characteristic of Bertrand competition is that in any Nash equilibrium both firms must be earning zero expected profits. The reason is simple: otherwise, one firm can almost double its expected profits by cutting its loan rates very slightly, raising its deposit rates very slightly, and thereby attracting every depositor and every borrower from its competitor. Combining the zero-profit condition with equation (19.11) implies that R^{D*} and R^{L*} must satisfy the relation

$$R^{D*} = p^*(R^{L*}) \cdot R^{L*} + (1 - p^*(R^{L*})) \cdot -\$0.50. \qquad (19.12)$$

exactly break even on every policy sold. This strategy on the part of the insurance company is referred to as "screening."

Exercise 19.4. This is a continuation of Exercises 19.2 and 19.3. How could the National Savings Bank "screen" borrowers according to their credit-worthiness?

• CHAPTER 20 •

Strikes and Other
Bargaining Breakdowns

20.1 • Introduction

In Chapter 6 we developed a model in which two bargainers reached a mutually advantageous exchange. The model, as you might recall, had the two players making alternating offers under conditions of perfect information. In equilibrium the first offer made in the bargaining process would be accepted by the other player. Wasteful back-and-forth bargaining was avoided by the ability of both parties to look ahead and calculate the consequences of rejecting an offer. Strikes, lockouts, and other break-downs in bargaining seem to contradict the theory of bargaining we developed in Part Two. Yet we know that in the real world these things occur.

In this application we will relax what was perhaps the strongest, and most unreal-istic, of the assumptions made in the bargaining application in Chapter 6, that of perfect information. When the players in a game have imperfect information, particu-larly about the payoffs, the players cannot perfectly predict what their opponents will accept or reject. But players can gain information about the game being played by observing their opponent's behavior, and they can reveal private information to other players through their own behavior. Three things often happen under these circum-stances.

First, a player may probe her opponent in order to gauge his preferences, even though this probing can be costly. Second, a player may try to signal her preferences credibly by engaging in some costly activity that would more likely be taken by someone with a certain set of preferences. Third, a player may try to bluff and pretend his preferences are different from what they are. This in turn implies players will have to call their opponent's bluff occasionally in order to discourage the opponent from bluffing excessively. Strikes and lockouts now can be seen as strategic acts intended either to alter the opponent's beliefs or to help solidify one's own beliefs about the opponent. In this chapter we will present a sequence of models of bargaining between a group of workers and a firm that demonstrates the role of strikes and lockouts in such negotiations.

20.2 • Game 1: Take-it-or-leave-it offers

Imagine a single shirt manufacturer, Welmade, Inc., bargaining over its wages with a labor union. The technology employed by the firm, the prices the firm pays for all inputs, and the price the firm receives for its output are all known to members of the union. That is, profits for the firm are common knowledge. This means that union members can predict the value of their labor to the firm. The owner and manager of Welmade, Bill Taylor, does not know how much the workers value their jobs with the firm. Using this simple framework we will show how the management of the firm can benefit by threatening a lockout.

There are three workers: Harry, Barry, and Moe. Each worker has a marginal value product (net of materials costs) of \$500 per week; because of the small size of the shop, a fourth worker would have a marginal product of zero. The fixed costs of running the shop are \$750 per week. Hence profits equal $3 \cdot (\$500 - W) - \$750 = \$750 - 3 \cdot W$, where W is the common wage paid. The fixed costs are not sunk costs. That is, if Mr. Taylor closes the shop completely, his total costs and profits are zero. We will assume Taylor is risk-neutral.

Harry, Barry, and Moe belong to a union that negotiates a contract with Mr. Taylor once a week. Bill Taylor, who does not like to negotiate, makes a single take-or-leave-it wage offer to the three workers. If they reject the offer, Taylor closes down his firm for the week (a "lockout"). He earns no revenue, but also has no costs—either fixed or variable.

The three workers decide whether to accept or reject the offer through a secret vote based on majority rule. If two or more of the workers accept the wage offered, then all three earn the accepted wage over the following week. If two or more reject it, however, then Mr. Taylor locks them out and they each have to find some other temporary employment to tide them over until they can negotiate again the following week.[1]

---

[1]In most states, workers involved in a labor dispute are not eligible for unemployment insurance.

The workers have alternative employment opportunities that change from week to week. At the time the members of the union vote whether to accept Taylor's wage offer for that week, they know what these alternative opportunities are. Denote these alternative wages for Harry, Barry, and Moe by $\underline{W}_H$, $\underline{W}_B$, and $\underline{W}_M$, respectively. Because each of the workers will prefer not to accept a wage below the wage paid in alternative employment, we will refer to $\underline{W}_H$, $\underline{W}_B$, and $\underline{W}_M$ as their **reservation wages**. These reservation wages are either \$100/week or \$200/week, and $\underline{W}_H \geq \underline{W}_B \geq \underline{W}_M$.

Suppose Taylor's offer is above Barry's reservation wage. In that case Moe and Barry will vote to accept the wage. Harry may or may not agree, but because decisions in the union are made by majority vote, Taylor's offer will be accepted. On the other hand, suppose Taylor's offer is below Barry's reservation wage. Obviously, Barry and Harry will vote to reject the offer. In this case Moe may or may not agree, but regardless of how Moe votes the wage offer will be rejected by the union. We will suppose that if Taylor's offer exactly matches Barry's reservation wage, he will vote in favor of accepting the offer. The result of this voting mechanism is that Barry is always happy with the outcome; in other words, the results of the union vote will always mimic Barry's vote. Barry is said to be the **decisive voter**.[2] We will use this fact to simplify the game tree by treating the three workers as a single decision maker having Barry's preferences. For this reason, we will actually refer to the three workers as "Barry."

The game we have described has three players: Taylor, Barry, and Nature. Nature determines Barry's reservation wage, $\underline{W}_B$. Although Nature's choice is observed by the workers, it is not observed by the management of the firm. We will suppose that Taylor has a prior belief that there is a 50% probability Barry will have a reservation wage of \$100 and a 50% probability it will be \$200. Taylor must make an offer without knowing $\underline{W}_B$. Once an offer is made, Barry either accepts or rejects it. The game tree is shown in Figure 20.1. Barry's payoff is either W or $\underline{W}_B$, and Taylor's payoff is either \$0 or \$750 − 3 • W.

As always, the best way to find the equilibrium strategies for either of the players is to start from the end of the game and work backwards. Because the highest reservation wage for any of the workers is \$200, any offer of \$200 or more will certainly be accepted by the union. Similarly, since the lowest reservation wage for any of the workers is \$100, any offer less than \$100 will certainly be rejected by the union. Finally, since Barry will have a reservation wage of \$200 half of the time, any wage between \$100 and \$200 will be accepted half of the time. Offering a wage of exactly

---

[2]The decisiveness of the "median voter" is an important property of the majority voting rule and appears repeatedly in the theory of social choice.

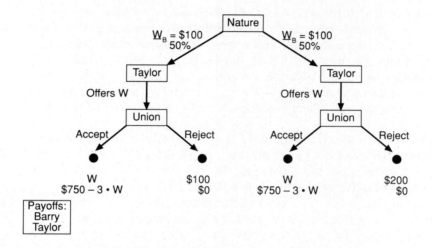

FIGURE 20.1 · The game tree when Taylor makes a take-it-or-leave-it offer.

TABLE 20.1   Equilibrium strategies in game 1

Probability that Barry's Reservation Wage equals $100	Taylor's Offer
Less than or equal to 1/3	$200
Greater than 1/3	$100

Barry's Reservation Wage	Union's Response to $100 Offer	Union's Response to $200 Offer
$100	Accept	Accept
$200	Reject	Accept

$100 dominates offering a wage between $100 and $200 and offering a wage of $200 dominates offering more than $200. So we can restrict our attention to the two offers: $100 and $200. If Taylor offers $200, then he will earn a profit of $750 − 3 · $200 = $150. If he offers $100, then he will earn $750 − 3 · $100 = $450 half the time and will earn $0 half the time; the expected profit is $225.

It follows that Taylor's optimal strategy is to offer $100 and risk having to lock out the workers—even though he makes a profit when he pays $200. In this equilibrium,

Barry always reveals his true reservation wage, for the offer is accepted if and only if $\underline{W}_B$ = $100. But because this revelation only occurs *after* Taylor makes his wage offer, Taylor cannot benefit from this information. As a result, Barry does not have to take this into account when forming his strategy.

The foregoing strategy remains optimal so long as the probability of a low reservation wage for Barry is greater than 1/3. The reader will be asked to verify this in the exercises at the end of the chapter. The reader will also be asked to verify that when this probability is below 1/3, then Taylor's optimal strategy changes and he offers $200, which is always accepted by the union. In this case, Barry's reservation wage is never revealed. These results are summarized in Table 20.1.

20.3 • Game 2: Alternating offers

One of the simplifying features of the previous game was the assumption that Taylor made only one take-it-or-leave-it offer. In many circumstances, a more realistic scenario is that the union and the employer make alternating offers to each other. We will now modify our game to allow both the union and the firm to make offers to each other. If they cannot come to an agreement, then there is a strike. The full story follows.

Mr. Taylor, who as you know hated to bargain, finally decides to retire and sells Welmade, Inc., to a group of Swedish investors. The workers take the opportunity to change the way wages are negotiated. They inform the new owners that *they*, the workers, will make an initial wage offer to Welmade. If Welmade does not like this offer, then it can make a counteroffer. If the workers find this counteroffer unacceptable, then negotiations will be suspended and the workers will strike for a week. Negotiations will be resumed with the firm the following week. As before, it is assumed that the workers know their reservation wages but that this is unknown to the new owners of Welmade. The resulting game tree is shown in Figure 20.2.

This game is much more complicated than the first one. In the previous game, the owner of Welmade had no chance to use the information embedded in the union's behavior to update his prior beliefs. In this new game, the initial union offer may reveal something about the union's preferences. Our problem is to find a union strategy that is optimal given Welmade's strategy, a strategy for Welmade that is optimal given Welmade's beliefs about the union, and beliefs for Welmade that are consistent with the union's strategy.

The workers have to take into account that their initial offer, W^I, will influence Welmade's belief about their reservation wages and that this belief will determine whether the firm will accept their offer or not. We will begin by finding constraints for the union's optimal strategy. Because the lowest reservation wage is $100, the union should never initially offer their services for less than $100. Also, the union

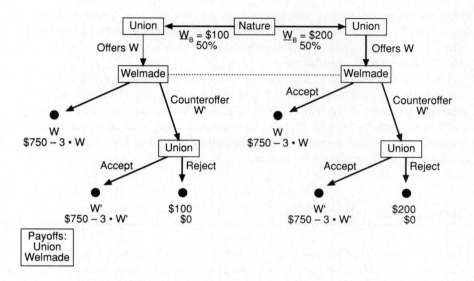

FIGURE 20.2 • The game tree when the union makes the first offer. The owners of Welmade can counteroffer, and the union can choose either to accept the counteroffer or to strike.

knows that Welmade will never accept any offer over $200 (since Welmade knows that a counteroffer of $200 will always be accepted). So the initial offer by the union must be between $100 and $200 (inclusive).

It is also worth noting that some results from the first game carry over to this game. For example, once the union's offer is made, if Welmade thinks that Barry's reservation wage equals $100 with a probability greater than or equal to 1/3, then Welmade should counteroffer with a wage of $100. On the other hand, if Welmade thinks there is less than a 1/3 chance that Barry's reservation wage is $100, then Welmade should just accept a $200 offer.

20.3.1   A nonequilibrium

Suppose the union makes an initial offer of $200. Suppose further that when the union offers $200, Welmade believes there is a 100% chance that Barry's reservation wage is $200. On the basis of this belief, the owners of Welmade might as well accept the offer and not make a counteroffer. Any counteroffer that saves them money, they believe, will be rejected. But this means that the union should always offer $200 regardless of what their reservation wage is. There is only a 50% chance that Barry has a reservation wage of $200 when the uninon offers $200. Thus, the proposed beliefs are inconsistent with the proposed union strategy. As a result, these beliefs cannot form part of a Bayesian equilibrium.

Clearly, if the union makes an offer of $200, then Welmade must believe there is *less than* a 100% chance that Barry's reservation wage is actually $200. How much less? Suppose Welmade believes there is a 75% chance that Barry's reservation wage is $200 if the union offers $200. Of course, this also means Welmade places a 25% probability on Barry's reservation wage being $100. Since 1/4 (25%) is less than 1/3, Welmade should simply accept the initial offer of $200. But if the union knew that Welmade had this belief, then the union would always offer to work for a wage of $200. Once again, the proposed beliefs are not consistent with the strategy chosen by the union. Welmade was assumed to believe that an offer of $200 meant that there was a 75% chance that Barry's reservation wage was $200, when in reality there was only a 50% chance.

20.3.2 Moving toward an equilibrium

The discussion in the previous section, though not complete, is at least moving us in the general direction of an equilibrium. Suppose the union offers to work for a wage of $200, and Welmade, when faced with this offer, believes there is a 50% chance that Barry has a reservation wage of $200. Since 1/2 (50%) is greater than 1/3, Welmade is best off countering with an offer of $100. This offer will be accepted (rationally) 50% of the time. Therefore, Welmade's beliefs correspond with the actions of the union.

We know the union will never offer to work for a wage above $200 because it will never be accepted. We have yet to determine if the union will ever offer to work for a wage strictly less than $200.

20.3.3 The Bayesian equilibrium

If Barry has a reservation wage equal to $200, the union will certainly never offer its services for less than $200. Therefore, if the union offers to work for less than $200, then it can only be the case that Barry has a reservation wage of $100. The only belief for Welmade consistent with this behavior is that they are certain that Barry has a reservation wage of $100, if the union offers to work for less than $200.

Given these beliefs, Welmade would certainly counter any offer strictly between $100 and $200 with an offer of $100. Since any offer strictly between $100 and $200 would only come from the union if Barry has a reservation wage of $100, Welmade's offer will be accepted by the union. Since, regardless of the initial offer by the union, the firm will counter with an offer of $100, the union might as well start the bargaining off with an initial offer of $200.

A complete Bayesian equilibrium is detailed in Table 20.2. This type of equilibrium is referred to as a **pooling equilibrium** because the union does not reveal any of its private information through its first offer. The union offers to work for a wage of $200 regardless of whether Barry's reservation wage is $100 or $200. Therefore, the owners of Welmade cannot tell anything about the union's preferences from the union's behavior. The outcome of this Bayesian equilibrium is the same as in game 1, where the union never had a chance to make an offer: Half the time there is a strike or lockout. Going first has not improved the union's expected payoff.

This game has other equilibria, but all of them have the following features: (1) The union always offers $200 when Barry's reservation wage is high, (2) Welmade never accepts any offer above $100, and (3) the union accepts any counteroffer above $100 when Barry's reservation wage is low and accepts only counteroffers above $200 when his reservation wage is high. Strategically, this game is no different from the first game we analyzed. By allowing the firm to make a counteroffer to the union's initial offer, Welmade's rejection of the initial offer is costless. In order to obtain an advantage from making the first offer, the union must structure the game so that there is a cost to Welmade from rejecting union offers above $100.

An obvious alteration of the game is to eliminate the firm's counteroffer. Now the union's offer is final. If the firm rejects it, the union does not work that week. No counteroffers, no renegotiations. In the exercises at the end of this chapter you will be asked to show that in this game, the union's optimal strategy is to offer a wage of $250 regardless of the worker's reservation wages, and the firm's optimal strategy is

---

TABLE 20.2   A Bayesian Equilibrium in the alternating offer game

The union strategy:
1. W^I = $200 always.
2. Accept a counteroffer of $200.
3. Reject a counteroffer of $100 if $\underline{W}_B$ = $200.
4. Accept a counteroffer of $100 if $\underline{W}_B$ = $100.

Welmade's beliefs:
1. $P(\underline{W}_B) = \$100 \mid W^I \geq \$200) = 0.5$.
2. $P(\underline{W}_B) = \$100 \mid W^I < \$200) = 1$.

Welmade's strategy:
Always accept an offer of $100 or less, and always reject offers above $100 and counter with an offer of $100.

to accept it. The problem with this "solution" is that the union may not be able to walk away from the negotiations should the firm reject this offer—especially if the workers' reservation wages are low that week. We cannot pursue this line of inquiry further without modeling the internal dynamics of the union and explicitly determining the circumstances under which members would leave the union and cross the union's picket lines.

Fortunately, the union has a less drastic way to punish Welmade for refusing its initial offer: Strike for a few days and then come back to the negotiating table. This approach has an additional advantage to the union: It makes it costly for it initially to pretend its reservation wage is high when, in fact, it is low. As a result, it allows the union to signal its true reservation wage to the firm. This new game is explored in the next section.

20.4 • Game 3: Incremental strikes

Consider a new game in which the union will punish the firm for rejecting its initial offer by striking for half a week. After this "mini-strike" is over, the union will consider a counteroffer from Welmade. If the union finds this wage offer unacceptable, then negotiations will be cut off and the strike will be continued for the rest of the week. The new game tree is displayed in Figure 20.3.

20.4.1 Groping toward an equilibrium

Although there is no set procedure, or algorithm, for finding an equilibrium in a Bayesian game, there are a number of things that should be kept clearly in mind while trying to find one. Most important is the requirement that beliefs and strategies be consistent with each other. The other is that one should use iterated dominance to eliminate strategies whenever possible.

Beginning at the end of the game, suppose the union makes an initial offer, it is rejected by Welmade, there is a half-week strike, and Welmade makes a counteroffer. If Barry's reservation wage is $100, then the union will accept any counteroffer greater than or equal to $100. On the other hand, if Barry's reservation wage is $200, then the union will accept any counteroffer greater than or equal to $200. In Table 20.3a we have begun to keep track of the equilibrium strategies and beliefs.

Initially, we will consider only pure strategies and **separating equilibria**. A separating equilibrium is one in which the union acts differently when its reservation wage is low than when it is high. In a separating equilibrium a low initial wage offer by the union, denoted by W_L^I (L for "low," and I for "initial"), will signal to Welmade that Barry's reservation wage is $100. In terms of Welmade's beliefs, if there is a

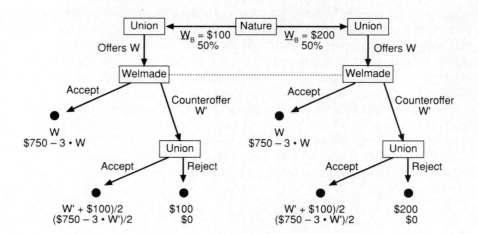

FIGURE 20.3 • The game tree for a game in which the union engages in a mini-strike if Welmade rejects its initial offer.

TABLE 20.3a   Bayesian equilibrium of game 3 (incremental strikes)

Union's initial offer:
   Unknown as yet.
Welmade's reaction and counteroffer:
   Unknown as yet.
Union's reaction to the counteroffer:
   Always accept a counteroffer of $200 or more. Always reject a counteroffer under $100,
   and accept a counteroffer between $200 and $100 if and only if $\underline{W}_B$ = $100.
Welmade's beliefs:
   Unknown as yet.

separating equilibrium, a low wage will imply that Welmade is *certain* that Barry has a $100 reservation wage. Similarly, a high initial wage offer by the union, W_H^1, will signal to Welmade that Barry has a reservation wage of $200. We have added these beliefs to Table 20.3b.

TABLE 20.3b   Bayesian equilibrium of game 3 (incremental strikes)

Union's initial offer:
  Unknown as yet.
Welmade's reaction and counteroffer:
  Unknown as yet.
Union's reaction to the counteroffer:
  Always accept a counteroffer of $200, always reject a counteroffer under $100,
  and accept a counteroffer between $200 and $100 if and only if $\underline{W}_B$ = $100.
Welmade's beliefs:
  $P(\underline{W}_B) = \$100 \mid W^I = W_L^I) = 1.$
  $P(\underline{W}_B) = \$100 \mid W^I = W_H^I) = 0.$

Having specified a set of beliefs for Welmade and determined how the union will react to any Welmade counteroffer, let us move up the game tree and determine Welmade's response to the union's initial offer. If the union has a low reservation wage and offers the wage $W_L^{\,I}$, and Welmade accepts it, then Welmade will make a profit of $\$750 - 3 \cdot W_L^{\,I}$. If Welmade rejects the offer, it will experience a half-week strike and then get a chance to make a counteroffer. Because Welmade believes that the offer of $W_L^{\,I}$ means the union will accept any counteroffer of $100 or more, Welmade should counter with an offer of $100. So if Welmade rejects the offer, it makes a profit of $(\$750 - 3 \cdot \$100)/2$. The initial wage offer, $W_L^{\,I}$, which makes Welmade exactly indifferent between accepting and rejecting the union's initial offer, satisfies

$$\$750 - 3 \cdot W_L^I = (\$750 - 3 \cdot \$100)/2. \tag{20.1a}$$

or

$$W_L^I = \$175. \tag{20.1b}$$

For simplicity we will assume that Welmade accepts the offer whenever it is exactly indifferent between accepting and rejecting it. The union will certainly not make a low-wage offer that is less than $175, since $175 will be accepted by Welmade. Nor will they offer more than $175, when Barry's reservation wage is low, because the firm will reject any offer greater than $175 and counter with an offer of $100. We have added this information to Table 20.3c.

We can use a similar logic to analyze the case where Barry has a high reservation wage of $200. If Welmade accepts a high wage offer, it will earn $\$750 - 3 \cdot W_H^{\,I}$; if it rejects the offer, then Welmade will suffer through a half-week strike and counter

TABLE 20.3c   Bayesian equilibrium of game 3 (incremental strikes)

Union's initial offer:
  If $\underline{W}_B$ = $100, then offer W_L^I = $175.
  If $\underline{W}_B$ = $200, then offer W_H^I = ?.
Welmade's reaction and counteroffer:
  If $W^I \leq$ $175, then accept.
  If $W^I >$ $175, unknown as yet.
Union's reaction to the counteroffer:
  Always accept a counteroffer of $200, always reject a counteroffer under $100,
  and accept a counteroffer between $200 and $100 if and only if $\underline{W}_B$ = $100.
Welmade's beliefs:
  $P(\underline{W}_B) = \$100 \mid W^I = W_L^I) = 1.$
  $P(\underline{W}_B) = \$100 \mid W^I = W_H^I) = 0.$

with an offer of $200 (remember Welmade now believes with certainty that the union has a high reservation wage) resulting in a profit of ($750 – 3 · $200)/2. The high wage that makes Welmade exactly indifferent between accepting and rejecting the offer is found by solving

$$\$750 - 3 \cdot W_H^{\ I} = (\$750 - 3 \cdot \$200)/2, \tag{20.2a}$$

or

$$W_H^{\ I} = \$225. \tag{20.2b}$$

Welmade is assumed to accept this offer. If the union proposes a wage above $225, it will be rejected, the workers will have to work elsewhere for half a week, and then Welmade will simply counter with an offer of $200. The workers end up earning a wage of $200 for the week. Because a proposal of $225 will be accepted, this is the union's best offer. This allows us to fill in the remaining gaps in the Bayesian equilibrium.

Having specified rational strategies given the beliefs of Welmade, we need to check whether the beliefs of Welmade are consistent with the rational strategies. In our example, this verification is easy. The union offers a wage of $175 only if Barry has a reservation wage of $100, and they offer a wage of $225 only if Barry has a reservation wage of $200. Therefore, Welmade's beliefs are accurate, given the chosen strategies.

TABLE 20.3d   Bayesian equilibrium of game 3 (incremental strikes)

Union's initial offer:
   If $\underline{W}_B$ = $100, then offer W_L^I = $175.
   If $\underline{W}_B$ = $200, then offer W_H^I = $225.
Welmade's reaction and counteroffer:
   If $W^I \le$ $175, then accept.
   If $175 < W^I <$ $225, then reject and counter with $100.
   If $W^I =$ $225, then accept.
   If $W^I >$ $225, then reject and counter with $100.
Union's reaction to the counteroffer:
   Always accept a counteroffer of $200, always reject a counteroffer under $100,
   and accept a counteroffer between $200 and $100 if and only if $\underline{W}_B$ = $100.
Welmade's beliefs:
   $P(\underline{W}_B)$ = $100 | W^I = W_L^I) = 1.
   $P(\underline{W}_B)$ = $100 | W^I = W_H^I) = 0.

The only problem with Table 20.3d is that the union strategy given—propose a wage of $175 when its reservation wage is low and a wage of $225 when its reservation wage is high—is not an optimal response to Welmade's strategy. Because Welmade will accept either offer, the union should always propose a wage of $225, regardless of its reservation wage. That is, when the union's reservation wage is low, it should simply bluff and act as if its reservation wage is high.

What we have found out is that there is no separating equilibrium for this game *in pure strategies*. In any separating equilibrium, the players must be using mixed strategies. Specifically, Welmade cannot always accept a union wage offer of $225. Sometimes it must call the union's bluff by rejecting this wage and forcing the union to call a strike. This strategy has the effect of making it costly for the union to bluff. Because calling the union's bluff is also costly for Welmade, the firm will want to do this as seldom as it can. We now need to determine the optimal amount of "calling" by Welmade and the optimal amount of "bluffing" by the union.

20.4.2   Finding a separating equilibrium

Because the correct separating equilibrium looks very similar to the "equilibrium" we derived in the previous section, we will begin by simply asserting what it is in Table 20.4. We will then show why it is an equilibrium as claimed. Notice that in this equilibrium the union sometimes bluffs (pretends to have a high reservation wage when it does not) and that sometimes Welmade calls the union's bluff by rejecting its high wage demands.

TABLE 20.4   Bayesian equilibrium of game 3 (incremental strikes) with mixed strategies

Union's initial offer:
  If $\underline{W}_B$ = $100, offer $225 with probability 0.5 and offer $175 with probability 0.5.
  If $\underline{W}_B$ = $200, always offer $225.
Welmade's reaction and counteroffer:
  Always accept an offer less than or equal to $175. Accept an offer of $225 with
  probability 0.6 and reject the offer and counter with $100 with probability 0.4.
  Always reject any offer over $225 or between $175 and $225 and counter
  with $100.
Union's reaction to the counteroffer:
  Always accept a counteroffer of $200, always reject a counteroffer under $100,
  and accept a counteroffer between $200 and $100 if and only if $\underline{W}_B$ = $100.
Welmade's beliefs based on the initial offer:
  $P(\underline{W}_B) = \$100 \mid W^I \neq \$225) = 1$.
  $P(\underline{W}_B) = \$100 \mid W^I = \$225) = 1/3$.

As you can see, the union has improved the outcome of the bargaining process very significantly over the outcome when they threaten no incremental strike. When the union's reservation wages are high, the union will ask and get $225 with probability 0.60 and will end up with $200 with probability 0.40; the expected wage is $215. When the union's reservation wages are low, then the union will ask and receive $175 with probability 0.5; will ask and receive $225 with probability $0.5 \cdot 0.6 = 0.3$; and will ask for $225 but end up accepting $100 with probability $0.5 \cdot 0.4 = 0.2$. The expected wage equals $175. Because in any given week there is a 50% chance of having a high reservation wage and a 50% chance of having a low reservation wage, expected equilibrium earnings, prior to knowing $\underline{W}_B$, equal $195.

No strike occurs under any of the following conditions: The union's reservation wage is low and it does not try to bluff; the union's reservation wage is low, it bluffs and asks for $225, and Welmade accepts it; or the union's reservation wage is high, it asks for $225, and Welmade accepts it. The probability any of these mutually exclusive events occur equals $0.5 \cdot 0.5 + 0.5 \cdot 0.5 \cdot 0.6 + 0.5 \cdot 0.6 = 0.70$. A short strike occurs when the union's reservation wage is low, it bluffs and asks for $225, but Welmade rejects the offer. The probability that this occurs is $0.5 \cdot 0.5 \cdot 0.4 = 0.10$. Finally, a long strike occurs when the union's reservation wage is high and it asks for $225, but Welmade turns the offer down. This happens with probability $0.5 \cdot 0.4 = 0.2$. The expected length of a strike equals $0.7 \cdot 0$ weeks $+ 0.1 \cdot 1/2$ week $+ 0.2 \cdot 1$ week $= 0.25$ week. That is, 25% of the time the workers will be on strike.

That the strategies and beliefs in Table 20.4 form a Bayesian equilibrium is easy to show. First, given the union's strategy, Welmade's beliefs are consistent with Bayes' theorem.

$$P(\underline{W}_B = \$100 \mid W = \$225) = \tag{20.3a}$$

$$\frac{P(W = \$225 \mid \underline{W}_B = \$100) \cdot P(\underline{W}_B = \$100)}{P(W = \$225 \mid \underline{W}_B = \$100) \cdot P(\underline{W}_B = \$100) + P(W = \$225 \mid \underline{W}_B = \$200) \cdot P(\underline{W}_B = \$200)}$$

$$= \frac{(1/2) \cdot (1/2)}{(1/2) \cdot (1/2) + (1) \cdot (1/2)}$$

$$= 1/3,$$

and

$$P(\underline{W}_B = \$100 \mid W = \$175) = \tag{20.3b}$$

$$\frac{P(W = \$175 \mid W_B = \$100) \cdot P(W_B = \$100)}{P(W = \$175 \mid \underline{W}_B = \$100) \cdot P(\underline{W}_B = \$100) + P(W = \$175 \mid \underline{W}_B = \$200) \cdot P(\underline{W}_B = \$200)}$$

$$= \left[\frac{1 \cdot 1/2}{1 \cdot 1/2 + 0 \cdot 1/2} \right]$$

$$= 1.$$

Next we consider Welmade's reaction to the union's initial offer. Suppose the union proposes a wage of $175. Given Welmade's beliefs, the probability of Barry's reservation wage being low is 100%. Therefore, Welmade's expected profit if it accepts the offer equals $750 − 3 · $175 = $225. By waiting the half-week, Welmade can counter with an offer of $100, which the union will accept. Welmade's expected profit equals ($750 − 3 · $100)/2 = $225. Since Welmade is indifferent, it might as well accept the offer. It follows that any offer between $175 and $225 will be rejected and followed by a midweek counteroffer of $100. In poker terminology, the union "blinked," and the firm is now calling its certain bluff.

Now consider an offer of $225 from the union. Welmade believes that Barry's reservation wage is $100 with probability 1/3. Welmade will use a mixed strategy only if it is exactly indifferent between accepting the offer and rejecting it and countering with $100. If it accepts the offer, its profit equals $750 − 3 · $225 = $75. If it rejects and counters with $100, then one-third of the time the counteroffer is accepted and two-thirds of the time it is rejected and the strike is extended to the whole week. The firm's expected profit equals

$$1/3 \cdot (\$750 - 3 \cdot \$100)/2 + 2/3 \cdot \$0 = \$75. \qquad (20.4)$$

Because the firm is indifferent between acceptance and rejection, a mixed strategy is optimal.

Finally, we must look at the union's strategy. Suppose $\underline{W}_B$ equals $200. Any initial offer less than $200 is senseless because it is below Barry's reservation wage. Any offer between $200 and $225 or over $225 will be rejected by Welmade and countered with an offer of $100. Because this is below Barry's reservation wage, the union will reject it and Barry will work the entire week at some other job for $200. If the union offers exactly $225, then Welmade will accept the offer 60% of the time. This implies that Barry's expected wage equals

$$0.6 \cdot \$225 + 0.4 \cdot \$200 = \$215. \qquad (20.5)$$

The union's optimal wage offer is $225.

If $\underline{W}_B$ is $100, then the situation is a little more complex. The union knows that, given Welmade's beliefs and strategy, any offer other than $175 or $225 is dominated. An offer of $175 will be accepted immediately. An offer of $225 will only be accepted with 0.6 probability, and when rejected it will be countered in midweek by a counteroffer of $100. This implies the expected wage for the week equals $0.6 \cdot \$225 + 0.4 \cdot \$100 = \$175$. Because Barry is indifferent between offering $175 and offering $225, it is optimal to randomize between them.

If you step back and reconsider Table 20.4, you will see that we have shown the strategies and beliefs in that table constitute a Bayesian equilibrium.

20.5 · Generalizations

Although we have assumed throughout this chapter that the firm's payoffs are common knowledge, this is clearly not true in real-world applications. When both sides have private information about their payoffs, then both sides will bluff, and the frequency and duration of bargaining impasses will only increase.

That the length of a strike or lockout can signal one's resolve to the opponent is an important insight into the labor negotiation process and has many testable implications. First, it implies that strikes will be more frequent and last longer during periods when the workers' reservation wages or the firm's profit function is changing than during periods when these factors are not changing. This is not because the two sides are confused about their optimal strategies, but because a long strike or lockout may offer the only credible way for one side to convince the other that the payoffs have changed. The bigger the change, the longer the strike or lockout may have to be.

20.6 • Summary

In this chapter we have seen the effect of private information on bilateral bargaining over a labor contract. When there is perfect information, a strike is unlikely. In more realistic settings in which the firm does not have information about the reservation wages of the members of the union (most importantly the median union member), there may be a delay in obtaining an agreement. The purpose of the delay is to communicate the payoffs to the opponent credibly. But the delay will be credible only if it is costly to the player threatening it.

Three models of increasing complexity were presented. The first model assumed a very short negotiation process, the second model allowed for alternating offers, and the third model allowed the union to threaten an incremental strike. Not surprisingly, as additional pieces of reality were introduced to what was initially a very simple model, the level of complexity of the equilibrium increased as well. It is not hard to think of additional pieces of reality, the most obvious being incomplete information about the firm on the part of the union. We leave it to the reader to pursue that topic at her leisure.

20.7 • Further Reading

For a review of the recent work on bargaining and private information, see John Kennan and Robert Wilson, "Strategic Bargaining Models and Interpretation of Strike Data," *Journal of Applied Econometrics* 4 (1989), pp. 87–130. Another survey of the literature can be found in Martin Osborne and Ariel Rubenstein, *Bargaining and Markets* (San Diego: Academic Press, 1990). The stategic option of holding out is explored in Peter Cramton and Joseph Tracy, "Strikes and Holdouts in Wage Bargaining: Theory and Data," *American Economic Review* 82 (1992), pp.100–121. A dated but still useful discussion of how private information affects the internal dynamics of the union and its decision to strike is Orley Ashenfelter and George Johnson, "Bargaining Theory, Trade Unions, and Industrial Strike Activity," *American Economic Review* 59 (1969), pp. 35–49.

20.8 • Exercises

Exercise 20.1   Show that in game 1, if the probability that Barry has a low reservation wage is below 1/3, then Taylor's optimal strategy is to offer a wage of $200, and the union's optimal strategy is to accept this offer.

Exercise 20.2   Consider game 2. Let π denote the probability that the union's reservation wage equals $100. For what values of π does this game have a "pooling" equilibrium in which the union offers $200, regardless of its true reservation wage?

Exercise 20.3   Alter game 2 in the following way: The union makes a take-it-or-leave-it offer. If the firm rejects the union's offer, then the union strikes for the entire week. Find a Bayesian equilibrium of this new game. Be sure to check: (i) that Welmade's strategy is optimal given its beliefs, (ii) that the union's strategy is optimal given Welmade's strategy, and (iii) that Welmade's beliefs are consistent with the union's strategy.

Exercise 20.4   In game 3, suppose the incremental strike lasts only one-third of a week instead of half a week. This new game has a separating Bayesian equilibrium similar to that described in Table 20.4. Find this equilibrium.

CHAPTER 21

Corporate Takeovers and Greenmail

21.1 · Introduction

There has been a great deal of popular interest in the most recent wave of corporate mergers. The stories of insider trading, of the gaining and losing of fortunes among investment bankers like Ivan Boesky and Michael Milken, and of the collapse of firms such as Drexel Burnham have made for fascinating reading. Alongside this expansive coverage of the corporate sector has arisen a flowery new language. Ten years ago economists simply talked about "mergers" and the "market for corporate control," and students' eyes would glaze over. Now we can talk about "greenmail," "white knights," "raiders," and "poison pills."

In this chapter we will first consider the conventional wisdom surrounding some of these strategies. We will then show some ways in which the conventional wisdom may be wrong. The credit for this unconventional viewpoint is due to two economists, Andrei Shleifer and Robert Vishny. We borrow liberally from their analysis.

21.2 · The current lexicon and conventional wisdom

Outside of curiosity about the act of one firm taking over another firm, there is a great deal of debate among economists and businesspeople about two aspects of merger activity. First, how does the threat of a merger affect shareholders of corporations? It has long been recognized that managers of corporations may have different objectives than corporate owners (the shareholders). Because managers seem to be able to engage in behavior that discourages merger activity or takeover attempts (such as "greenmail" or "poison pills"), the question arises as to whether these managerial strategies are in the best interest of the owners of the corporation. Second, what are the consequences of merger activity for the economy as a whole? Are mergers simply motivated by complicated tax laws or financial market gimmicks that make investment bankers rich at the expense of the rest of the world? Or do mergers serve the purpose of driving mediocre management and corporate structures out of existence and replacing them by more efficient managers and firms?

In this chapter we will make headway only on the first question. That is, we will concentrate on the conditions under which certain types of managerial responses to a takeover attempt are actually in the best interest of the shareholders.

Suppose that a firm is perceived by *someone* to be a target for a takeover attempt.[1] Perhaps this someone has reason to believe that better management could run the firm more profitably, or perhaps it is thought that the various operations that the firm performs could be sold off piecemeal at a profit, or perhaps it is thought that there will be a synergistic effect (one plus one equals more than two) by merging this firm with another. Whatever the reason, one possible action the acquirer might take is to begin buying up shares of the target firm (or threatening to do so). At some stage the acquirer then announces, or threatens to announce, a tender offer for a majority of the outstanding shares. In a **tender offer**, the acquirer promises to buy all shares tendered to it before a given date and time at a share price usually well above the current market price—*as long as* enough shares are tendered so as to transfer effective control of the corporation over to the acquirer. The "unfriendly" acquirer is often referred to as a **raider.**

To combat the raider's tender offer, the management of the target firm can buy back the raider's shares at a price above what the raider paid for them; this is known as a **repurchase agreement**. In addition, the management of the target firm almost always requires in this agreement that the acquirer not buy any new shares in the target firm for some fairly lengthy time period. In short, the target firm's management bribes the potential acquirer to get away and stay away! The profit the raider makes from accepting such an agreement is called **greenmail**.

On the surface it seems that greenmail helps the managers of the firm, who are worried about their future employment, but is bad for the shareholders, who are prevented from selling their shares for a relatively high price. All the acquirer wants to do, so the conventional wisdom goes, is to offer the shareholders a share price

---

[1]*Someone* can refer to an individual investor, a consortium of investors, or the management of another firm using the financial capital of their stockholders.

above the current market price. The shareholders will tender their shares only if they perceive that it is in their interest to do so. So they must be made better off if they choose to tender their shares. It follows, therefore, that self-interested management must be protecting its own narrow interests by engaging in greenmail.

21.3 · Why the conventional wisdom might be wrong

The reason shareholders of the targeted firm might be made better off if the management pays greenmail to a raider is that by doing so they might be able to induce other firms to start bidding for the ownership of the firm. The entry of these other firms may result in a higher share price than would have resulted if only the raider made an offer. A **white knight** is a special type of bidder who has been *invited* by the target firm to submit a bid. The cynical view is that the white knight is invited in by the firm in distress in order to save the jobs of senior managers. But we will show that another possible reason for the invitation is that it can increase the level of competition for the rights of the distressed firm. The payment of greenmail turns out to be a signal to the white knight about the economic status of the target firm, which is known only to the target firm.

21.4 · Greenmail without white knights

Imagine a target firm, Bull's Eye Inc., which is being considered for acquisition by two potential acquirers, Carnivore Inc. and Appetite UnLtd. Two important aspects of this model are that these two potential acquirers are not identical and that each is uncertain about the profitability of a takeover.

The owners of Carnivore have no concrete idea how they would go about making Bull's Eye more profitable. They do know, however, that if they spend $12,000 on a consultant, there is a 50% chance that the consultant will uncover some hitherto unknown scheme that will increase Bull's Eye's market value by $120,000.[2] There is also a 50% chance that the consultant will come up empty and Carnivore will have spent $12,000 for nothing.

The expected gross gain from hiring the consultant is

$$0.5 \cdot \$120,000 + 0.5 \cdot \$0 = \$60,000. \tag{21.1}$$

---

[2]This is the present value of the increased profits Bull's Eye would earn after reorganization. In a more general model we would model the expected payoff as an increasing, continuous function of the amount spent by Carnivore for financial consulting services.

The consultant costs only $12,000, so there is an expected net gain of $48,000. As long as the expected gain is nonnegative, the purchase of the consultant's services is rational.

The other potential acquirer, Appetite UnLtd., is in a similar but not identical position. It has access to another consultant who has a 50% chance of finding a way to increase the market value of Bull's Eye by $200,000. The cost of this consultant is $48,000. As in the previous case, if Appetite UnLtd. were the sole proprietors of Bull's Eye, then these consulting fees would be worth paying. As owners of Bull's Eye they would have an expected gross gain from hiring the consultant of

$$0.5 \cdot \$100,000 + 0.5 \cdot \$0 = \$50,000. \tag{21.2}$$

Because the consultant costs $48,000, the net gain is $2,000.

21.4.1 Digression: The splitting of the gains

Before we can calculate the payoffs for the game, we must have a brief discussion of who gains from the acquisition of the target firm. The split will depend on how many firms are bidding for Bull's Eye.

If both Carnivore and Appetite try to acquire Bull's Eye, then they will get into a **bidding war**. We will suppose that this war takes the form of an auction in which the shares of Bull's Eye are sold to the highest bidder. Under conditions of perfect information (remember, we are at the final stage of the game), it is recognized by all that the firm that is willing to pay the most for Bull's Eye must pay at least what the second highest bidder is willing to offer—but no more than this. Since at this stage the consultants' fees are "water under the bridge," the value to Carnivore of acquiring Bull's Eye equals $120,000, and the value to Appetite of acquiring Bull's Eye equals $200,000. It follows that Appetite will win the auction by paying $120,000 for Bull's Eye's shares. Bull's Eye's current stockholders gain $120,000, Appetite gains $200,000 – $120,000 = $80,000, and Carnivore gains nothing.

It is much less clear what the outcome will be if only one of the two potential acquirers makes a bid for Bull's Eye. Shareholders may rationally hold onto shares to participate in the increased value of the firm rather than sell them to a bidder. For simplicity, we will assume that if there is only one bidder, then Bull's Eye's increased value is split 50/50 between the acquirer and the current shareholders. There are a wide variety of other splits that could also be rationalized, but that is left to another book. Although our specific numerical solutions depend on how these gains are divided, the qualitative features of the equilibria we will obtain below remain unchanged if other splits are used. What is important is only that the acquirer gain *something* from taking over Bull's Eye.

21.4.2 Back to our story

Having described the players, their possible actions, and the outcomes of these actions, it is time to describe the game tree. In the first stage, Carnivore and Appetite simultaneously decide whether to hire their respective consultant(s). In the second stage, Nature decides whether the consultant(s) hired is (are) successful. Finally, in the third stage, Carnivore and Appetite make tender offers to shareholders of Bull's Eye and the final payoffs are generated. The first two stages of the game tree are shown in Figure 21.1.

The third stage in which the acquirer(s) bids for Bull's Eye's shares is not shown in Figure 21.1. Instead, in the interest of simplicity, this part of the game tree has been replaced by terminal nodes. The payoff triples (Carnivore, Appetite, Bull's Eye) assigned to those nodes are the payoffs that result from optimal play in the bidding subgame. In the bidding subgame, a potential acquirer makes a bid for Bull's Eye if and only if it knows how to make Bull's Eye more profitable. An acquirer has this information if and only if its consultant has been successful.

With the bidding game solved out, the game is reduced to a simultaneous-move game between Appetite and Carnivore. In this game, the firms must decide whether or not to hire the consultant. Their joint decision results in the playing of one of four

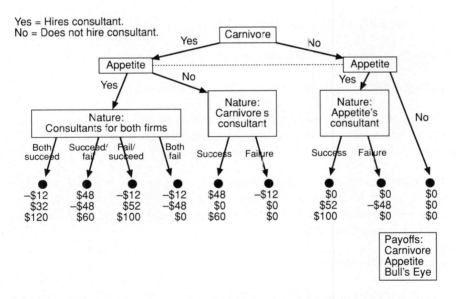

FIGURE 21.1 • Game tree for the takeover game between Bull's Eye, Carnivore, and Appetite.

lotteries. Either one can separately hire a consultant, both can hire consultants, or neither one can hire a consultant. Their choices will depend on the expected payoffs to both of them from playing each of the lotteries.

It is worthwhile to verify the payoffs asserted in Figure 21.1. We will move from right to left. If neither firm acquires a consultant, then neither will try to take over Bull's Eye, so the payoffs to all three players are zero. If Carnivore does not hire a consultant but Appetite does, and the consultant fails, then again neither firm bids for Bull's Eye. Carnivore's and Bull's Eye's payoffs are zero, and Appetite suffers the loss of its $48,000 consultant's fee. If only Appetite's consultant is successful, then only Appetite will bid for Bull's Eye's stock. As we have already discussed, we assume the $200,000 gain from acquiring Bull's Eye is split evenly between Appetite and Bull's Eye. So Carnivore's payoff equals zero, Bull's Eye's payoff equals $0.50 \cdot \$200,000 = \$100,000$, and Appetite's payoff equals $0.50 \cdot \$200,000 - \$48,000 = \$52,000$.

Suppose both firms hire a consultant. Then the lottery played has four possible outcomes: Both consultants are successful, only Carnivore's consultant is successful, only Appetite's consultant is successful, or both consultants are unsuccessful. We will assume the success or failure of Carnivore's consultant is independent of the success or failure of Appetite's consultant. As a result, each of these four outcomes is equally likely. From Figure 21.1 we see that Carnivore's expected payoff equals:

$$0.75 \cdot -\$12,000 + 0.25 \cdot \$48,000 = \$3,000, \tag{21.3}$$

and Appetite's expected payoff equals

$$0.25 \cdot \$32,000 + 0.25 \cdot \$52,000 + 0.50 \cdot -\$48,000 = -\$3,000. \tag{21.4}$$

If only Carnivore hires a consultant, there are two equally likely outcomes: The consultant is successful, or the consultant is unsuccessful. Carnivore's expected payoff equals

$$0.50 \cdot \$48,000 + 0.50 \cdot -\$12,000 = \$18,000, \tag{21.5}$$

and Appetite's expected payoff equals $0. Similarly, if only Appetite hires a consultant, then its expected payoff equals

$$0.50 \cdot \$52,000 + 0.50 \cdot -\$48,000 = \$2,000, \tag{21.6}$$

and Carnivore's expected payoff equals $0.

The resulting payoff matrix for the simultaneous-move game played in stage 1 is shown in Table 21.1. You can confirm that Carnivore has a strongly dominant strategy: Hire the consultant. Appetite does not have a dominant strategy, but it does have

TABLE 21.1   Expected payoffs from takeover game

		Carnivore, Inc.	
		Hire Consultant	Don't hire consultant
Appetite UnLtd.	Hire Consultant	($3,000, –$3,000)	($0, $2,000)
	Don't Hire Consultant	($18,000, $0)	($0, $0)
		Payoffs: (Carnivore, Appetite)	

an iterated dominant strategy: Don't hire the consultant. So this game has an iterated dominant strategy equilibrium in which only Carnivore hires a consultant. This consultant has a 50% chance of successfully figuring out how Carnivore can make Bull's Eye more profitable. The expected payoff to Bull's Eye shareholders when Carnivore and Appetite play their equilibrium strategies equals

$$0.50 \cdot \$60,000 + 0.50 \cdot \$0 = \$30,000. \tag{21.7}$$

Now let us suppose that the management of Bull's Eye can "bribe" Carnivore not to play the takeover game we have just analyzed. The only way Bull's Eye could benefit from paying such a bribe is if doing so would induce Appetite to hire a consultant and explore the feasibility of taking over Bull's Eye. We already know that Appetite will hire a consultant if and only if Carnivore is removed from the game. But taking a potential acquirer out of the takeover game is exactly what greenmail is meant to do! What has been missed in the conventional analysis of takeovers is that the stockholder might actually benefit from removing an acquirer. It will benefit if doing so induces a better acquirer to enter the picture.

The new game tree that includes the potential payment of greenmail is shown in Figure 21.2. In the first stage, Bull's Eye offers Carnivore greenmail of G to stay out of the takeover game against Appetite. Paying $0 to Carnivore is equivalent to not offering greenmail. Carnivore can either accept or reject this offer. If Carnivore accepts the offer, then Appetite can decide whether to hire the consultant confident that there will be no bidding war against Carnivore. If Carnivore rejects the greenmail offer, then Carnivore and Appetite play the takeover subgame analyzed previously. In Figure 21.2, we have replaced this entire subgame with a terminal node. The payoffs assigned to this node are the expected Nash equilibrium payoffs of the subgame. The first payoff listed in each triple belongs to Carnivore, the second to Appetite, and the third to Bull's Eye's stockholders.

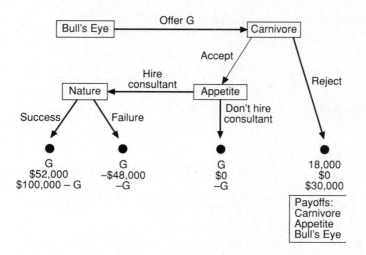

FIGURE 21.2 • Game tree for the takeover game between Bull's Eye, Appetite, and Carnivore that explicitly allows for the payment of greenmail by Bull's Eye.

This game is a sequential-move game, so we can find its equilibrium using backwards induction. We begin with Appetite's decision as to whether or not to hire the consultant knowing that Carnivore has accepted the greenmail offer. The expected payoff from hiring the consultant equals

$$0.50 \cdot \$52,000 + 0.50 \cdot -\$48,000 = \$2,000. \tag{21.8}$$

Because this is positive, Appetite will hire the consultant. Moving up the game tree, the next decision node belongs to Carnivore. Carnivore will accept any greenmail offer of \$18,000 or more. If Bull's Eye offers \$18,000 to Carnivore, the offer will be accepted and Appetite will hire the consultant. The expected payoff to Bull's Eye's stockholders equals

$$0.50 \cdot (\$100,000 - \$18,000) + 0.50 \cdot -\$18,000 = \$32,000. \tag{21.9}$$

On the other hand, if Bull's Eye offers less than \$18,000 to Carnivore, the offer will be rejected, only Carnivore will hire a consultant, and the expected payoff to Bull's Eye's stockholders will equal \$30,000. It follows that payment of \$18,000 in greenmail to Carnivore is in the best interests of the shareholders![3]

---

[3]If you don't love game theory when you see results like this, you are just not cut out to be a game theorist.

21.5 • Greenmail with white knights

While the model just presented seems logically sound, it does not conform well to empirical data. The model predicts that when the stockholders of a takeover target observe a raider accepting a greenmail offer from their firm, they should infer that a more suitable acquirer exists and is being enticed into exploring the firm's takeover. As a result, the stockholders should immediately revise their evaluation of the firm's worth upward, and the firm's stock price should increase. Unfortunately, that is not what the data show. Instead, the acceptance of greenmail is usually followed by a *drop* in the stock price of the target firm. Second, when a target refuses to pay greenmail to a raider, the target often seeks out a "white knight"—a potential acquirer that is *requested* by the targeted firm to make an offer for its shares.

In this section we will try to account for these two stylized facts by introducing private information into our takeover game. This modification will allow us to account for the two empirical facts we have just cited.

First, however, we need to make a few other modifications to our takeover game. We will assume there are *three* potential acquirers for Bull's Eye: Carnivore Inc., Appetite UnLtd., and Jacob Pickens. We will also modify the informational structure of the game and the payoffs. Assume that Carnivore *already knows* how to increase Bull's Eye's market value by $140,000. Appetite and Pickens do not know how to do this, but both can hire a consultant to help them. As before, a consultant has a 50% chance of figuring out how to increase Bull's Eye's market value by $200,000 and a 50% chance of being completely unsuccessful. A consultant costs $10,000.

We will make the same assumptions about how the gains from an acquisition are split between the acquiring firm and the current stockholders of Bull's Eye. If only one firm makes an offer for Bull's Eye's shares, then the gains are split 50/50. But if there is a bidding war between two or more bidders, then the winner must pay what the second highest bidder would have been willing to pay to take over Bull's Eye. For example, if the bidders are Carnivore and Appetite, then Appetite will win the auction for Bull's Eye by paying $140,000. Appetite gains $60,000, Bull's Eye's stockholders gain $140,000, and Carnivore gains nothing. On the other hand, if the bidders are Appetite and Pickens, both of which are willing to pay up to $200,000 to acquire Bull's Eye, then the winner must bid $200,000 for the stock, and the stockholders capture all the gains from the acquisition.

Now comes the interesting informational assumption. Bull's Eye's management is in a good position to know what needs to be done to increase its profits. As a result, Bull's Eye may know *from the very beginning* whether Appetite or Pickens can make a profit from taking over the firm. We will refer to this knowledge as "having a white knight." If Bull's Eye possesses this information, Bull's Eye can share it with the "white knight," thereby ensuring that the white knight will bid for Bull's Eye's shares.

The new game tree is displayed in Figure 21.3. Nature begins the game by deciding whether or not Bull's Eye has a white knight and, if so, who it is. The white knight is either Appetite or Pickens, but never both. Nature's move is observed only by Bull's Eye. Knowing whether or not there is a white knight, Bull's Eye then makes a greenmail offer to Carnivore, which Carnivore can either accept or reject. Upon observing Bull's Eye's offer and Carnivore's acceptance, Appetite and Pickens simultaneously decide whether to hire consultants. Immediately afterward, Nature decides whether the consultants are successful or not. The three firms then decide whether they will make a bid for Bull's Eye. Only then can Bull's Eye reveal any information it has to any of the three potential acquirers. The game now ends and payoffs are realized.

As always, we will begin our analysis with the last move in the game. This move belongs to Bull's Eye when Bull's Eye has a white knight. It must decide whether or not to share its knowledge of how to increase its market value with the white knight. At this point in the game, two things are possible: Either the white knight already knows how to increase Bull's Eye's value, or it does not. In the first case, sharing Bull's Eye's information is moot. In the second case, however, sharing the information turns the white knight into an active bidder for Bull's Eye's shares. This can only increase the price paid by the acquirer, no matter how many firms are bidding.

Therefore, Bull's Eye will always share its private information with its white knight, when it has one. When Bull's Eye does not have a white knight, the firms must base any bids they make on whatever information they have learned privately through their consultants. As a consequence, Carnivore's, Appetite's, and Pickens'

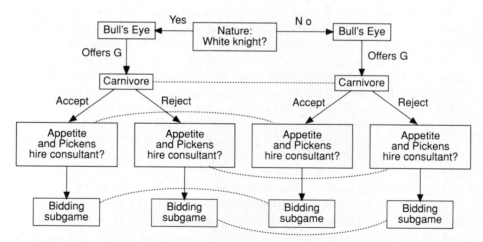

FIGURE 21.3 · The game tree for the takeover game played between Bull's Eye, Carnivore, Appetite, and Pickens where Bull's Eye may have a white knight.

payoffs will depend, among other things, on whether or not Bull's Eye has a white knight. In order to evaluate the expected payoff of each of their strategies, these three players must form a belief about Bull's Eye's knowledge. This belief consists of a probability p that Bull's Eye has a white knight. The belief may depend on Bull's Eye's greenmail offer to Carnivore. An example of a belief is: "Bull's Eye does not have a white knight for certain whenever if offers $50,000 or more in greenmail, and has a white knight for certain whenever it offers less than $50,000 in greenmail."

This belief is the same for all three players. In order for the belief to be rational, it must be consistent with Bayes' theorem and Bull's Eye's optimal strategy. So if Carnivore, Appetite, and Pickens all believe Bull's Eye has a white knight if and only if it offers less than $50,000 in greenmail, then Bull's Eye's strategy must be of the form: "Offer $50,000 in greenmail when there is no white knight, and offer no greenmail when there is a white knight."

We will show that if Appetite and Pickens believe Bull's Eye has a white knight, then they both have a dominant strategy: Do not hire a consultant, regardless of whether or not Carnivore accepts Bull's Eye's greenmail. If Appetite and Pickens believe that Bull's Eye does not have a white knight, then they have a different dominant strategy: Hire a consultant, regardless of whether or not Carnivore accepts Bull's Eye's greenmail.

It now follows that Carnivore's optimal strategy will also depend on its belief about the existence of a white knight. If Carnivore believes there is a white knight, then it can foresee that it will lose the bidding war for Bull's Eye. As a result, it will accept any greenmail offer Bull's Eye makes. On the other hand, if Carnivore believes there is no white knight, then it can foresee that it has some chance of successfully taking over Bull's Eye (namely, when Appetite's and Pickens' consultants are both unsuccessful). As a result, Carnivore will accept any greenmail offer of $17,500 or more.

It remains only to determine Bull's Eye's optimal strategy. This strategy consists of one greenmail offer when there is a white knight and another greenmail offer when there is no white knight. Bull's Eye's optimal strategy depends on what the other players infer from Bull's Eye's greenmail offer. We are looking for consistency: The other player's beliefs must be consistent with Bull's Eye's strategy and Bayes' theorem, and Bull's Eye's strategy must be an optimal response to the other player's beliefs. We will show that the following strategy for Bull's Eye and beliefs for Carnivore, Appetite, and Pickens have the mutual consistency we desire: Bull's Eye offers $50,000 in greenmail when there is no white knight and offers nothing when there is. The other three players believe there is no white knight when Bull's Eye offers $50,000 or more and believe there is a white knight if Bull's Eye offers less than $50,000.

Notice that in this equilibrium the payment of greenmail signals Bull's Eye does *not* have a white knight. When Bull's Eye *has* a white knight, no greenmail is paid to

Carnivore. Instead Bull's Eye reveals its private information to the white knight. This equilibrium not only reveals the role of the white knight but also shows why paying greenmail is bad news for the target firm's stockholders: In this equilibrium, the stockholders' expected payoff is *higher* when there is a white knight than when there isn't. Not only is the expected price paid for Bull's Eye's stock higher when there is a white knight, but no greenmail needs to be paid to Carnivore.

We must now establish our claims about the optimal strategies of our four players. We will begin with Appetite and Pickens. Suppose both of them believe Bull's Eye has a white knight. Then they can foresee that Bull's Eye will eventually tell one of them how to make it more profitable. Consider Appetite's position. If it is the white knight, then hiring a consultant is a waste of money. And if Pickens is the white knight, then Appetite can take over Bull's Eye only by getting into a bidding war with Pickens and paying $200,000. Because this again results in a loss, Appetite has a dominant strategy: Don't hire a consultant. Because of the symmetry between the two firms, the same is true for Pickens.

Now suppose both firms believe that Bull's Eye does *not* have a white knight and Carnivore turned down Bull's Eye's greenmail offer. If Appetite does not hire a consultant, then it will never find out how to make Bull's Eye more profitable, and its payoff will be zero. If both it and Pickens hire consultants, then three outcomes of relevance to Appetite are possible: (1) Appetite's consultant is unsuccessful, (2) both consultants are successful, and (3) only Appetite's consultant is successful. Appetite's payoff in the first case is zero. But so is Appetite's payoff in the second case, because Appetite and Pickens will end up in a bidding war with each other. In the third case, Appetite will find itself in a bidding war with Carnivore and therefore will have to pay $140,000 for Bull's Eye. Its profit from the acquisition equals $200,000 – $140,000 = $60,000. Because the consultant costs $10,000, Appetite's expected profit from hiring a consultant if Pickens hires one also equals

$$0.5 \cdot 0 + 0.25 \cdot 0 + 0.25 \cdot \$60,000 - \$10,000 = \$5,000. \qquad (21.10)$$

Appetite does even better if Pickens chooses not to hire a consultant, for now Pickens will never bid for Bull's Eye and Appetite avoids a bidding war against it. Now either Appetite's consultant is unsuccessful and Appetite's payoff is zero, or the consultant is successful and Appetite plays a bidding war against Carnivore. It follows that Appetite's expected profit equals

$$0.5 \cdot 0 + 0.5 \cdot \$60,000 - \$10,000 = \$20,000. \qquad (21.11)$$

The payoff matrix of the simultaneous-move game played between Appetite and Pickens when both believe Bull's Eye has no white knight is given in Table 21.2.

TABLE 21.2 Payoff matrix of simultaneous-move game played between appetite and Pickens when both believe Bull's Eye has no white knight

| | | Appetite, UnLtd. | |
		Hire Consultant	Don't Hire Consultant
Pickens	Hire Consultant	($5,000, $5,000)	($20,000, $0)
	Don't Hire Consultant	($0, $20,000)	($0, $0)
		Payoffs: (Pickens, Appetite)	

Table 21.2 makes clear that both firms have a dominant strategy in this case: Hire the consultant. Both firms' profits increase only if Carnivore accepts Bull's Eye's greenmail offer and does not bid against Bull's Eye for Bull's Eye's stock. We leave it as an exercise to calculate the payoff matrix in this case and verify that it remains a dominant strategy for both firms to hire a consultant.

We next need to examine Carnivore's behavior. Suppose Carnivore believes Bull's Eye has a white knight. It can foresee that it will be the loser in a bidding war against either Appetite or Pickens. As a result, it will accept any greenmail offer Bull's Eye makes. Now suppose Carnivore believes Bull's Eye does not have a white knight. It knows that both Appetite and Pickens will choose to explore a takeover. As a result, it will be able to take over Bull's Eye if and only if both of their consultants are unsuccessful and it is the only bidder. The probability of this happening equals 25%. In the event Carnivore is the only bidder, it will have to share half the value it adds to Bull's Eye with the current stockholders. So Carnivore's expected payoff equals

$$0.25 \cdot 0.50 \cdot \$140,000 = \$17,500. \tag{21.12}$$

It follows that Carnivore will only accept greenmail payments of $17,500 or more in this case.

For the equilibrium we asserted to be an actual equilibrium, we need to show why the beliefs we asserted were held by Carnivore, Pickens, and Appetite are rational. To restate them in a more general form: Carnivore, Pickens, and Appetite believe Bull's Eye definitely has a white knight if it offers less than G^* to Carnivore, and that it does not have a white knight if it offers G^* or more. G^* is some unspecified positive number. We assume only that $G^* \geq \$17,500$.

Suppose Bull's Eye has a white knight and offers less than G^* to Carnivore. Carnivore will accept this offer, and both Appetite and Pickens will choose not to hire a consultant because they will believe, correctly, that the firm has a white knight. The result is that the white knight makes the only bid for Bull's Eye, and the stockholders gain half of $200,000 minus the greenmail payment, G^*, or

$$\$100,000 - G^*. \tag{21.13}$$

If Bull's Eye offers G^* or more to Carnivore, then Carnivore will accept the offer and Appetite and Pickens will both hire consultants because they believe, incorrectly in this case, that Bull's Eye does not have a white knight. There are four equally likely outcomes: (1) Both consultants are successful, (2) only the white knight's consultant is successful, (3) only the white knight's consultant is unsuccessful, and (4) neither consultant is successful. In the first and third cases, Appetite and Pickens will get into a bidding war, and the stockholders will gain $200,000. In the second and fourth cases, only the white knight will bid for Bull's Eye, and the stockholders will share half of the gain from the acquisition or $100,000. Bull's Eye's expected payoff equals

$$0.50 \cdot \$200,000 + 0.50 \cdot \$100,000 - G^* = \$150,000 - G^*. \tag{21.14}$$

A comparison to (21.13) and (21.14) reveals that Bull's Eye's best greenmail offer depends on the value of G^*. If $G^* \geq \$50,000$, then it is optimal for Bull's Eye not to pay any greenmail to Carnivore when it knows it has a white knight. On the other hand, if $G^* < \$50,000$, then Bull's Eye *will* pay G^* in greenmail to Carnivore when it has a white knight in order to get Appetite and Pickens to hire consultants, thereby producing higher bids. So a necessary condition for the three players' beliefs to be rational is that $G^* \geq \$50,000$.

Suppose Bull's Eye does not have a white knight, and Carnivore's, Appetite's, and Pickens' beliefs are as before. Again, if Bull's Eye offers Carnivore less than G^*, the offer will be accepted and neither Pickens nor Appetite will hire a consultant because they will believe, incorrectly, that Bull's Eye has a white knight. As a result, no one will make a bid for Bull's Eye and the firm will simply be out its greenmail payment, G^*.

On the other hand, if Bull's Eye offers at least G^* to Carnivore, then Carnivore will accept it. Subsequently, Appetite and Pickens will both hire consultants because they will believe, correctly, that Bull's Eye does not have a white knight. There are three possible outcomes of relevance to Bull's Eye: (1) Both consultants are successful, (2) only one consultant is successful, and (3) neither consultant is successful. The payoff to the stockholders in the three cases are, respectively, $200,000, $100,000, and $0. Bull's Eye's expected payoff equals:

$$0.25 \cdot \$200,000 + 0.50 \cdot \$100,000 + 0.25 \cdot \$0 - G^* = \$100,000 - G^*. \tag{21.15}$$

As we saw earlier, Bull's Eye's optimal offer depends on the value of G^*. As long as $G^* \leq \$100,000$ (given the beliefs by the three firms), Bull's Eye will offer G^* to Carnivore when it knows it does not have a white knight. But if $G^* > \$100,000$, then Bull's Eye will not offer any greenmail to Carnivore when it does not have a white knight.

Combining all our results, we find that there is a *continuum of Bayesian equilibria* for this game. Each equilibrium depends on a number G^* that lies between $\$50,000$ and $\$100,000$, inclusive. The equilibrium strategies are the following:

> *Bull's Eye:* Offer greenmail of G^* to Carnivore when there isn't a white knight, and offer nothing when there is.
>
> *Carnivore:* Accept any greenmail offer made by Bull's Eye.
>
> *Appetite and Pickens:* Hire consultants if and only if Bull's Eye offers G^* or more to Carnivore.

The equilibrium belief is:

> Bull's Eye has a white knight if and only it if offers at least G^* in greenmail to Carnivore.

The payment of greenmail correctly signals to both Appetite and Pickens that the target does not have a white knight. This creates a contest between Appetite and Pickens to find a way to get at the potential profits. Conversely, the lack of a greenmail payment correctly signals to both firms that there is a white knight in the wings. In this case they simply wait for Bull's Eye to inform them who it is; the firm chosen as the white knight successfully fends off the raider, and the other firm walks away without fighting.

In this model the true purpose of greenmail is to serve as a credible signal. Getting Carnivore to leave the market is incidental. This is made more vivid by the surprising fact that when Bull's Eye pays greenmail to Carnivore, it pays much more than it has to. Carnivore will accept any greenmail offer over $\$17,500$. But a payment of at least $\$50,000$ in greenmail is required to send a *credible signal* to Pickens and Appetite that it does not have a white knight.

21.6 • Summary

This application presented a game-theoretic analysis of corporate takeovers. Using this framework, we showed how the payment of greenmail to a corporate raider might be in the best interests of the firm's stockholders if it resulted in a better offer from another firm. The reason one acquirer might have to be eliminated in order to get another acquirer to make a bid is that the acquiring firm often must first invest some time and money to see if taking over the target firm makes economic sense. A firm will not be willing to make this investment if the probability is too high that it will face a bidding war against a raider.

Unfortunately, our first takeover model failed to conform to one well-documented fact about greenmail: The payment of greenmail to a raider is usually followed by a *decline* in the market value of the firm. Our first model, by contrast, predicted that greenmail would be associated with an increase in the firm's value.

We modified our model by introducing asymmetric information. In our new model the target firm may or may not have a white knight. The target has a white knight if it knows the identity of an acquirer that can make the firm much more valuable. In our model the target firm uses the greenmail payment to the initial raider to signal whether or not it has a white knight. If the target has a white knight, then it does not pay greenmail and simply informs the white knight of its private information about how the white knight can make the target more valuable. If it does not have a white knight, however, then the target firm needs to signal this to the group of potential white knights by paying greenmail to a raider. Once they see the greenmail payment, the potential white knights begin exploring the possibility of acquiring the firm. Without the greenmail payment, they run the risk of being drawn into a bidding war against the white knight and will not explore a takeover attempt.

21.7 • Further reading

This application is based in large measure on Andrei Shleifer and Robert W. Vishney, "Greenmail, White Knights, and Shareholders' Interest," *Rand Journal of Economics*, 17 (1986), pp. 293–309.

21.8 • Exercises

Exercise 21.1   Consider the takeover game diagrammed in Figure 21.3. Assuming Appetite and Pickens both believe Bulls Eye has no white knight and Carnivore accepts Bulls Eye's greenmail offer, derive the payoff matrix for the simultaneous-move subgame played between Appetite and Pickens.

Exercise 21.2   Consider the takeover game with a white knight diagrammed in Figure 21.3. Suppose when only one firm bids for Bull's Eye, the shareholders obtain 10% of the gains from the acquisition, and the acquiring firm gets 90%. Determine the new payoffs and find a Bayesian equilibrium for the new game.

Exercise 21.3   Bill Raider is considering whether to acquire a company, Bull's Eye Inc., which has a single stockholder, John Jay. Bull's Eye's value to Jay, denoted V_J, is either $10/share or $100/share, depending on the outcome of a risky project codenamed "Crapshoot". Regardless of the outcome of the project, Bull's Eye is worth 50% more to Raider than it is to Jay. That is, $V_R = 1.5 \cdot V_J$, where V_R is the value of Bull's Eye to Raider. It is common knowledge that John Jay already knows the outcome of the project and hence V_J, but Raider knows only of the existence of Crapshoot and that there is a 50% chance it was successful. Raider makes a single take-it-or-leave-it offer to Jay for all of Bull's Eye's stock, at a price P, which Jay can either accept or reject. Both Raider and Jay are risk-neutral wealth maximizers. If Jay accepts the offer, Jay's payoff equals $P - V_J$ and Raider's payoff equals $V_R - P$. If Jay rejects the offer, the payoff to both players is 0.

(a) Draw the game tree for this game. Be sure to show all the nontrivial information sets of each player.

(b) Determine Jay's optimal acceptance/rejection rule conditional on the outcome of the Crapshoot project.

(c) Use Bayes' theorem and the rule you found in (b) above to calculate the probability that Crapshoot was successful conditional on Jay accepting an offer of P by Raider.

(d) Use the conditional probability you found in (c) to determine the expected payoff to Raider from offering P. Find the price that maximizes this expected payoff. Show that if both players act optimally, then Raider will acquire Bull's Eye if and only if Crapshoot is *unsuccessful*.

• CHAPTER 22 •

Public Goods and
Preference Revelation

22.1 • Introduction

Most of the economic applications in this book have dealt with resource allocation in
a market economy. In some instances markets work fairly well, at least by the criterion
of Pareto optimality. In other instances the markets will fail to achieve Pareto
optimality. For much of the last century—particularly because Arthur Pigou's work on
the social loss caused by any divergence between marginal private costs and benefits,
and marginal social costs and benefits—the policy response to market failure has been
to call for government intervention. Recent research from a group of economists
working in the subfield called public choice economics has identified some conditions
under which government intervention will either fail to improve on non-Pareto optimal
market results, or will actually make things worse.

In this chapter we will develop a model in which markets fail to provide a type of
product referred to as a public good. This market failure can be viewed as the outcome of a game. We will also find that simple voting mechanisms designed to correct
the market failure will also usually fail to achieve a Pareto optimal outcome. Finally,
we will show that the government can ensure an efficient outcome by employing a
seemingly bizarre scheme called a Clarke tax.

22.2 • Public goods

A **public good**, by definition, has two characteristics: It is **nonrival**, which means that
if one person consumes the product, then anyone else can consume the same product

at no additional cost; and it is **nonexcludable**, which means that it is prohibitively expensive to keep an additional person from consuming the good when it is being consumed by someone else. An example of a good that is nonrival is a television signal. It costs the same for a television station to provide a television signal to the George Bush household in the downtown Washington, D.C., area, as it does to provide a television signal to both the George Bush household *and* any other resident of the downtown Washington, D.C., area, say the Ted Kennedy household.

In contrast, consider the provision of a hamburger by a fast food restaurant to George Bush or Ted Kennedy. It is impossible for the restaurant to sell George Bush a hamburger, for George Bush to consume that hamburger, and then for Ted Kennedy to consume *that same* hamburger.[1] In fact, the thought of their trying to do this is rather disgusting. Whereas George Bush and Ted Kennedy do not compete with each other over a television signal, they certainly compete with each other over the consumption of a hamburger. Hamburgers, unlike television signals, are *rival* in consumption.

The second characteristic of a public good is that it is nonexcludable. Although it may not cost HBO, a subscription television broadcaster, any more to transmit a signal to one household in Chicago than it costs to transmit a signal to 100,000 households in Chicago, it may be possible for either HBO or a cable television provider to employ a scrambling device to exclude some people from receiving that signal.

In some instances, however, exclusion is simply not feasible. For example, suppose that a household is sufficiently worried about the prospects of an invasion into the United States that it chooses to buy an MX missile for its backyard. It is their sense, perhaps misguided, that they will receive some additional security from the missile. The "security" they receive will also be received by their neighbors. Therefore, their consumption of the services provided by the MX missile is nonrival. But, unlike the case of the HBO signal, it is impossible for this household to keep their neighbors from obtaining the same security services provided by the MX missile that they receive. Nor is there any way for the neighbors to avoid the increased likelihood that the neighborhood has become a target.[2] Therefore, there is nonexclusion in the consumption of the services this MX missile provides. Many types of military expenditures are thought to be examples of public goods.

It is a common mistake to confuse public goods with publicly provided goods. Many states, for example, now sell lottery tickets. They are a *publicly provided* good. Yet the benefits of a lottery ticket go only to the ticket holder. That is, lottery tickets are both rival and excludable and, therefore, *not* a public good.

---

[1] George could share the hamburger with Ted, but then each would be consuming only a fraction of it. George and Ted still cannot share the same physical fraction of the same hamburger.

[2] Neighbors can avoid the "benefits" of being near an MX missile site by moving, but then they are no longer neighbors. The fact remains that *neighbors* always get this "benefit."

22.3 • Public goods and the problem of market failure

To see why markets will typically fail to produce an efficient output of a public good, imagine the following situation: Residents of East Isle, a small island town just off the coast of Maine, are considering putting up a new bridge from the mainland to their town. The existing bridge is a drawbridge, and it is annoying for motorists to have to wait for fishing boats to pass while the drawbridge is up. A new bridge would use the old moorings but it would be raised high enough so that fishing boats could pass under it. The cost of the new bridge is $30,000. There are 10 households on the island, each of whom would be willing to pay $5,000 for the services provided by the bridge. Because the bridge is nonrival, the benefits from building it, measured by the amount each household is willing to pay for the bridge, would be $5,000 • 10, or $50,000.[3] Because the cost of building the bridge is only $30,000, it makes sense to build it. That is, if a dictator could take over the town, tax everyone an additional $3,000, take the money, and build a bridge, then each individual household would be better off by $2,000.

Let us suppose, however, that the bridge is nonexcludable as well as nonrival, making it a public good. Although it is conceptually and technically possible to have a toll booth controlling access to the bridge, making its use excludable, we will assume that the operation of the toll booth is prohibitively expensive.

Consider the possibility of a private firm building the bridge for the residents of East Isle. Suppose a representative from a bridge-building firm visits different households on East Isle with the intent of getting the head of the household to sign a bridge-building agreement. The agreement is designed to assure the firm of enough revenue to cover the cost of building the bridge. Because the construction cost is $30,000, the firm must be assured of at least $30,000 in revenues to make it worthwhile for it to build the bridge. To increase the number of households who will sign the agreement, the firm promises that the price it will charge per agreeing customer will just allow the firm to break even. Therefore, any household that signs the agreement will pay $30,000 divided by N, where N is the number of households who sign. To be specific, suppose the agreement reads as follows:

The bridge agreement   I, the undersigned, agree to pay an equal share of $30,000 for a new bridge from the mainland to East Isle, along with other households who sign this agreement, up to a maximum of $5,000. I understand that the bridge will not be built unless 6 households sign this agreement.

---

[3]The bridge is nonrival in the sense that the additional cost of an additional motorist using the bridge is usually zero. If, however, there is a sufficient amount of congestion, then an additional motorist will impose nonzero costs on other motorists and consumption of the services of the bridge will become rival.

Because the payment that any household makes to the firm depends upon the number of households who sign up, the decision of one household to sign up has implications for other households and vice versa. In short, this is a game. As you know, a game is not well defined unless the informational structure of the game is completely specified. We will suppose that all 10 households make their signing decision "simultaneously" (that is, ignorant of each other's decision).

Consider a single household, the Addams family. In order for this household to know what it should do, it must consider the strategies that the other nine households might choose. One possible combination of strategies for the other households is that they all sign the agreement. Given these conditions, if the Addams family were also to sign, then the net benefit they receive would equal $2,000 (the $5,000 they were willing to pay minus the $3,000 fee to the bridge-building firm). But if the Addams family does not sign the agreement, then the bridge will still be built, but now the Addamses pay nothing! The net benefit from not signing is $5,000.[4] Under these circumstances, the Addamses' best strategy is not to sign.

Yet another combination of strategies by the other 9 households is that 8 of them sign the agreement and 1 does not. In this case, if the Addams family signs, its net benefit equals $5,000 − $30,000/9 = $1,666.67. But if it does not sign, the bridge will still be built and the family's net benefit will equal $5,000. Again the Addams family is better off not signing the agreement. Clearly, the same conclusion results if 7 or 6 other households sign up. On the other hand, if 4 or fewer households sign the agreement, then the bridge will not be built regardless of what the Addams family does. Again, the best strategy is not to sign the agreement.

The only combinations of strategies left to consider involves exactly 5 other households signing the agreement. When this happens, then the Addams family must sign the agreement in order for the bridge to be built. The net benefit to the family from signing is now $5,000 − $30,000/6 = $0, but the net benefit of not signing is also $0 because the bridge will not be built. Again, there is no advantage to signing up. The payoffs to the Addams family are summarized in Table 22.1.

It is easy to see from Table 22.1 that the Addams family has a weakly dominant strategy: Do not sign up. Because all the other households face exactly the same incentive structure, it is a Nash equilibrium for all 10 households not to sign the agreement. The sad result is that the bridge is not built and everyone is worse off than if the bridge had been built.

Notice that if each household could collectively *commit* to signing the agreement, then they would all be better off. The problem they face is making that commitment *credible*. That is, any individual household will always have an incentive, when push comes to shove, to renege on the agreement. As long as the decision to sign the

---

[4]This implies there is no retribution from their neighbors.

TABLE 22.1   Payoffs Addams family

Number of Households Who Sign Up (Excluding Addams)	Net Benefit to the Addams Family from Signing Up	Net Benefit to the Addams Family from Not Signing Up
9	$2,000	$5,000
8	$1,667	$5,000
7	$1,250	$5,000
6	$714	$5,000
5	$0	$0
4	$0	$0
3	$0	$0
2	$0	$0
1	$0	$0
0	$0	$0

agreement takes place simultaneously (in game time), the credibility problem remains. There may be some cooperative mechanism for making such credible commitments, but that is outside the realm of this book.

This problem is referred to as the **free-rider problem**. When there is a public good that is of benefit to all members of a group, then each individual has an incentive to take a "free ride" at the expense of those willing to provide the good. When everyone feels this way, the good is never produced.

22.4 • Public goods and the problem of government failure

The inability of the bridge construction firm to come to terms with the residents of East Isle in the previous section had nothing to do with the assumption that there was only one firm trying to produce the bridge. Indeed, we assumed the one firm was willing to produce the bridge for $0 in profit; it behaved as a perfect competitor. Nevertheless, the free-rider problem made it unlikely that *voluntary* exchanges would take place.

Because governments have the power to coerce people, they can circumvent the requirement that exchange be voluntary and, thereby, avoid the free-rider problem. For this reason it can be argued that the decision whether or not to build the bridge should be left to the government. In particular, *if the government knew* that each of the 10 households was willing to pay up to $5,000 for a bridge that cost only $30,000, then it could simply tax everyone $3,000 and use the money to build the bridge.

Social welfare would be improved by this result.[5] Unfortunately, the government does not generally observe how much people are willing to pay for a public good.

Consider the hypothetical neighboring town of West Isle. West Isle, an island community of five families, is also deciding whether to build a bridge to the mainland. Unlike the homogeneous population of East Isle, however, the five West Isle families have very different willingnesses-to-pay for the bridge, as shown in Table 22.2

Suppose the town officers of West Isle decide to hold a referendum to decide whether or not to build a bridge that costs $50,000. The referendum passes if a majority of the voters vote in favor of it. If the referendum passes, each individual will be taxed $10,000 to pay for the construction. Each household's willingness-to-pay for the bridge is not known by anybody else. The net benefit of the bridge to any individual, which is simply the willingness-to-pay for the bridge for any individual minus the tax cost, is given in Table 22.3.

TABLE 22.2 The hypothetical population of West Isle

Household	Willingness-to-Pay for a Bridge
Ames	$1,000
Baum	$4,000
Coos	$9,000
Dawes	$14,000
Elwin	$27,000

TABLE 22.3 The hypothetical population of West Isle

Household	Net Benefits from Bridge
Ames	−$9,000
Baum	−$6,000
Coos	−$1,000
Dawes	$4,000
Elwin	$17,000

[5]We are ignoring distributional concerns. We are also ignoring the question of whether or not the government will act in the best interests of its taxpayers. These issues are complicated ones from which we will politely beg off.

Each household can vote either for the proposal (to build the bridge) or against the proposal. Assuming that secret balloting takes place and that households choose not to buy each other's votes, everyone has a weakly dominant strategy: Vote in favor of the proposal if and only if the net benefit is nonnegative. So three households (Ames, Baum, and Coos) will vote against the proposal, and two households (Dawes and Elwin) will vote for the proposal. Under the election rules, the bridge is not built.

If voters can bribe each other, the situation is much more complex. It is possible to imagine Elwin paying Coos to vote for the proposal in return for a bribe of between $1,000 and $17,000. Of course, Elwin will want an assurance that Coos will actually vote in favor of the proposal. Unfortunately, there is no obvious end to the side payments that various combinations of people might offer each other. We will not analyze this vote-buying game any further on the grounds that it is illegal in the United States to bribe voters, and all the good citizens of West Isle are law-abiding.

Notice that in the foregoing example the outcome of the referendum was in accord with Coos' preferences (it was also in accord with Ames' and Baum's). Suppose, instead, that Coos had positive net benefits from the bridge. In that case the referendum would have passed and Coos would have been satisfied with the outcome (as would Dawes and Elwin). In either case, Coos is happy. Coos is the **median voter**: the voter for whom the number of voters with a greater willingness-to-pay equals the number with a lower willingness-to-pay. As a general rule, when a decision is made by majority vote, and each voter votes according to her preferences, then the outcome of the vote will always be in accord with the median voter's preferences. You saw this result used earlier in Chapter 21 on strikes.

One immediate problem with using referenda to make social decisions is that it can give results that are not Pareto optimal. In the example given, the three people who prefer not to build the bridge would be made, collectively, $16,000 worse off if the bridge were built. On the other side of the ledger, the two people who prefer to have the bridge built would be made, collectively, $21,000 better off if it were built. We can imagine an exchange in which those people who prefer to have the bridge built would pay the people who prefer not to have the bridge built an amount between $16,000 and $21,000 to get the recalcitrants to change their minds. Everyone could be made better off if this were to occur. Because the possibility of mutually advantageous exchange still exists after the voting has taken place, there is **government failure**. In the previous section the private sector failed to build a bridge that "should" have been built. Here the government fails to do the same thing.[6]

---

[6]More generally, public goods will typically be underprovided by the private sector. In contrast, referendum voting like that described in the text may generate outputs below *or* above the efficient level. It all depends on whether the median voter has preferences that are below or above the efficient level.

We argued at the beginning of this section that one important problem facing the government is how to get a population to reveal its preferences for public goods. Majority voting, as we have described it, induces people to reveal their preferences qualitatively, but the intensity of their preferences remains hidden. We have seen that the qualitative revelation is not enough to guarantee efficient resource allocations. In order for the government to make intelligent resource allocation decisions, it needs to know the amount people are willing to pay for a public good, not just the proportion of voters willing to pay a positive amount.

22.5 • The Clarke tax: A weak solution

In response to this problem, economists have tried to come up with ways to lead rational voters to reveal honestly the intensity of their preferences. One such mechanism is the **Clarke tax**. We will look at the incentive properties of this voting scheme using West Isle's decision of whether or not to build a bridge to the mainland.

Imagine that on the West Isle ballot each voter is asked to express his or her willingness-to-pay for the bridge. An example of such a ballot is shown in Table 22.4. If the bridge is built, each voter is taxed $10,000 to cover the construction costs. The ballot is secret, so that any individual's expressed willingness-to-pay cannot be used later to alter his tax burden.

The initiative passes if the total willingness-to-pay of those voters who want the bridge built is greater than the total willingness-to-pay of those who do not want the bridge built. In such an election, those voters who want the bridge built have nothing

---

TABLE 22.4   Willingness-to-pay ballot for West Isle

In the space below, please write down the amount of money you would be willing to pay—above any taxes you may be assessed—to build a bridge to the mainland, recognizing that if the bridge is built your taxes will increase by $10,000.

$\$_____$

In the space below, please write down the amount of money you would be willing to pay—above any taxes you may be assessed—to ensure that the bridge is *not* built to the mainland, recognizing that if a bridge is built your taxes will increase by $10,000.

$\$_____$

to lose by writing down the largest numbers they can. The same is true for those who do not want the bridge built. Such a ballot provides no incentive for people to be truthful. Indeed, it creates every incentive for people to vastly exaggerate their preferences.

In a surprisingly overlooked article, Edward Clarke suggested an ingenious voting system in which individuals are given the correct incentives to reveal willingly their true willingness-to-pay. This solution to one of the more vexing problems facing government officials ties a tax payment, referred to as a *Clarke tax*, to each voter's reported preferences.

The ballot in a Clarke tax referendum is somewhat different from the ballot displayed in Table 22.4. Voters are still asked to write down on the ballot how much they would be willing to pay either to ensure that the bridge is built or to ensure that it is not built. But now the voter is warned that *he or she may have to pay an additional tax on the basis of the vote cast*. This additional tax is the "Clarke tax." Because the voter may have to pay something as a result of casting a vote, the ballot can no longer be anonymous. As before, the outcome of the election is determined not by counting the number of ballots for and against the bridge proposal, but by counting the total willingness-to-pay of those who want the bridge built and the total willingness-to-pay of those who do not want the bridge built. The side with the highest collective willingness-to-pay wins. A hypothetical ballot is shown in Table 22.5.

TABLE 22.5   The ballot for a Clarke tax referendum

Name:_____

Social Security Number: _____

Signed: _____   Date: _____

In the space below, please write down the amount of money you would be willing to pay—above any taxes you may be assessed—to ensure a bridge to the mainland, recognizing that if a bridge is built your taxes will increase by $10,000. ***Please note*: You may be subject to an additional Clarke tax.**

$_____

In the space below, please write down the amount of money you would be willing to pay—above any taxes you may be assessed—to ensure that a bridge to the mainland is not built, recognizing that if a bridge is built your tax liability will increase by $10,000. ***Please note*: You may be subject to an additional Clarke tax.**

$_____

text. There is an extremely large literature on voting models that is remarkably interdisciplinary. It seems economists, political scientists, philosophers, and mathematicians all have a great deal to say on the subject. The most famous reference is Kenneth Arrow, *Social Choice and Individual Values,* 2nd ed. (New York: Wiley, 1963). Much of this literature is highly technical.

The original article on the Clarke tax by Edward Clarke is "Multipart Pricing of Public Goods," *Public Choice* 11 (1971), pp. 17–33. The exposition is clearer in T. N. Tideman and G. Tullock, "A New and Superior Process for Making Social Choices," *Journal of Political Economy* 84 (1976), pp. 1145–1160.

23 8 · Exercises

Exercise 22.1   Which of the following are public goods and why: (I) a radio broadcast, (2) a musical tune, (3) a mathematical theorem, (4) a view of the Grand Canyon, (5) a campsite in Yosemite National Park.

Exercise 22.2   Consider the hypothetical town of North Isle, which consists of 15 households, each of whom is willing to pay $5,000 for a bridge. The bridge will cost $75,000. Does a free-rider problem still exist? Explain your answer.

Exercise 22.3   Suppose that the West Isle bridge proposal discussed in Section 4 requires a two-thirds majority to pass and that votes, not willingness-to-pay, are counted. What would be the outcome of a referendum on building a bridge that cost $50,000? What if the bridge cost $30,000? How would your answers to either of the previous questions change if Ames were willing to pay $1 million for the bridge?

Exercise 22.4   Suppose the citizens of West Isle use a willingness-to-pay referendum to decide whether or not to build a bridge to the mainline. But instead of adopting a Clarke tax, they decide to simply assess every decisive voter $5000. What is the optimal strategy of each of West Isle's five voters? Explain why this tax does not induce voters to be truthful about their preferences.

· PART FIVE ·

Repeated Games

• CHAPTER 23 •

Subgame-Perfect Equilibrium

23.1 • Introduction

You have probably been bothered by the one-shot nature of the strategic situations we have considered so far. In the real world, most interactions between people are repeated. We negotiate with the same employer repeatedly; we shop at the same food store repeatedly; and we buy the same brands repeatedly. Other examples of repeated interactions are a sequence of new firms assessing whether to enter a market and compete against a monopolist and a group of countries negotiating tariff reductions under the GATT.

Games in which players meet in strategic interactions repeatedly are referred to as **repeated games**. Unfortunately, the terminology used by economists who work in the area is still unsettled. When we talk about a repeated game we will mean a situation like the following: Two vegetable stands are located near each other on the same highway. The owners of the two stands must simultaneously choose their vegetable prices each morning. Once the prices are chosen, they cannot be changed until the next day. Therefore, each day both stands must choose among the same set of actions. They may or may not choose the same actions all the time. For example, the weather may influence the price they charge. Yet each day the structure of the daily pricing game is the same. The information they have on any morning will be different from the information they have on other mornings, but the sequence of moves, the timing of those moves, and the actions that can be taken are the same every day. We will refer to the play that takes place in the course of a day as a **stage** of the repeated game. A stage in the game just described is shown in Figure 23.1.

The entire sequence of stages constitutes the complete repeated game. As you might imagine, drawing a game tree for a repeated game with even a relatively small number of stages can be an absurdly large task. Frequently, identifying a portion of the game tree that describes a single stage will be sufficient to clarify the game. Sometimes the number of stages is even infinite. When the game is infinite, all the players are strategic, and they are all informed about each other's past actions, then the game is called a **supergame**.

To analyze repeated games, tools that have been developed in all the previous chapters will be used. As in Part Four, a player's move at one stage in the game may reveal information about that player that is useful to other players at later stages in the game. This may be the case even though any stage in the game resembles a simultaneous-move game similar to those we studied in Part Three or a sequential-move game like those in Part Two. The inferences a player's opponents make about how that player will behave in the future will depend on the history of previously observed actions. The predictions the other players make about the future behavior of a player that are based on her previous actions in the game constitute that player's **reputation**. Depending on the game, it may be advantageous to acquire a reputation for being "tough," "nice," or "crazy." Reputations have no value unless the players are uncertain against whom they are playing. As a result, games where reputations matter are games in which there is asymmetric information about the characteristics of the players—particularly their payoffs.

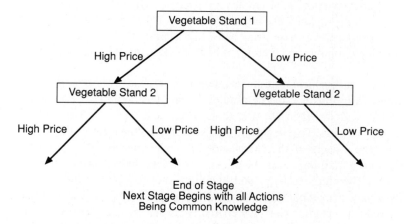

FIGURE 23.1 · A stage in a daily vegetable pricing game.

The techniques developed in Part Four to find a Bayesian equilibrium apply just as well to repeated games. When one player is deciding which action to take at any stage of a game, that player will rationally take into account the effect each action will have on the behavior of her opponents in future stages of the game. If the player wants her opponents to believe something about her, her actions must *credibly* signal to her opponents what type of player she is. If a player does not want her actions to reveal information about her to her opponents, she must also choose actions that credibly do not signal her type. If a player wants to make it clear to her opponents that she is committed to **retaliation** if her opponents choose a particular course of action, *this commitment must be credible*. The test for credibility is the same as always: Is the player made better off by retaliating than by not retaliating?

23.2 • Example: Duopoly revisited

Let us begin by looking at a one-stage duopoly game between two specialty U.S. jean manufacturers: Rip Jeans (R) and Torn Jeans (T). The "worn" jeans manufactured by the two firms are perfect substitutes that sell at a common world market dollar price P. The inverse market demand curve is given by

$$P = 22 - (Q_R + Q_T), \tag{23.1}$$

where the output of the two firms, denoted Q_R and Q_T, is measured in millions of jeans per year.[1] Both firms face the same marginal cost of $10 per pair and fixed costs of $15 million. These fixed costs, however, are not sunk costs. Should the firm shut down completely, the firm could reduce its costs to zero. If we measure costs in millions of dollars, the cost function for Rip Jeans, denoted $C_R(Q_R)$, is given by

$$C_R(Q_R) = \begin{cases} 15 + 10 \cdot Q_R, & \text{if } Q_R > 0 \\ \\ 0 & \text{if } Q_R = 0. \end{cases} \tag{23.2}$$

---

[1] In case you have not seen the term *inverse demand curve* before, let us assure you that you have seen the graphs of many inverse demand curves. Usually we think of the quantity demanded of any product as a function of the price of that product (among other things). Following typical mathematical convention, this would mean that the quantity demanded (the dependent variable) would be measured on the vertical axis and price (the independent variable) on the horizontal axis. As you well know, economists ignore this convention and draw demand curves with price on the vertical axis and quantity demanded on the horizontal axis. That is, they have graphed the inverse demand curve.

and the cost function for Torn Jeans, denoted $C_T(Q_T)$, is given by

$$C_R(Q_T) = \begin{cases} 15 + 10 \cdot Q_R, & \text{if } Q_T > 0 \\ \\ 0 & \text{if } Q_R = 0. \end{cases} \tag{23.2}$$

If the two firms could collude—a big *if*—they could maximize their combined profits by agreeing to produce 3 million jeans each. We will hereafter refer to this output level as the **cartel output level.** When both firms produce at the cartel output level, the world market price for "worn jeans" is $16/pair and each firm earns an annual profit of $16 · 3,000,000 – $15,000,000 – $10 · 3,000,000 = $3,000,000.

Of course, any such cartel agreement would be not only unenforceable in U.S. courts but illegal as well! Therefore, the firms cannot rely on the courts to help them enforce binding agreements. If a commitment to produce at the cartel output level by one firm is to be believable to the other firm, it must be in the best interest of that firm to produce that output. That is, the commitment must be a subgame-perfect equilibrium strategy for the firm. This type of multiplayer agreement, in which all the players agree to a particular behavior, and in which the behavior is consistent with a subgame-perfect equilibrium, is said to be a **self-enforcing agreement.**[2]

Suppose both jean companies must sign binding contracts for factory space, fabric, and labor at the beginning of the year. Then both firms will be forced to choose their annual output at the beginning of the year without prior knowledge of the other firm's decision. Both firms are assumed to maximize the present value of the stream of profits (long-run profits). Because we are temporarily limiting ourselves to a one-stage game, short-run and long-run profits are the same. As we saw in Chapter 13 of Part Three, in which we studied a simultaneous-move Cournot duopoly game, this game has a unique Nash equilibrium. It is found by deriving both firms' reaction functions, which in this case are

$$Q_R = 6 - 0.5 \cdot Q_T, \tag{23.4a}$$

$$Q_T = 6 - 0.5 \cdot Q_R. \tag{23.4b}$$

Solving equations (23.4a) and (23.4b) for the two unknown variables results in both firms producing 4 million jeans, which they sell for $14, and earn an annual profit of $1 million each. We will refer to this output level as the **Cournot output level.**

---

[2]It must also be executed in such a manner that the firms cannot be successfully prosecuted by the U.S. Justice Department under the antitrust laws. We will ignore this complication in what follows.

Let us now reanalyze this game from a different angle. To make our example more vivid, let us imagine that the CEOs (chief executive officers) of the two companies, Bob Sharp of Rip and Ruth Lessing of Torn, meet in December at a holiday party. Off in a corner, Ruth quietly points out to Bob that "producing 4 million jeans each, which we are bound to do if we do not cooperate, is in neither of our firms' self-interest. If we were to both cut our production to 3 million jeans," she goes on, "we would force the market price up to $16 and triple our profits." Bob says that her implicit proposal sounds like a great idea to him and that he will advise his firm to reduce its output for the coming year. Talk, however, is cheap!

As soon as Bob gets home from the party he calls his chief financial officer, Aye Shade, and tells him about his conversation with Lessing. What should they do? Should they go ahead with their plan to produce 4 million jeans, or should they reduce their output to 3 million jeans as Lessing has proposed? Of course, there are many other output options the two executives could also consider, but for simplicity we will limit the choice to just these two. We will call the decision to reduce output **cooperation** and the decision to keep output at the Cournot equilibrium level **defection.** The payoffs associated with these two output choices, assuming Torn Jeans is also only considering these same two options, is given in Table 23.1[3]

If Rip Jeans were to cooperate, the optimal action for Torn Jeans would be to defect. On the other hand, were Rip Jeans to defect, then Torn Jeans should defect as well. Torn Jeans has a dominant strategy to defect, as does Rip Jeans. Therefore, there is a unique Nash equilibrium in which both firms defect, produce 4 million

Table 23.1 Cournot duopoly game Between Rip Jeans and Torn Jeans

		Rip Jeans	
		Cooperation $Q_R = 3$ million	Defection $Q_R = 4$ million
	Cooperation $Q_T = 3$ million	(3, 3)	(0, 5)
Torn Jeans			
	Defection $Q_T = 4$ million	(5, 0)	(1, 1)
		Payoff: (Torn Jean profits, Rip Jean profits)	

[3]It may have occurred to the reader that if a player is going to cheat on his cooperating opponent, then the optimal cheating output is higher than the Cournot output level. We have chosen to ignore this and limit ourselves to two output levels, rather than three, in the interests of simplicity.

jeans apiece, and earn only $1 million each in profits. These firms seem to be stuck in a prisoner's dilemma.

The problem with this purported equilibrium is that it seems to depend on the assumption that the firms both make one output decision and then never meet again. It is, of course, much more realistic to suppose that Rip Jeans and Torn Jeans do not meet just once, but meet in the marketplace year after year. Unless the CEOs are congenitally myopic, they should be interested not only in their current profits but in their future profits. The question is: How does the equilibrium change if the game described in this section is just a single stage of a larger game in which this stage is repeated? In particular, is it possible for firms to commit credibly to the cooperative outcome in a dynamic setting? If so, how?

23.3 • Finitely repeated games

As our story goes, Rip and Torn share a duopoly in the worn jean market because they foresaw the advent of a fad ahead of other jean manufacturers. This good fortune will last only as long as the fad does. Suppose experience suggests the fad will last only two years. Then the Cournot stage game will be repeated exactly twice. The extensive form of the repeated game is shown in Figure 23.2.

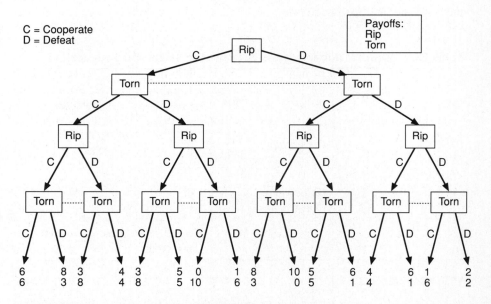

FIGURE 23.2 • A game tree for a two-stage repeated game.

In the first stage of this two-stage repeated game, Rip and Torn simultaneously decide whether to cooperate or defect. The respective outputs are observed, and the first stage comes to an end. The second stage is qualitatively the same as the first stage. Again, Rip and Torn simultaneously choose whether to cooperate or defect. Then the game ends. Payoffs are listed at the end of the game, not because that is when they are realized, but because it is assumed that the firms care about long-run profits and not short-run profits. We have ignored discounting over the two time periods. Consider the payoffs to the two firms if they both choose a strategy in which they cooperate in both stages. In that case, they can both expect to earn $3 million per year, or a total of $6 million. Alternatively, if Rip always chooses to cooperate in the first time period but to defect in the second, whereas Torn always chooses to cooperate, then Rip will earn $3 million in the first year and $5 million in the second, for a total of $8 million. Torn will earn $3 million in the first year and $0 in the second. We leave it to the reader to calculate the other payoffs.

As you can see, this game involves both simultaneous play (at each stage) and sequential play (between stages). A strategy consists of a choice of output in period 1 (in ignorance of the output chosen by the opponent) and a choice of output in period 2 (in ignorance of the output chosen by the opponent in that period), *where the choice in period 2 can depend on the opponent's observed output choice in period 1.* We wish to determine whether one player can affect the other player's behavior by threatening the other player. A **threat** consists of the promise to take some action in the second stage of the game if the opponent takes some given action in the first stage of the game. In order for the threat to affect the opponent's behavior, it must be credible.

Because this repeated game is partially sequential, the technique of backwards induction can be used to find a subgame-perfect equilibrium. Therefore, we will try to solve the second stage of the game first, prune the game tree, and then solve the first stage of the game. Even though the subgame played in the second stage involves simultaneous moves, it has a unique (dominant strategy) Nash equilibrium in which both players defect and choose the Cournot output levels. Each will earn only $1 million in the second year. It is important to note that the optimality of this action is independent of what happened in period 1. Regardless of what transpires in stage 1, rational play in stage 2 is now known. The game tree can be pruned back. When this is done we are left with the first stage, which is now just a single-period simultaneous-move Cournot game. The payoffs of this game consist of the first-period payoffs plus the second-period payoffs of $1 million. Since the same amount is being added to all the first-period payoffs, maximizing these new payoffs is equivalent to maximizing the first-period payoffs. So the "reduced" game is equivalent to a one-stage Cournot game. But we know the only Nash equilibrium for this game is for both firms to choose the Cournot output levels. So in equilibrium both firms defect in both stages. Repetition does not generate cooperation.

You may think the problem is that we did not repeat the game enough times. For example, suppose both firms expect the market to evaporate in two years, but they choose their outputs only a week in advance. The simultaneous-move stage game is now repeated 104 times. It is left as an exercise for the reader to derive this game tree (just kidding!). Remarkably, backwards induction selects the same type of subgame-perfect equilibrium as before. At the last stage in the game both firms will find it to their advantage to choose the Cournot output. Pruning the tree back one stage leaves us at stage 103. Now that the 103rd stage is the last stage of the game, it is still in both firms' best interest to choose the Cournot output, allowing us to prune back the tree yet another layer. This process, of course, keeps being repeated all the way to the first stage of the game, when it is still in both firms' best interest to choose the Cournot output. The only subgame-perfect equilibrium, solvable using backwards induction, has both firms choosing the Cournot output in every period. The argument is valid no matter how many times the game is repeated.

Besides being counterintuitive, the prediction that both players will never cooperate when playing a finite number of repetitions of a prisoner's dilemma-type stage game is inconsistent with the outcomes of numerous experiments. When people play such games in experimental settings, they usually cooperate until near the end of the game, at which point cooperation finally breaks down.[4]

There are at least three ways to reconcile our theory with the evidence. The backwards induction argument we used earlier is valid only if: (1) neither player can fix his second-period output at the same time he sets his first-period output, (2) both players know each other's payoffs, and (3) both players know how many times they will repeat the stage game. Normally, at least one of these conditions is violated. We can never be sure how frequently we interact with someone else; we can never be certain about our opponent's payoffs or about our opponent's beliefs about our payoffs; and we can sometimes enter into binding commitments about our future actions.

We will now examine how the relaxation of any of these three conditions can make it rational to cooperate with an opponent—at least to some extent and at least for a while.[5]

23.4 • A first modification: Precommitment

Return to the example in which Rip Jeans and Torn Jeans are embroiled in a repeated game with just two stages. Each stage looks like a Cournot simultaneous-move game. What distinguishes the model presented in this section is that each firm can make a

---

[4]This research is part of a fast-growing field called experimental economics.
[5]More is not better here. Too much uncertainty can actually destroy the incentives for cooperation.

binding commitment at the first stage of the game to its output in the second stage. It is crucial to note that the binding commitment in period 2 may depend on the choice of output the firm's opponent makes in period 1. For example, a binding commitment to a second-period output might consist of promising to choose the cooperative output if the opponent chooses to cooperate in the first time period, but to defect if the opponent chooses to defect in the first time period. We will discuss later the means by which the firm could make such irrevocable commitments.

By assuming binding commitments are possible, the two-stage repeated game is transformed into a one-stage, simultaneous-move game. The strategies of the two firms in this one-stage game consist of: (1) a level of output in period 1, denoted Q_1^R and Q_1^T, and (2) a level of output in period 2 that depends on the output of the rival in period 1, denoted $Q_2^R(Q_1^T)$ and $Q_2^T(Q_1^R)$. If the commitment is truly binding, the firms choose their strategies simultaneously at the beginning of period 1 and cannot alter them in period 2.

This game has many subgame-perfect equilibrium strategies. One of these equilibrium strategies is for both firms to set output at 4 million jeans in both periods regardless of what the rival does in the first period. Symbolically, this pair of strategies is shown in Table 23.2. To verify this, imagine that you are the CEO of Rip Jeans and that you believe Torn Jeans is irrevocably committed to producing 4 million jeans in both periods. Your best response to this strategy is to produce 4 million jeans in each period also.

Consider now the strategies in Table 23.3. If both firms follow these strategies, then each will produce 3.5 million jeans in the first period. Though not fully cooperating, they are at least not producing the full Cournot output. In the second period

TABLE 23.2   Noncooperative Nash equilibrium strategies for the repeated Cournot game with precommitment

$Q_1^R = Q_1^T = 4$ million

$Q_2^R(Q_1^T) \equiv Q_2^T(Q_1^R) \equiv 4$ million

TABLE 23.3   Cooperative Nash Equilibrium strategies for the repeated Cournot game with precommitment

$Q_1^R = Q_1^T = 3.5$ million

$Q_2^R(Q_1^T) = \begin{cases} 4 \text{ million} & \text{if } Q_1^T = 3.5 \text{ million} \\ 5 \text{ million} & \text{otherwise} \end{cases}$

$Q_2^T(Q_1^R) = \begin{cases} 4 \text{ million} & \text{if } Q_1^R = 3.5 \text{ million} \\ 5 \text{ million} & \text{otherwise} \end{cases}$

they both produce 4 million jeans. They both defect in the second stage. Profits for each firm will be $2.5 million in the first period and $1 million in the second period, or $3.5 million overall. To verify that this is indeed a subgame-perfect equilibrium of the game, we need to show that neither firm can unilaterally alter its strategy and earn total profits of more than $3.5 million.

Because the two firms are identical and the proposed equilibrium strategies are the same, we need only show that Rip Jeans cannot earn more than $3.5 million when Torn follows the "cooperative" strategy. First, suppose Rip produces 3.5 million jeans in the first period; then it knows that Torn will produce 4 million in the second period, to which its best response is to defect and produce 4 million jeans as well. Given Torn's first-period proposed strategy, suppose Rip decides to consult its reaction function shown in equation (23.4a) and to maximize its first-period profits by increasing production to 4.25 million jeans. It will boost its first-period profit to $3.063 million, but it will also trigger retaliation by Torn in the second period. Indeed, it knows that Torn will flood the market with 5 million jeans in the second period, driving down the price so much that Rip cannot make a positive profit at any output level! Rip's best response is to shut down completely and earn nothing in the second period. Its profit over the two periods is $3.063 million, which is less than the $3.5 million it earns when it "cooperates" with Torn. This shows that each firm's strategy is a best response to the other firm's strategy.

In the proposed equilibrium, if the threats made are ever carried out, they will hurt the "avenger" as much as the "avenged." In other words, if either player, at the end of the first stage, actually observed an output other than 3.5 million jeans on the part of its opponent, it would really like to produce an output other than 5 million jeans in the second stage. In fact, however, the first stage is water under the bridge. It is rational for a player to make such threats only if she is very confident the threats will never need to be carried out. But they will never be carried out only if the rival firm is convinced both that the threat will be made *and* that it will be carried out. In order to believe the latter, however, the rival firm must believe the threat is irrevocable. If the rival firm has doubts about the irrevocability of the threats, then it may be rational to call the other firm's bluff. And if the firm believes its bluff will be called, then it will not be rational to issue it. Draconian threats about how the firms will act in the second period are rational only if they can be committed to *before* the two firms choose their first-period outputs.

23.5 • A second modification: Uncertainty about the future

When we showed earlier that Rip Jeans and Torn Jeans would never cooperate, we assumed not only that the number of interactions was finite, but also that the number of interactions was fixed and common knowledge.[6] But fads are mercurial by nature, and so the length of their popularity is unpredictable. If the two firms do not know how long "worn jeans" will be popular, then they do not know many stages the repeated game will have. How will they behave now?

This question cannot be answered without introducing this uncertainty rigorously into our repeated game. To be specific, suppose that at the beginning of every year, and regardless of how many years both have been in business, Rip and Torn both believe the probability the worn jean fad will end that year is 0.5. This number is known as the **continuation probability** for the repeated game. The continuation probability is common knowledge. In the interest of simplicity, we will also continue to assume that the two firms restrict themselves to either the collusive output level of 3 million jeans per year or the Cournot output level of 4 million jeans per year.

Because, at the beginning of *any year*, both firms believe there is a 0.5 chance the worn jean fad will last exactly one more year, they must also believe there is a $0.5 \cdot 0.5 = 0.25$ chance the worn jean fad will last exactly two more years, and that there is a $0.5 \cdot 0.5 \cdot 0.5 = 0.125$ chance the worn jean fad will last exactly three more years. More generally, they believe the probability the fad will last exactly N more years is 0.5^N. The *expected number of additional years* the fad will last, starting from the beginning of the current year, equals the following infinite series:

$$(1 \cdot 0.5) + (2 \cdot 0.25) + (3 \cdot 0.125) + \ldots = 2. \qquad (23.5)$$

The two firms will no longer play the Cournot game exactly twice. Instead, they will play the game twice *on average*. No matter how many times they have played the game, the firms always expect the game to last for two more years. The probability the game will go on forever is zero, but there is some chance (however small) the game will last longer than any given length of time (even, say, 100 years). As a result, there is no final fixed end point at which we can begin our backwards induction to determine the firm's equilibrium strategies.

An unfinished game tree for our new game is presented in Figure 23.3. In every period, Rip and Torn simultaneously determine their outputs. Nature then determines whether the game ends at that stage, or goes on for at least one more period. Since the probability the game goes on forever is zero, eventually the two firms end up at a terminal node. The payoffs to the players at this node are simply the present value of the profits the two firms have earned up to that point.

Suppose that both firms use only pure strategies. When forming beliefs about the type of rival one is playing against, it probably makes sense to consider what

---

[6]Remember this means that both players are rational, each believes that the other is rational, each believes that the other believes that he is rational, and so on, *ad infinitum*.

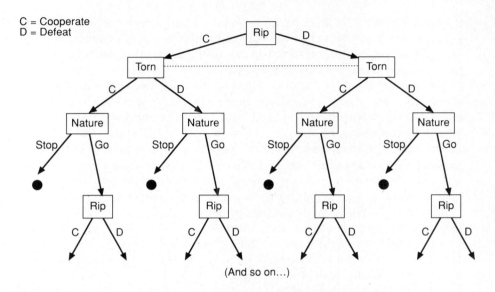

FIGURE 23.3 • The game tree for a repeated Cournot game when the stopping point for the game is uncertain.

decisions that player has made in the past. Call the sequence of choices the two firms have made previous to period N, the *history* of the game up to N, and denote it by H_N. Since the game goes on indefinitely, a pure strategy for firm i consists of the following:

1. A choice of output in period 1, Q_1^i
2. A choice of output in period 2 (assuming that nature has let the game advance this far), which may depend on the history of the game up to that point, $Q_2^i(H_2)$;
3. A choice of output in period 3 (assuming that nature has let the game advance this far), which may depend on the history of the game up to that point, $Q_3^i(H_3)$;

   .
   .
   .

N. A choice of output in period N (assuming that Nature has let the game go this long), which may depend on the history of the game up to that point $Q_N^i(H_N)$.

A pure strategy for firm i is a sequence of output choices $\{Q_1^i, Q_2^i(H_2), \ldots, Q_N^i(H_N),\ldots\}$ and will be denoted by S_i; S_R is Rip Jeans' strategy and S_T is Torn Jeans' strategy. Any two pure strategy pairs, S_R and S_T, determine a sequence of quantities for both firms (depending on how long the game lasts). For example, suppose Rip and Torn select strategies that result in both choosing the Cournot output every period. If the fad lasts only one year, then the two firms will earn a total profit of $1 million each. If the fad lasts exactly two years, then the two firms will earn $1 million in each year. If the fad lasts N years, each of the two firms will earn $1 million for N years. Although the payoff from the selection of this pair of strategies is uncertain, the *expected (von Neumann-Morgenstern) utility* to each firm is well defined. Assuming for the moment that neither firm discounts the future and both are risk-neutral profit maximizers, the expected utility for each firm when both choose the Cournot output level every period equals:

$$(\$1 \text{ million} \cdot 0.5) + (\$2 \text{ million} \cdot 0.25) + \ldots + (\$N \text{ million} \cdot 0.5^N) + \ldots \qquad (23.6)$$

$$= \$2 \text{ million}.$$

More generally, suppose p is the probability that the game continues for another period. Then at the initial node of the game, the probability the game lasts exactly 1 period equals $1 - p$; the probability the game lasts exactly 2 periods equals $(1 - p) \cdot p$; and the probability the game lasts exactly N periods equals $(1 - p) \cdot p^{(N-1)}$. Suppose a pair of pure strategies results in a VNMU to player i of u_1 in period 1, u_2 in period 2, and so on. The expected utility to the player from this pair of strategies equals:

$$(1 - p) \cdot u_1 + p \cdot 1 - p) \cdot (u_1 + u_2) \qquad (23.7)$$

$$+ \ldots + p^{N-1} \cdot (1 - p) \cdot (u_1 + \ldots + u_N) + \ldots +$$

$$= (1 - p) \cdot (1 + p + p^2 + \ldots) \cdot u_1 + (1 - p) \cdot (p + p^2 + \ldots) \cdot u_2$$

$$+ \ldots + (1 - p) \cdot (p^{N-1} + p^N + \ldots) \cdot u_N + \ldots +$$

$$= u_1 + p \cdot u_2 + p^2 u_3 + \ldots + p^{N-1} u_N + \ldots$$

In deriving equations (23.6) and (23.7), we assumed that neither firm discounted the future. That assumption was made to simplify the mathematics. But the sort of potentially lengthy stage game presented here requires that we take account of the firms' time preferences. Suppose the players discount utility t periods from now by $1/(1 + r)^t$, where r is the interest rate. The present value of utility in period 2 equals $u_2/(1 + r)$; in period 3 it equals $u_3/(1 + r)^2$; etc. Therefore, the expected present value of utility from the given pair of pure strategies equals:

$$u_1 + p \cdot u_2/(1 + r) + p^2 u_3/(1 + r)^2 + \ldots + p^{N-1} \cdot u_N/(1 + r)^{N-1} + \ldots \qquad (23.8)$$

$$= u_1 + (p/1 + r) \cdot u_2 + (p/1 + r)^2 \cdot u_3 + \ldots + (p/1 + r)^{N-1} \cdot u_N + \ldots$$

$$= u_1 + \tau \cdot u_2 + \cdot \tau^2 u_3 + \ldots + \tau^{N-1} \cdot u_N + \ldots,$$

where $\tau = p/(1 + r)$. Hence, by replacing p with $p/(1 + r)$, we can immediately extend everything we have done so as to incorporate discounting.

23.5.1   A noncooperative equilibrium

In previous sections, the noncooperative output—the Cournot output—frequently ended up being a subgame perfect equilibrium. Consider two firms that adopt a *stubbornly* noncooperative strategy. Such a strategy is shown in Table 23.4.

When playing against a stubbornly noncooperative opponent, the best response in each period is to choose the Cournot output level. Any choice other than the Cournot output leads to lower profits in the current period and has no offsetting future benefit because it does effect the behavior of the opponent.

This equilibrium is somewhat disturbing because it relies on completely dogmatic behavior. No matter what the other firm does, neither firm will change its beliefs about what the other firm will produce next period. If your opponent were to produce at the collusive output level for ten years in a row, it would appear silly to ignore this history and conclude that she will be noncooperative from now on. It seems more likely that either she doesn't know what she is doing or that she is trying to tell you something (such as "collude with me"). In both cases, you can probably increase the likelihood of future cooperation by cooperating today.

23.5.2   A cooperative equilibrium

We now will consider a cooperative equilibrium in which all threats are credible. The equilibrium strategy of both players is rather vindictive: Each player cooperates only as long as its rival cooperates. Once the other player breaks ranks, the first player produces the Cournot output forevermore. Such a strategy is accurately referred to as a **grim strategy**. In order to state this strategy more rigorously, let HC denote the set of all histories (of whatever length) in which both firms have always chosen the collusive output level (3 million jeans). Then the grim strategy is described in Table 23.5.

Suppose both firms adopt the grim strategy. In period 1, neither firm has yet defected; therefore, both firms will produce 3 million jeans. In period 2, neither firm has yet defected, so once again both firms will choose 3 million jeans. In fact, in year

TABLE 23.4   Stubbornly noncooperative strategy

$Q_1^i = 4$ million jeans,

$Q_t^i(H_t) \equiv 4$ million jeans,   for all histories H_t, and $t > 1$.

TABLE 23.5 The grim strategy

$$Q_1^i = 3 \text{ million jeans}$$
and for $t > 1$,
$$Q_1^i(H_t) = \begin{cases} 3 \text{ million jeans} & \text{if } H_t \, \varepsilon \, HC \\ 4 \text{ million jeans} & \text{otherwise} \end{cases}$$

N, neither firm will have defected, so both firms will choose to be cooperative one more time. In short, the outcome when both firms adopt the grim strategy is that both firms always cooperate. Assuming, once again for simplicity, that neither firm discounts its future profits, the expected profits to each firm when both adopt the grim strategy equal

$$\$3 \text{ million} + \$ 3 \text{ million} \cdot 50\% + \$3 \text{ million} \cdot 25\% + \ldots = \$6 \text{ million}. \tag{23.9}$$

Of course, it remains to be shown that the grim strategy can be part of a Nash equilibirium.

Let us suppose Rip Jeans believes Torn Jeans has adopted a grim strategy. If Rip were *ever* to defect, then Rip will expect Torn to defect forever after. Therefore, it would be rational for Torn, once having chosen to defect, also to defect forever after. So it remains only to be shown that Rip's best response to Torn's grim strategy is to cooperate initially and to continue to do so as long as Torn cooperates.

We already know that a player that adopts a grim strategy, in this case Torn, will choose the cooperative output in the first time period. Suppose Rip starts out by defecting. Rip will earn a profit of $5 million in the first period, but, as we saw in the previous paragraph, because both firms defect from then on, Rip's profits will be $1 million per year from period 2 until the game ends. These low future profits are the cost of obtaining the big payoff in the first period.

If the game ends immediately, then Rip's strategy of defecting right from the start pays off. If the game lasts exactly two periods, then Rip ends up with a payoff of $5 million + $1 million = $6 million, exactly what it would have obtained by following the grim strategy ($3 million + $3 million). But if the game lasts any longer than two periods, then Rip does strictly worse by defecting than by cooperating.

Of course, Rip does not know how long the game will last. The expected utility from adopting any strategy that calls for Rip to defect in period one equals:

$$\$5 \text{ million} + \$1 \text{ million} \cdot 0.5 + \$1 \text{ million} \cdot 0.25 + \ldots \tag{23.10}$$

$$= \$5 \text{ million} + \$1 \text{ million} \cdot (0.5 + 0.25 + \ldots)$$

$$= \$6 \text{ million},$$

which exactly equals the expected utility to Rip from cooperating with Torn every period (see equation (23.9)). Hence, there is no benefit to Rip from departing from the grim strategy in period 1.

But if there is no benefit from defecting in the first period, then there is no benefit from defecting in subsequent periods. To see this, suppose it is the beginning of some subsequent period and both players have cooperated up to that point. *From that point on to the end of the game*, the game they play is formally identical to the game they face in period 1. As we just saw, Torn gains nothing from defecting at this stage of the game.

In summary, Torn might as well be cooperative unless Rip is uncooperative, at which point Torn is unforgiving and becomes uncooperative thereafter. But this is just the grim strategy! This proves that the grim strategy is a best response to an opponent that has also adopted the grim strategy. It follows that a subgame-perfect equilibrium for this game is for both firms to use the grim strategy.

23.5.3   And now the bad news: The folk theorem

In a neat world there would be a only one equilibrium. In the repeated duopoly game we have been describing, we have already found two subgame-perfect equilibria. Are there more? Are there a great many more? To begin to answer this very important question, let us try to limit the set of possible strategies either firm might choose.

Take a look at this game from a somewhat different perspective. By employing the grim strategy, both firms are opening themselves up to the possibility of low profits in period 1. Alternatively, each firm can guarantee itself an expected profit of zero by choosing not to produce in every period.

In general, suppose two players in a game, A and B, can employ a variety of strategies, 1 through N. Regardless of the strategy chosen by player A, if player B chooses strategy 1, B will receive a minimum expected payoff of $\underline{u}_1$. If B chooses strategy 2, B will receive a minimum expected payoff of $\underline{u}_2$, and so on. The collection of minimum expected payoffs can be written $\{\underline{u}_1, \underline{u}_2, \ldots, \underline{u}_N\}$. The *maximum* of these *minimum* expected payoffs is referred to as the player's **maximin utility**. Any payoff combination, for both players, that gives both players no less than their minimax utility is said to be **individually rational**.

In addition, Rip and Torn cannot together earn an expected profit of more than $6 million because this is the maximum they can earn collectively by cooperating with each other in every period. A payoff combination to the two players that can be achieved by the selection of *some* combination of strategies (not necessarily equilibrium strategies!) is said to be **feasible**. In the case of the jean duopoly game, the feasible payoffs are precisely those in which Rip's and Torn's expected utility is nonnegative and does not sum to more than $12 million. We have drawn the individually rational and feasible payoff vectors for the jean duopoly game in Figure 23.4. As you can see, there are a very large number of feasible and individually rational payoffs. Each of these payoff combinations is associated with some strategy combination.

Now for the answer to our question about the number of subgame-perfect equilibria. It turns out that—subject to some technical restrictions[7]—any given individually rational and feasible payoff vector is also a subgame-perfect equilibrium payoff vector for the repeated game as long as p, the probability that the game continues for one more period, is sufficiently close enough to one.[8] Ugh! This result is known as the **folk theorem** because early versions of it have been around for so long that no one quite remembers who first stated it or proved it. We will not prove it here.

How bad a problem is the folk theorem? There is some evidence that the folk theorem may not be as bad a problem as was once thought. In many applications, it is possible to pare down the number of reasonable equilibria by using criteria such as symmetry between the players. In addition, when the continuation probability is *not*

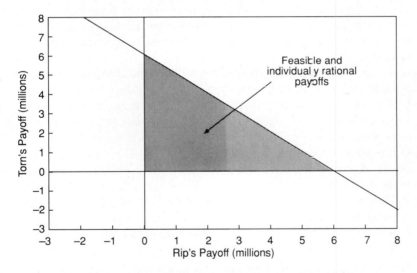

FIGURE 23.4 • A set of feasible and individually rational payoffs.

[7]If you think you can handle it, these can be found in Fudenberg and Maskin (1986), but this paper is very difficult.

[8]If the players are discounting future payoffs with a discount rate $1/(1 + r)$, then r must also be close to zero.

close to one, then the set of equilibrium payoff vectors may be *much smaller* than the set of all feasible and individually rational payoffs. Indeed, if p is sufficiently small—that is, if future interactions are sufficiently unlikely—then the repeated game is almost a one-shot game, and its set of equilibrium payoff vectors will simply coincide with the payoff vectors of the one-shot stage game.

23.6 • A final modification: Uncertainty about the payoffs

Suppose Rip Jeans and Torn Jeans make the production decisions only a week in advance. Then they will make 102 such decisions over a two-year period. For simplicity we will assume that the annual demand and cost functions used earlier are now the weekly demand and cost functions. As we saw earlier, as long as both firms know the game will end with certainty at some specific date, there is only one subgame-perfect equilibrium the one in which the firms produce the Cournot output every period.

This conclusion, however, rests on the assumption that both firms know the payoffs with certainty. In particular, each firm is assumed to know the payoffs of the other firm with certainty, each firm is assumed to know that the opponent knows its payoffs with certainty, and so on. But suppose each firm is uncertain about the opponent's payoffs.

Specifically, suppose there are two types of firms: "altruistic" firms and "greedy" firms. Greedy firms are interested only in maximizing their profits. As a result, their payoffs are those found in Table 23.1. But altruistic firms have an "intrinsic" desire for cooperation and behave as if their payoffs in the stage game are those given in Table 23.6. The numbers in Table 23.6 are just VNMU values in which the altruistic firm's utility depends on more than economic profit.

In the one-shot Cournot duopoly game, greedy firms have a dominant strategy: Defect. Because defection is a dominant strategy, it does not depend on the greedy firm's beliefs about the opponent's payoffs. Altruistic firms, on the other hand, do not have a dominant strategy. Such firms will defect if they believe their opponent will defect and will cooperate if they believe their opponent will cooperate.

TABLE 23.6   Stage game payoffs to an altruistic firm

| | | Altruistic Firm | |
		Cooperation	Defection
Other Firm	Cooperation	7	5
	Defection	0	1

Suppose it is common knowledge that Rip Jeans is an altruistic firm, but Torn's type is known only to itself. Then Rip and Torn are playing a game with imperfect and private information. We will assume it is common knowledge that, at the first stage of the game, Rip believes there is a 0.8 chance that Torn is a greedy firm and only a 0.2 chance that Torn is an altruistic firm like itself.

Suppose both firms interact only once. Consider a set of beliefs for Rip about Torn's behavior that are as favorable toward a cooperative equilibrium as possible: Rip believes that Torn will always choose to cooperate when Torn is an altruistic firm and will always choose to defect when Torn is a greedy firm. Given these beliefs, Rip can calculate that its expected utility from cooperating equals $0.8 \cdot 0 + 0.2 \cdot 7 = 1.4$ and its expected utility from defecting equals $0.8 \cdot 1 - 0.2 \cdot 5 = 1.8$. Hence, Rip's best strategy is to defect. Because we started with beliefs that were most likely to support a strategy of cooperation, it follows that Rip's optimal strategy is to defect regardless of his beliefs. Because Torn can see this, Torn's best strategy is to defect even if it is an altruistic firm.

The existence of altruistic firms does not provide enough of an incentive for Rip to cooperate unless Rip believes it is very likely that Torn is also an altruistic firm. You can verify that Rip must believe there is a greater than $1/3$ chance that Torn is also an altruistic firm before Rip is willing to risk cooperating in the one-shot Cournot game.

Fortunately, meeting over and over again at different stages of a repeated game allows Rip to condition its behavior on past play by Torn, and such conditioning can give Torn an incentive to develop a reputation for being an altruistic firm—regardless of its true type. As we will see, even if altruistic firms are rare, as long as there are enough stages in the game, the repeated game will possess a Bayesian equilibrium in which the firms start out cooperating—regardless of their type. Behavior at the end of the game will depend on Torn's true type. If Torn is truly altruistic, then Rip and Torn can continue to cooperate until the end of the game. But if Torn is actually a greedy firm, then eventually the future benefits of an altruistic reputation fall below the immediate benefits of defection, and Torn will give up its reputation and revert to defecting for the rest of the game.

Let us examine this logic in detail by considering two repetitions of the Cournot stage game. Because this is a game with asymmetric information, Rip must form a belief about Torn's type from the action taken in the first period. This belief can be represented by two numbers (π_C, π_D), where π_C is, according to Rip, the probability that Torn is an altruistic firm if the firm cooperated in the first period, and π_D is the probability that Torn is an altruistic firm if the firm defected in the first period.

As we saw in Part Four, many Bayesian equilibria involve mixed strategies ("bluffing"), and the one we will present here is no exception. Therefore, instead of considering strategies in which actions are taken with certainty, we will consider probabilistic behavior from the outset. A mixed strategy for Rip in this repeated game can be represented by three numbers: (r_1, r_2^C, r_2^D), where r_1 is the probability Rip will cooperate in period 1, r_2^C is the probability rip will cooperate in period 2 if Torn cooperated in period 1, and r_2^D is the probability Rip will cooperatine in period 2 if Torn defected in period 1. A mixed strategy for Torn can be represented by six numbers: $(g_1, g_2^C, g_2^D, a_1,$ $a_2^C, a_2^D)$, where g_1 is the probability Torn will cooperate in period 1 if Torn is a greedy firm, g_2^C is the probability Torn will cooperate in period 2 if Rip cooperated in period 1 and Torn is an greedy firm, g_2^D is the probability Torn will cooperate in period 2 if Rip defected in period 1 and Torn is a greedy firm, and so on.

A Bayesian equilibrium for this game is presented in Table 23.7. After describing what this equilibrium implies about each firm's behavior, we will go on to explain why it is an equilibrium. In this equilibrium, Rip always cooperates in the first period, cooperates in the second period half of the time if Torn cooperated in the first period, and always defects in the second period if Torn defected in the first period. Rip believes a first-period defection by Torn implies Torn is a greedy firm for certain, whereas first-period cooperation implies there is a 1/3 chance Torn is an altruistic firm. Torn's optimal strategy is to cooperate in both periods if it is an altruistic type of firm; otherwise, it cooperates half of the time in the first period but always defects in the second period. The reason Torn behaves in this way is to develop a reputation for cooperation, which it can then exploit in the second period.

A first condition for a Bayesian equilibrium is that Rip's beliefs must comply with Bayes' theorem. This means

$$
\begin{aligned}
\pi_D \; &= \; P\{\text{Torn is altruistic} \mid \text{Torn defects}\} \qquad\qquad\qquad (23.11)\\
&= \; P\{\text{Torn defects} \mid \text{Torn is altruistic} \cdot P \; \{\text{Torn is altruistic}\}\\
&\quad \div P\{\text{Torn defects}\}\\
&= \; 0 \cdot 0.2 \div P\{\text{Torn defects}\}\\
&= \; 0
\end{aligned}
$$

and

$$
\begin{aligned}
\pi_C \; &= P\{\text{Torn is altruistic} \mid \text{Torn cooperates}\}\\
&= P\{\text{Torn cooperates} \mid \text{Torn is altruistic}\} \cdot P\{\text{Torn is altruistic}\}\\
&\quad \div P\{\text{Torn cooperates}\}\\
&= 1 \cdot 0.2 \div 0.6\\
&= 1/3
\end{aligned}
$$

since

CHAPTER 23 • SUBGAME-PERFECT EQUILIBRIUM

TABLE 23.7 Bayesian equilibrium of the repeated Cournot game when Rip Jeans is uncertain about Torn Jean's payoffs

Rip's strategy:
$$r_1 = 1 \qquad r_2^C = 0.5 \qquad r_2^D = 0$$
Rip's beliefs:
$$\pi_C = 1/3 \qquad \pi_D = 0$$
Torn's strategy:
if a greedy firm: $\quad g_1 = 0.5 \qquad g_2^C = g_2^D = 0$
if an altruistic firm: $\quad a_1 = 100\% \qquad a_2^C = a_2^D = 100$

$$P\{\text{Torn cooperates}\} = P\{\text{Torn cooperates} \mid \text{Torn is altruistic}\} \qquad (23.13)$$
$$\cdot \; P\{\text{Torn is altruistic}\}$$
$$+ \, P\{\text{Torn cooperates} \mid \text{Torn is greedy}\} \; \cdot \; P\{\text{Torn is greedy}\}$$
$$= \cdot \; 1 \; \cdot \; 0.2 + 0.5 \; \cdot \; 0.8$$
$$= 0.6$$

Therefore, Rip's beliefs are consistent with Bayes' theorem.

We next need to check if Rip's strategy is optimal given Rip's beliefs and Torn's strategy. We start with period 2. Suppose Torn cooperated in period 1. Then Rip believes there is a 1/3 chance that Torn is altruistic and will continue to cooperate in period 2. If Rip cooperates in period 2, then its expected payoff equals $1/3 \cdot 7 + 2/3 \cdot 0 = 2.33$, and if Rip defects in period 2, then its expected payoff equals $1/3 \cdot 5 + 2/3 \cdot 1 = 2.33$. Because Rip is indifferent between defecting and cooperating, it is optimal for Rip to randomize. On the other hand, if Torn defected in period 1, then Rip believes the firm is greedy for certain and so will defect this period. In this case, Rip's best action is to respond in kind and defect as well.

Torn's second-period actions are independent of Rip's first-period actions; hence, Rip should choose the first-period action that maximizes its expected first-period utility. There is a $0.2 \cdot 1 + 0.8 \cdot 0.5 = 0.6$ chance that Torn will cooperate in the first period. As a result, if Rip cooperates in the first period, its expected utility will equal $0.6 \cdot 7 + 0.4 \cdot 0 = 4.2$, and if Rip defects in the first period its expected utility will equal $0.6 \cdot 5 + 0.4 \cdot 1 = 3.4$. It follows that Rip's best response to Torn's strategy is to cooperate in the first period.

Given Rip's strategy, it is clearly optimal for Torn to cooperate in the first period when it is an altruistic firm and to defect in the second period when it is a greedy firm. If it is an altruistic firm then the expected second-period payoff from cooperating equals $0.5 \cdot 7 + 0.5 \cdot 0 = 3.5$; if the firm defects, its expected second-period payoff equals $0.5 \cdot 5 + 0.5 \cdot 1 = 3$. It follows, then, that Torn should always cooperate in the second period when it is an altruistic firm.

If Torn is a greedy firm and it defects in the first period, then it knows Rip will defect in the second period, resulting in a total payoff of $5 + 1 = 6$. On the other hand, if it cooperates in the first period, then its first-period payoff equals 3 and its expected second-period payoff equals $0.5 \cdot 5 + 0.5 \cdot 1 = 3$. So Torn's expected total payoff over the two periods equals 6 regardless of the action it takes, and randomization is optimal.

23.7 · The economic role of reputation

Reputations are a type of game-strategic investment. As with all other types of investments, in order to develop a reputation a player must accept a lower current payoff in order to obtain a higher future payoff. Reputations work by altering the opponents' beliefs about the player's future actions and thereby altering their future actions as well. A player is more likely to make a reputational investment if she values the future highly and has a long planning horizon.

Because a reputation takes time to create, it is valuable. Unfortunately, a reputation can be easily destroyed by a wrong move. For example, in the repeated Cournot game, the first time that Torn defects it reveals itself to be a greedy firm and can never get Rip to cooperate with it again. In the two-period Cournot game we just examined, the reputation had no real value because Torn was indifferent between cooperating and obtaining the reputation in period 1, on the one hand, and defecting and foregoing it, on the other. But this is no longer true once the game lasts longer than two periods. As a rule, the larger the number of repetitions, the more valuable a good reputation will be.

23.8 · Summary

We have proceeded far from the simple sequential games we first analyzed in Part Two. We can now incorporate in our models repeated interaction between players. This allows us to find conditions under which it is rational for selfish players to cooperate with their opponents and ignore the incentives to cheat. These conditions are unsurprising: The players must place a high weight on the future so that they are sufficiently fearful of future retribution by an opponent. Retribution need not be due to any "psychic" desire for revenge. Instead, retribution simply provides the proper incentives for cooperation. If you do not punish noncooperative behavior, you invite this behavior in the future.

Unfortunately, although cooperation is consistent with subgame-perfect equilibrium, the folk theorem shows that *many* other outcomes of a repeated game are also generated by subgame-perfect equilibrium strategies. In the worst case, almost any payoff vector that is both feasible (attainable by the execution of some set of strategies) and individually rational (gives to each player at least what each can guarantee for herself) can be attained as the outcome of some subgame-perfect equilibrium of the game. Paring down this huge set of possible outcomes is a problem receiving great attention by game theorists at the moment.

23.9 • Further reading

The idea that players in repeated games should never invoke threats that they will not want to carry out when forced to is due to Reinhard Selten, "Reexamination of the Perfectness Concept for Equilibrium Points in Extensive Games," *International Journal of Game Theory* 4 (1975), pp. 25–55. It is now a standard assumption in game theory, and we have employed it throughout this book. Selten went on to show that the only subgame-perfect equilibrium of the finitely repeated prisoner's dilemma that does not involve incredible threats is the one in which both players never cooperate.

The effect of uncertainty about the payoffs in a finitely repeated prisoner's dilemma was explored in a path-breaking paper by David Kreps, Paul Milgrom, John Roberts, and Robert Wilson, "Rational Cooperation in the Finitely Repeated Prisoner's Dilemma," *Journal of Economic Theory* 27 (1982), pp. 245–252.

There are many statements of the folk theorem for repeated games. One of the more recent is by Drew Fudenberg and Eric Maskin, "The Folk Theorem in Repeated Games with Discounting or with Incomplete Information," Econo*metrica* 54 (1986), pp. 533–554. This paper is very difficult. A less general but more readable discussion of the folk theorem can be found in Chapter 5 of Eric Rasmusen, *Games and Information* (New York: Basil-Blackwell, 1989).

23.10 • Exercises

Exercise 23.1   Verify the payoffs for the two-stage game displayed in Figure 23.2.

Exercises 23.2, 23.3, and 23.4 are based on the repeated Cournot stage game between Rip and Torn jeans presented in Section 23.2. The payoffs of the stage game are given in Table 23.4.

Exercise 23.2   Suppose the two firms repeated the stage game exactly twice, but before they move, they issue irrevocable threats. The threat {C, D} means "If my opponent chooses C in period 1, then I will choose C in period 2, and if my opponent chooses D in period 1, then I will choose D in period 2." Find (most of) the Nash equilibria, with credible threats, of this game as follows:

(a) There are 16 possible pairs of threats the two firms could issue in the first stage of the game (4 for Rip times 4 for Torn). Once the two firms choose their first-period outputs, their second-period outputs are determined by their previously issued threats. So, once the two firms choose their first-period outputs, outputs and profits in *both periods* are determined. For each pair of threats and each pair of first-period outputs, calculate the sum of the profits the two firms earn over the two periods. For example, suppose the threats are Rip = {D, D} and Torn = {C, D} and first-period outputs are Rip = C and Torn = D. Then second-period outputs will be Rip = D and Torn = C. Table 23.4 implies that Rip's total profits are 0 + 5 = 5 and Torn's total profits are 5 + 0 = 5.

(b) The profits you calculated in (a) are the firms' payoffs in the output selection game they play *after* they issue their threats. Use your calculations from (a) to form the payoff matrices for each of the 16 simultaneous-move games played after the issuance of *each* of the 16 possible pairs of threats. For example, if the threats are Rip = {D, D} and Torn = {C, D}, then the payoff matrix of the subgame the two firms play when they choose their first-period outputs is:

| | Rip's first-period output | |
	C	D
Torn's output C	(3+5, 3+0)	(0+5, 5+0)
Torn's output D	(5+1, 0+1)	(1+1, 1+1)

where the payoff vectors mean: (Rip's first-period profit + Rip's second-period profit, Torn's first-period profit + Torn's second-period profit).

(c) For each of the sixteen subgames constructed in (b), find a pure-strategy Nash equilibrium, if one exists. If no pure-strategy Nash equilibrium exists, then find the mixed-strategy Nash equilibrium (one is guaranteed to exist). For example, in the case of the subgame played after the two firms threaten Rip = {D, D} and Torn = {C, D}, it is a dominant-strategy equilibrium (hence the unique Nash equilibrium) for both players to choose C (the cooperative output) in the first period. The equilibrium payoffs are 8 for Rip and 3 for Torn.

(d) Now use backwards induction and use the Nash equilibrium payoffs of the 16 subgames analyzed in (c) as the payoffs of the simultaneous-move "threat game" played between the two firms before either firm chooses its output. Find all the pure-strategy Nash equilibria for this game, if any exist. If none exist, discuss how you could find a mixed-strategy equilibrium (which is guaranteed to exist). *Hint*: First, eliminate all sequentially dominated strategies.

Exercise 23.3   Suppose there is a fixed positive probability p that the stage game will be repeated at least one more time and that this probability does not change with the number of times the game has been repeated so far. The game tree is shown in Figure 23.3. A pair of strategies for this game are *collusive* if they result in both firms choosing C every period. Show that this game has a collusive subgame-perfect Nash equilibrium if and only if $p \geq 1/2$. Proceed as follows: The grim strategy provides the toughest *credible* punishment to an opponent for choosing D. As a result, a collusive subgame-perfect equilibrium exists if and only if the grim strategy is a perfect Nash equilibrium (don't formally prove this statement, just accept it as true). So your task reduces to showing that if Rip Jeans adopts the grim strategy, then adopting the grim strategy is a best response for Torn Jeans if and only if $p \geq 1/2$. (The reverse then is true as well, by symmetry).

(a) Show that if Torn Jeans ever defects, then it should defect forever after.
(b) Calculate Torn's expected total profit if it cooperates in every period. You will want to make use of the following facts: (1) if a pair of strategies results in the sequence of stage payoffs to Torn of $u_1, u_2, ...$, then Torn's total expected profit equals

$$u_1 + p \cdot u_2 + p^2 u_3 + \ldots + p^N u_{N+1} + \ldots,$$

and (2) if A is some constant, then

$$A + p \cdot A + p^2 \cdot A + \ldots + p^N \cdot A + \ldots = A \div (1 - p).$$

(c) Calculate Torn's expected total profit if it defects in every period.
(d) Calculate Torn's total expected profit if it cooperates for the first N periods of the game and then defects forever after. Use the fact that:

$$A + p \cdot A + p2 \cdot A + \ldots + p^{N-1} \cdot A = A \cdot (1 - p^N) \div (1 - p).$$

(e) Now show that the expected profit calculated in (b) is greater than or equal to that calculated in (c) and (d) if and only if $p \geq 1/2$. You are then done.

Exercise 23.4   Suppose the two firms are playing the repeated game described in Exercise 23.2 with $p = 0.5$. The Tit-for-Tat (TFT) strategy is as follows: Choose C in the first period; thereafter, choose in this period what your opponent chose in the last period. That is, if your opponent cooperated (defected) last period, then you cooperate (defect) this period. Determine whether or not it is a Nash equilibrium (not necessarily subgame-perfect) for both firms to adopt TFT strategies. That is: If Rip Jeans adopts a TFT strategy, can Torn Jeans do strictly better by using some other strategy than by adopting TFT? Proceed as follows (this is sometimes called *dynamic programming*):

(a) Calculate Torn's profits if it adopts TFT. You will want to make use of the formulas given in Exercise 23.2.

(b) Now let V^* denote the highest expected profit Torn can earn if Rip uses the TFT strategy. Suppose Torn's best response to Rip's strategy is to choose C in the first period. Show this implies: $V^* = 3 + 0.5 \cdot V^*$. Solve for V^* and compare to your answer with (a).

(c) Now suppose Torn's best response to Rip's strategy is to choose D forever. Calculate Torn's expected profit and compare with your answer in (a).

(d) Now suppose Torn's best response to Rip's strategy is to choose D in the first period and choose C in the second period. Show that this implies: $V^* = 5 + 0.5 \cdot 0 + 0.5^2 \cdot V^*$. Solve for V^* and compare your answer in (a).

Exercise 23.5 According to the folk theorem, as long as the probability that the game continues is high enough, then any payoff vector lying in the shaded region of Figure 23.4 can be attained by playing some pair of Nash equilibrium strategies. Which of these many equilibria do you consider most likely to be observed in practice? Does the notion of a *focal point* apply?

Exercise 23.6 In Section 23.6, we assumed that Rip was uncertain about Torn's payoffs. Suppose it is period 2 and Rip believes the probability that Torn is an altruistic firm equals π. Show that Rip is willing to risk cooperating in period 2 if and only if $\pi \geq 0.5$.

• CHAPTER 24 •

Cartel Enforcement

24.1 • Introduction

A **cartel** consists of a group of suppliers who have made an explicit agreement to limit competition among themselves for their mutual benefit. A cartel is similar to a monopoly—indeed, the goal of a cartel is to act as if it were a monopoly—but with one important difference. A monopoly consists of a single decision maker, whereas a cartel consists of a voluntary association of decision makers, each of which is aware that its profits depend on the behavior of all the other cartel members. Because of this, management of a cartel involves much more than simply selecting the profit-maximizing level of output and price. Cartel management also includes the allocation of production among the members, the allocation of cartel profits among the members, and the policing of the cartel agreement.

These three aspects of a cartel's operation are not independent of each other. For example, the allocation of profits must take into account the incentives this may provide for members to cheat on the agreement or even to leave the cartel. Similarly, the allocation of production quotas is constrained by the degree to which such allocations will either be adhered to voluntarily or can be policed at low cost.

Complicating the cartel's problem is the fact that in most countries collusive agreements are considered criminal conspiracies. Where this is the case, domestic cartels cannot enforce their agreements through the courts and must hide their activities so as to avoid prosecution. Although collusive agreements among governments, such as between the countries in the Organization of Petroleum Exporting Countries (OPEC) cartel, are legal, such agreements are not legally enforceable. As a result, whether they are domestic or international in scope, cartel agreements must almost always be *self-enforcing*. Game theoretically, this means the allocation of output and profits among the members of the cartel must constitute a Nash equilibrium of the noncooperative game being played. Furthermore, we would like the Nash equilibrium to involve only credible threats.

Between October 15, 1973, and November 1, 1974, OPEC succeeded in raising the average price of Persian Gulf crude oil from $2.05/barrel to $10.35/barrel, or over 500%. Although probably the most successful cartel to date, OPEC is simply the latest in a long series of international cartels. In the twentieth century alone, cartels (that we know of) have been formed in the production and marketing of natural rubber, tin, mercury, aluminum, tea, sugar, copper, platinum, potash, diamonds, and coffee.

In a study by Paul Eckbo of 51 cartel agreements involving 18 internationally traded commodities, only 19 were able to raise prices by more than 100%. These "efficient" cartels did not last very long. Although the formal agreements remained in place for many years, these cartels were not able to control prices for more than five years. According to Eckbo, cartels lasted more than four years when concentration of production was high, the demand for the commodity was inelastic, the cartel's market share was high, the cartel members had a cost advantage over nonmembers, and governments did not get involved in the operation of the cartel. Cartels have been most successful where they have had tight control of the distribution of the commodity. For example, the iodine cartel lasted over fifty years by having all iodine sales conducted out of a single cartel office in London.

In this application we will present a simple game-theoretic model of cartel enforcement proposed by Robert Porter and Ed Green that can account for the instability of cartels. Their model suggests that the source of the problem is the limited ability of cartel members to monitor each other. But before we examine their game, let us review what we already have learned about cartels where the members can perfectly monitor each other.

24.2 · Cartel enforcement with perfect monitoring

In Chapter 23 we analyzed a repeated Cournot game between two jean manufacturers, Rip Jeans and Torn Jeans. This type of game—in which the players move simultaneously each period, the payoff matrix never changes, both players can observe each other's previous actions, and the number of repetitions is random—is often called a **repeated prisoner's dilemma with discounting.** One of the perfect Nash equilibria of this game results in both players always producing the Cournot equilibrium output each period. We will refer to this as the **noncooperative equilibrium.**

Repeated prisoner's dilemmas often have other equilibria as well. We will call any noncooperative equilibrium in which the players earn higher (discounted) profits than they do in the noncooperative equilibrium as a **self-enforcing cartel agreement.** As we saw in Chapter 23, such cartel agreements exist as long as both players have a sufficiently low discount rate, the short-term benefits of defection from the collusive output level are sufficiently low, and the cartel profits are sufficiently higher than the Cournot equilibrium profits.

When the cartel contains more than two members, enforcement becomes a problem. Now some subset of the cartel membership must enforce enforcement. That is, cartel members who do not follow through on punishing the defector must themselves be punished, members who do not punish those who do not punish the defector must be punished, and so on. Although rigorous analysis becomes much more complicated, our earlier results on repeated prisoner's dilemmas with two players can be extended to models in which there are many players. In particular, the folk theorem can be extended.

24.3 • Cartel enforcement with imperfect monitoring

Colombia and Brazil currently produce about 40% of the world's raw coffee beans.[1] Suppose they decide to organize a coffee cartel, the Coffee Alliance to Foster Exports (CAFE). Let P_t denote the market-clearing world price of coffee beans in period t (in dollars per kilogram), let $D(P_t)$ denote the quantity of coffee beans demanded worldwide during period t, let Q_t denote the quantity of coffee supplied by CAFE, and let $S(P_t)$ denote the quantity of coffee beans supplied by all noncartel members. All quantities are in millions of kilograms. P_t is defined by the requirement that supply equals demand or

$$D(P_t) = Q_t + S(P_t). \tag{24.1a}$$

Equation (24.1a) implicitly defines the market price P_t as a function of cartel output Q_t. Alternatively, we could rewrite equation (24.1a) as

$$Q_t = D(P_t) - S(P_t). \tag{24.1b}$$

This equation says that the output that the cartel can sell depends on the residual demand for coffee—that is, the difference between the amount of coffee demanded

---

[1]The other 60% is produced primarily by the Central American countries, Kenya, and Indonesia.

and the amount supplied by other producers. The residual demand for coffee is the demand facing CAFE. As the price falls, we would expect world demand for coffee to rise (the demand for coffee is downward-sloping) and non-CAFE supply to fall (the supply of non-CAFE coffee is upward-sloping). Therefore, the residual demand curve for CAFE coffee is downward-sloping. Furthermore, the elasticity of the residual demand will increase as the elasticity of world demand increases and as the elasticity of supply from other producers increases.

Because we would expect both demand and noncartel supply to vary randomly over time, the relationship between P_t and Q_t is not deterministic, but random. That is, P_t is a function of both Q_t, the cartel's output, and an unobservable random variable θ_t that represents shifts in the residual demand for the cartel's coffee. Specifically, we will assume here that the residual demand for coffee, $D_t(P_t) - S_t(P_t)$, equals $10 - (P_t \div \theta_t)$. This implies

$$P_t = (10 - Q_t) \cdot \theta_t, \tag{24.2}$$

where θ_t is a positive random variable with a mean of 1. So, for example, if CAFE sells 8 million kilograms in some period, the market price in that period will be, on average, $2 per kilogram.

Equation (24.2) implies that neither Colombia nor Brazil can exactly determine the other's current output from the knowledge of its own level of production and its observation of the current world price for coffee beans. For example, if Colombia's output in any time period was low and yet there was a low market price, this could mean: (1) Brazil's output is high, or (2) world demand is low, or (3) the combined supply of all other world coffee producers is high, or (4) some combination of (1), (2), and (3).

24.3.1 The game tree

The game tree for this repeated Cournot game with uncertainty and imperfect information is shown in Figure 24.1. In the first period, Colombia and Brazil simultaneously select their output for that year. We will denote the output levels chosen in year t by q_t^C and q_t^B. In Figure 24.1 we have simplified their choices to choosing "high" or "low" output levels. Their combined output $q_t^C + q_t^B$ equals Q_t.

After the two countries select their first-period output Nature determines θ_t and, thereby, the world price of coffee P_t according to equation (24.2). Figure 24.1 presents a simplified schematic of our game, in which Nature's choice of residual demand and each cartel member's choice of its output results in either a "low," "moderate," or "high" price of coffee. If both countries choose a high output, then, depending on residual demand, the price will be either moderate or low; if both countries

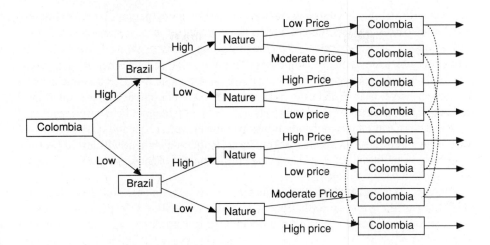

FIGURE 24.1 • A portion of the game tree for the dynamic cartel output game.

produce a low output, then the price will be either high or moderate; otherwise, the price will be either low or high.

Initially, both countries observe the market price, but since they do not directly observe θ_t, they cannot directly determine the other country's output. They then simultaneously choose their output level for year 2. Figure 24.1 shows four of Colombia's information sets. The first information set contains of a single decision node, that corresponding to Colombia's output decision in year 1. In year 2, Colombia could be at one of eight decision nodes. These eight nodes are partitioned into three information sets. One information set consists of the three decision nodes that follow a low coffee price. A second set consists of the two decision nodes that follow a moderate coffee price, and a third set consists of the three decision nodes that follow a high coffee price. Only one of Brazil's information sets is displayed in Figure 24.1. This set contains Brazil's two decision nodes for year 1, representing the fact that when Brazil moves, it is ignorant of Colombia's output decision.

24.3.2 Strategies

A strategy for Colombia consists of: (1) an output level for year 1, q_1^C; (2) an output level for year 2 that depends on the world price observed in year 1, $q_2^C(P_1)$; (3) an output level for year 3 as a function of the world price in years 1 and 2, $q_3^C(P_1, P_2)$; and so forth. The possible strategies for Brazil are analogous to those for Colombia. In general, these strategies could be very complex. We will focus in this application on **trigger price**

strategies. In a trigger price strategy, a firm makes inferences (perhaps incorrect) about rival firms from the observation of market price. If market price remains above some critical value—the trigger price—then the firm will not infer cheating on the collusive agreement and will maintain a cooperative output level. If, on the other hand, market price falls below the trigger, then some punishment must be imposed on the cheater. In our two-player case, the cheater's identity is known, of course. But as soon as the number of players is three or more, the cheater's identity cannot be determined.

Trigger price strategies depend on four parameters, p^R, T, q^N, and q^O, where p^R is the trigger price, T is the number of time periods the punishment will last, q^O is the cooperative output and q^N is the noncooperative output. The trigger price strategy works as follows:

Each year is designated as either "cooperative" or "noncooperative" depending on the history of the game up to that point. In a noncooperative year the country produces an output level q^N, and in a cooperative year it produces an output level q^O, where $q^O < q^N$. The first year is always a cooperative year. After that, if year t iscooperative and the world price P_t is above the **trigger price** p^R, then year t + 1 is also cooperative. If year t is cooperative but the world price P_t fell below the trigger price p^R, then the next $T - 1$ years would be noncooperative and year t + T would again be cooperative. The trigger price strategy will be denoted by the four-tuple: (p^R, T, q^N, q^O).

The trigger price strategy we have described is a less extreme version of the *grim strategy* discussed in Chapter 23. Both strategies call for the player to cooperate initially and to continue to cooperate as long as there is evidence that the other member of the cartel is cooperating. With the trigger price strategy, the evidence that the other player is cheating consists of a suspiciously low market price P_t. When such evidence is observed, the strategy requires the player to "punish" the other player by producing at the higher Cournot level. Unlike the case of the grim strategy, this punishment is of limited duration. After a fixed period of time has elapsed, the player begins cooperating again.

A great many pairs of trigger price strategies can form subgame-perfect Nash equilibria of this cartel game, but some of these equilibria result in higher cartel profits than do others. In the next three sections we will show how to find the "optimal" trigger price agreement.

24.3.3 Payoffs

Because Nature's actions are unpredictable, any pair of strategies for Colombia and Brazil will result in a random sequence of prices and profits for both countries. We will assume that both countries are risk-neutral and seek to maximize the expected present value of the stream of profits they will earn now and in the future. We will assume both countries discount a dollar in profits t years in the future by 0.9^t. That is, $1.00 one year from now is worth $0.90 today, $1.00 two years from now is worth $0.81 today, and so forth. The interval of time between successive output decisions is a week. Both countries choose the quantity of coffee beans they will sell at the beginning of each week. Since $1.00 one year from now is worth $0.90 today, $1.00 one week from now is worth $0.90^{1/52} = $0.998 today.

We will also assume the cost of growing coffee is the same in Colombia as it is in Brazil. There are no fixed costs, and the variable cost is constant at $1.00 per kilogram. It follows that if Colombia produces q_C million kilograms of coffee, and Brazil produces q_B million kilograms of coffee during any given week, then Colombia's expected profit that week, π_C, will equal (in millions of dollars)

$$\pi_C(q_B, q_C) = (9 - q_C - q_B) \cdot q_C \tag{24.3}$$

and Brazil's expected profit that week, π_B, will equal (in millions of dollars)

$$\pi_B(q_B, q_C) = (9 - q_C - q_B) \cdot q_B. \tag{24.4}$$

In order to find a trigger price strategy equilibrium we first need to know the Nash equilibrium of the simple one-shot, Cournot stage game in which Colombia's and Brazil's payoff functions are given by (24.3) and (24.4). This we know readily how to do. First, we find Colombia's reaction function by maximizing (24.3) over q_C, Colombia's output, holding q_B, Brazil's output, fixed. Colombia's reaction function is

$$R_C(q_B) = (9 - q_B)/2. \tag{24.5}$$

Secondly, we find Brazil's reaction function in a similar manner, which is

$$R_B(q_C) = (9 - q_C)/2. \tag{24.6}$$

These reaction functions have been plotted in Figure 24.2.

The desired equilibrium output levels consist of those values of q_B and q_C for which

$$q_C = R_C(q_B), \tag{24.7}$$
$$q_B = R_B(q_C).$$

As Figure 24.2 shows, at the unique Nash equilibrium (assuming that both countries can only employ pure strategies), both Colombia and Brazil produce 3 million

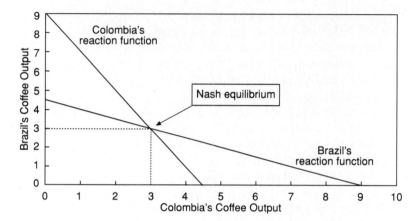

FIGURE 24.2 • Reaction functions for the one-shot Cournot game between Brazil and Colombia.

kilograms per period and earn \$9 million in profits per period. For future reference, we will denote this unique Cournot equilibrium output level by s^*.

24.3.4 Some equilibria

As is the case when both firms' previous moves are common knowledge, one equilibrium of this game is for both countries to adopt the "stubbornly noncooperative" strategy of producing s^* every year regardless of the price history. To see that this pair of strategies constitutes a Nash equilibrium, notice that the past is informative only to the extent that it affects a player's beliefs about what the opponent will do in the future. If one player believes the other is never going to cooperate, then the past is completely uninformative. Furthermore, if the other country is stubbornly noncooperative, then there is no future benefit from giving up any expected profits today. Hence, the best response to a stubbornly noncooperative opponent is to be stubbornly noncooperative oneself. This equilibrium amounts to not forming a cartel. We will refer to this as a **noncollusive equilibrium.**

Fortunately, our game has many more interesting cartel-like equilibria. In particular, this game has an entire family of Nash equilibria with credible threats in which both countries adopt a common trigger price strategy of the form (p_R, T, s^*, q^*). That is, during noncooperative periods both countries set their output level at s^*, the one-shot Cournot equilibrium of 3 million kilograms, and during cooperative periods both countries set their output level at q^*, where $q^* \leq s^*$. We will refer to such an equilibrium as a self-enforcing trigger price cartel agreement, or **cartel agreement** for short. Notice that if $q^* = s^*$, then the "cartel agreement" collapses to the noncollusive equilibrium.

Before we establish that nontrivial cartel agreements exist, we will examine how a cartel operating under such an agreement would behave. The agreement is designed to discourage both firms from cheating and producing more than the cooperative output level q^O during cooperative periods. When all cartel members are following the cartel agreement, they can deduce that a fall in the market price below the trigger price p^R *must* be due to a fall in residual demand. It is never due to cheating by one of the cartel members. Nevertheless, when such a price drop occurs, *all cartel members must follow through and simultaneously increase their output to the Cournot level for T – 1 periods*. Otherwise, everyone will have an incentive to cheat on the agreement during the cooperative periods. The agreement will result in the periodic outbreak of price wars that are caused by an unexpected fall in demand, *not* by cheating on the part of one of the members of the cartel. Such behavior is consistent with the historical record we presented earlier.

Now we will show that nontrivial trigger price cartel agreements exist and will provide a numerical example of what they look like. In the process we will present a technique for finding the equilibria of this type of dynamic game.

We will proceed in two steps. First, we will show that if one of the two cartel members, say Brazil, adopts the trigger price strategy (p^R, T, s^*, q_B), then an optimal response of the other member, Colombia, is to adopt the trigger price strategy (p^R, T, s^*, $R_{TP}(q_B)$). That is, Colombia will use the same trigger price and period of noncooperation as does Brazil. As a result, one of the countries cooperates when and only when the other does. The function $R_{TP}(q)$ is analogous to the reaction functions R_C and R_B of the one-shot Cournot game studied earlier. For this reason, we will refer to it hereafter as the **trigger price reaction function**. It is not hard to believe that because the two countries are assumed to have the same costs, both countries have the same trigger price reaction function. We will proceed to show this.

Suppose Brazil adopts the trigger price strategy (p^R, T, s^*, q_B). In the first week after the agreement comes into force, Colombia knows that Brazil will cooperate and produce q_B units of coffee. If Colombia produces $R_C(q_B)$, then it will have maximized its expected profits in the first week. But this output level ignores the future. By increasing its output, Colombia has increased the likelihood that the market price will be low enough to trigger retaliation by Brazil. If Brazil retaliates (and Colombia may luck out), then it will produce $s^* > q_B$ in period two. As a result, Colombia will end up with lower profits next period than if Brazil had continued to cooperate and produced q_B. As a result, Colombia is faced with a trade-off: Either it can exploit Brazil's cooperation in the first week, produce a lot of coffee, and risk retaliation, or it can increase the likelihood of getting Brazil's cooperation in the future by producing relatively little coffee. There is an output level between 0 and $R_C(q_B)$ that maximizes the expected present value of the stream of profits Colombia will earn over its entire (infinite) lifetime. This output level we denoted earlier as $R_{TP}(q_B)$.

After the first week, Colombia's optimal output during any week depends on whether Brazil is cooperating or not. If in week t Brazil is not cooperating, then nothing Colombia does *that week* will affect Brazil's future pattern of cooperation. Remember that we are assuming that Brazil employs a trigger price strategy, that the length of Brazil's periods of noncooperation is fixed at $T - 1$ weeks, and that its output during this period of noncooperation is stubbornly fixed at s^*. As a result, Colombia's best course of action is to maximize its expected current profits and produce $R_C(s^*) = s^*$ units of output. That is, the best response to Brazil's production of the Cournot (one-shot) equilibrium output is to produce the Cournot output as well.

If Brazil cooperates in week t, then the situation facing Colombia for the $t + 1$ weekly stage of the game is essentially equivalent to the game the two countries faced in the first week. But this means that Colombia's optimal output is $R_{TP}(q_B)$, since this was its optimal output in week 1 and essentially nothing has changed. The conclusion is that Colombia's best response to Brazil's strategy is to produce $R_{TP}(q_B)$ in cooperative weeks, produce s^* in noncooperative weeks, and cooperate if and only if Brazil cooperates. This means Colombia's optimal strategy is the trigger price strategy $(p^R, T, s^*, R_{TP}(q_B))$, as we claimed.

24.3.5   Calculating the trigger price reaction function

Now we can derive the reaction function $R_{TP}(q)$. Let $V_C(q_B, q_C)$ denote the expected present value of Colombia's profit stream when it adopts the trigger price strategy (p^R, T, s^*, q_C) and Brazil adopts the trigger price strategy (p^R, T, s^*, q_B). As we will explain, $V_C(q_B, q_C)$ satisfies the recursive equation

$$V_C(q_B, q_C) = \pi_C(q_B, q_C) + P\{p^R \le P_1\} \cdot 0.998 \cdot V_C(q_B, q_C) \qquad (24.8)$$
$$+ P\{p^R > P_1\} \cdot [0.998 \cdot \pi_C(s^*, s^*) + \ldots +$$
$$0.998^{T-1} \cdot \pi_C(s^*, s^*) + 0.998^T \cdot V_C(q_B, q_C)].$$

where $P_1 = (10 - q_B - q_C) \cdot \theta_1$, $\pi_C(q_B, q_C)$ is Colombia's expected profit during any week in which Colombia sells q_C units of coffee and Brazil sells q_B units of coffee, and $P\{\cdot\}$ equals the probability that the event within brackets occurs.

Before we use equation (24.8) to find an expression for V_C, we will first show how the equation was derived. Because both countries begin by cooperating with each other, $\pi_C(q_B, q_C)$ equals Colombia's expected profit in the first week. This explains the first term on the right-hand side of (24.8). After the first week, one of two things can occur: Brazil and Colombia can continue to cooperate, or they can begin a period of noncooperation.

The first possibility will occur if and only if P_1 does not fall below the trigger price p^R. If this should occur and the two countries continue to cooperate in week 2, then the second stage of the game beginning in week 2 is equivalent to the game that begins in week 1 (only one week later). This means the expected present value of Colombia's profit stream beginning in week 2—conditional on the two countries continuing to cooperate with each other—equals $0.998 \cdot V_C(q_B, q_C)$. Multiplying this by the probability that Brazil will cooperate in period 2 yields the second term on the right-hand side of equation (24.8).

If P_1 falls below the trigger price, then the two firms are required by their trigger price strategies to increase their output to the Cournot level of s^* for the next $T - 1$ weeks and to revert to cooperation in week $T + 1$. As we already pointed out, the $t + 1$ stage of the game is identical to the first stage of the game. As a result, the expected present value of the profit stream that begins at week $T + 1$—conditional on both countries cooperating this week—equals $0.998^T \cdot V_C(q_B, q_C)$, the expected present value of the entire profit stream must be discounted by 0.998^T because the profits are delayed by the intervening price war. It follows that the present value of the stream of expected profits beginning in week 2 equals $0.998 \cdot \pi_C(s^*, s^*) + \ldots + 0.998^{T-1} \cdot \pi_C(s^*, s^*) + 0.998^T \cdot V_C(q_B, q_C)$. Multiplying this sum by the probability that a price war begins in week 2 yields the third and final term in expression (24.8).

With some algebraic manipulation, expression (24.8) can be rewritten

$$V_C(q_B, q_C) = \pi_C(s^*, s^*) \div 0.002 + [\pi_C(q_B, q_C) - \pi_C(s^*, s^*)] \qquad (24.9)$$
$$\div [0.002 + (0.998 - 0.998^T) \cdot F(p^R \div (10 - q_B - q_C))]$$

where $F(x) = P\{\theta_t \leq x\}$.

Earlier we found $\pi_C(s^*, s^*)$ equals \$9 million per week and $\pi_C(q_B, q_C) = (9 - q_C - q_B) \cdot q_C$. In what follows we will assume the random variable θ_t has the cumulative distribution function

$$F(x) = 2 \div [1 + \exp(-\ln 3) \cdot x^{15}] - 1. \qquad (24.10)$$

The cumulative distribution function, you may recall, measures the probability that a random variable, θ_t, takes on a value less than x. Associated with the cumulative distribution function is a probability density function. The area under density function between two numbers, say x_1 and x_2, measures the probability of a random variable, θ_t, falling between x_1 and x_2. This cumulative distribution function defined

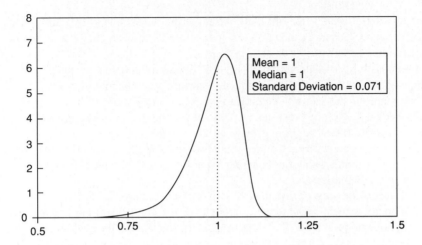

FIGURE 24.3 • The probability density function associated with the cumulative distribution function defined in equation (24.10).

in equation (24.10) has a bell-shaped density function, a median and mean of 1, and a standard deviation of 0.071.[2] A graph of the density is given in Figure 24.3.

Substituting our expressions for $\pi_C(q_B, q_C)$ and $\pi_C(s^*, s^*)$ into (24.9) results in

$$V_C(q_B, q_C) = \$4{,}500 + [(9 - q_C - q_B) \cdot q_C - 9] \tag{24.11}$$

$$\div [0.002 + (0.998 - 0.998^T) \cdot F(p^R \div (10 - q_B - q_C))].$$

Colombia's optimal cooperative output $R_{TP}(q_B)$ is the output level that maximizes V_C holding q_B fixed. In Figure 24.4 we have plotted six of Colombia's isopayoff curves for the case where $p^R = \$3.62/Kg$ and $T = 150$ weeks (3 years). An **isopayoff curve** consists of the cooperative output combinations that result in the same expected discounted profits for Colombia. The graph of the trigger price reaction function, $R_{TP}(q_B)$, consists of those points on each isopayoff curve at which the tangent line to the curve is perfectly horizontal. Notice that unlike many of our previous reaction functions, R_{TP} is not monotonic but, rather, has a serpentine graph.

It now follows that the pair of trigger price strategies (p^R, T, s^*, q_B^*) and (p^R, T, s^*, q_C^*) form a subgame-perfect Nash equilibrium for this game if and only if $q_C^* =$

---

[2]This distribution function was chosen over a more familiar one, such as the log-normal distribution, because of the greater ease with which it can be manipulated analytically and numerically.

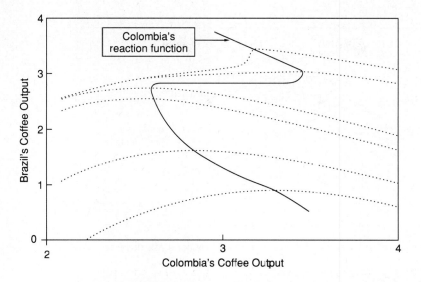

FIGURE 24.4 • Several isopayoff curves for Colombia and its associated reaction function.

$R_{TP}(q_B^*)$ and $q_B^* = R_{TP}(q_C^*)$. This implies $R_{TB}^{-1}(q_C^*) = q_B^* = R_{TB}(q_C^*)$. Graphically, this means the functions R_{TB} and R_{TB}^{-1} intersect at the point (q_C^*, q_B^*). One intersection point is (s^*, s^*), which represents the noncooperative equilibrium, which we already know to be a (trivial) trigger price equilibrium for this game.[3]

Figure 24.5 plots both R_{TB} (Colombia's trigger price reaction function) and R_{TB}^{-1} (Brazil's trigger price reaction function). There are three intersection points, each of which corresponds to a Nash equilibrium in trigger price strategies. Notice that all three points fall on the 45° line through the origin (implying that the firms will behave identically in equilibrium). The point B corresponds to the noncollusive equilibrium in which both countries always produce 3 million Kg. The point A corresponds to a nontrivial cartel agreement in which the countries produce 2.54 million Kg of coffee during cooperative periods and 3 million Kg during noncooperative periods. The point labeled C corresponds to a third Nash equilibrium in which the two countries

---

[3]It can be shown with more sophisticated mathematical techniques that (q_C^*, q_B^*) is an intersection point of R_{TB} and R_{TB}^{-1} if and only if $q_C^* = q_B^* = q^* = R_{TP}(q^*)$. That is, any cartel agreement requires that the two countries adopt the same strategy. This is a consequence of our assumption that the market demand function is linear and that the two countries have identical costs. If R_{TP} has two fixed points, say q_1^* and q_2^*, with $q_1^* < q_2^*$, then it can be shown that the equilibrium associated with the q_1^* will be strictly preferred by both countries to the equilibrium associated with q_2^*.

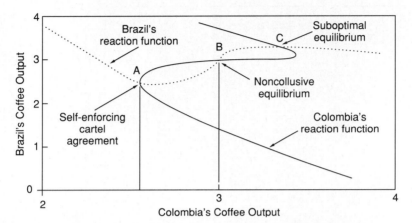

FIGURE 24.5 • Brazil and Colombia's reaction functions are drawn.

are actually stuck producing *more than* the Cournot output of 3 million Kg during the cooperative periods. Perversely, this results in both countries earning lower profits on average during the cooperative periods than during the noncooperative ones.

Having now identified all the possible self-enforcing cartel agreements into which Brazil and Colombia could enter, the second step is to find the Pareto optimal one.[4] This is the agreement we would expect the two countries to select. We will now show how to find this optimum numerically.

24.3.6   The optimal cartel agreement

For every possible trigger price p^R and penalty T there exists an optimal self-enforcing trigger price cartel agreement in which both countries agree to produce 3 million Kg of coffee during noncooperative periods and to produce some amount q^* during cooperative periods. The cooperative output q^* is a function of p^R and T. For example, as we showed above, when p^R equals \$3.62/Kg and T equals 150 weeks, $q^*(p^R,T) = 2.54$ million Kg. For some trigger prices and penalties the best agreement is not to collude. That is, for these trigger prices and penalties $q^*(p^R,T)$ equals s^*. This is the case, for example, if p^R equals \$3.62/Kg and T equals only 10 weeks.

Define $V^e(p^R,T) = V_C(q^*(p^R,T),q^*(p^R,T), p^R,T)$. This is the payoff Brazil and Colombia each receives if they adopt the best self-enforcing cartel agreement in which

---

[4]Be careful—we are currently defining Pareto optimality in terms of these two firms, not in a societal sense.

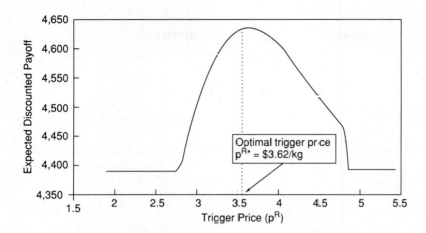

FIGURE 24.6 • Holding T at 150 weeks, the expected present value of Colombia's profits are plotted against p^R. The maximum occurs at $3.62/Kg.

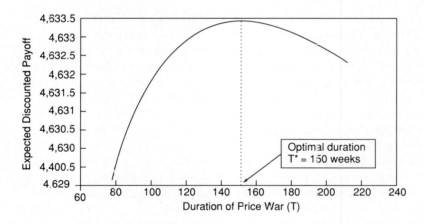

FIGURE 24.7 • Holding p^R at $3.62/Kg, the expected present value of Colombia's profits are plotted against T. The maximum occurs at T = 150 weeks.

the trigger price equals p^R and the penalty equals T. The optimal cartel agreement is the one which maximizes V^e. Using numerical methods, it is possible to determine that the optimal trigger price, p^{R*}, equals $3.62/Kg and the optimal penalty, T^*, equals 150 weeks. This can be verified by inspecting Figures 24.6 and 24.7. In Figure 24.6, the parameter T has been set to 150 weeks and then $V^e(p^R, 150)$ has been plotted against the first parameter, p^R. A maximum is reached at $\$3.62/kg = p^{R*}$. Similarly, in Figure 24.7, p^R has been set equal to $\$3.62/kg$ and $V^e(3.62, T)$ has been plotted against the second argument, T. A maximum is reached at 150 weeks $= T^*$.

24.4 · Summary

It has been known for some time that producers would like to limit competition among themselves. The problem they face in doing this is that the incentives to cheat on such agreements is usually very strong, and such agreements, even when they are not outright illegal, are almost never legally enforceable.

As a result, any group of producers who try to form a cartel are constrained to agreements that are self-enforcing: That is, it is in each member's own self-interest not to cheat. When the producers can costlessly monitor each other's activities, this constraint is not that onerous. As long as the members are sufficiently forward-looking, the cartel can get its members to collude so effectively as to mimic a pure monopoly.

Once monitoring is costly, however, this is no longer the case. Nevertheless, under a wide range of circumstances, cheating can be deterred even though it cannot be detected directly. We have demonstrated this with an example in which the cartel members can only observe the world market price. Cheating by cartel members can be detected only through its effects on the market price. Because prices can change for other reasons—such as fluctuations in demand and in the supply of noncartel members—there is some probability that a decline in the market price will occur even though no cheating took place. Nevertheless, unless the cartel periodically responds to such price movements as if they were caused by cheating, all members will have an incentive to cheat. The resulting price wars are the price of maintaining the cartel.

We showed that a trigger price strategy could result in a self-enforcing pricing agreement. Such a strategy works as follows: As long as the market price stays above some fixed level, called the trigger price, all members act "cooperatively," produce a relatively small quantity of the good, and earn relatively high profits. But once the market price falls below the trigger price, then all members revert to "noncoopera-tion" and produce the Cournot equilibrium output, earning the relatively low Cournot profit. However, they do not do this forever (as would be dictated by the grim strategy). Instead, the period of noncooperation is of limited duration.

The result is that the cartel oscillates between periods of cooperation and nonco-operation, where the periods of noncooperation are triggered by unexpected drops in residual demand. In its broadest outlines, such behavior seems to be consistent with what we observe in the real world.

24.5 • Further reading

Any recent treatment of industrial organization will devote a significant number of pages to the problem of cartels. See, for example, Dennis Carlton and Jeffrey Perloff, *Modern Industrial Organization* (Glenview, Ill.: Scott Foresman, 1990), pp. 208–257. A somewhat dated, but still useful, survey article was written by G. Hay and D. Kelley, "An Empirical Survey of Price-Fixing Conspiricies," *Journal of Law and Economics* 17 (1974), pp. 13–38. Also helpful is George Stigler, "A Theory of Oligopoly," *Journal of Political Economy* 72 (1964), pp. 44-61.

The model used in this application was patterned after Robert Porter, "Optimal Cartel Trigger Price Strategies," *Journal of Economic Theory* 29 (1983), pp. 313-338. There are, not surprisingly, a very large number of recent theoretical studies designed to predict cartel behavior. Among the better known are those by Edward Green and Robert Porter, "Noncooperative Collusion under Imperfect Price Information," *Econometrica* 52 (1984), pp. 87-100, and S. Salop, "Practices That (Credibly) Facilitate Oligopoly Coordination," in Joseph E. Stiglitz and G. Frank Mathewson, eds., *New Developments in the Analysis of Market Structure* (Cambridge, MA: MIT Press, 1986).

For a history of cartels, see Paul Eckbo, *The Future of World Oil* (Cambridge, MA.: Ballinger, 1976).

24.6 • Exercises

Exercise 24.1 Suppose you worked for the Justice Department's antitrust division. And suppose you suspected that a group of firms were colluding using trigger price strategies. How might you prove this was the case?

Exercise 24.2 Suppose Colombia and Brazil can tell whether or not the other is selling any coffee in any period. They just cannot determine the amount being sold. Determine whether the following is a self-enforcing cartel agreement: Brazil sells only in odd years and Colombia sells only in even years.

Exercise 24.3 Another family of strategies for the cartel enforcement game are *harsh trigger price* (HTP) strategies. This family of strategies is parameterized by two numbers: a trigger price p^R and an output level q^O. A country using an HTP strategy is in one of three states each period: cooperative, noncooperative, and cutthroat. In the cooperative state the country produces q^O. In the noncooperative state the country

TABLE 24.1   Transition between states under a harsh trigger price strategy

Last period		This period
State	Price	State
Cooperative	$P_{t-1} \geq p^R$	Cooperative
Cooperative	$P_{t-1} < p^R$	Cutthroat
Cutthroat	$P_{t-1} = 0$	Cooperative
Cutthroat	$P_{t-1} > 0$	Noncooperative
Noncooperative	All prices	Noncooperative

produces 3 million Kg of coffee. In the cutthroat state, the country produces 5 million Kg of coffee. The country starts out cooperating and changes states as follows: Suppose Brazil adopts the HTP strategy (q_B^O, p^R) and Colombia adopts the HTP strategy (q_C^O, p^R). How will the game evolve over time? (Hint: Does either country ever become non-cooperative?)

Exercise 24.4   This is a continuation of Exercise 24.3. Let $V_i(q_B^O, q_C^O)$ denote the expected present value of country i's profit stream when Brazil adopts the HTP strategy (q_B^O, p^R) and Colombia adopts the HTP strategy (q_C^O, p^R). Using equation 24.8 as a guide, find a recursive expression for $V_i(q_B^O, q_C^O)$.

Exercise 24.5   This is a continuation of Exercise 25 .3 . Suppose Brazil adopts the HTP strategy (q_B^O, p^R) and suppose there exists an output level q_C^O such that

(i) $V_C(q_B^O, q_C^O) \geq V_C(q_B^O, q)$, for all $q \geq 0$.

(ii) $\pi_C(5,5) + 0.998 \cdot V_C(q_B^O, q_C^O) \geq$

$\pi_C(5, R_C(5)) + 0.998 \cdot \pi_C(3,3) + 0.998^2 \cdot \pi_C(3,3) +$

$+ \ldots + 0.998^T \cdot \pi_C(3, 3) + \ldots$

Show that Columbia's best response to Brazil's strategy is to adopt the HTP strategy (q_C^O, p^R).

Exercise 24.6   It would appear Brazil and Colombia could prevent debilitating price wars if they could only monitor each other's coffee sales. Since, each country could give the other the right to monitor its sales, what might it mean if each chooses not to?

• CHAPTER 25 •

Durable Goods and Monopoly Power

25.1 • Introduction

When we think of firms in a competitive situation, we almost invariably take a particular point in time for our frame of reference. That is, a firm in a competitive market is competing at a given time and place with other firms producing a similar good or service. But competition can exist over time as well. In and of itself, this is not a terribly profound observation. What is profound is that the single provider of a durable good—often referred to as a **durable good monopolist**—might end up *competing against itself* over time, thereby reducing or even eliminating its market power. The monopolist self-destructs.

The origins of this notion that a monopolist, under some circumstances, might end up competing against itself comes from Ronald Coase,[1] who speculated that a monopolist producing an infinitely durable good, a diamond ring perhaps, was in just such a position. Consumers interested in buying a diamond are interested not only in the price of a diamond today, but also in the price of a diamond tomorrow, next year, next decade, and so on. If consumers think the price of a diamond is likely to fall in the near future, then they will wait and not buy the diamond today. The potential diamond buyer will buy the diamond today only if the monopolist can convince her

---

[1]Yes, the same Ronald Coase of Coase theorem fame.

that it will not lower its price much in the near future. Of course, the monopolist's promise not to lower the price in the future must be credible for it to be convincing.

Under conditions of perfect information, however, the monopolist may find it very difficult to convince consumers that the price will remain high. After all, most of the consumers who would be willing to pay a lot for a diamond have probably already bought one; those consumers who have not yet bought a diamond value one much less. Once the really profitable consumers are gone, the monopolist may be willing to sell diamonds for a price just above marginal cost.

As we have seen time and time again, rational game players will look to the future before deciding what to do today. Consumers, even those with a very high desire for a diamond, will be aware that the monopolist will eventually have a strong incentive to sell diamonds at a lower price. As a result, even consumers who are willing to pay a lot for a diamond have an incentive to wait for the price to fall. The monopolist is stuck. Because in the future it will want to charge a low price (in order to sell a few more diamonds), it may be forced to charge a low price today in order to sell any diamonds today. We will now proceed to put some game-theoretic flesh on the bones of the foregoing logic and see if it holds up to rigorous analysis.

25.2 • A naive game

Imagine a company, call it Big Blue, that has just begun producing a new model of its line of microcomputers (PCs). Their new PC is capable of running programs at twice the speed of existing PCs. A PC is an example of a **durable good**: a good that provides a stream of services over an extended period of time. For the sake of simplicity, we will assume that this period of service is unlimited. We will also assume that every consumer wants at most one computer. This allows us to abstract away from the decision of *how much* to buy in order to focus on the more important decision of *when* to buy.

There are 1,500 consumers interested in buying this product who differ in the maximum amount they are willing to pay for this new PC model. It is important to understand why this is so. This new computer provides each consumer i with a marginal benefit of V_i at the end of every year. Different consumers have different marginal benefits. For example, the marginal benefit of a personal computer is low for most college students, because they have ready access to college-provided computers, but high for the business executive who needs to do job-related work at home. Because dollar values in the future are not the same as dollar values today, it is important that we make the dollar benefits in every year comparable with the dollar costs, which are paid at the beginning of the year in which the computer is purchased. Consumer i discounts future dollar benefits and costs by r_i per year. That is, \$1 in benefits at the end of this year is equal to $1/(1 + r_i)$ in benefits immediately; $1 in benefits at the end of two years is worth $1/(1 + r_i)^2$ in benefits today, and so forth. So the sum of the discounted values of the future benefits from using the computer equals:

$$V_i/(1 + r_i) + V_i/(1 + r_i)^2 + \ldots = V_i/r_i. \tag{25.1}$$

A second difference among consumers is that they have different marginal discount rates. Those students who have studied the problem of intertemporal choice will recognize that this is possible only if the capital market is Pareto inefficient. If the capital market were Pareto efficient, then in equilibrium all consumers would have the same marginal discount rate, which would equal the common interest rate each faces for both borrowing and lending. But as we already saw in Part Four, asymmetric information can result in serious imperfections in the capital market. In particular, credit rationing can result in consumers' discount rates diverging from the interest rates they face for borrowing and lending. For example, many college students face high borrowing costs because of their short credit histories and low net wealth, whereas many business executives face low borrowing costs because they have long credit histories and high net wealth.

For simplicity, we will assume that there are only two types of PC buyers: *high-value* buyers and *low-value* buyers. The high-value buyers get a marginal benefit of $200 per year and have a discount rate of 10%. As a result, their maximum willingness-to-pay equals $200/10\% = \$2,000$. The low-value buyers obtain a marginal benefit of only $120 per year *and* have a discount rate of 20%. It follows that their maximum willingness-to-pay equals $120/20\% = \$600$. There are 1,000 low-value buyers but only 500 high-value buyers.

Suppose the marginal cost to Big Blue of making a PC is only $100. Clearly, there is a great deal of room for mutually advantageous exchange. We will hereafter assume Big Blue is barred from charging different customers different prices at the same point in time, perhaps as a consequence of antitrust legislation.[2]

Suppose Big Blue could commit itself never to change its initial price for the PC. Then the game between Big Blue and its customers would be very simple. Big Blue would make the first move and set the price, which it could never alter. Once Big Blue chose its price, then the high-value and low-value buyers would simultaneously decide whether to buy the PC at this price immediately, buy it at this price at some future time, or never buy it. The game would then end.

The analysis of this game is straightforward. Because the price will never change, buying the PC in the future is weakly dominated by buying the PC today. A typical

---

[2]In the United States, price discrimination is illegal.

TABLE 25.1 Sales and profits in the durable monopoly game when Big Blue can fix its future prices in advance

Price	Unit Sales	Profit
$600	1,500	$750,000
$2,000	500	$950,000

high-value buyer purchases the PC immediately if and only if the price is less than or equal to $2,000, and the low-value buyer buys the PC immediately if and only if the price is less than or equal to $600.[3] Table 25.1 shows Big Blue's profit from charging either $600 or $2,000 for the PC.

Clearly, Big Blue's optimal strategy is to charge $2,000, sell PCs only to the high-value buyers, and make a profit of almost $1 million. The problem with this outcome is that none of the low-value buyers end up with a PC even though each is willing to pay $500 more than it costs to produce it. As a result, the outcome is *Pareto inefficient*, resulting in a welfare loss of $500,000 (= $500 per low-value buyer × 1,000 low-value buyers).

The assumption that Big Blue can commit itself to shutting down permanently after one time period begs the question of whether such a commitment is credible. Sometimes a seller can make such a credible commitment. For example, consider the case of a professional photographer who destroys his negatives after a certain number of prints have been made from them. This ensures potential buyers that the market will not be flooded with prints in the future, thereby driving down the price. It is hard to see how Big Blue could accomplish something similar. Although it could destroy the factory that makes the PCs, nothing would prevent it from building another factory later.[4]

It is far more realistic to assume that Big Blue *cannot* commit itself to keeping its prices constant but is, instead, free to change its prices at any time. In the next section we will show that such price flexibility will force Big Blue to charge much lower prices from the very beginning, exactly as Professor Coase conjectured.

25.3 · The pricing game with fully flexible prices

We will now suppose that everything is the same as before *except* that Big Blue cannot set its future prices in advance. Instead, in every period the firm has full price flexibility.

---

[3]As we have done in the past, we have assumed that the consumer buys the good whenever she is indifferent between buying it and not buying it.

[4]An example of this type of behavior is the recent videotape release of Walt Disney Productions' *Fantasia.* The Disney company claims this is a limited-release offer and that *Fantasia* will never be offered for sale again. We will see.

25.3.1   Actions

Big Blue sets its price at the beginning of the year and does not change it until the following year. The price charged in any year is completely unconstrained by the prices charged in the past. The firm's only constraint is that, at any point in time, every buyer must be charged the same price. The price charged in year t will be denoted P_t.

Consumers must decide if and when to buy a PC. B_t^i denotes consumer i's PC purchase decision in year t. B_t^i can take one of two values: "Buy now" or "wait."

At the beginning of every year, each consumer either has already bought a PC and is no longer in the market, or has not yet bought a PC and is still a potential customer. We will call those consumers still in the market **active** consumers. Consumers who are not active are **inactive.** The variable A_t^i denotes the status of consumer i at the beginning of year t and takes on one of two values: "active" or "inactive." Because customers are assumed to buy at most one PC, if A_t^i = inactive (that is, the consumer already owns a PC at the beginning of year t), then A_s = inactive and B_s^i = wait for every $s \geq t$ (the consumer is forever inactive and never buys another PC). If B_t^i = buy now, then A_s^i = inactive and B_s^i = wait for every $s > t$ (the consumer is inactive thereafter and never buys another PC).

25.3.3   Information

Every year, after Big Blue sets its price for that year, the active consumers simultaneously decide whether to buy a PC that year or to wait. All past buy/wait decisions are common knowledge. In addition, it is common knowledge which active consumers are high-value buyers and which are low-value buyers. As a result, at the beginning of every year, before any decisions are made by either Big Blue or the consumers, it is common knowledge exactly how many active low-value buyers and high-value buyers there are. This is a stronger informational assumption than we need, but it allows us to sidestep complicated informational issues. The number of active high-value buyers at the start of year t will be denoted HU_t, and the number of active low-value buyers will be denoted LU_t.

25.3.3   The order of moves

The game tree is shown in Figure 25.1. In order to make the game tree understandable, we have assumed there is only one high-value buyer and one low-value buyer. Note that the low-value buyer's decision nodes are connected by a dotted line, signifying that the two nodes are in the same information set. This means that when the low-value buyer makes his first purchase decision, he does not know what the high-value buyer has

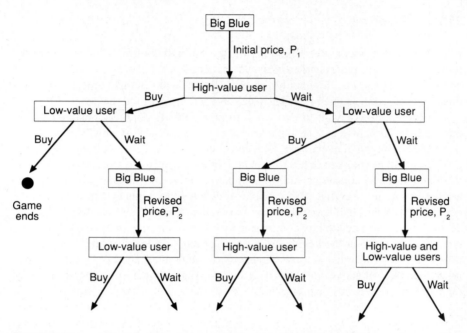

FIGURE 25.1 • Game tree for the game between a durable good monopolist and two types of consumers.

decided to do. And since the tree shows the low-value buyer moving after the high-value buyer, the high-value buyer is similarly ignorant of the low-value buyer's decision when making her purchase decision.

Once the customers make their purchase decisions, Big Blue can then change the price of the PC for the following year. Big Blue's inability to bypass this move by setting this price in advance is a crucial feature of the game. The game ends when there are no more active consumers.

25.3.4 Payoffs

Let S_t denote sales in year t. Profits accrue at the end of the year. Big Blue discounts future profits by 15% a year. Big Blue's payoff equals the present value of its stream of net profits, or

$$\sum_{t=i}^{\infty} S_t \cdot (P_t - \$100)/(1.15)^{-t}. \tag{25.2}$$

As before, V_i denotes the annual marginal benefit to consumer i from owning a PC and r_i denotes the discount rate of the ith buyer. Let $s(i)$ denote the year in which consumer i buys a PC. Then the consumer's payoff is the present value of her stream of net benefits, or:

$$(\sum_{t=s(i)}^{\infty} V_i/(1 + r_i)^t) - P_{s(i)}/(1 + r_i)^{s(i)}, \qquad (25.3)$$

which can be rewritten more compactly as

$$(V_i/r_i - P_{s(i)})/(1 + r_i)^{s(i)}. \qquad (25.4)$$

25.3.5 Strategies

A pure strategy for Big Blue consists of a price to charge each year depending on the history of the game up to that point. Because the only thing about the past that really matters is the number of active low-value and high-value buyers (which is common knowledge among all the players), we will restrict Big Blue to strategies of the form $P_t = P(HU_t, LU_t)$.

A pure strategy for a buyer consists of a purchase decision in every year as a function of the history of the game up to that point. These strategies can be extremely complicated. In order to make the analysis tractable, we will restrict the buyers to strategies of the form $A_t^i = A(P_t, HU_t, LU_t, B_t^i, V_i, r_i)$. That is, when deciding whether to buy the good or not, all that matters is the current price being charged by Big Blue, the number of active low-value and high-value buyers, whether the consumer has already bought a PC or not, and the consumer's value for the PC. This is an example of what is sometimes called a **stationary strategy** in the durable goods monopoly literature.

If consumer i's strategy in year t is to buy a PC now if the price is below some number $\underline{P}_t^i$, and to wait if the price is above $\underline{P}_t^i$, then the strategy is called a **reservation price strategy**, and the number $\underline{P}_t^i$ is called the consumer's reservation price in year t. The consumer's reservation price in year t will not necessarily equal the consumer's maximum willingness-to-pay for a PC. The reservation price involves a comparison of the marginal benefit of buying the PC today with the marginal benefit of buying the PC in the future at a lower price. Because each consumer's reservation price will depend on the price the consumer expects Big Blue to charge in the future, it will generally depend on the number of active high-value buyers, the number of active low-value buyers, the consumer's willingness-to-pay for a PC, and the consumer's discount rate.

25.3.6 Equilibrium

We will begin by presenting one of the many Nash equilibria for this game. The strategies are shown in Table 25.2.

As you know, a Nash equilibrium consists of a collection of strategies, one for each player, such that each player's strategy is optimal given the other player's strategies. Let us verify that this holds for the strategies in Table 25.2. Given Big Blue's strategy of keeping the price constant, a consumer never benefits by waiting to buy a PC. And given the consumers' strategies, if Big Blue ever charges more than $600, it will sell no PCs in that period but will not alter the future behavior of the consumers. This can only reduce its profit stream. This shows that the strategies are a Nash equilibrium.

Unfortunately, this Nash equilibrium is not subgame perfect, as it involves a noncredible threat by the high-value buyers. The threat is that they will not buy a PC whenever the price is above $600. But suppose Big Blue were to charge $700. Because this is more than the PC is worth to any low-value buyer, none of them will buy it at this price. But $700 is *less* than the PC's present value to any high-value buyer. Clearly, a high-value buyer should buy the PC immediately if she believes Big Blue will never lower its price below $700. But the buyer should also buy the PC immediately even when she expects the price to drop to $600 next year. The reasoning behind this last claim is as follows. The payoff to the high-value buyer if she buys the PC today equals $(\$2,000 - \$700)/(1.10) = \$1,181.81$. Her payoff if she waits until next year and Big Blue drops the price to $600 equals $(\$2,000 - \$600)/(1.10)^2 = \$1,157.02$. Because $1,157.02 is less than $1,181.81, her best action is to *buy the PC for $700 immediately and not wait*. This shows that the high-value buyers' threat not to pay more than $600 for a PC today is not credible.

A collection of subgame-perfect equilibrium strategies is presented in Table 25.3. In describing these strategies, we have left unspecified two functions, P^* and $\underline{P}^*$, whose ranges lie in the interval [$600, $2,000]. Both functions are hard to derive explicitly. Fortunately, their exact specification is not needed to demonstrate that the strategies in Table 25.3 form a subgame-perfect equilibrium.

Big Blue's equilibrium strategy is to charge a price that depends on the relative number of active high-value buyers and active low-value buyers. The price is never

TABLE 25.2   A Nash equilibrium for the durable monopoly game when Big Blue's future prices are perfectly flexible

Big Blue's pricing strategy:
$\quad P_t = \$600$, all t.
Active consumer i's reservation price strategy:
$\quad \underline{P}_t^i = \$600$, all t.

TABLE 25.3   A subgame-perfect equilibrium for the durable monopoly game with flexible prices

Big Blue's strategy:

$$P_t = \begin{cases} \$600 & \text{if (1) holds} \\ P^*(LU_t, HU_t) & \text{if (2) holds} \\ \$2,000 & \text{if (3) holds} \end{cases}$$

Active high-value buyer's strategy:

$$\underline{P}_t^i = \begin{cases} \$727.27 & \text{if (1) holds} \\ \underline{P}^*(HU_t, LU_t) & \text{if (2) holds} \\ \$2,000 & \text{if (3) holds} \end{cases}$$

Active low-value buyer's strategy:

$$\underline{P}_t^i = \$600$$

where:

(1) $LU_t \geq 1.95 \cdot HU_t$,

(2) $1.95 \cdot HU_t > LU_t > 0$,

(3) $LU_t = 0$.

below $600 or above $2,000 and is an increasing function of the relative number of high-value buyers. The low-value buyers' strategy is to wait until the price falls to their maximum willingness-to-pay ($600) and then buy immediately. The high-value buyers' strategy is the most complex. Their lowest reservation price is $727.27 and their highest is $2,000. They adopt their lowest reservation price whenever the low-value buyers make up more than two-thirds of the active buyers (approximately), and they adopt their highest reservation price whenever there are no low-value buyers among the remaining active buyers. Whenever the proportion of low-value buyers among the active buyers is positive but less than two-thirds (approximately), the reservation price and the probability of buying at that price depends on the proportion of low-value and high-value buyers among the active buyers.

The outcome of playing the equilibrium strategies in Table 25.3 is simple. Initially, the low-value buyers make up more than two-thirds of active buyers ($LU_t = 1,000 > 975 = 1.95 \cdot HU_t$), Big Blue charges $600 for the PC despite the fact that the high-value buyers have a reservation price above this figure. All consumers buy a PC immediately at this price. The game then ends. 1,500 PCs are produced and sold *versus* only 500 when Big Blue can keep itself from cutting its price in the future.

Table 25.4 compares the equilibrium payoffs in this flexible-price game with the equilibrium payoffs in the fixed-price game. The table shows that the $500,000 welfare loss incurred when the fixed-price game is played disappears once prices are flexible. This overall welfare gain is at the expense of the monopolist and to the benefit of the high-value ("high marginal utility and patient") buyer. The welfare of the low-value ("low marginal value and impatient") buyer is the same in both equilibria. These qualitative features of the equilibrium continue to hold under much less restrictive assumptions.

25.3.7 Verification of the equilibrium

First we will establish that the collection of strategies in Table 25.3 form a Nash equilibrium. To do this, we will assume that every player but one adopts these strategies and then show that the remaining player cannot do better by adopting another strategy.

Because Big Blue will never reduce its price below $600, once the price reaches $600, a low-value buyer cannot gain anything by waiting further. This shows that the low-value buyer's strategy is optimal at every point in the game.

If a high-value buyer waits, then next year she will be the only active buyer in the market and will face a price of $2,000 for a PC—a decidedly inferior outcome compared to the current price of $600.

If Big Blue charges $600 initially, it will make an immediate profit of 1,500 · ($600 − $100) = $750,000. If Big Blue charges more than $727.27 in the first year, then it will sell nothing and next year will be forced to sell its PCs for $600. All it has done is to delay earning profits for a year. If it charges between $600 and $727.27 in the first year, it will sell only to the high-value buyers. The firm's best option in the

TABLE 25.4 Subgame-perfect equilibrium payoffs of the durable monopoly game with both fixed and flexible prices

Player	Equilibrium payoffs		Change
	Fixed Prices	Flexible Prices	
Big Blue	$950,000	$750,000	−$200,000
High-value buyer	$0	$700,000	+$700,000
Low-value buyer	$0	$0	$0
Total	$950,00	$1,450,000	+$500,000

second year is to charge $600 and sell to the remaining low-value buyers. The present
value of the profits from doing this equals

$$500 \cdot (P_1 - \$100) + 1{,}000 \cdot (\$600 - \$100)/1.15 \qquad (25.5)$$

$$\leq 500 \cdot (727.27 - \$100) + 1{,}000 \cdot (\$600 - \$100)/1.1$$

$$= 748{,}417.61$$

$$< \$750{,}000.$$

It follows that the best price to charge initially is $600.

Although we have shown that these strategies constitute a Nash equilibrium, we
now need to verify that they are also subgame-perfect. Since we have already shown
that the low-value buyer's strategy is optimal at every point in the game, we can limit
ourselves to examining the strategies of the high-value buyers and Big Blue. Since
the players' strategies depend on the proportion of high-value and low-value buyers
among the active buyers, there are three cases to consider: (1) $LU_t \geq 1.95 \cdot HU_t$,
(2) $1.95 \cdot HU_t > LU_t > 0$, and (3) $LU_t = 0$.

Case 1 $LU_t \geq 1.95 \cdot HU_t$. The actions called for by the player's equilibrium
strategies are shown in Table 25.5.

We will first establish the optimality of the high-value buyer's reservation price. If
a high-value buyer buys a PC at time t at the price P_t, then her payoff equals ($2,000
$- P_t$) $\cdot (1.10)^{-t}$. If $P_t \leq \$600$ and she waits, then next year she will be the only active
buyer left. In this case, Big Blue's equilibrium strategy is to charge $2,000 from then
on and the high-value buyer's equilibrium strategy is to buy the PC at this price. So

**TABLE 25.5   Actions called for by equilibrium strategies when $LU_t \geq$
$1.95 \cdot HU_t$**

Big Blue:
  Charge a price of $600

High-value buyers:
  Wait   if $P_t > \$727.27$
  Buy now   if $P_t \leq \$727.27$

Low-value buyers:
  Wait   if $P_t > \$600$
  Buy now   if $P_t \leq \$600$

the payoff from waiting equals $(\$2{,}000 - \$2{,}000)/(1.05)^{t+1} = \$0$. Clearly, if the price is below $600, it is better to buy the PC this year rather than to wait.

Now suppose $\$727.27 \geq P_t > \$600$ and the high-value buyer waits. In this case, no low-value buyer will buy a PC this year, but every other high-value buyer will. As a result, $LU_{t+1} = LU_t \geq 1.95 \cdot HU_t \geq 1.95 \cdot HU_{t+1} = 1.95$. Big Blue's equilibrium strategy calls for it to charge $600 next year, and the high-value buyer's equilibrium strategy calls for it to buy the PC at this price. The payoff from waiting equals $(\$2{,}000 - \$600)/(1.10)^{t+1}$. The payoff from buying the machine now equals $(\$2{,}000 - P_t)/(1.10)^t$. This equals the payoff from waiting if and only if $P_t \leq \$727.27$. So it is optimal to buy the PC this year whenever the price equals or is below $727.27.

Finally, suppose $P_t > 727.27$. If all consumers follow their equilibrium strategies, then none of them will buy the PC at this price. As a result, next year $LU_{t+1} = LU_t \geq 1.95 \cdot HU_t = 1.95 \cdot HU_{t+1}$, and so Big Blue will charge $600 for the PC (assuming it reverts back to its equilibrium strategy). But we just saw that if $P_t > \$727.27$ and $P_{t+1} = \$600$, then the high-value buyers should wait until next year. This shows that a reservation price of $727.27 is optimal.

We now will establish the optimality of Big Blue's $600 price. If the firm charges $600, then all the active buyers will buy the PC at this price, yielding a payoff of $(HU_t + LU_t) \cdot (\$600 - \$100)/(1.10)^t$; of course, all the active buyers will also buy the PC at a lower price, but this yields lower profits. If Big Blue charges $727.27, then only the high-value buyers will buy a PC. With the high-value buyers out of the market, next year Big Blue's equilibrium strategy is to charge $600. The payoff from charging $727.27, therefore, equals $HU_t \cdot (\$727.27 - \$100)/(1.15)^t + LU_t \cdot (\$600 - \$100)/(1.15)^{t+1}$. Finally, if Big Blue charges more than $727.27, then no one will buy a PC this year, and $HU_{t+1} = HU_t$ and $LU_{t+1} = LU_t$. As a result, next year Big Blue will charge $600 and sell to the remaining consumers. The payoff is $(HU_t + LU_t) \cdot (\$600 - \$100)/(1.15)^{t+1}$, which is lower than the payoff from charging $600 this year. So Big Blue should charge either $600 or $727.67 this year. It is better to charge $600 rather than $727.27 if and only if

$$(HU_t + LU_t) \cdot \$500/(1.15)^t \tag{25.6a}$$
$$\geq HU_t \cdot \$627.27/(1.15)^t + LU_t \cdot \$500/(1.15)^{t+1}$$

or

$$LU_t \geq 1.95 \cdot HU_t. \tag{25.6b}$$

Since (25.6b) is satisfied, Big Blue's optimal price is $600, as claimed.

Case 2 $0 < LU_t < 1.95 \cdot HU_t$.   The actions called for by the player's equilibrium strategies are shown in Table 25.6.

TABLE 25.6   Actions called for by equilibrium strategies when $0 < LU_t$ $< 1.95 \cdot HU_t$

Big Blue:
  Charge the price $P^*(HU_t, LU_t)$

Active high-value buyers:
  Wait   if $P_t > \underline{P}^*(HU_t, LU_t)$
  Buy now   if $P_t \leq \underline{P}^*(HU_t, LU_t)$

Active low-value buyer:
  Wait   if $P_t > \$600$
  Buy now   if $P_t \leq \$600$

Generally, in this book we have explicitly computed all equilibria. But we will not do so here. The functions P^* and $\underline{P}^*$ are defined by complex recursive equations whose solution is both beyond the level of this book and unnecessary for determining the equilibrium outcome of this game. In the problems at the end of this chapter, we have left it as an exercise to show that when $HU_t = LU_t = 1$, then $P^* = \underline{P}^* = \$2,000$.

Case 3 $LU_t = 0$.   The only active buyers left are high-value buyers. Clearly, Big Blue cannot do better than to charge $2,000 and sell to the remaining active buyers. Conversely, given that Big Blue will never lower its price below $2,000, no high-value buyer can gain by waiting. So the optimal reservation price is the buyer's maximum willingness-to-pay.

25.4 · A folk theorem

So far, we have restricted the buyers to a very simple class of strategies. Under our assumption that the low-value buyers value the PC above its marginal cost (the so-called **gap case**), this restriction is innocuous. The Coase conjecture will continue to hold even if the buyers' strategies are allowed to be arbitrarily complex.

But our restriction on buyer strategies is not innocuous once there are buyers whose valuation for the PC is below Big Blue's marginal cost. This is known as the **no-gap case.** In the no-gap case the Coase conjecture will hold if and only if the buyers are restricted to stationary strategies. Worse still, if the buyer strategies are unrestricted, then there is a folk theorem. This result is due to Lawrence Ausubel and Raymond Deneckere. Their theorem is too complicated to state fully here, but the essence of it is this: Let π^* be Big Blue's static monopoly profit ($950,000 in our case) and let δ be any positive number, however small. As long as the time between offers is short enough that both Big Blue and the buyers discount the immediate future very little, there exists a subgame-perfect equilibrium in which Big Blue's profit is greater than $\pi^* - \delta$. As Ausubel and Deneckere put it, "It is possible, even in the durable goods market, that a monopoly *is* a monopoly."

It is not clear what to make of this remarkable result. On the one hand, the no-gap assumption seems more realistic than the assumption of a gap between the buyers' valuations and the seller's costs. On the other hand, the assumption that the buyers' strategies can have an unrestricted degree of complexity seems unreasonable. It seems more reasonable to assume that the buyers limit themselves to relatively simple rules. Unfortunately, there is as yet no good way to model strategy complexity. Our own opinion is that monopolists should draw little comfort from this folk theorem.

25.5 • Summary

The future presents a serious problem for Big Blue. As we have seen, if the players ignored the future, then the firm could offer the PC for sale at a price of $2000 and make a profit of almost $1 million. But time marches on, and the consumers are well aware of this fact. Year 2 is bound to come, Big Blue will still be selling PCs when it does, and all the consumers are aware of it. By looking ahead, the consumers can anticipate a price decline. As a result, the decision to buy in year 1 depends on the price in year 2. Big Blue, in this model, cannot get out of the problem created by its strong desire to sell to the low-value buyer in year 2. Therefore, Big Blue ends up with profits of $750,000 instead. From the perspective of the efficient allocation of society's scarce resources, Big Blue's problem is a good thing. In particular, the welfare loss discussed at the beginning of this chapter is eliminated.

Under certain conditions, the monopolist may actually be induced (by his own greed!) to charge a price only slightly above marginal cost (that is, the "competitive price") right from the first day of production. Alas, however, our good cheer is tempered somewhat by Ausubel and Deneckere's folk theorem. If buyer strategies can have arbitrary complexity and if some buyers value the good at less than its marginal cost, then the monopolist may be able credibly to commit itself to charging a price close to the static monopoly price and keeping it there.

25.6 • Further reading

The Coase conjecture first appeared in a paper by Ronald Coase, "Durability and Monopoly," *Journal of Law and Economics* 15 (1972), pp. 143-149. Other fairly advanced treatments of this issue are Eric Bond and Larry Samuelson, "Durable Good Monopolies with Rational Expectations and Replacement Sales," *Rand Journal of Economics* 15 (1984), pp. 336–345, and J. Bulow, "Durable Goods Monopolists," *Journal of Political Economy* (1982), pp. 314–332.

Two good literature surveys are Richard Schmalensee, "Market Structure, Durability, and Quality: A Selective Survey," *Economic Inquiry* 17 (1979), pp. 177–196, and S. J. Liebowitz, "Durability, Market Structure, and New–Used Goods Markets," *American Economic Review* 72 (1982), pp. 816–824.

The folk theorem for the durable good monopolist is reported in Lawrence Ausubel and Raymond Deneckere, "Reputation in Bargaining and Durable Good Monopoly," *Econometrica* 57 (1989), pp. 511–532. A simpler exposition of their theorem (though still difficult) can be found in Drew Fudenberg and Jean Tirole, *Game Theory* (Cambridge, Mass.: MIT Press, 1991), Chapter 10.

25.7 • Exercises

Exercise 25.1 Suppose Big Blue offers price protection to its customers: If it ever lowers the price on its current model, it will rebate to previous buyers the difference between the new lower price and the price they paid when they bought the PC. Show that, even if Big Blue has perfect price flexibility, its optimal strategy is to charge $2,000 forever and for the high-value buyers to buy a PC immediately.

Exercise 25.2 Continuation of 25.1. Can you think of ways that Big Blue could cheat on its price protection plan? If such cheating is possible, what type of strategic problem do Big Blue's customers face?

Exercise 25.3 Verify that equation (25.4) is algebraically equivalent to equation (25.3).

Exercise 25.4 Suppose Big Blue refuses to sell its PCs. Instead, it rents them. The high-value buyers are willing to pay a rental fee of up to $200 per year, and the low-value buyers are willing to pay a rental fee of up to $120 per year. Show that it is no longer rational for the buyers to consider Big Blue's future rental rates when deciding whether to rent a PC this year. Use this to find the unique subgame-perfect equilibrium for this game.

Exercise 25.5 This problem concerns the equilibrium of the durable monopoly pricing game with flexible prices. Show that if at any point in the game there exists exactly one high-value and one low-value active buyer ($HU_t = LU_t = 1$), then the optimal strategy of Big Blue is to charge $2,000, and the high-value buyer's reservation price equals $2,000. (*Hint*: Given Big Blue's strategy, show that the high-value buyer will accept any price below $2,000; and given this reservation price, Big Blue's optimal strategy is to charge $2,000 and sell to the low-value buyer next year for $600.)

Name Index

Page numbers in **bold face** refer to bibliographic references.

Subject Index